Saving Wisdom

Saving Wisdom
Theology in the Christian University

BRIAN W. HUGHES

With a foreword by Brian E. Daley, SJ

☙PICKWICK *Publications* · Eugene, Oregon

SAVING WISDOM
Theology in the Christian University

Copyright © 2011 Brian W. Hughes. All rights reserved. Except for brief quotations in critical publications or reviews, no part of this book may be reproduced in any manner without prior written permission from the publisher. Write: Permissions, Wipf and Stock Publishers, 199 W. 8th Ave., Suite 3, Eugene, OR 97401.

The Scripture quotations contained herein are from the New Revised Standard Version Bible, copyright © 1989 by the Division of Christian Education of the National Council of the Churches of Christ in the U.S.A., and are used by permission. All rights reserved.

Part of chapter four has been previously published as "The Contemplative Function of Theology within Liberal Education: Rereading Newman's Idea of a University," *HORIZONS* vol. 32. No. 1 (Spring 2005) 7–25. It is used by permission.

Pickwick Publications
An Imprint of Wipf and Stock Publishers
199 W. 8th Ave., Suite 3
Eugene, OR 97401

www.wipfandstock.com

ISBN 13: 978-1-60608-958-3

Cataloguing-in-Publication data:

Hughes, Brian W.

Saving wisdom : theology in the Christian university / Brian W. Hughes ; with a foreword by Brian E. Daley, SJ.

xvi + 354 pp. ; 23 cm. Includes bibliographical references and index.

ISBN 13: 978-1-60608-958-3

1. Universities and colleges—Religion. 2. Church and education. I. Daley, Brian E., 1940–. II. Title.

BV1610 .H75 2011

Manufactured in the U.S.A.

Para Rosario, mi querida mujer

gracias por todo . . .

Contents

Foreword by Brian E. Daley, SJ / *ix*
Acknowledgments / *xv*
List of Abbreviations / *xvi*

Introduction / 1
1. Friedrich Schleiermacher—The Possibility of Theology / 13
2. Friedrich Schleiermacher—Theology and Its Place in the University / 59
3. John Henry Newman—The Possibility and Nature of Theology / 99
4. John Henry Newman—Theology in the University / 163
5. Avery Cardinal Dulles—Ecclesial-Transformative Theology and the University / 187
6. Edward Farley—Theology as Sapiential Hermeneutic in the University / 229
7. University Theology as Saving and Sapiential / 289

Bibliography / 327
Index / 341

Foreword

ONE OF THE QUESTIONS academic theologians repeatedly ask themselves is how the theology they study and teach fits into the business of a university. The question, which has been in the air since the origin of Western universities in the twelfth century, really concerns the central meaning of both terms: it asks what a university is really about, and how theology, as a form of learning, fits into what a university does. Thomas Aquinas begins his *Summa Theologiae*, his monumental survey of the Church's tradition of "sacred learning" (*sacra doctrina*), by insisting theology is a genuine science, as sciences were then understood: it arranges what is known through revelation about God, the ultimate source and goal of all things in the world, in terms of causal explanation and deduction, just as geometry or physics arranges what is known about the visible world on the basis of a few basic assumptions (ST I, q. 1, a. 2). Aquinas's approach to the organization of our knowledge about God rests on the Christian Bible, as received and interpreted by the tradition of the Catholic Church. In his view, such knowledge communicates an understanding of ultimate truth, ultimate reality, because it reflects on what God has shared with the human race about the Mystery of his own being. "Sacred doctrine essentially treats of God viewed as the highest cause—not only so far as he can be known through creatures, as philosophers knew him ..., but also so far as he is known to himself alone, and revealed to others. Hence sacred doctrine is especially called wisdom" (ibid., a. 6). Wisdom, in the classical usage of Augustine and the West, is an understanding of truth that transforms the knower, by enabling him or her to participate personally and actively in the truth that is known. But because it is communicated to us first as a science, an organized body of human knowledge, theology—"sacred learning"—has a legitimate and indeed a centrally important role in the study and life of the university, where all human knowledge of the truth of creation is investigated.

Since the Enlightenment, religious faith has been understood less in terms of knowledge or wisdom than in terms of feeling: private convictions and assumptions, important to a person's individual choices and actions and to those of the community in which he or she is situated, but essentially inaccessible to the critical, public edge of reason. The university, on the other hand, has come to be seen, since the early nineteenth century, more and more as the institution where the objectified knowledge and empirically based thought strategies central to a liberal, secular, technologically advanced society are pursued and shared. Religious people, certainly, participate in any university's life, just as they participate in the civil society that supports and sanctions it; but just as civil societies in Europe and America have tended, since the eighteenth century, to insist more and more on an institutional separation between Church and state, and so effectively to insulate public life from the teachings and practices of religion, Western culture has come more and more to assume that the business of universities is not to reflect directly on religious faith or to promote religious practice. Religious thought and behavior, certainly, both individual and social, are understood to be worth studying in a scholarly way, as a highly influential aspect of human culture, a part of human history. But in a university, it is generally assumed, religion must be considered objectively, from the safe distance of the neutral observer; religious phenomena may be observed and measured, religious language analyzed, but the basic conviction of a worshipping community, living from and in a tradition of faith, needs to be kept separate from academic study, if the rules of scientific inquiry are to be rightly observed. Empirical "religious studies," in other words, or philosophical reflection on the possibility and meaningfulness of religious belief, may belong in a university; but theology, if it is understood in the traditional Augustinian sense as "faith seeking understanding," does not. The place for theology is taken by most academics to be the seminary—the institution dedicated to forming ministers for pastoral leadership within religious communities—not the university.

This growing sense of alienation between theology, as an academic discipline, and the work of the university raises difficult questions, of course, for those universities whose historic origin and public identity are connected with a particular religious tradition—especially in the United States, where such institutions are most numerous. The general pattern of development in religiously affiliated universities, as has been painstakingly pointed out by James T. Burtchaell, CSC,[1] has been a gradual move towards secularization. Many colleges and universities—founded by a Church or a religious group in the nineteenth or early twentieth century primarily to help educate people of that religious tradition and to empower them to participate fully in American life—have chosen to de-emphasize their religious ties in the past half-century or so and to cultivate the intellectual habits and attitudes of larger or more prestigious secular institutions. The result has been that the religious identity of these institutions has become marginal or largely symbolic: a campus chapel, perhaps, or a prayer by the chaplain at graduation, but little if any continuing influence by that Church or religious group on the university's intellectual culture. The reason for the distancing of these institutions from their religious base, Burtchaell argues, has generally not been any external pressure by the state, nor the influence of benefactors or trustees, but the desire of faculty and administrators to make their institutions conform to the wider secular pattern, and so to win increased respect among academic peers. One effect has been the transformation of departments of theology, in many universities with a religious origin, into departments of religious studies, with the assumption that the study of religion should be carried out from then on in an objective way, without specific confessional orientation.

For Catholic universities, the result of this trend has been a great deal of soul-searching, especially in the last two decades, centered on questions of religious identity. To a large degree, the origin of this discussion was the debate within the Catholic hierarchy about the implementation of Pope John Paul II's Apostolic Constitution on Catholic universities, *Ex corde ecclesiae*, published on August 15, 1990. Besides giving a ringing endorsement of the importance of higher education and academic research for the life of the Church, the document also lays down norms for the conduct and official recognition of Catholic institutions of learning. Among other things, it emphasizes the central importance of the teaching of theology in Catholic universities, and defines Catholic teachers of the theological sciences as bearers of an official mission to uphold and develop the authentic Catholic tradition of faith. This mission is to be expressed, the Constitution specifies, in an official

---

1. *Dying of the Light*. For the argument that some religiously founded universities in contemporary America have managed both to cultivate their academic values and to retain their ecclesial identities, see Benne, *Quality with Soul*.

document or "mandate" signed by both a theologian and his or her local bishop, marking a mutual commitment to loyalty and support, as bearers of distinct but essential roles in the Church's witness to the Gospel. Although the implementation of *Ex corde* occasioned heated debates in American academic circles and in the media, its stipulations seem to have been absorbed smoothly into the life of traditionally Catholic universities, and its affirming vision of the importance of the intellectual life for the Church's healthy functioning holds out real promise for a change in mood in both diocese and academy.

Meanwhile, the recent proliferation of "Catholic studies" programs at Catholic colleges and universities suggests a growing sense on the part of administrators, parents, and supporters that the Catholic identity of these institutions—so central to their continuing appeal and plausibility—is not always fully sustained on the intellectual level by existing departments of theology or religious studies. Catholic studies programs seem to many educational institutions a way to offer students a broad vision of the Church's history, literature, and culture, as well as an opportunity to study its theological tradition from the standpoint of thoughtful commitment rather than critical distance—from "within" the tradition rather than "outside" it.

At heart in these recent discussions, of course, is the double question of what theology really is, and how a university, in a pluralistic and technologically sophisticated society, best fulfills its mission. As "faith seeking understanding," theology clearly begins in the conviction that God—however mysterious, however ineffable and unreachable by the human mind—is the most real of all realities. To speak about God is to attempt to give voice to truth perceived, to point to what Newman calls the ultimate "fact." Theology relies on the canonical writings and interpretive traditions of a worshipping community as the source of its knowledge of God, and finds the ratification of its principles and conclusions in each believer's experience of a new and greater freedom to live a hopeful, productive, purposeful life. The university is a complex institution dedicated to the study and analysis of the reality we live in, the search for better ways of conceiving the truth and building our lives on it. So for a university whose history is bound up with a religious tradition, and whose continuing sense of its own identity affirms that tradition as central to what it is and wants to be, the serious study of theology is indispensable.

The difficult questions arise, though, when one tries to take this line of argument further. What does a university with a religious history and identity understand by theology? Is it essentially the reflective assimilation of its own community's traditional doctrine, a kind of academically refined catechesis? Is it the speculative exploration of new possibilities for applying traditional ideas? Is it philosophical consideration of our human ability to ask ultimate questions, the development of what Edward Farley calls "a hermeneutic self-consciousness," in which the believer might frame all the rest of his or her knowledge of the world? How is the study of theology, based on the faith of a historical worshipping community, and exposing that faith to all the questions intelligent modern people feel moved to raise about it, to be integrated with the other pursuits and practices a university undertakes? How does it shape the university's expectations of success at its task, its hopes for the kind of graduates it tries to produce? What part does theology play in forming the university's distinctive culture?

Brian W. Hughes's book, *Saving Wisdom*, helps ask some of these questions with greater depth and a wider perspective than we might otherwise do. It is fundamentally a detailed engagement with the thought of four major theologians of the nineteenth and twentieth century who spent much of their academic careers in universities: Friedrich Schleiermacher, John Henry Newman, Avery Dulles, and Edward Farley. Schleiermacher and Farley come from the Protestant tradition; Newman and Dulles are Catholics (and were both made cardinals of the Church in later life). Each of them represents a distinctive, well-articulated understanding of what authentic Christian theology is; of how theology is related to philosophy, Christian doctrine, and the other branches of human knowledge; and of how theology might play a central programmatic role in the intellectual life of a university. Hughes's achievement here is not simply to analyze the details of each of these four views of theology's place in the university, but also to show similarities and differences between them, continuing trajectories and new approaches, common concerns and particular perspectives, in ways that might surprise us. This is not a book that promotes a thesis of its own, so much as an engagement with four epochal thinkers who have asked an enduring modern question for intelligent people of faith: what is theology's real place in a university? May it teach us to seek our own answers to that question with a wisdom that will help save both our universities and ourselves.

Brian E. Daley, SJ
Department of Theology
University of Notre Dame

Acknowledgments

No book is written without sacrifice and support. This project started as a doctoral dissertation, inspired by working with Fr. Michael J. Buckley, SJ. Over the years, many friends provided gracious help. Brian E. Daley, a friend and mentor, suggested I publish the manuscript. Grant Kaplan read the entire book critically and largely translated portions of Schleiermacher's difficult Fraktur script. Dominic Doyle and Ted Kepes provided welcome suggestions and criticism. Rebecca Frey copyedited the manuscript, making fine observations and corrections that have only improved it. I am grateful to the late Avery Cardinal Dulles, SJ, Michael J. Himes, Robert J. Daly, SJ, Edward Farley, John Jones, and Bryan Le Beau for their varied forms of assistance. Staffs at the Johnson County Library, Kansas, and the National Institute of Newman Studies, Pittsburgh, have been tremendously supportive. Colleagues at the University of Saint Mary have been generous with their encouragement: Robert Schimoler, Kathleen Wood, SCL, Rosalie Curtin, SCL, Rosemary Kolich, SCL, Barbara Sellers, SCL, Marie Brinkman, SCL, Diane Steele, SCL, and Susan Rieke, SCL. Former Academic Vice President of the University of Saint Mary, Sandra Van Hoose, provided key summer research grants to sustain my efforts. Two graduate assistants, Darby O'Neil and Ryan Reed, proved competent and unflagging in the final stages of completion. Aside from my loving parents, I am deeply grateful to my extraordinary wife, Rosario Garriga. She has sacrificed, shown patience, and contributed beyond my expectations. Whatever shortcomings remain are solely mine.

Abbreviations

BO	Schleiermacher, *Brief Outline on the Study of Theology*.
CF	Schleiermacher, *The Christian Faith*, edited by H. R. Mackintosh and J. S. Stewart.
Craft	Avery Cardinal Dulles, *The Craft of Theology: From Symbol To System*, exp. ed.
DE	Edward Farley, *Divine Empathy: A Theology of God*.
EM	Edward Farley, *Ecclesial Man: A Social Phenomenology of Faith and Reality*.
ER	Edward Farley, *Ecclesial Reflection: An Anatomy of Theological Method*.
FK	Edward Farley, *The Fragility of Knowledge: Theological Education in the Church & the University*.
GA	John Henry Newman, *An Essay in Aid of A Grammar of Assent*, 1985.
Idea	John Henry Newman, *The Idea of a University*, 1976.
OT	Schleiermacher, *Occasional Thoughts On Universities in the German Sense*.
Speeches	Schleiermacher, *On Religion: Speeches To Its Cultured Despisers*, (1799). The 1799 edition will be cited as *Speeches*. The revised Oman translation of 1821 will be cited as *SP*.
ST	Thomas Aquinas, *Summa Theologiae*.
TH	Edward Farley, *Theologia: The Fragmentation and Unity of Theological Education*.
US	John Henry Newman, *Fifteen Sermons Preached at the University of Oxford*, edited by James David Earnest and Gerard Tracey.
VM	John Henry Newman, *The Via Media of The Anglican Church*, 1990.

Introduction

L'illumination n'est que la vision soudaine, par l'esprit, d'une route lentement préparée.

—Antoine de Saint Exupéry, *Pilote de Guerre*

PROBLEMATIC SITUATION: HISTORICAL AND CONTEMPORARY CRITICISMS OF THEOLOGY IN THE UNIVERSITY

IN NOVEMBER OF 1997, *The Boston Globe* reported a controversy over a course at the Massachusetts Institute of Technology offered by Dr. Anne Foerst in the engineering department. Its title was "God and Computers," and the readings for the course were taken largely from Christian theology. Dr. Foerst, a postdoctoral associate, theologian, and Lutheran minister, designed the course to examine "the role that Western assumptions about God and religion may play in the development of artificial intelligence, which seeks to build machines that have human-like capabilities." Although the course proposal won a prestigious Templeton Award in 1997, Professor Marvin Minsky—also of MIT and "widely known as father of artificial intelligence"—was quoted as saying that "'God and Computers' was 'not a serious discussion' and questioned whether it was a 'proper subject for an MIT credit course, rather than a possible ... extracurricular activity.'"[1] This dispute over the place of theology in the university, however, finds a peculiar parallel among certain Christian theologians.

In his book, *On Theology*, distinguished theologian Schubert Ogden reflects on the place of theology within the university. After distinguishing between philosophical and systematic theology, he concludes that "constructive *Christian* theology as such does not necessarily have any place in the liberal arts curriculum of the university. As rightly as it may

---

1. Ribadeneira, "Spirited Study of Science, Religion," B1, B8.

claim such a place in the curriculum of the explicitly Christian university, it seems quite out of place in the curriculum of any university that is not explicitly Christian."[2] How theology secures a place within the Christian university Ogden leaves unexplained. Thus, on a fundamental level, some Christian theologians like Ogden and a distinguished computer scientist, Minsky, seem to agree that Christian theology as such does not belong in the university.

But the comments of a distinguished educator earlier this century make such remarks appear quite mild. In 1936, noted educational leader Robert Hutchins castigated the growing specialization and fragmentation of university disciplines within higher learning in an attempt to discover something that might re-order and unify the university as a whole. In his attempt, he assessed the situation of theology and the modern university in a description that comes close to a dirge.

> The medieval university had a principle of unity. It was theology. The medieval theologians had worked out an elaborate statement in due proportion and emphasis of the truths relating to man and God, man and man, and man and nature . . . But these are other times; and we are trying to discover a rational and practical order for the higher learning of today. Theology is banned by law from some universities. It might as well be from the rest. Theology is based on revealed truth and on articles of faith. We are a faithless generation and take no stock in revelation. Theology implies orthodoxy and an orthodox church. We have neither. To look to theology to unify the modern university is futile and vain.[3]

For contemporary Protestant thinkers like Ogden and Hutchins, the exclusion of theology from the university is almost taken for granted. This view of theology and the university is in startling contradiction to the earlier universities of Europe in which theology held a premier place. What each of these distinct but related positions indicates is that for different reasons, Christian theology was found to be irrelevant or inappropriate or arcane or something done outside the university.

The line of criticism and controversy concerning theology's place within the university, however, has its seeds in the early discussions

---

2. Ogden, *On Theology*, 132.

3. Hutchins, *Higher Learning in America*, 96–97. For a good overview of the relationship between religion, theology, and the university, see the articles in Marsden and Longfield, *Secularization of the Academy*.

about the division of theology from philosophy reaching back into the disjunction between university culture and theology. Curiously, it was at the point in German history when universities were at their nadir that theology first fell seriously from its prestigious place alongside law and medicine.[4] The first modern university, the University of Halle (1694), was the setting. There, the philosopher Christian Wolff made modern philosophy usurp the place of theology by an enlightened appeal to reason alone.[5] "There are two kinds of truths, natural and supernatural. We know the former through reason, the latter through Holy Scripture. Philosophers who have trained their reason are the ones who are qualified to judge of the former; and the theologians, who are conversant with the true meaning of the Scriptures, are the ones who are qualified to judge the latter. Whoever wishes to judge both kinds of truth must be a philosopher and a theologian at the same time."[6]

The distinction that Wolff drew between philosophy and theology was hardly unknown. But its influence and power within the university was new.[7] While not hostile to the existence of theology per se, Wolff so sharply separated philosophical truth from theological truth that he fashioned their relationship as one of alienation rather than accord.

---

4. Paulsen, *German Universities and University Study*, 42ff. "At the end of the seventeenth century the German universities had sunk to the lowest level which they ever reached in the public esteem and in their influence upon the intellectual life of the German people. The world of fashion, which centered at the princely courts, looked down upon them from the heights of its modern culture as the seats of an obsolete and pedantic scholasticism. A man like Leibniz, who had secured his scientific education at Paris and London, disdained a position at a University, although, as the most distinguished scholar and philosopher of Germany, such a place was naturally open to him anywhere. He preferred the courts, where he could hope to find readier appreciation and assistance for his intellectual strivings..."

5. Ibid., 45.

6. Wolff, unpaginated dedication to the first edition of the "German Teleology," *Vernünfftige Gedanken von den Absichten der natürlichen Dinge, den Liebhabern der Wahrheit mitgetheilet*, as quoted in Saine, *Problem of Being Modern*, 130.

7 See Saine, *Problem of Being Modern*, 130ff.; Cf. Paulsen, 44ff.; Joseph Hough maintains, based on Paulsen, that: "[R]ational knowledge was to be advanced by research. Knowledge was no longer seen to be the wisdom of the past that was simply to be transmitted to students, nor was it the function of the university to preserve and secure ancient truths against challenge. The assumption on which the new university instruction was to be based was that truth was to be discovered." "Marginalization of Theology in the University," 42–43.

Wolff's disjunction of theology and philosophy controverts what Thomas Aquinas classically argued in the *Summa Theologiae*. He differentiates two senses of theology: "theology that belongs to sacred doctrine differs according to kind from that theology which is placed as part of philosophy."[8] But here theology was both part of revelation *and* philosophy. There is not alienation but a distinction and a certain harmony. In contrast, Wolff eliminates this distinction so that theology becomes all revelation and philosophy becomes utterly rational. Though Aristotle subsumed theology under metaphysics, Aquinas not only adheres to his division but enriches it by holding a theology proper to *sacra doctrina*. Both kinds of theology existed in the medieval university but in different ways. Wolff's division effectively collapses the distinction between revelation and the theology that pertains to revelation so that the distinction now becomes revelation over and against rational philosophy. Philosophy now usurped the place that theology previously held as a university discipline.

Prior to Wolff, philosophical studies at German universities were propadeutic to theology—philosophy organically connected with and gave way to theology. But because of the influence of Wolff's argument, the relationship between philosophy and theology changed. Philosophy became an enterprise entirely independent of theology.[9] The great historian of the German university, Friedrich Paulsen, describes something of this new alienation between philosophy and theology when he writes of Wolff: "Basing himself upon the modern sciences of mathematics and physics, he declares that philosophy should seek the truth free from all assumptions, regardless of what may happen to the theologians. Similarly as in the case of theoretical philosophy, the theological basis of practical philosophy was also positively repudiated: law and morals, he declared, must be based upon a rational knowledge of human life and society."[10] Philosophy and other university research were thus emancipated from the influence of or relationship to theology. The ascendancy of Wolff's re-organization of the university relationship between philosophy and

---

8. *ST*, I. Q. 1., art. 2. "Unde theologia quae ad sacram doctrinam pertinet, differt secundum genus ab illa theologia quae pars philosophiae ponitur."

9. Saine, *Problem of Being Modern*, 130.

10. Paulsen, *German Universities and University Study*, 45.

theology was enormous. His system would soon enter and dominate every Protestant university in the eighteenth century.[11]

There is a strange concordance, however, between the influential argument advanced by a rational philosopher into the university setting and the essential practice of at least one major ecclesiastical leader. Wilhelm Emmanuel Ketteler, a significant nineteenth-century Neo-Scholastic and Catholic bishop of Mainz, judged the Mainz seminary rather than the university to be the proper place for theological study. Not only was he "convinced that the university was not a beneficial environment in which to form loyal and good servants of the Church" but he also believed that "academic theology possessed only secondary importance in the education of priests." What Ketteler carried out as a necessary strategy, namely, of preserving the church from secularizing forces, stridently in continuity with the Catholic church's defensive reaction to rationalism and liberalism, was virtually raised to the level of doctrine. Ketteler saw the universities dominated by modern philosophy—the legacy of Wolff—as a threat to theological and ministerial training.[12] Thus, what compounded the alienation of theology from philosophy and other university disciplines partly emerged from within theology itself. In practice, Ketteler conceded the validity of Wolff's argument. Not only was Ketteler's decision an instance of intellectual retreat on the part of theology, but it finds odd support among contemporary critics of theology's place in the university. What had once been the unifying feature of university education—theology—now parted company from university disciplines and their claim to comprehensive knowledge.

Significantly, however, theology's recent history of exclusion from the university is partly a judgment not about the university but a judgment about the nature of theology itself. Historically, within Protestant and Catholic churches and among their theologians, critical judgments

11. Ibid. Paulsen further maintains that "The reception of the new philosophy and science marks a turning point for the German universities. Through it they were enabled to struggle out of the bog in which they had lain at the close of the seventeenth century; and under the leadership of the Wolffian system they won the ascendancy in the intellectual life of the German people," 46.

12. Madges, "Does Theology Belong in the University? The Nineteenth-Century Case in Ireland and Germany," 167. Gerald McCool contends that "Rome was more interested in securing a doctrinally sound ultramontanist education for the priests who would be the spiritual leaders of the loyal Catholics of the lower and middle classes than it was in developing a sophisticated university theology aimed at the aristocracy and the upper bourgeoisie." *Nineteenth-Century Scholasticism*, 133.

about theology were made that help explain some of the confusion and controversy concerning the place and nature of theology in the contemporary university.

SHIFTING THEOLOGICAL LOCATIONS IN PROTESTANT AND CATHOLIC HISTORY: PAST AND PRESENT

In the latter decades of the nineteenth century, the place of American Protestant theological training shifted from theological tutors to seminaries to university-related divinity schools. Earlier emphasis upon the spiritual formation of ministers, classical training in a kind of theological *paideia*—piety with learning—collided with later ideals of "impartial scientific scholarship." Ideas about how theology should be done evolved. When theology changed from something that different denominations did to a historical discipline, many ecclesiastical leaders thought this shift was an advance in the direction of religious and inter-denominational unity. This shift from theology as primarily a denominational preserve also helped lessen the American public's perception of Protestant theology as "contentious, sectarian, and divisive."[13] This past perception had restricted the ability of Protestant theology to speak with unity and authority upon important issues. As Clark Gilpin maintains: "In both seminaries and colleges at mid-century [1850s], scholars proposed to transcend sectarian debate and avoid the divorce of religious belief from the academy by advancing a new understanding of religion based on historical scholarship, which could exert unifying intellectual influence in church and society.[14]" Moreover, there were calls for theology to be socially useful. Many believed that the horizon of theology needed to be broader and reach beyond its narrow contraction to individual congregations or denominations. Protestant theology needed to become more credible to different communities and different disciplines. It needed to enter into the political and civic discourse that was shaping the nation. In short, theology needed to become more public.[15]

Different ideals of scientific, disciplined scholarship and application, in turn, meant that more specialized and professional training displaced the setting of serious and rigorous theology from particular localities to centers of theological inquiry: university-related divinity schools.

---

13. Gilpin, *Preface to Theology*, 45.
14. Ibid., 51f.
15. Ibid., 46–53.

As liberal theologians, the primary proponents of this change, sought harmony between the Christian tradition and the broader intellectual culture, they insisted on reinterpreting the doctrines of Christianity to fit the needs and the language of the time.[16] But as theological scholarship advanced, a rupture within the unity of theological contexts—between church and academy—developed. As Clark Gilpin writes, "The academic theologian sought historical understanding through critical appraisal of evidence. The religious inquirer sought guidance for the impending spiritual and ethical judgments of social life."[17] According to one observer, Gerald Birney Smith, the "truths" that both directions pursued "are so different in their psychological aspects that the teaching of the one does not necessarily involve the teaching of the other."[18] Pastoral, spiritual formation and academic rigor began to separate.[19]

American Protestant theology moved into the university through its lodging in professional and divinity schools and seminaries related to or affiliated with universities. This transition, however, initiated the legacy of what Edward Farley calls the "clerical paradigm" of theology. That is, theology was to be realized through a course of studies leading to practical ministry.[20] As schools of medicine train doctors and schools of law train lawyers, so divinity schools train clergy, a professional occupation.[21] In the late nineteenth and early twentieth centuries of American Protestant theological history, professionalization and specialization became necessary to meet the pluralism of issues and challenges fac-

16. Ibid., 95f.
17. Ibid., 103–4.
18. Quoted in ibid., 104.
19. It should be noted that the number of ministers going to divinity schools or seminaries who were highly educated from the start was not terribly large. One suspects, therefore, that the number of ministers affected by changes which occurred in the teaching and nature of Protestant theology was not large either. According to William Adams Brown and Mark A. May's four volume study, "An analysis of the 1926 Religious Census figures for seventeen of the largest white Protestant denominations in the United States, shows that two out of five of all the ministers of these denominations were graduates neither of college nor of theological seminary, while only one in three was a graduate of both. One need not exaggerate the importance of purely academic training in a profession in which personal qualities count for so much as in the ministry to feel that a situation like this must cause serious concern." *Education of American Ministers*, I:4, as quoted in Kelsey, *Between Athens and Berlin*, 55.
20. Farley, *TH*, 127–35.
21. Harvey, "On the Intellectual Marginality of American Theology," 185.

ing the Christian church.²² But how academic theology figured into the increasingly complex intellectual and social situation and served professional ministry became the source of much controversy. Clark Gilpin maintains that

> the recurrent question of whether or not academic theology contributed to the proper equipment of the church's ministry came to focus in this era on the authority that should be attributed to technical expertise achieved through specialized university research. What sort of education do ministers really need? This was a question with high stakes, since the narrowing of theology to a specialized expertise not only heightened doubts about its pastoral utility but also reduced the clergy to theologians-at-second-hand, something akin to backyard astronomers, who looked to academic theologians for "original," constructive religious thought.²³

What had taken place was a progressive hibernation of theology. Theology was less and less in evidence in the university curriculum as a whole. Near the turn of the century, liberal theologians envisioned theology as rigorous, critical historical scholarship and tried to reconnect it to the canons of academic inquiry; but this inevitably involved de-emphasizing confessional doctrine.²⁴ Theology as pastoral thus became increasingly sequestered in the divinity schools and thus more removed from university disciplines. Indeed, given the growing number of contemporary criticisms of classically "Protestant" theological education, it seems clear that the question over this hibernation remains ongoing even today.²⁵

Similar to the course of American Protestant theology, there was a parallel in American Catholic theological history. Something comparable to the historically pastoral intent of Protestant theology can also be seen in Catholic theology. Since the anti-modernist movement, theology's "hibernation" within Catholic universities and colleges generally subsided only after Vatican II.²⁶ The setting for Catholic theology was

---

22. Gilpin, *Preface to Theology*, 87.
23. Ibid., 88.
24. Ibid., 98ff.
25. See Farley, *TH*; *FK*; Wheeler and Farley, *Shifting Boundaries*; Griffin and Hough, *Theology and the University*; Wood, *Vision and Discernment*.
26. I borrow the term "hibernation" from Hennesey, *American Catholics*, 203.

almost without exception the seminary, despite its exceptional appearance at the Catholic University of America at the turn of the century.[27] The character of Catholic theology pursued in these seminaries before Vatican II was apologetic and pastoral. Moral theology in the manualist tradition was largely the focus because of its immediate applicability to practical problems.[28] The demand for priests to help resolve the laity's moral questions surpassed all other theological concerns. Charles Curran describes something of this environment concerning ecclesiastical training during nineteenth-century American Catholic life.

> Bishops needed priests and were even willing to cut short their study if they were trained in moral theology. In 1813 John Carroll, the archbishop of Baltimore, writing to a Jesuit superior called for the early ordination of priests even if they had not studied all the treatises on divinity provided they knew the obvious and general principles of moral theology. Archbishop Samuel Eccleston of Baltimore in writing about a particular seminarian in 1845 told the seminary president that he could not ordain the seminarian until he had a good course in moral theology. Give preference to moral theology and postpone dogmatic theology if necessary. Not only was the practical ministry of the priest the primary criterion of seminary training but the needs of the ministry could shorten that training provided the preparation in moral theology was adequate.[29]

With few exceptions, serious academic and rigorous Catholic theology, what was called at the time "dogmatic," was not a priority for clerics before and beyond the crisis of modernism up to Vatican II. Catholic theology would have been studied by laypersons even less. Indeed, according to eminent historian of Catholic higher education, Philip Gleason, theology "was strictly a seminary subject, which had never been taught to collegians. All they had traditionally gotten was the catechism for an hour a week. Religion, many Catholic educators held, was not an academic subject at all—it was a way of life."[30]

---

27. Gleason, "Catholic Higher Education as Historical Context for Theological Education," 26.

28. Curran, *Origins of Moral Theology in the United States*, 63.

29. Ibid., 63–64.

30. Gleason, "Catholic Higher Education as Historical Context for Theological Education," 26.

What did pass for the most rigorous "theological" reflection, in contrast, occurred in Catholic universities prior to the mid-1960s as "philosophy."[31] Its heritage and influence was Aquinas, and it energized many important Thomist and Neo-Thomist philosophers and theologians. This history is well known and need not be repeated here. In any case, if philosophy was the integral discipline in Catholic universities for much of this century, during the 1960s the role shifted to theology. "Before long," writes David O'Brien, "the newly diverse philosophy departments lost their way and theology was left alone to provide the distinguishing intellectual component of Catholic higher education."[32] This shift intensified during and after Vatican II. As students and professors of theology were increasingly no longer clerics, so Catholic theology was no longer strictly clerical nor was it limited to seminaries. Theology was being studied, taken-up, and transformed by university and college educated men and women.

The heritage of Bishop Ketteler still continues to affect the understanding of theology's place in the university to some extent. One must recognize that even in the Catholic church itself there is—among some—suspicion and reserve about Catholic theology in the university. Again, this is because of a judgment made about theology—not about universities. In January 1998, Catholic theologian Thomas Rausch observed as serious problems not only "the growing chasm between professional theology and the life and faith of the church" but also the increasing polarization among "liberals" and "conservatives." For liberals, he sees that "the contextual emphasis in contemporary scholarship has led to increasingly specialized theologies—liberation, feminist and ecological—focusing on interests of particular disadvantaged groups." Moreover, he criticizes the focus of these theologies as "more ideological than evangelical or religious." As for conservatives, he maintains that they "do not trust the theology of the academy; they object that it has demythologized the Bible into meaningful stories rather than narratives that have anything to do with history, deconstructed the authority of the church and its ordained ministry, substituted a permissive sexual ethics

---

31. For a good overview, see Gleason, *Contending With Modernity*, 114–15, 138–45, 163–66. It is noteworthy that theology courses were only urged as a way to unify undergraduate Catholic curricula in 1939. See O'Brien, *From The Heart of the American Church*, 43.

32. O'Brien, *From the Heart of the American Church*, 48.

for traditional Catholic morality, and transformed Catholic theology into the ideological agenda of contemporary liberal culture." Furthermore, he adds distressingly that "so many Catholic students are unable to give an account of what salvation means or summarize the message of the Gospel in concrete terms seems to them [conservatives] to confirm their negative judgment. Nor are such critics simply exaggerating. They have some legitimate concerns."[33] Rausch's comments indicate what is symptomatic in Catholic higher education: concern over the function, place and future of theology—externally and internally—is widespread and urgent.

AIMS OF THIS STUDY

The question of whether theology belongs in the university or the dubious consequences of its residence in divinity schools or seminaries spark ongoing debate. But there is an even more basic issue: what precisely *is* theology? The problematic situation sketched above is multi-dimensional: there is ambiguity concerning whether theology belongs in the university, the relationship of theology in the university to religious faith, to church authority, and to other academic disciplines. In important ways, Friedrich Schleiermacher, John Henry Newman, Avery Cardinal Dulles, SJ, and Edward Farley consider these issues in different historical periods. Certainly, there are differences in educational assumptions, ecclesial denomination, academic culture, technology and social demographics that separate the two centuries and the theologians themselves. Unlike Avery Cardinal Dulles and Edward Farley, each of whom taught in Christian universities, Schleiermacher helped found and taught theology in the first modern secular university in Europe—the University of Berlin—without any religious affiliation.[34] Newman, though deeply

---

33. Rausch, "Divisions, Dialogue, and the Catholicity of the Church," 21–29. Rausch corroborates the observation of Arthur L. Kennedy. "It is evident today that most students are unfamiliar with the most important teachings about Catholic faith and that the expectations among college faculty regarding prior catechesis has been accordingly weakened," "Introduction of Theology in the Catholic Tradition," 90. David O'Brien echoes the same problems. "Appeals to form Catholic lay leaders and to offer Catholic perspectives on contemporary culture ignore the yawning chasm between campus ministry and the research and teaching at the center of university life, as well as between theology and the other academic departments and professional programs." *From the Heart of the American Church*, 119.

34. Howard, *Protestant Theology and the Making of the Modern German University*, 130.

involved in university and elementary education, was never a formal university professor.[35] However, allowing for these and other cultural differences in time and place, each theologian not only formulates an important view of theology but also combines it with a robust stance of how theology inhabits the university.

Precisely because these theologians treat aspects of the larger problematic situation, the main question of this inquiry can be raised: can a comparative and critical exposition of their thought yield fundamental patterns about theology's academic meaning and purpose? Secondly, if fundamental patterns are operative within their thinking, do these patterns persist as general norms? If they do persist, then this study can valuably illuminate options and implications about the future of theology in the university for the twenty-first century. It is my contention that viewing these different conceptions of theology's presence in the university together rather than in isolation has exactly this advantage of tracing deeper currents that escape notice within the contemporary discussion.

In pursuit of this goal, this investigation explores a range of diverse topics: the relationship of theology to religious experience; theology and church authority; a theologian's ecclesial and academic commitments; the connection between faith and theological understanding; participation in a religious symbol system; theology as wisdom; and the difference between religion and theology. To conclude, let me provide a contextual disclaimer. Though I am shaped by the Catholic theological tradition, I believe the implications of this study for theology as an academic entity necessarily extend beyond Catholic theology and Catholic institutions. For this reason, the argument of the book is not confined to the nature of theology in a Catholic university but, more broadly, in a Christian institution of higher learning.

---

35. Newman was rector of the short-lived Catholic University of Ireland and also established the Oratory school in Birmingham.

1

Friedrich Schleiermacher—The Possibility of Theology

> Since each person, as an individual, is the not-being of the other, it is never possible to eliminate non-understanding completely.
>
> —Friedrich Schleiermacher

My purpose in this chapter is to establish Friedrich Schleiermacher's approach to Christian theology from the perspective of its possibility. The scope of the chapter is not comprehensive; it enlists primarily two works: the *Brief Outline of the Study of Theology* and *The Christian Faith*.[1] This chapter is, however, a necessary preliminary to understanding how Schleiermacher situated theology within the university. I contend that Schleiermacher reinterpreted Christianity and Christian theology from within the Reformed tradition. He initiated a reform in theological argumentation at the center of this reinterpretation. Schleiermacher adduced the religious experience of God as the warrant for theology. Radically simplified, he considered the Christian religious self-consciousness and its relation to the redemption of Jesus Christ the content of theology. As with every particular content, Schleiermacher also posits a complex expression. I maintain that it is precisely this expression that allows Christian theology to be a legitimate area of human and ecclesial reflection. Furthermore, this expression gives evidence of prior conditions. And it is precisely these conditions that I identify as theology's possibility.

---

1. Schleiermacher, *Brief Outline of the Study of Theology*, cited hereafter as *BO*. *Christian Faith*, hereafter cited as *CF*. German editions will be indicated by adding a "g" to the reference. German references are taken from Schleiermacher, *Universitätsschriften. Herakleitos. Kurze Darstellung des theologischen Studiums*, *KGA* with number; and *Der Christliche Glaube* cited as *CB*.

As certain contents of Christian theology find realization in *The Christian Faith*, the *Brief Outline* expresses the different aspects of theological reflection. In the *Brief Outline*, Schleiermacher distinguishes three branches of theology: philosophical, historical, and practical. The text is not a profound investigation into a single question or topic proper but rather an overview. He intended the work to be a student textbook, but its context is now that of a new church. In the preface to the first edition, which Schleiermacher left unrevised when the second edition was published, the outline seeks to call the "students' full attention to matters of form, so that they may better apprehend the significance of the particular parts and their interrelation."[2] What Schleiermacher attempts in the *Brief Outline* is merely to give a kind of shape or design to serious theology.

Schleiermacher defines theology broadly at the beginning of the *Brief Outline* as "a positive science, whose parts join into a cohesive whole only through their common relation to a particular mode of faith, i.e., a particular way of being conscious of God. Thus, the various parts of Christian theology belong together only by virtue of their relation to 'Christianity.'"[3] The main ideas that contribute to the possibility of theology are evident: theology as *Wissenschaft*; the integrity of its different branches; the origin of theology in the religious experience of God; and the social expression of the relationship between humans and God in history as Christianity and the church. Schleiermacher's understanding of theology as a discipline is possible only if it is an entity related and ordered to the historical reality of Christianity—specifically the existence of the Christian church. There is, however, another element equally fundamental to the possibility of theology, namely the theologian. In the *Brief Outline*, Schleiermacher not only describes the different branches of theology but also attends—less systematically—to theological and "scientific" formation. The formation of the theologian, the requisite skills, habits of mind, and other scholarly qualities are major factors in Schleiermacher's view of theology. How the theologian is formed and disposed to carry out the tasks of theology invariably affect

---

2. *BO*, "Preface to the First Edition," 17. It is difficult to know whether Schleiermacher thought it should be widely used or simply a helpful interpretation that finds a place among others. He does tell us, however, that "I am in no position to claim that other teachers should use it [the Outline]."

3. Ibid., §1, 19.

theology's meaning and entailments.[4] In short, theology will be shown to be possible for several reasons: 1) the religious consciousness of God as piety, the feeling of absolute dependence; 2) human nature as religious nature—spirituality; 3) piety as social, historical, and ecclesial; and 4) the character of the theologian.

THE PROBLEM OF AUDIENCE

As inquirers seek to discover and reveal, they must also view their subject matter within its context as well as elucidate its proper characteristics. For my purposes, part of this inquiry involves acknowledging those intellectual currents antecedent to and coextensive with Schleiermacher's own work. Most of these currents originated in the eighteenth century. Historians of theology and ideas note familiar recurrent themes: Enlightenment optimism in rationality, criticism of authority, historical criticism of the Bible, deism, pietism, Romanticism, individualism, the successes of empirical science, rejection of supernatural revelation, and insistence on rational morality.[5] These ideas and movements form the philosophical and theological background of Schleiermacher's theology and that of the nineteenth century. Claude Welch maintains that the "theological problem of the 19th century" was precisely "How is theology possible?"[6] Schleiermacher recognized this question early in his career.[7] His philosophical and theological education enabled him to grasp Enlightenment attitudes toward theology and religion, especially from his early thorough and sympathetic reading of Kant to his subsequent criticism of the philosopher.[8] How Schleiermacher presents Christian

---

4. I agree with John Thiel, who, in defining *theological authorship*, argues that "the theologian is a creative agent whose talent is essential to the performance and the results of the theological task." The importance of the theologian's role in Schleiermacher's thought has also been argued by Thiel and Bradford E. Hinze. See *Imagination and Authority*, ix; and "Theological Responsibility," 573–98; Hinze, *Narrating History, Developing Doctrine*, 177–89.

5. See K. Barth, *Protestant Theology in the Nineteenth Century*, 80–173; Welch, *Protestant Thought in the Nineteenth Century*; González, *History of Christian Thought*, 318–46; Evans et al., *History of Christian Theology*, 206–29; Gay, *Enlightenment*; and Vidler, *Church in an Age of Revolution*.

6. Welch, *Protestant Thought*, 59.

7. Cf. Schleiermacher, *Speeches*. For a good account of how the problematic situation of theology affected Schleiermacher, see Redeker, *Schleiermacher*, 2f.

8. *Speeches*, 19–20. For a critical stance toward Kant, see Schleiermacher, *On Freedom*.

theology, then, must be situated within and in important ways viewed as standing in opposition to this intellectual milieu.[9] Attempts to grasp Schleiermacher's thought must consider the totality of the immediate context—a fundamental tenet of his own hermeneutics.[10] The readers of his *On Religion: Speeches to Its Culture Despisers* (1799), a new kind of apologetical dialogue with the philosophical currents critical of Christian religion and theology, cannot escape engaging these currents in grasping Schleiemacher's main points.[11]

A grasp of Schleiermacher's general intellectual environment is one thing; uncovering the precise identity of the thinkers to whom Schleiermacher paid his intellectual debts is another.[12] Scholarly debate over this question has never been resolved. From the beginning to the present day, interpretations of Schleiermacher's thought have not yielded a consensus. He is not unlike Hegel in that wildly different evaluations have circulated about his writings. His first letter to Lücke shows how varied and contradictory were the initial interpretations of *The Christian Faith*. "[O]ne calls me a gnostic; another an Alexandrian, which is the opposite of a gnostic; one traces my thought back to Schelling; another, to Jacobi; one claims I teach the principles of monastic morality, whereas another considers me a Cyrenian, even though he does not explicitly say so—to these persons I could only say that they should first come to agree among themselves, an apt piece of advice for such situations, which a friend recently used with good success in a similar debate with opponents.[13]" Contemporary interpretations virtually mirror the first ones. In 1995, Thandeka summarized the findings of Ulrich Barth concerning present interpretations of Schleiermacher.

> The barrage of mutually exclusive and conflicting claims about Schleiermacher's theology has persisted . . . scholars and theologians have concluded that Schleiermacher's link between self-consciousness and God-consciousness is basically adequate

---

9. For a fine overview of the intellectual milieu concerning his idea of religion, see Crouter, "Introduction," *Speeches*, 1–39.

10. See Schleiermacher, "General Hermeneutics," *Hermeneutics and Criticism*, 231.

11. See *Speeches*, "First Speech: Apology," 88–90. There Schleiermacher contends that the cultured despisers have really misunderstood the nature of religion from the beginning.

12. Jaqueline Mariña argues that Kant and Leibniz are "two of the greatest influences" upon his philosophical thought. *Transformation of the Self*, 15.

13. See Schleiermacher, *On the Glaubenslehre*, 36.

(Johann Friedrich Röhr); inadequate (Friedrich Wilhelm Gess); ontological (Marlin E. Miller); a specific mode of time-consciousness (Hans-Richard Reuter); the basis for interpreting religion as mystical, anti-moral and anti-intellectual (Emil Brunner); philosophic ethics (Emmanuel Hirsch); the basis for a system of aesthetics as the process of an ethical activity (Rudolf Odebrecht); inadequate as the basis for a philosophic doctrine of art (Edmund Husserl); platonic (Berhard Todt); Kantian (Wilhelm Dilthey); Fichtean (Immanuel Hermann Fichte); Spinozistic and Schellingian (Christoph von Sigwart); and Jacobian (Eilert Herms).[14]

Perhaps what accounts for this diversity of opinion is not simply the often nontechnical language of the *Brief Outline* and the *Glaubenslehre*, but also the thinkers Schleiermacher engaged before writing them. A brief glance at his early writings reveals his reading in and writing on Plato, Aristotle, Spinoza, Leibniz, Kant, and Jacobi.[15] If one adds to Schleiermacher's diverse philosophical interests the contradictions and plurality among his commentators, any interpretation put forward at this point in time must be mindful of its limits. One should also be mindful of the present age, in which all textual interpretation inevitably contains conscious and unconscious projections as well as prior theological and philosophical commitments. My own interpretation is no exception to these cautionary realities.

This contentious atmosphere might also result from the span of Schleiermacher's corpus. The *Speeches* was first published in 1799, when its author was thirty-one. He revised the work twice, in 1806 and 1821. There are two editions of both the *Brief Outline* (1810, 1830) and *The Christian Faith* (1821/1822 and 1829/1830). Revisions make the problem of interpretation double-barreled: the "what" question now combines with "when." Regarding Schleiermacher's major works, Richard Crouter notes that his habit of revising reflects his interest in meeting new problems and new audiences. He did not simply repeat himself but changed his thinking over time.[16] If this perspective is accurate, then which currents did Schleiermacher consciously confront in his understanding of

---

14. Thandeka, *Embodied Self*, 9. Information is condensed from Barth, *Christentum und Selbstbewußtsein*.

15. Schleiermacher, *Jugendschriften 1787–1796, KGA* I.1; *Schriften aus der Berliner Zeit 1796–1799, KGA* I.2. Editions cited hereafter as *KGA* with number.

16. *Speeches*, 57. See also Crouter, "Rhetoric and Substance," 285–306.

theology? Since his life and work overlap the eighteenth and nineteenth centuries, the task seems daunting, especially concerning the relationship of theology to philosophy.[17] One way to determine the philosophical influences on Schleiermacher's work entails modifying the question: with whom was Schleiermacher conversing in the *Brief Outline* and *The Christian Faith*? Who was his audience?

It is astonishing that Schleiermacher does not explicitly mention a single name in either edition of the *Brief Outline*.[18] This omission means that commentators and readers have fewer built-in checks and controls on their interpretations. The reader must infer which theologians he followed or critiqued. This principle also holds for any philosophical principles that he used or language he employed. The prefaces of each edition are not helpful since neither reveals much about his audience except that it included his immediate students. Instead, he tells about his programmatic intent. The preface to the first edition indicates that the current array of textbooks did not meet his lecture needs, so he is embarking in a different "order of treatment."[19] Schleiermacher was also the first professor of dogmatics at the Prussian University of Berlin. He stopped dealing with an established department curriculum and set down something of his own.

The Christian Faith gives us more interesting information, especially the index of names and the preface. If the index is used to adduce evidence about his audience, one recognizes immediately that it cannot be professional philosophers. In a book of some 751 pages, Plato, Aristotle, Leibniz, and Cicero are each mentioned only once. There is an even more telling omission; Schleiermacher does not refer even once to his philosophical contemporaries, namely Kant, Fichte, Schelling, and F. H. Jacobi. As for the controversial introduction, it contains only two references to philosophers: one to Plato and the other to Moses Mendelssohn—hardly a dialogue. If Schleiermacher was not speaking to philosophers or addressing philosophical subjects, what about theologians? Again the index is revealing. Contemporaries are named: Baumgarten-Crusius, Bretschneider, de Wette, Daub, Delbrück, Sack, Steffens, and Wegscheider. But all receive passing mention in a single reference—like the philoso-

---

17. Crouter, "Rhetoric and Substance," 285.

18. *KGA*, 1.6. See "Namen," 468–73. All the names listed in both editions are in the editor's footnotes.

19. *BO*, "Preface to the First Edition," 17.

phers. Other Protestant theologians, however, are cited more frequently, namely Johann Gerhard (1582–1637) and closer to his own time, Franz Volkmar Reinhard (1753–1812).[20] Reinhard, surprisingly, appears more often than Calvin. Yet the vast majority of references are to traditional theologians: Augustine, Calvin, Luther, Melanchthon. Furthermore, the confessions, creeds, and catechisms of the church are the most frequently cited of all.[21] Still, what about the preface? In the preface to the second edition, Schleiermacher states unequivocally his hope that "the book might contribute to an ever clearer understanding as to the meaning of our Evangelical Faith." Opposing his critics of the first edition, he writes: "I must protest most emphatically against the honour recently done me in some quarters of bringing me forward as the head of a new theological school. I protest against this, because I am without either of the two requisite qualifications. In the first place, I have invented nothing, so far as I remember, except my order of topics and here or there a descriptive phrase; and similarly in my thinking I have never had any other aim than that of communicating my thoughts by way of stimulus, for each to use in his own fashion."[22]

Schleiermacher insists he does nothing new except for rearranging topics. The index and his references certainly bolster the claim. There is, however, another clue that indicates his presentation was more original than it may initially appear. King Frederick William III of Prussia decreed in 1817, only four years earlier than the first edition of *The Christian Faith* (1821), the merger of the Reformed and Lutheran churches into a

---

20. Johann Gerhard, whom Bossuet called "le troisième homme de la Réforme," was the major Protestant theologian of the seventeenth century. Professor at the University of Jena from 1616 until his death, his massive nine-volume *Loci theologici* was the standard text of Lutheran orthodoxy. In it, Gerhard brought the received thinking concerning Scripture into conversation with Aristotle and employed "all the available tools of philology, grammar, and philosophy." Scharlemann, *Thomas Aquinas and John Gerhard*, 4–7. See also the entry "Gerhard, Johann," *Oxford Dictionary of the Christian Church*, 666–67. Franz Volkmar Reinhard was a professor of philosophy and theology at the University of Wittenberg who later become part of the supreme consistory of Dresden. The work Schleiermacher refers to, often as a foil, is his *Vorlesungen über die Dogmatik*. In his dogmatic work and copious sermons, Reinhard sought to harmonize Lutheran faith and doctrine with reason. See "Reinhard, Franz Volkmar," *New Schaff-Herzog Encyclopedia of Religious Knowledge*, 449.

21. See *CF*, 756–57.

22. *CF*, viii.

single Prussian united church.[23] So for Schleiermacher, a new dogmatics was required for a new church. Indeed, *The Christian Faith* was written "with special reference to the Union of the two Protestant communions—the Lutheran and the Reformed."[24] What, then, can be concluded provisionally?

The evidence from the prefaces and indexes to the *Brief Outline* and *The Christian Faith* do not prove that Schleiermacher avoids philosophy absolutely. What the references do show, however, is that claims that Schleiermacher engages in philosophical reflection to counter the philosophers of his time are difficult to sustain. It is reasonable to conclude that just as his primary sources are ecclesial, so is his audience. The question then emerges: is it feasible to explain the possibility of theology from internal and specifically Christian evidence? Must one, in other words, correlate the tenets of Christian doctrine with the philosophical idealism of Fichte, Schelling, Jacobi, and others to understand how theology is possible?[25] No. Moreover, there is no need to rely on prefaces or indices alone for support. Schleiermacher offers two compelling statements about the fact that his theology does not rely on philosophical presuppositions for its integrity. In the introduction to *The Christian Faith*, Schleiermacher states: "[T]he present work entirely disclaims the task of establishing on a foundation of general principles a Doctrine of God, or an Anthropology or Eschatology either, which should be used in the Christian church though it did not really originate there, or which should prove the propositions of the Christian Faith to be consonant with reason."[26] If the work adheres to this principle, then Schleiermacher

---

23. Rouse and Neill, *History of the Ecumenical Movement 1517–1948*, 286. For the official documents, see Huber and Huber, *Staat und Kirche im 19. und 20. Jahrhunderts: Dokumente zur Geschichte des deutschen Staatskirchenrechte*, I:576–78.

24. *CF*, "Author's Preface to the Second Edition," viii.

25. Such questions raise the complicated issue of the relationship between philosophy and theology in Schleiermacher's thought—a difficult area meriting the kind of reflection beyond the scope of this section. I propose instead to take up more basic considerations and leave this discussion to later sections.

26. *CF*, 3. According to F. Lichtenberger, a similar separation can also be found in Schleiermacher's friend and pupil August Twesten in his *Vorlesungen über die Dogmatik der evangel. lutherischen Kirche*, quoted in *History of German Theology in the Nineteenth Century*, 196–97. But by no means was Schleiermacher the only theologian struggling with the Enlightenment. Some theologians repudiated the influence of Enlightenment trends on the side of traditional biblical revelation, such as Gottfried Menken. Others tried to harmonize Christian faith and doctrine with the laws of reason, like Franz

is doing something other than philosophy. Faithful to the intellectual heritage of the early Reformers who also grasped the intellectual currents of their day, he does not synthesize faith and reason.[27] Furthermore, he does not demonstrate the "truth and necessity of Christianity," for he presumes "that every Christian, before he enters at all upon inquiries of this kind, has already that inward certainty that his religion cannot take any other form than this."[28] Schleiermacher assumes as a given that the subject matter of Christian theology has a cognitive dimension. It is intelligible and can be communicated.[29] The *Brief Outline* and *The Christian Faith* do not attempt to justify their subject matter before reason as a natural theology might undertake to do.

The second statement Schleiermacher offers about his reasons for separating philosophy from Christian doctrine appears in one of his letters to Gottfried Lücke. At the time of writing this letter, Schleiermacher was revising the first edition of *The Christian Faith*. In an exasperated tone, he writes: "The last thing I ever expected was that I would be associated at so many points with the speculative dogmaticians, among whom I would not be able to appear even as a dilettante, for I am not at all inclined to philosophize in dogmatics." A bit further on, he continues:

Reinhard and J. A. L. Wegscheider. According to Karl Barth, Wegscheider "wanted to be an *apologist* and to interpret Christianity in such a way that it never came into conflict with the modern consciousness." Barth, *Protestant Theology*, 519–21; 475.

27. Schleiermacher's thought discloses a fundamental continuity with the thought of the early Reformers on the futility of reason or natural knowledge in Christian doctrine. Though acknowledging pagan authors have treated rational knowledge of God and recognized its truth, Melanchthon eschews rational warrants in the service of Christian doctrine and grounds the knowledge of God "in his revelations and his clearly expressed words." Philipp Melanchthon, *Melanchthon on Christian Doctrine: Loci Communes 1555*, 7. Huldreich Zwingli thundered against the theologians at Paris, indicating that human wisdom has no part in Christian doctrine: "Philosophy has been forbidden in the schools of Christ [Cf. Col. 2:8], but these people have made it the arbiter of the heavenly word, and that, indeed, a philosophy which they have drawn from the last dregs of the pool." *Commentary on True and False Religion*, 52, 56. Calvin indicates the futility of human nature to even gain natural or rational knowledge of God, asserting that "in order that true religion may shine upon us, we ought to hold that it must take its beginning from heavenly doctrine and that no one can get even the slightest taste of right and sound doctrine unless he be a pupil of Scripture." John Calvin, *Institutes of the Christian Religion* (1559), 72; esp. I:v–vi.

28. *CF*, 60.

29. Consistent with this principle, Schleiermacher's understanding of "polemics" and "apologetics" is different from traditional practices that seek to engage and refute non-Christian philosophy or heterodox argument. *CF*, 52ff.; *BO*, §41–§44.

> Even if I had referred more often to the domain of philosophy, I would still follow the rule of not allowing philosophy to influence the content of the *Glaubenslehre*. Of course, how faithful I have been to my resolution is another matter, but, for the time being, the signs are fairly good. One person firmly maintains that I based my work on Jacobi and another contends it is based on Schelling, and the only proof these two can adduce are strange insertions and unwarranted suppositions. Even someone as knowledgeable as our friend Bonn can come to no other view of my way of philosophizing than that I would start out not with a feeling but with a notion and that in other respects it is about the same as the church's doctrine of faith. All things considered, then, it would seem that very little of philosophy or philosophers is to be encountered in my work. And in this matter I am far from wanting anything else. Were I to find that the content of even one proposition was speculative or could justly be considered so, I would remove this inappropriate garment from it or strike it out.[30]

Schleiermacher denies repeatedly that he employs philosophy as a foundation for dogmatics. He is aware, however, that some may construe his thought as philosophically influenced but it was not his interest or intent to do so. He wanted to keep philosophy and theology as two distinct realms of intellectual discourse.

Proposition §2 of the *Brief Outline* sketches the elements of the way theology will be treated and calls explicit attention to the issues of subject matter and expression. Schleiermacher records:

> Whether any given mode of faith will give shape to a definite theology depends upon the degree to which it is communicated by means of ideas rather than symbolic actions, and likewise on the degree to which it attains historical importance and autonomy. Theologies, moreover, may differ according to every particular mode of faith, in that they correspond to the distinctiveness of each both in content and in form. A real theology will develop only on the two conditions stated. For, in the first instance, no need for one will arise in a community of small extent; and in the second, where a preponderance of symbolic actions exists

---

30. Schleiermacher, *On the* Glaubenslehre, 45, 87. Cited as *LU*. It is very likely Schleiermacher has in mind representatives of the so-called speculative school like Carl Daub (1765–1836) and Philipp Marheineke (1780–1847). For a discussion of the speculative school, see Lichtenberger, *History of German Theology*, 221–41.

the ritual which interprets these hardly deserves to be called a science.[31]

He specifies several conditions for theology to exist. Fundamentally, it must be something communicable "by means of ideas rather than symbolic actions." It must be transmitted, expressed, and understood in language more than in ritualistic signs or symbols. Theology cannot have a private meaning or be restricted to a few—it must be something broad and accessible to people. In other words, theology is possible when it is public discourse. Correspondingly, its possibility hinges upon "the degree to which" the "particular mode of faith . . . attains historical importance and autonomy."[32] Consequently, its viability requires communication and the reality and historicity of faith. In short, theology is possible precisely because the church and Christianity have a place and meaning within human history. Expressed in the historical experience of believers, faith precedes theology. If so, then theology radically depends upon history for its subject matter and warrant.

The possibility of theology as knowledge, however, does not refer primarily to independent academic criteria determinative of its intellectual legitimacy or cultural validity. Theology as knowledge or as a science [*Wissenschaft*] takes its fundamental character as theological from the church. "When this same knowledge is acquired and possessed without relation to the 'government' of the Church, it ceases to be theological and devolves to those sciences to which it belongs according to its varied content."[33] Schleiermacher maintains that only in, under, and related to church organization is theology valid. As ecclesial origin and relationship remain paramount, theology is therefore a special kind of ecclesial knowledge emerging from within the historical experience of the church and in service to it. At the same time, the church and Christianity represent more than bureaucratic and hierarchical structures of human cooperation, though they certainly include them. What Schleiermacher

---

31. *BO*, 19.

32. Ibid. Terrence Tice provides an illuminating note to the latter point by stating that in the first edition, Schleiermacher added the words, "i.e., is formed as a Church," n. 4.

33. *BO*, 20; "Depending on the subject matter, such knowledge would be referred to linguistic and historical studies, psychology and ethics, together with general studies on various sorts of technique and philosophy of religion—two disciplines which are based on psychology and ethics."

means by Christianity is "a particular way of being conscious of God" that forms the church as a social collective. This social and historical expression becomes possible because there is an experience of God famously described as the consciousness of being absolutely dependent.

PIETY, HUMAN NATURE, AND SPIRITUALITY

Schleiermacher develops his widely recognized treatment of religion in the introduction to *The Christian Faith*. "Religion's" placement there, however, has generated controversy among its readers and misgivings by the author.[34] What causes confusion and disparate criticisms is the relationship of the introduction to the body of the text:[35] Schleiermacher's discussion of piety, feeling, and the notion of absolute dependence "lies outside of the discipline of dogmatics itself."[36] It was to some of his critics "a strange and unfamiliar drink" (*einem ... fremdartigen und ungewohnten Getränke*).[37] In large part, this confusion arises because Schleiermacher borrows language and concepts from the sphere of "free human action." More precisely, these terms are from "that speculative presentation of Reason, in the whole range of its activity, which runs parallel to natural science." This speculative presentation is what Schleiermacher calls ethics.[38] This idiosyncratic usage is important to note. Schleiermacher's

---

34. See *LU*, 56. The German edition is Schleiermacher, *Theologisch-dogmatische Abhandlungen und Gele-genheitsschriften*, cited as *LU*(g).

35. See *LU*, 55–8.

36. *LU*, 56.

37. *LU*(g), 341. Translation mine.

38. *CF*, 3–5. Tice distinguishes four different meanings of *Ethik* in Schleiermacher's thought. The first definition is the one that Schleiermacher employs here. Tice writes that "ethics refer to theoretical, philosophical, and methodological study of the entire human domain, which Wilhelm Dilthey (1833–1911), following his lead, called the *Geisteswissenschaften* or 'human sciences.'" *Schleiermacher*, 57. Brian Gerrish argues that ethics for Schleiermacher more closely resembles what we would call "social theory" today. See Brian Gerrish, *Tradition and the Modern World*, 42. John C. Shelley goes further. He maintains that Schleiermacher conceives ethics as "the process through which nature gradually becomes the organ of reason ... the process by which reason permeates nature and gives it shape or form ... Ethics is not one corner of life or simply the province of the individual. It quite literally encompasses all of finite reality." Shelley also indicates that Schleiermacher's categories are dependent on philosophy, adding more support to my contention that Schleiermacher cannot evade the use of philosophical terms or categories. *Introduction to Christian Ethics*, 22–23.

use of the term *ethics* is liable to be misunderstood as referring to moral reasoning and behavior.

The introduction comprises two parts: definition and method.[39] Regarding the former, insofar as Schleiermacher elaborates an understanding of dogmatic theology, he employs analysis and information of different sciences that help establish its definition and content. These sciences belong to philosophical theology.[40] Many of his contemporaries could not understand that Schleiermacher is simply following the program of his theological encyclopedia. His theological encyclopedia clearly specifies that philosophical theology *precedes* historical and dogmatic theology.[41] *The Christian Faith* is thus a completion of the structure of philosophical and historical theology developed in the *Brief Outline*.[42] In terms of historical theology described in the *Brief Outline* which includes dogmatic theology, it is clear that Schleiermacher's theological project requires a fuller definition of dogmatic theology.[43] Yet he also undertakes something more. Schleiermacher argues that the Introduction is a scientific investigation dealing with "piety and Church, like other things," that "are a subject matter for knowledge" (*ein Stoff sind für das Wissen*).[44] And like those "leaders of the state or of science" (*Leitenden*

---

39. Proposition §1 asserts: "The purpose of this Introduction is, first, to set forth the conception of Dogmatics which underlies the work itself; and secondly, to prepare the reader for the method and arrangement followed in it." *CF*, 1.

40. *BO*, §22-24; in proposition §33, Schleiermacher states his position explicitly. "The point of departure of philosophical theology, therefore, can only be taken 'above' Christianity, in the logical sense of the term, i.e., in the general concept of a religious community or fellowship of faith." Cf. *LU*, 78. He writes that "the Introduction belongs to the realm I customarily call 'philosophy of religion,' although others use that term differently."

41. See *LU*, 76–79.

42. The content of practical theology is developed in a separate work. Schleiermacher, *Die Praktische Theologie nach den Grundsätzen der evangelischen Kirche im Zusammenhange dargestellt*. Some of it has been translated into English. Schleiermacher, *Christian Caring*.

43. "It would doubtless be a natural thing for me to take as my basis the definition of Dogmatics given in my *Outline*; but that book is so short and aphoristic that it is not superfluous to come to its aid with some elucidations." *CF*, 1.

44. *CF*(g), 15. The English translators, Mackintosh and Stewart, render this phrase rather loosely as "material for scientific knowledge," which, while not precise enough, does capture the sense of the its meaning given its total context. See *CF*, 6. The German term for "science," namely, *Wissenschaft*, has several different senses. I understand the term as Schleiermacher and others of his time who use it to broadly denote a compre-

im Staat oder die in der Wissenschaft) who examine those aspects of religion, namely, "piety and the communion relating to it, and determining their proper place in the total field of human life," Schleiermacher too undertakes the same type of "consideration" (*Betrachtung*).

What does this consideration mean and why is it significant? There are several crucial points to consider. First, Schleiermacher's form of argumentation in the first section of the introduction is what he considers philosophical theology. This distinction is crucial: he is not writing dogmatics. His re-description of universal human nature as pious through its experience of the feeling of absolute dependence is already a provisional and nondogmatic claim.[45] Therefore, the analysis of the church and of his own philosophical theology arising from the religious experience of God in human nature remains heuristic. Referring to the first section of the introduction, Schleiermacher maintains: "[E]ven here at the very beginning there is plenty of opportunity for very diverse definitions and conceptions of Dogmatics, each of which can only regard itself as preparatory for a future one when the scientific studies of which it has to take account will be more firmly established, while, nevertheless, Christianity remains entirely the same.[46]" Admittedly, his interpretation stands as one of many in a developmental historical process. Different and plural interpretations of dogmatics and theological topics are then legitimate. Yet what justifies this confidence? For Schleiermacher, what holds true concerning the historical content and reality of Christianity remains the same while changing in expression and form. In other words, the representation of genuine Christian teaching can retain its inner integrity while the vehicle of meaning, namely language, changes. How this representation gets worked out in greater detail, I leave for the discussion of theology's nature and necessity. It suffices to indicate the central role that creative expression and reformulation play in developing the possibility of theology.

Schleiermacher describes the feeling of absolute dependence as the essence of piety in propositions §3–§6 of *The Christian Faith*. The

---

hensive, rigorous, and consciously rational body of organized knowledge or information. It does not mean, first and foremost, the empirical-hypothetical scientific method. Law, history, medicine, philosophy, and theology are all sciences in this sense.

45. *LU*, 77. He refers to "truly dogmatic propositions" in the context of a disagreement with Dr. Baur concerning Christ in the *Glaubenslehre*. He refers to them broadly: "the Introduction does not contain even a single one of these."

46. *CF*, 5.

subject matter of the discussion is given in §3: "The piety which forms the basis of all ecclesiastical communions is, considered purely in itself, neither a Knowing nor a Doing, but a modification of Feeling, or of immediate self-consciousness." Propositions §4, §5, and §6 disclose characteristics of piety that gradually move from its place in the soul to its theological meaning and character, to its experience in the totality of lived consciousness, and then finally to its expression and social nature as church. Faithful to his theological hermeneutic of part and whole, he begins with the whole, analyzes the elements that comprise it, then relates the parts back to the whole again. To understand the essence of piety, it is critical to see how Schleiermacher describes piety in this dialectical interplay. Schleiermacher makes distinctions in order to unite. Ultimately, the structure of Schleiermacher's analysis provides an overview of the nature of piety.

Robert Williams argues that Schleiermacher considers piety phenomenologically.[47] Within the realm of free human activity, the character of the feeling of absolute dependence is different from knowing and doing.[48] Again, it bears repeating that Schleiermacher selects the topics of knowing and doing to compare with feeling because he is describing a phenomenon of human self-consciousness within "the entire sphere of human life [*im Gesamtgebiet des menschlichen Lebens*]"[49] Besides feeling, knowing and doing coexist within human self-consciousness. Consequently, these elements are abstracted from but not unintelligible to a commonsense view of conscious experience.[50] Though employing philosophical language from the sphere of "ethics," Schleiermacher is conscious of his audience.

Schleiermacher introduces two critically important terms, "feeling" and "self-consciousness." In part, he does so because he needs to purify his terminology. "The term 'feeling' (*Gefühl*) has in the language of com-

---

47. *Schleiermacher the Theologian*, 6–8. To say that Schleiermacher's treatment of piety finds a parallel in phenomenological thinking is the point I most agree with. But I disagree that Schleiermacher is to be read anachronistically as a phenomenologist.

48. Here, Schleiermacher's treatment coheres with his comments in the *Speeches* about the conception and reality of feeling as something utterly different from metaphysics and morals, see *Speeches*, 98.

49. *CB*, 15.

50. Schleiermacher appeals to the reader's lived experience in defining feeling and self-consciousness. See *CF*, 7. It must also be kept in mind that the audience of the *Glaubenslehre* is believers.

mon life been long current in this religious connexion; but for scientific usage it needs to be more precisely defined."[51] In the historical constellation of religious discourse, such terms tend to have a semantically complex career.[52] Since "feeling" is one of them, "self-consciousness" assigns a sharper meaning and precision it would otherwise lack. Though not simply synonymous, "self-consciousness" specifies the definition of "feeling" more adequately. He writes, "Feeling is not to be thought of as something either confused or inactive; since, on the one hand, it is strongest in our most vivid moments, and either directly or indirectly lies at the root of every expression of our wills, and, on the other hand, it can be grasped by thought and conceived of in its own nature.[53]" This description is quite general, indicating a certain scale of intensity to self-consciousness. To understand piety more clearly, I need to unpack critical aspects of self-consciousness as such in order to clearly establish Schleiermacher's treatment as relatively traditional.

The propositions from §3 to §5 concern human consciousness and mental states. Three elements frame the parameters of Schleiermacher's examination, namely, "Knowing, Doing, and Feeling." They are discussed in terms coordinated with psychology.[54] What Schleiermacher means by psychology refers to premodern analysis of the soul and its powers, not the contemporary social-scientific discipline. The description of human self-consciousness that builds to the feeling of absolute dependence indirectly parallels Plato's tripartite understanding of the soul and its powers.[55] Though Schleiermacher's language is not Platonic and his understanding of the mind differs from his Greek predecessor's, nevertheless, Plato's influence upon his thought was immense.[56] Because Plato's

51. *CF*, 6.

52. For the history of *Gefühl*, see Lamm, "Early Philosophical Roots of Schleiermacher's Notion of *Gefühl*, 1788–1794," 67–105.

53. *CF*, 11–12.

54. Ibid., 8.

55. Plato argues that the soul is tripartite. It possesses appetitive, spirited, and rational natures. In some ways following Plato, Schleiermacher distinguishes the three different grades of consciousness: animal, sensible, and the feeling of absolute dependence. See *Republic*, 110–17 [435c–441c].

56. "There is no author," writes Schleiermacher, "who has affected me so deeply and who has initiated me into the holy of holies not only of philosophy but of humankind in general, as has this divine man [i.e., Plato]." *Aus Schleiermachers Leben. In Briefen*, 72, as quoted in the "Introduction," *Speeches*, 28 n. 92. Schleiermacher was not only a theologian and philosopher, but also one of the most distinguished classical philologists of his

view of the soul is well known, I suggest that Schleiermacher's analysis of the soul [*Seele*] or mind should be understood along similar lines.⁵⁷

The foundational constituents of "every" self-consciousness can be summarized. There are two elements in human self-consciousness, writes Schleiermacher, "a self-caused element *(ein Sichselbstsetzen)* and a non-self-caused element *(ein Sichselbstnichtsogesetzhaben)*; or a Being and a Having-by-some-means-come-to-be *(ein Sein und ein Irgendwiegewordensein).*"⁵⁸ One expresses the existence of the subject for itself; the other entails its coexistence with an Other. In lived time, these two elements are termed "Receptivity and its (spontaneous) Activity." Of these, receptivity is primary, as we shall see.⁵⁹ Determinations of self-consciousness that correspond to receptivity share a feeling of dependence; those that indicate activity involve the feeling of freedom.⁶⁰ These two elements anchor Schleiermacher's analysis.⁶¹ All other aspects that bear upon the meaning of piety and the feeling of absolute dependence derive from this oppositional scheme. He writes: "Life, then, is to be conceived as an alternation between an abiding-in-self *(Insichbleiben)* and a passing-beyond-self *(Aussichheraustreten)* on the part of the subject.

---

time. He was the first to translate all of Plato's works into German except the *Timaeus* and the *Laws*. Translating Plato occupied him at intervals from 1804 to 1828. His translation would become the standard German edition of Plato's works for many years. For more on Schleiermacher and Plato, see *Speeches*, 28–29; Redeker, *Schleiermacher*, 181–85. For the influence of Plato on aspects of Schleiermacher's thought, see Williams, *Schleiermacher the Theologian*, 60–64.

57. *CB*, 17.

58. *CF*, 13.

59. What Schleiermacher means here resembles what Henry David Thoreau would later write concerning the relationship of human experience to the surrounding world. "I think that the man of science makes this mistake, and the mass of mankind along with him: that you should coolly give your chief attention to the phenomenon which excites you as something independent of you, and not as it is related to you. The important fact is its effect on me. He thinks that I have no business to see anything else but just what he defines the rainbow to be, but I care not whether my vision of truth is a waking thought or a dream remembered, whether it is seen in the light or in the dark. It is the subject of my vision, the truth alone, that concerns me. The philosopher for whom rainbows, etc., can be explained away never saw them. With regard to such objects I find that it is not that they themselves (with which the man of science deal) that concern me; the point of interest is somewhere *between* me and them (i.e., the objects). *Journal of Henry David Thoreau*, 164–65 (his italics); as quoted in *Uncommon Learning*, 61–62.

60. *CF*, 13–14.

61. *Speeches*, 79–81.

The two forms of consciousness (Knowing and Feeling) constitute the abiding-in-self, while Doing proper is the passing-beyond-self.⁶²" So conceived, life as conscious existence constitutes a totality of diametrical forces, each manifesting a particular kind of expression.

Schleiermacher uses psychological categories to describe a series of relationships concerning the experiences of knowing and doing. His aim is not to elaborate capacities proper to intellect and will but to define piety negatively. "Thus both hypotheses lead to the same point: that there are both a Knowing and a Doing which pertain to piety, but neither of these constitutes the essence of piety."⁶³ Knowing and doing are instances of the drive outward toward an other that might range from something so intimate as the objectification of one's own self-consciousness to the activity one engages in upon a person, thing, place, or the like. In each experience of knowing and doing, "an Other is determined by us, and without our spontaneous activity could not be so determined."⁶⁴ Broadly considered, knowing and doing are activities of the subject *upon the world*, an exercise of self-consciousness coordinate with intellect and will.⁶⁵ Each term belongs to the whole of human consciousness yet differs from the essence of piety. Knowing and doing presuppose the "feeling of freedom."⁶⁶ The feeling of freedom entails a certain modification of self-consciousness. It is something "self-caused"—the subject's influence upon the world and hence determined by the subject responding to external determinations.

Having distinguished knowing and doing but united their differences through the common element of freedom, Schleiermacher indicates more exactly how feeling differs from thinking or acting. At its center, he conceives self-consciousness as primarily receptive and thus as *being determined*. "But as we never do exist except along with an Other, so even in every outward-tending self-consciousness the element of receptivity, in some way or other affected, is the primary one; and even the self-consciousness which accompanies an action (acts of knowing included), while it predominantly expresses spontaneous movement and activity, is always related (though the relation is often a

62. *CF*, 8.
63. Ibid., 10.
64. Ibid., 14.
65. Ibid., 7.
66. Ibid., 14.

quite indefinite one) to a prior moment of affective receptivity, through which the original 'agility' received its direction."[67] Ultimately, what remains prior to doing and knowing in human consciousness is the "non-self-caused element." Consciousness is already being influenced prior to the counter-movement of human freedom. Something is always already *given* in each experience of consciousness. This fact means that receptivity precedes activity or reaction. Understanding this fact about one's experience occurs only retrospectively. In other words, since the attempt to understand a particular event is an activity of the subjective consciousness upon the content of experience, the feeling of dependence can never be expressed in the same way as one's experience of it. One's experience is always bigger, larger, more textured than the words one can find to describe it. Concepts and language remain limited instruments in human efforts to express reality. Indeed, language can never exhaust let alone describe the content of even discrete experience.[68] For this reason, the experience of piety as a feeling of dependence is not only pre-reflective but also somehow absolute. But what does absolute mean in this context? Employing a different vocabulary, Schleiermacher refers again to the "non-self-caused" element in human consciousness

---

67. Ibid., 13.

68. Bryan Magee illustrates this truth. "For most of my waking day my conscious awareness is a predominantly visual experience—as Fichte puts it, 'I am a living seeing'—but there are no words to describe the irregular shapes of most of the objects I see, nor are there any words to describe the multiple, coexisting three-dimensional spatial relationships in which I directly see them as standing to one another. There are no words to the infinitely different shadings and differentials of color that I see, nor for the multifarious densities of light and shadow. *Whenever* I see, all that language can do is to indicate with the utmost generality and in the broadest and crudest of terms what it is that I see. Even something as simple and everyday as the sight of a towel dropped on to the bathroom floor is inaccessible to language—and inaccessible to it from many points of view at the same time: no words to describe the shape it has fallen into, no words to describe the degrees of shading in its colors, no words to describe the differentials of shadow in its folds, no words to describe its spatial relationships to all the other objects in the bathroom. I see all these things at once with great precision and definiteness, with clarity and certainty, and in all their complexity. I possess them all wholly and securely in direct experience, and yet I would be totally unable, as would anyone else, to put that experience into words. It is emphatically not the case, then, that 'the world is the world as we describe it,' or that I 'experience it through linguistic categories that help to shape the experiences themselves' or that my 'main way of dividing things up is in language' or that my 'concept of reality is a matter of our linguistic categories.'" *Confessions of a Philosopher*, 76–77.

to indicate what conditions obtain for feeling as absolute. In so doing, Schleiermacher begins to distinguish the finite from the transcendent.

The positive account of feeling and piety as the consciousness of being absolutely dependent or "which is the same thing, of being in relation with God" starts in proposition §4.[69] Both feelings of freedom and dependence comprise a unity in the human person. Thus the other is not many different objects, but the same object for both. The feelings of freedom and dependence relate to the same thing precisely as a unified self-consciousness. Reciprocity between feelings of freedom and dependence adequately characterizes the reality of self-consciousness. As such, there is a unity of subjectivity and a unity of orientation. Consciousness is dynamic—it acts and it undergoes. Each aspect mutually influences and determines the other. There is therefore a coherence between dependence and freedom. Yet because this is so, there cannot be any pure absolute feeling of dependence or freedom without the opposite feeling having a counter-effect.[70] This mutual conditioning is the critical point.

To illustrate, Schleiermacher selects the topics of nature and society. Whether the example is a child's dependence upon her parents or a single individual's influence upon "heavenly bodies," it makes no difference. For Schleiermacher, "we ourselves . . . exercise a counter-influence." In each instance, degrees of reciprocity exist between feelings of freedom and those of dependence. However, some factors determine receptivity more than activity. Most of the time human beings experience their world as acting on them. There are noises and sounds and smells that people do not choose but still experience, whether pleasantly or unpleasantly. Whatever the case may be, the crucial point here is that "neither of the two members will ever completely disappear."[71] It follows, then, that a feeling of absolute freedom is impossible. Why? The feeling of freedom always presupposes a prior object given to human beings and as already affecting receptivity. The feeling of dependence is always already involved, and thus necessarily limiting the feeling of freedom to some degree. But is the same true for the feeling of absolute dependence? Schleiermacher maintains: "[F]or just the same reason, this

---

69. It should be noted that in his first letter to Lücke, Schleiermacher provides yet another expression for piety or pious feeling, namely, an "immediate existential relationship." *LU*, 40.

70. *CF*, 16.

71. Ibid., 15.

feeling cannot in any wise arise from the influence of an object which has in some way to be *given* to us; for upon such an object there would always be a counter-influence, and even a voluntary renunciation of this would always involve a feeling of freedom. Hence a feeling of absolute dependence, strictly speaking, cannot exist in a single moment as such, because such a moment is always determined, as regards its total content, by what is *given*, and thus by objects towards which we have a feeling of freedom."[72] A total feeling of dependence cannot be "purely absolute." An absolute feeling of dependence would negate the reciprocal unity of consciousness precisely because the feeling of freedom is partly constitutive for the feeling of dependence to exist at all. Nevertheless, there is the self-consciousness which "accompanies all our activity, and therefore, since that is never zero, accompanies our whole existence, and negatives absolute freedom, is itself precisely a consciousness of absolute dependence; for it is the consciousness that the whole of our spontaneous activity comes from a source outside of us in just the same sense in which anything towards which we should have a feeling of absolute freedom must have proceeded entirely from ourselves."[73] The vector of absolute dependence is not in any respect an object against which a genuine feeling of freedom can "push," so to speak. The vector of absolute dependence is the meaning of "relation to God." God is "the *Whence* of our receptive and active existence, as implied in this self-consciousness, is to be designated by the word 'God,' and that this is for us the really original signification of that word."[74] Hence the directionality or the orientation of the soul is not ultimately toward the world or a part of the world. If so, then God would be an object, something "thrown up" over against consciousness. This is precisely what God is *not*. "God" does not denote an object that human beings can influence through freedom or something that affects their receptivity in such a way that their feeling would be annulled. Rather, the movement of human consciousness is ultimately beyond limitations and conditions. This is why the feeling of absolute dependence is not modified by some previous knowledge of God (though that might exist) "but simply to set it aside as something with which, in a system of Christian doctrine, we could never have any concern, because plainly enough it has itself nothing to do directly with

72. Ibid., 16.
73. Ibid.
74. Ibid.

piety."[75] The experience of absolute dependence precedes concept formation and reflexive thought. Concepts do emerge, hence the designation of "God" as an idea. Still, this act always follows the occurrence of the feeling, spacing the time when self-consciousness can reflect, apprehend, and objectify its meaning.

The idea of God expresses the feeling of absolute dependence. There are a few points to note. First, God is a co-determinant in the feeling. The feeling of absolute dependence is "the fundamental relation which must include all others in itself. This last expression includes the God-consciousness in the self-consciousness in such a way that, quite in accordance with the above analysis, the two cannot be separated from each other."[76] God must be a co-determinant for human consciousness to constitute a reciprocal relation between the feeling of dependence and freedom. Again, if God were the sole determinant, Schleiermacher believes that the feeling of freedom would be negated. "For every moment which is made up of a partial feeling of freedom and a partial feeling of dependence places us in a position of co-ordinate antithesis to a similar Other."[77] Put in more traditional categories, human beings are creatures who differ from their Creator. Creaturehood comprises these feelings of freedom and dependence. Take away either and the notion of creature or human person ceases to exist. This is why God cannot be the sole determinant of human experience.

Second, as I indicated above, Schleiermacher follows Plato and Aristotle in differentiating powers of the soul. But while Plato argues for three—irrational, spirited, and rational—and Aristotle has at least four (nutritive, sensory, locomotive, and cognitive), Schleiermacher distinguishes only three powers—namely, animal, sensible, and the feeling of absolute dependence—the highest level.[78] The feeling of absolute dependence is the "highest grade of human self-consciousness."[79] Through these categories, Schleiermacher locates and explains the feeling of absolute dependence in concrete human experience. How and why do they fit together?

---

75. Ibid., 17.
76. Ibid.
77. Ibid., 20.
78. Aristotle *De anima* II:3.
79. *CF*, 18–19.

Schleiermacher is describing forms of consciousness that lie within a broader evolution of human consciousness. In the development of human consciousness, distinct stages coexist within the fundamental antithesis between feelings of dependence and freedom. These stages span a qualitative range of pleasure and pain. The range of pleasure and pain is part of the descriptive framework within the general antithesis. Schleiermacher specifies the form of human religious consciousness in general—but not yet as a particular instance. The framework and form must be general—one could even say archetypal—precisely so that individual determinations of human religious consciousness within the antithesis may appear in their diversity. In turn, the diversity of determinations is closely connected to the common form of human religious consciousness. This connection means that the further specification of "the antithesis of the pleasant and the unpleasant" merely continues a dialectical scheme coordinate not only with the primary elements of nature and human nature begun in the *Speeches*, but also with the oppositional pairs: receptivity/activity, freedom/dependence, and feeling/knowing-doing. Not all conscious experience as receptivity is pleasant and vice-versa. Nevertheless, any activity can be plotted along such a qualitative spectrum of consciousness, as can thinking, acting, and the like.

Animal, sensible, and the feeling of absolute dependence structure general self-consciousness. In animal consciousness, there is no distinction between feeling and perception. This is because immediate self-consciousness does not reflect upon the content of experience. Consequently, this mode remains "in a state of unresolved confusion." Schleiermacher provides two analogies. Animal self-consciousness is like the experience of children prior to speech and "those dreamy moments which form the transition between sleep and waking." In contrast, human sensible self-consciousness involves determining and being determined by the range of human phenomena, or what Schleiermacher states as "the social and moral feelings no less than the self-regarding." This social dimension is the main difference between sensible and animal consciousness. The realm of everyday, concrete, lived consciousness is precisely the mode of sensible self-consciousness. It is the locus of the fundamental antithesis between freedom and dependence. More specifically, sensible self-consciousness is the mode in which "feeling and perception are clearly distinct from each other, and thus make up the whole wealth of man's sensible life, in the widest sense of the term."[80] Sensible self-consciousness differs from the feeling of absolute dependence in an important way, however. It is always particular, individual, and remains within the antithesis of freedom and dependence, "the realm of reciprocal action." But as I have shown, there is no antithesis within the feeling of absolute dependence. For Schleiermacher, the feeling of absolute dependence as such "is not the consciousness of ourselves as individuals of a particular description, but simply of ourselves as individual finite existence in general."[81] There cannot be any reciprocal determination of self-consciousness upon the immediate self-consciousness of being in relation to God. God is not an object, an idea, a particular force like those met in sensible self-consciousness. Consequently, for Schleiermacher, "all antithesis between one individual and another is in this case done away."[82] In other words, the highest grade of self-consciousness in terms of its general form exists equally in human consciousness as such.

Thus far I have tried to trace the general form of piety—the feeling of absolute dependence. Schleiermacher distinguishes it from such cognitive and performative activities as knowing and doing. It is only when he distinguishes moments or levels within human self-consciousness that the feeling of absolute dependence as the highest grade of human self-consciousness achieves concrete historical meaning. At this stage of his argument, Schleiermacher can be misunderstood to be reducing the feeling of absolute dependence or "being in relation to God" to religious emotion. In fact, the feeling of absolute dependence, while not identical with religious emotion, nonetheless manifests itself within the sphere of human affectivity and emotion.

Schleiermacher stands in a lengthy and rich tradition of religious and spiritual thinkers who describe piety and "being in relation with God" as affective.[83] This doctrine is neither new nor uniform within the

---

80. Ibid., 19.

81. Ibid., 18–19.

82. Ibid., 19.

83. This meaning emerges especially when Schleiermacher refers to the ministry. "Others of us, however, see the task of ministry as that of giving a clear and enlivening description of a common inner experience, and what emerges as doctrinal teaching is really only a preparation and a means to this end. We do not fancy that we are introducing into our church communities something completely new, as though in the first course of study we communicate the ideas to them and then in a second course we based piety on the ideas. Rather, what is possessed is shared in common, and we serve

history of Christian spirituality. Numerous and varied accounts of the religious experience of God span the history of Christian spirituality. St. Paul describes the "fruit of the Spirit" as affective evidence of being in the presence and Spirit of God.[84] In late antiquity, a representative of monastic and ascetical spirituality like Evagrius Ponticus will counsel an examination of the dynamics of affective consciousness in the monk's struggle for virtue and purity.[85] Similar dynamics recur in the drama of St. Augustine's restless heart and its movement toward God in the *Confessions*.[86] In the Middle Ages, human affectivity figures strongly in the mystical-ascetical writing of Richard of St. Victor's *The Twelve Patriarchs* and St. Bonaventure's *Itinerarium mentis in Deum*.[87] The great spiritual contemplative and mystic, Meister Eckhart, remarks on the affective experience of God when he writes: "For you will have peace to the extent that you have God, and the further you are away from God the less you will be at peace. Anything that is at peace has God in it to the extent that it is at peace. Thus you may measure your progress with God by measuring your peace or the lack of it. When you have unrest within you, you will be restless visibly, but the unrest comes from the creature and not from God."[88] It was, however, the spiritual genius of St. Ignatius Loyola to articulate precisely these experiences of affective consciousness of God as consolation and desolation in his *Autobiography* and to codify them in the *Spiritual Exercises*.[89] In eighteenth-century New England, Jonathan

---

our brothers only by explaining more clearly to them what it is and so awaken in them the joy in it as well as concern for it." *LU*, 41. In taking this position, I disagree with Karl Barth, who does not place Schleiermacher in the tradition of Reformation thinkers on the theme of religion. See Barth, *Word of God and the Word of Man*, 195–96. For other perceived discontinuities, see Barth, *Theology of Schleiermacher*, 39, 158.

84. Gal 5:22–26: "By contrast, the fruit of the Spirit is love, joy, peace, patience, kindness, generosity, faithfulness, gentleness, and self-control. There is no law against such things. And those who belong to Christ Jesus have crucified the flesh with its passions and desires. If we live by the Spirit, let us also be guided by the Spirit. Let us not become conceited, competing against one another, envying one another."

85. Ponticus, *Praktikos & Chapters on Prayer*, 29–30.

86. Compare, for example, Augustine's self-diagnosis before his moral conversion in the beginning of book three of the *Confessions* with that of his serenity in books eight and nine.

87. Cf. *Twelve Patriarchs*, in *Richard of St. Victor*, 53–147; Bonaventure, *Itinerarium mentis in Deum*.

88. Eckhart, "Talks of Instruction," *Meister Eckhart*, 41–42.

89. See *Ignatius of Loyola*; see also "Rules for the Discernment of Spirits," *Spiritual Exercises*, #313–#351.

Edwards likewise expounded a guide to true religion concerning the Spirit of God and human affections.[90] Even closer to Schleiermacher's own time stands Jean-Pierre de Caussade, S.J., who in his *L'abandon à la Providence Divine* virtually prefigures Schleiermacher's treatment of absolute dependence when describing the soul's passive surrender to the will of God.[91]

The more obvious parallel to Schleiermacher within the Reformed tradition is Calvin. In the preface to the reader (*lectori*) in a later Latin edition of the *Instituto christianae religionis*, Calvin remarks that his work is a "sum of religion in all parts" [*religionis summam omnibus partibus*].[92] "Religion" here is probably better understood as "piety." This interpretation is more consonant with the translation of the 1536 edition, whose subtitle runs "Embracing almost the whole sum of piety, & whatever is necessary to know of the doctrine of salvation: A work most worthy to be read by all persons zealous for piety, and recently published."[93] Indeed, the entire work, as the editors of the 1559 edition relate in their introduction and Calvin himself indicates, "is not a *summa theologiae* but a *summa pietatis*."[94] Religion in this sense does not mean a particular historical phenomenon like Judaism or Islam. The titles of the works in Latin lack the definite article *le* which French editions possess. Calvin's meaning is closer to the medieval conception of religion as virtue that one finds in Aquinas as a quality relating a person to God.[95] In a profound way, as Calvin's text is about Christian piety, so also is Schleiermacher's *Christian Faith*.

For Schleiermacher, the experience of being immediately in relation to God, though not in itself an emotion, ingeniously recasts a recurrent phenomenon in the tradition of Christian spirituality. His interpretation of piety as feeling is neither Gnosticism nor esoteric mysticism.

---

90. Edwards, *Religious Affections*, 91–124.

91. De Caussade, *Sacrament of the Present Moment*, 10. "For obedience to God's undefined will depends entirely on our passive surrender to it. We put nothing of ourselves into it apart from a general willingness that is prepared to do anything or nothing, like a tool that, though it has no power in itself, when in the hands of a craftsman, can be used by him for any purpose within the range of its capacity and design."

92. Calvino, *Institutio Christianae religionis* (1637).

93. John Calvin, *Institutes of the Christian Religion* [1536] (1986).

94. John Calvin, *Institutes of the Christian Religion*, 2 vols. (1559), li.

95. For the French editions, see the index of the 1559 translation by Battles and edited by McNeill, Vol. 2, 1527–28. For Aquinas on religion, see *ST*, II–II, Q. 81, arts. 1–2.

Schleiermacher describes the experience of God as constitutive of the human condition, or what the Christian tradition variously identifies as spiritual consolation and desolation. The feeling of absolute dependence entails real historical experience.[96] Schleiermacher's account of human self-consciousness is not, therefore, a philosophical bastard stepchild of "religious experience" that ignores the historical grounding of Christians' everyday relationships with God. His description is simply a different expression of traditional Christian teaching.

This interpretation seems to be evident in Schleiermacher's treatment of the relation between the feeling of absolute dependence—the highest form of self-consciousness—to the sensible grade of human self-consciousness. Schleiermacher specifies moments concerning the feeling of absolute dependence that fall at an intermediate point within the range of pain and pleasure as a "particular religious emotion" (*besondere fromme Erregung*).[97] Within the stages of self-consciousness, he describes experiences of "being in relation to God" that occur within lived experience. Consider a specific relationship, namely, how the higher consciousness and sensible consciousness comprise a coherent unity.

> The sensibly determined self-consciousness splits up of itself, in accordance with its nature, into a series of moments that differ in their content, because our activity exercised upon other beings is a temporal one, and their influence upon us is likewise temporal. The feeling of absolute dependence, on the other hand, being in itself always self-identical, would not evoke a series of thus distinguishable moments; and if it did not enter into relation with such a series in the manner described above, either it could never become an actual consciousness in time at all, or else it must accompany the sensible self-consciousness monotonously without any relation to the manifold rising and falling variations of the latter ... That is to say: being related as a constituent factor to a given moment of consciousness which consists of a partial feeling of freedom and a partial feeling of dependence, it thereby becomes a particular religious emotion, and being in another moment related to a different datum, it becomes a different religious emotion; yet so that the essential element, namely, the feeling of absolute dependence, is the same in both, and thus throughout

---

96. *LU*, 45.

97. *CB*, 37. It must be noted that the editors of the English edition, Stewart and Mackintosh render *Erregung* here as "emotion." It can also mean "agitation," "stimulation," or "excitement."

the whole series, and the difference arises simply from the fact that it becomes a different moment when it goes along with a different determination of the sensible self-consciousness.[98]

Normal everyday human consciousness involves feeling and perception. It coexists with the feeling of absolute dependence. In reality, there is no such thing as a pure feeling of absolute dependence, no epiphany of immediate or pure divinity precisely because all self-consciousness is temporal. Because it is temporal, everyday consciousness is thus conditioned by the antithesis of dependence and freedom.[99] When the feeling of absolute dependence breaks through into sensible self-consciousness, it always emerges as a "particular religious emotion." As I have said, it is my contention that this view of absolute dependence accords with what the spiritual tradition has sometimes termed consolation or desolation. The religious experience of God in all its plurality can be understood within the range of pleasure and pain. Generally conceived and in myriad ways, what Schleiermacher argues that human beings experience in the feeling of absolute dependence concerning God, Christians have maintained from the beginning as an awareness of grace and sin.[100]

The coexistence of the feeling of absolute dependence and sensible self-consciousness for Schleiermacher "forms the feeling-content [*Gefühlsgehalt*] of every religious life, so that it seemed superfluous to illustrate these formulae by examples." Indeed, this point seems so evident to Schleiermacher that he finds it unnecessary to illustrate it with more examples! He assumes that believers would understand the subject matter given how obvious and fundamental the experience of God is within the Christian life. The effects of this coexistence within religious experience can be as generally and diversely characterized in Christian spirituality as one's movement toward or away from God.

> [O]ur religious consciousness, as we actually find it, is not of that character [pure feeling of absolute dependence without change] but is subject to variation, some pious emotions approximating more to joy, others to sorrow. Thus this antithesis refers simply

---

98. *CF*, 22–23.

99. Ibid., 131–32.

100. "Considered as finite being and hence as representing all finite being, this consciousness of the absolute dependence of the self as an inward permanent datum which can be made apparent at any moment, is a state of our heart or soul (*Gemüthszustand*)." *CF*, 140.

to the manner in which the two grades of self-consciousness are related to each other in the unity of the moment. And thus it is by no means the case that the pleasant and the unpleasant, which exist in the sensible feeling, impart the same character to the feeling of absolute dependence. On the contrary, we often find, united in one and the same moment (as a clear sign that the two grades are not fused into each other or neutralized by each other so as to become a third) a sorrow of the lower and a joy of the higher self-consciousness; as, e.g., whenever with a feeling of suffering there is combined a trust in God.[101]

Schleiermacher also describes the emergence of absolute dependence as occurring easily, with difficulty, as having life-giving effects, or as varying in degree.[102] Though he employs different language, his account of piety is consistent with what spiritual masters hold concerning the movements of the soul and human affectivity when encountering God. His portrayal of piety is not something foreign to ordinary experience or limited to mystics. It is the normal human encounter with the divine. Indeed, for Schleiermacher, the achievement of "an uninterrupted sequence of religious emotions can be required of us, as indeed Scripture actually requires it; and it is confirmed every time a religious soul laments over a moment of his life which is quite empty of the consciousness of God (since no one laments the absence of anything which is recognized to be impossible). Of course, it goes without saying in this connexion that the feeling of absolute dependence, when it unites with a sensibly determined self-consciousness, and thus becomes an emotion, must vary as regards strength."[103] Attempts to view Schleiermacher's account of piety and the feeling of absolute dependence outside the tradition of Christian spirituality miss the entire point of Schleiermacher's treatment of piety and disregard his later remarks concerning Christian religious consciousness.[104] The interpretation Schleiermacher gives to religion,

101. Ibid., 23–24.
102. Ibid., 24–25.
103. Ibid., 24.
104. See for example ibid., 356. "The religious consciousness of the Christian . . . is composed of the consciousness of sin . . . and the consciousness of grace." Louis Roy, while making distinctions within Schleiermacher's notion of consciousness, hints at Schleiermacher's connection to Christian thinkers like Augustine and Eckhart in the treatment of religious consciousness but does not situate him clearly within the Christian spiritual tradition. See Roy, "Consciousness According to Schleiermacher," 217–32.

religious consciousness, and the feeling of absolute dependence must be seen precisely within this spiritual-theological context.[105] His analysis and description of piety cannot be abstracted from his personal Pietist roots.[106] In short, Schleiermacher's analysis of religion as piety, then, reinterprets and describes a classic topic within the history of Christian spirituality. As he states in the second preface to *The Christian Faith*, "I have invented nothing, so far as I remember, except my order of topics and here or there a descriptive phrase..."[107]

Schleiermacher's dialectical description of human religious experience as consciousness of being in relation to God or piety builds from an abstract analysis of elements to its historical form as positive religion. In part, his methodology demonstrates the universality of human religious self-consciousness. It indicates a profound awareness of God's activity in human history as something that transcends the particular experience of the Christian—what Schleiermacher considers to be the highest particular religion. While he insists on the superiority of Christianity over other religious traditions, he does not repudiate his fundamental principle, namely, that piety is a universal human phenomenon.[108] What remains decisive, however, is the historical location and social organization for such a universal human piety to have any definite meaning.

While Schleiermacher holds that human beings do in fact experience God at some level of consciousness, he does not mean that piety exists as a vague "religion in general." Human piety exists and is meaningful only from the perspective of social organization and historical continuity. Schleiermacher considers "the general susceptibility of individual souls to religious emotion" to inhabit only particular religious traditions and communions.[109] As a general tendency, piety lacks historical continuity and definition. This fact means that the only way that human beings can interpret and give meaning to their piety stems from the historical nexus of traditions and languages into which they are born, reared, and find

105. This interpretation agrees with Brian Gerrish. See *Continuing the Reformation*, 7f.

106. Gerrish, *Tradition and the Modern World*, 17.

107. *CF*, viii.

108. Schleiermacher explains the relationship between piety and other positive religions, namely, Islam and Judaism, in the context of delineating Christianity's distinctive essence. Different religious communities are examined generically and developmentally. See *CF*, 31–44.

109. Ibid., 30.

their identity. Human religious self-consciousness, in other words, must always and everywhere assume a definite shape and form. It is an identity that possesses and expresses an essence. This essence distinguishes one form of religion from another. Consequently, human piety emerges in history as something radically particular and definite. When the religious self-consciousness becomes historically continuous in expression and growth, it manifests a twofold aspect. "[T]he organization of the communicative expressions of piety in a community is usually called *Outward Religion*, while the total content of the religious emotions, as they actually occur in individuals, is called *Inward Religion*."[110]

Piety becomes more fully historical and concrete when inner experience takes outward form. As noted earlier, Schleiermacher posits the human experience of God as so central to the meaning of the human being that he describes it "as an original and innate tendency of the human soul."[111] As constitutive of human nature, piety also emerges more clearly in social life. This communal form of piety is "a Church."[112] The feeling of absolute dependence can be communicated socially.

> Fellowship . . . is demanded by the *consciousness of kind* which dwells in every man, and which finds its satisfaction only when he steps forth beyond the limits of his own personality and takes up the facts of other personalities into his own. It is accomplished through the fact that everything inward becomes, at a certain point of its strength or maturity, an outward too, and, as such, perceptible to others. Thus feeling, as a self-contained determination of the mind (which on the other side passes into thought and action, but with that we are not here concerned), will, even *qua* feeling, and purely in virtue of the consciousness of kind, not exist exclusively for itself, but becomes an outward, originally and without any definite aim or pertinence, by means of facial expression, gesture, tones, and (indirectly) words; and so becomes to other people a revelation of the inward.[113]

Schleiermacher's thought is consistent. In some respects, a church results from the reciprocal nature of the antithesis between freedom and dependence. External influences upon one's consciousness within experience, that is, modifying feeling, must manifest themselves for the external

110. Ibid.
111. Ibid., 22.
112. Ibid., 26.
113. Ibid., 27.

determination to have validity. For the best explanation, Schleiermacher notes the intrinsic relationship between lived experience becoming manifest in ethics. But he defers the issue, recognizing that it merits separate treatment.[114]

In any case, unlike such theorists as Hobbes or Rousseau, Schleiermacher agrees with Aristotle and medieval thinkers who argue that human nature is naturally social. If human nature is social, so also is piety.[115] Again, this theme reveals how central ethics as social theory is in Schleiermacher's reflections. As social creatures, individuals incorporate into religious communion in two basic ways. Some are naturally drawn toward fellowship because of the degree to which they are conscious of God. Piety is something dynamic and can increase, decrease, vary, and emerge within consciousness as different emotions at different places and times. Other people enter religious communities because of the clarity of their own prior religious experience by "the communicative and stimulative power of expression or utterance."[116] Important consequences follow. In each case, the social aspect of religious experience remains crucial for the inner unity of experience and outward unity of historical form.[117] The identity of the feeling of absolute dependence and the identity of a particular religious communion, in other words, requires social relationships to recognize and convey it. Religious communities in turn generate meaningful religious communication, namely language, symbols, art, liturgy, and music. When the God-consciousness of social groups takes definite and continuous form, such particular religions emerge as Christianity, Judaism, and Islam. Positive religions, in other words, do not emerge prepackaged.[118] What all share besides an

---

114. Schleiermacher holds in *Christian Faith* that "The truth that every essential element of human nature becomes the basis of a fellowship or communion, can only be fully explicated in the context of a scientific theory of morals [*wissenschaftlichen Sittenlehre*]," 27. He states this position elsewhere, particularly in his *Introduction to Christian Ethics*, 33f. In this work, Schleiermacher notes the problematic nature of the historical separation between systematics and ethics.

115. *SP*, 148. "If there is religion at all, it must be social, for that is the nature of man, and it is quite peculiarly the nature of religion. You must confess that when an individual has produced and wrought out something in his own mind, it is morbid and in the highest degree unnatural to wish to reserve it to himself. He should express it in the indispensable fellowship and mutual dependence of action."

116. *CF*, 27.

117. Ibid., 48–49.

118. Ibid., 49, 29.

original experience of God is the need for communal discernment and interpretation.

Here Schleiermacher makes several important distinctions among religiosity, subjective and objective religion, and natural religion. First, the "individual's susceptibility (which admits of different degrees) to the influence of the fellowship or communion, as also his influence upon the latter, and thus his participation in the circulation and propagation of the religious emotions—this is designated *Religiosity (Religiosität)*."[119] Schleiermacher calls the inward experience of God-consciousness "subjective" and the outward form of expression "objective." This outward form is also the "common element." The inner necessity that takes outward expression always assumes, as I have said, a definite form. Consequently, Schleiermacher seems to reject what has been called natural religion in philosophical and theological discourse. As such, Schleiermacher—at his most sympathetic reading—simply states concerning religion in general or natural religion that: "It is only that tendency, the general susceptibility of individual souls to religious emotion, that could be called 'religion in general.'"[120] The character of religious feeling, however, remains intrinsically ecclesial; it naturally seeks definiteness, form, organization, and communication. Yet having argued this point, Schleiermacher goes on to hold that such definitions and explanations are preliminary, arbitrary, and "indeterminate." One suspects that Schleiermacher drops the question not simply because it leads into murky territory, but also because doing so would contradict his assertion that his introduction is not constructing an anthropology. The consideration of natural religion falls outside the kind of ecclesial reflection he works out.[121]

In sum, if Schleiermacher is not doing speculative dogmatics or rational philosophy but reinterpreting the experience of God within the tradition of Christian spirituality, then piety as human religious experience exists concretely within everyday human consciousness and has roots in Christian historical experience.[122] He is laying the groundwork

119. Ibid., 30.

120. Ibid.

121. See ibid., 3.

122. It is indicative of the priority accorded to religious experience over reflective thought become doctrine that anthropomorphic speech about God is inevitable. Schleiermacher contends precisely that affective experience of God cannot but speak about God anthropomorphically given its effect on religious consciousness. See *CF*, 25–26.

for linking his description of the feeling of absolute dependence from human nature as naturally religious to a historical realization of it as formed by biblical revelation and Christian spirituality. The burden of the argument is to explain the bond, as Schleiermacher writes, "between Christian piety in itself, on the one hand, and both Christian belief (so far as it can be brought into the form of knowledge) and Christian action, on the other."[123] This link is where theory seeks verification in praxis. Indeed, Schleiermacher maintains repeatedly that attention to one's own mind and consciousness is crucial precisely because it is the evidence to which he appeals.[124]

THE THEOLOGIAN: RELIGIOUS INTEREST AND SCIENTIFIC SPIRIT

One fundamental condition that makes theology possible is the scientific and careful delineation of Christian piety and doctrine. Another condition is what Schleiermacher designates as the theological disposition [*der theologischen Gesinnung*] of the theologian.[125] Why is it important? It is essential because "there is a special talent required for every true art."[126] If theology is a subject matter and a complex of qualities brought to bear upon it, then a theological disposition is a key condition for theology and Schleiermacher's theological ideal. He provides a general description. "If one should imagine both a religious interest (*religiöses Interesse*) and a scientific spirit (*wissenschaftlichen Geist*) conjoined in the highest degree and with the finest balance for the purpose of theoretical and practical activity alike, that would be the idea of a 'prince of the Church.'"[127] These two attributes are essential to the theologian.

Religious interest is one of the two elements that comprise a "prince of the Church." Unfortunately, it is not a term Schleiermacher explains in sufficient detail. His descriptions and references tend to be diffused throughout the text and remain somewhat indefinite. What Schleiermacher identifies at the beginning of the *Brief Outline* as a *religiöses Interesse*, he uses interchangeably with "*kirchliches Interesse*," or

---

123. Ibid., 7.
124. Ibid., 7, 13, 25.
125. *BO*, § 262, 92.
126. Schleiermacher, *Christian Caring*, 112.
127. *BO*, § 9, 21.

"ecclesiastical interest" in different sections of the work.[128] It should also be noted that the German word *Interesse* has a stronger meaning than its English counterpart. Schleiermacher is referring to a deep, ongoing concern with one's general direction in life. In discussing Kantian philosophy, Jürgen Habermas speaks of the meaning of "interest" that matches the sense of Schleiermacher's use of the word. He writes, "Interest in general is the pleasure that we connect with the idea of existence of an object or an action. Interest aims at existence, because it expresses a relation of the object of interest to our faculty of desire." Habermas goes on to describe pure interest as an intellectual "permanent attitude."[129] With this meaning as background, I want to focus on several aspects that will shed light on its meaning and significance for doing theology: belief, perception, and vocation.

First, a theologian must be a person of faith, a believing and practicing Christian. One cannot, according to Schleiermacher, do theology and lack personal belief in the teachings of Christianity. An illustrative example occurs in his explanation of how one approaches dogmatic theology.

> A dogmatic treatment of doctrine is not possible without personal conviction [*eigne Ueberzeugung*], nor is it necessary that all treatments which relate to the same period of the same Church community should agree among themselves. One might wish to draw both statements from the fact that the dogmatic treatment only has to do with the doctrine current at a given time (see §§ 97 and 98). Only this would not suffice, for the person who is not convinced of this doctrine, though he might well provide a report on it, and even on the manner in which the ordered structure of the doctrine is conceived, cannot establish the truth of this structure through the disposition he makes of it. Yet it is only the latter factor which makes the treatment dogmatic. The other is merely a historical treatment of the sort which a person who knew enough could give similarly of all systems.[130]

There is a certain outlook that a believing theologian brings to bear upon his work that somehow enables her to establish the warrant for

---

128. See *BO*(g) §12, §193, §258, §262, and §330.

129. Habermas, *Knowledge and Human Interests*, 198–99. For a general overview of the term, see Gerhardt, "*Interesse*," 4:479–94.

130. *BO*, §196, 72. Tice renders *eigne Ueberzeugung* as personal conviction, but it can also mean "personal belief."

its doctrinal truth.[131] Only believers and theologians, par excellence, can therefore ground the validity of dogmatic claims. Schleiermacher immediately indicates, however, that his statement must be understood within a broad communal context of doctrinal judgment. He is not simply asserting that an individual's theological pronouncements enjoy authoritative veracity and become immediately binding on particular churches.[132] He is expressing the orthodox Christian conviction that the one who has not believed and thus experienced God cannot understand.[133]

Second, theologians must also be perceptive to the changes, movements, and problems within their own local church. Schleiermacher's insistence on the integrity of the theoretical and practical is especially evident here. As the goal of all theological study is practical theology—a point we shall consider later—the ecclesial interest of the theologian needs to press beyond abstract speculative ideas. It should influence the life of the theologian's own faith community.[134] A concrete ecclesial commitment of active service is inscribed within the identity and function of the theologian. "If, accordingly, all true theologians also participate in the leadership of the Church, and all who are active in Church government live also within the theological arena, it follows that both an ecclesial interest and a scientific spirit must be united in each person, despite any tendency to lean toward the one side or the other. If the opposite were the case, then the scholar would no longer be a theologian; he would merely be engaged in working over various theological subjects in the spirit of whatever particular science is proper to them."[135] Theologians

---

131. Cf, *LU*, 40.

132. See *BO*, §197, 72. "The statement and support of a body of propositions which are preponderately deviant and which express merely the conviction of an individual we would not term a "Dogmatics"; nor would we use the word for any such presentation which is offered in a time marked by a divergence of views but which would only admit what is uncontroversial."

133. The classic statement is Anselm's. "For I do not seek to understand that I may believe, but I believe in order to understand. For this also I believe,—that unless I believed, I should not understand." Anselm, *Proslogium; Monologium; and Appendix in Behalf of the Fool by Gaunilon; and Cur Deus Homo*, 53. For a modern and penetrating interpretation, see Karl Barth, *Anselm: Fides Quaerens Intellectum*.

134. *BO*, §259, 91. "The tasks of any person who is to exert influence of a genuinely deliberative character arise out of the way in which he appraises the actual condition of the Church at the present time, according to his conception of the essence of Christianity and of his own particular Church community."

135. Ibid., §12, 22.

are more than believers—they are clerics or ministers. Removed from an ecclesial context and a clerical framework, intellectual pursuits of theologians lose their theological character. Schleiermacher thus seems to exclude the possibility of lay theologians in part because dogmatics ultimately serves preaching and thus primarily designates pastors.[136] In any case, this ecclesial role is not for anyone, even among church members. Some of the theologically trained members tend toward more scholarly pursuits, while others incline toward more pastoral endeavors. Schleiermacher evinces a practical awareness of the ecclesial situation joined with the relative gifts and merits of the theological students addressed in the *Brief Outline*.[137]

Finally, in addition to personal belief and ecclesial sensitivity, the theologian should possess a vocation to theology [*innern Beruf*]. There is a sense of being summoned by God to a specific work.[138] Inevitably, it would seem, the theologian's vocation shares affinities with that of the prophets and others specially called by God. Individual discernment concerning one's ability and talent determines "the function his is to perform." [139] For Schleiermacher, this function means not only a calling to theological scholarship but also serious participation in church government. Even if one cannot personally realize the ideal of a prince of the church, a sense of vocation remains essential. In a frank comment, Schleiermacher remarks: "If one thinks of this balance as having broken down [ecclesial interest and scientific spirit], then the one who has primarily cultivated the knowledge of Christianity is a theologian, in the narrower sense; and, on the contrary, the one who has primarily cultivated activity which pertains to Church government is a clergyman ... Without such an inner calling, no one is truly either a theologian or a clergyman."[140] A vocation to theological study and ecclesial participation remains a prerequisite for theology. Whether "clergyman" in this context means special preparation for church administration or preaching,

---

136. See ibid., §11, 22, especially the explanatory note; Cf. §3 and §10, 20–21; § 279–80, 98; Editor's Postscript, 124.

137. *BO*, §13, 22.

138. This is also a strong theme in Calvin; see *Institutes* (1559), 3.10–11.

139. *BO*, §13, 22. The German term *Beruf* joined with *innere* evokes a deeply theological meaning and can be rendered "inner voice" or "divine summons." It could also refer to *Beruf* as the technical theological term for vocation.

140. Ibid., §10; §13, 21–22.

Schleiermacher indicates that the office of the ministry requires communication. Personal belief in the truth of the Christian faith obliges the theologian to share it with others.[141] Communication of the faith supported by personal conviction and scholarly study thus constitutes part of what leadership means within the Christian Church.

Though important and vital for theology to be properly "theological," the ecclesial interest presupposed for theologians is not Schleiermacher's main concern in the designation of the theologian. Most of Schleiermacher's statements about the theological disposition refer to the other element of the theological ideal, namely, the scientific spirit. It is precisely here that one encounters the decisive element of Schleiermacher's "prince." But there is a problem. The *Brief Outline* does not provide a clear and unambiguous definition of this desideratum. One finds a clue in his brief, earlier work on universities. There he described "scientific spirit" as "the feeling ... of the inner connectedness of all knowing" [*Gefühl von dem innern Zusammenhange alles Wissens*].[142] It reads almost as an intuitive quality or sense. Although this statement surfaces in the context of the philosophy faculty of a university, it is central to understanding Schleiermacher's theological ideal.

The scientific spirit encompasses certain habits of mind and scholarly skills. First, a theologian with a scientific spirit needs to cultivate a view of the whole. In the Introduction to the *Brief Outline*, Schleiermacher makes a fascinating and daunting assertion. He maintains that "[I]f one is to deal with any one of the theological disciplines in a truly theological sense and spirit [*theologischem Sinn und Geist*], he must master the basic features of them all. Only when each person in a general way comprehends the whole along with his own special discipline, can each and all communicate. Only thus can each person exert an influence upon the whole through his main field."[143] Theologians must seek a certain general perspective on the enterprise that is theology. That is, they must understand how a part relates to the whole and vice-versa. This drive toward a comprehensive and relational unity of knowledge is an essential characteristic of the scientific spirit. For Schleiermacher, it is a serious prerequisite for anyone undertaking theological study at all. An interest in the manifold ways in which elements cohere and affect one another

---

141. Ibid., §39, 31.
142. Friedrich Schleiermacher, *OT*, 35; *KGA*, 54.
143. *BO*, §16, 23.

discloses a crucial theological habit of mind. True understanding resides in knowing the whole. Schleiermacher conceives the character of theology's subject matter as a "whole" [*Ganzen*] repeatedly.[144] The reach and significance of one theological branch depends on a higher viewpoint that grasps unity within plurality.

Second, in addition to this holistic ability to discern part and whole in general, Schleiermacher insists more specifically that a theologian should have "an adequate perspective over the ways in which the various parts of theology interrelate, and of the particular value of each for serving the overall aim of theology." The grasp of theology's interconnecting parts is "indispensable for every theologian."[145] Hence, to engage any one of the different dimensions of theology—philosophical, historical, practical—theologians must know the basic subject matters and meaning of them all. This is an idealistic rather than a realistic proposal. Schleiermacher acknowledges that the notion of one theologian grasping and mastering all the theological disciplines is something impossible. Still, Schleiermacher cautions against the dangers of specialization. One ought not to immerse oneself in the details of one's area of expertise while overlooking other fields. Scriptural exegetes must understand the necessity of articulating doctrine and its relationships to church government. Pastors should discern the distinctiveness of Christianity in comparison with other modes of faith. Moral theologians should recognize the materials for common worship, the theological concepts embodied in symbol and liturgy. Indeed, one's command of a particular area—not simply of theological knowledge but of any knowledge that loses sight of the interrelationships of different parts—will suffer distortion.[146] In short, Schleiermacher demands that theologians acquire a generalist's breadth and specialist's depth. Lacking these skills, "the whole of theology would exist neither in one person nor in all together." Even more problematic, however, the absence of this scientific spirit would lead to a

---

144. Ibid., §1, §8, §15, §16, §17, §18, §20. §31; *OT*, 9; 15–19; 21.

145. Ibid., §18, 23.

146. *OT*, 2–3: "In the domain of knowing, everything fits together and interrelates with sufficient exactness that one can say that to the degree something is presented for itself alone it is bound to be distorted and incomprehensible. This is true because, strictly speaking, every particular admits of thorough inspection only in combination with all the rest, and consequently even the improvement of each aspect is dependent on all the rest."

situation in which specialists from different fields "would not be able to communicate at all."[147]

This demand for a comprehensive viewpoint is not important simply for theological competence or interdisciplinary dialogue. It is critical because such a habit of mind advances the theology and church leadership of the Evangelical Church. The vitality of reflection joined with present and future government is at stake. This trait of the scientific spirit also generates a humble receptivity to extra-evangelical knowledge and truth, guarding theologians against scholarly myopia and religious bias. Schleiermacher states: "Among us, students of theology only too often restrict their knowledge to the condition of the evangelical Church, even to that part of it within which their own activity lies. Such a restriction has a highly injurious effect upon the practice of the Church. Nothing so much favors persistence in the customary and traditional as the ignorance of strange and yet kindred circumstances. And nothing brings on a more uncouth fanaticism than the fear of having to recognize elsewhere something good which is lacking in one's own circle."[148] Given the history of mistrust between the Reformed churches and other Christian denominations, this statement is remarkable. Anticipating modern efforts toward Christian ecumenical dialogue and cooperation, Schleiermacher wants the theologian to have "[a] general knowledge of the condition of Christendom as a whole."[149] For him, this knowledge entails understanding the basic tenets and fundamental theological principles of other Christian denominations. It is interesting to note that what makes these statements logical is their connection to Schleiermacher's richly catholic theological viewpoint.

Third, the theologian must possess a disposition of historical consciousness [*geschlichtlichen Bewußtsein*] that is critical [*Historische Kritik*].[150] The most basic reason is because the content of Christian theology, or what Schleiermacher initially refers to as "a particular mode of faith," discloses itself in and through Christianity—a definite and historical phenomenon. Such modes of faith are not simply private and singular epiphanies but social experiences of God that are handed down over time. Since everything that develops and changes is by definition

---

147. *BO*, §14–15, 22–23.
148. Ibid., §243, 85.
149. Ibid., §244, 85.
150. Ibid., §8; §102.

historical, an adequate grasp of any present phenomenon must understand the past as a necessary context. Phenomena within contemporary Christianity, then, like a piece of writing, can only be understood as a part of a larger whole, namely, its historical past and context.[151] Familiarity with history is so important for Schleiermacher that he maintains that the theologian "should also practice some personal research and use of sources, on at least one small part of history."[152] He thus repeats the call for a generalist's breadth married to a specialist's depth.

The habit of historical-critical consciousness is more than a facile acquaintance with historical change; it also involves interpretation. Because theologians must identify the essence that makes Christianity distinctive as a mode of faith and experience of God—a constituent part of the theological discipline Schleiermacher calls philosophical theology—this kind of consciousness is required. Insofar as historical-critical consciousness bears upon the subject matter of theology in thought and language—that is, in texts—it is also hermeneutical. All written texts and language fall under the purview of historical interpretation. "The full understanding of a discourse or piece of writing is a kind of artistic achievement, and thus requires an 'art doctrine,' or technology, which we designate by the term 'hermeneutics.'"[153] Consequently, historical-critical consciousness entails identifying and analyzing similarities and differences between those realities unique to Christian faith and those of other religions.[154] Content can vary from doctrine to liturgy to morality. In all, however, the skills of judging, comparing, ruling items in or out as consistent with or contradictory to Christian faith—these activities are what Schleiermacher normally means by criticism in the usual sense. This is, moreover, a *sine qua non* for doing theology at all—an essential condition of its possibility.[155] The implications of this disposition,

---

151. The dialectical relationship between part and whole is integral to Schleiermacher's thought and especially to his hermeneutics. Though referring specifically to biblical interpretation, the principles for understanding apply equally to his work in theology. He writes, "Every utterance or text is only to be understood in a larger context . . . the understanding of the whole is not only conditioned by that of the particular, but also, vice versa, that of the particular by that of the whole." Schleiermacher, *Hermeneutics and Criticism*, 231.

152. *BO*, §190, 70.

153. Ibid., §132, 56.

154. Ibid., §32, 29.

155. Ibid., §33, 29.

however, are extensive and make demands on theologians. Theologians must be able to handle and interpret primary sources, which makes a working knowledge of Greek and Hebrew essential.[156] Historical-critical consciousness as part of the scientific spirit, then, requires more than familiarity with the genesis of the particular Christian mode of faith. Theologians must understand the past and present ideas of Christianity comparatively.

Fifth, the scientific spirit holds that theologians are independent in their inquiries. Theologians study and master many different elements of the discipline, aiming to appropriate the requisite habits and skills concerning parts and wholes as their own judgment. Dependence on specialists and the opinions of others contributes only so much. For example, it is crucial to possess a generalist's competence in making theological interpretations that rely on languages within theology. Indeed, remarking on biblical hermeneutics, Schleiermacher states: "Every theologian must do his own exegesis for himself, on account of its close connection with philosophical theology, regarded as the locus of all basic principles for theological work; thus, there is very little here, too, that one can allow himself to take over directly from the specialists."[157] Self-reliance stands as a critical attribute of the theologian and thereby indispensable for genuine scientific work. There is an important sense in which confidence in one's own skills and habits generates a richer, more vital disposition for serious theological reflection. Yet independent appropriation and formation of scientific habits and discipline does not mean isolation. Far from working in imaginary solitude or driven by individual gratification, Schleiermacher conceives theological inquiry—as with any scientific pursuit—as being conducted within a community.[158] Different views and perspectives need to be considered, sifted, and determined.

---

156. "In the area of language proficiency, it is to be expected that every theologian will attain (a) a basic knowledge of Greek, especially of the various developments of Greek prose, (b) a knowledge of both the original languages of the Old Testament, and, by this means, a clear insight into the nature and compass of Hebraism in the New Testament, and (c) finally, in order to make use of the work of specialists, not only an acquaintance with the literature of the entire field but especially an independently formed judgment regarding what is excessive and insufficient, natural and artificial, in the employment of oriental material." *BO*, §131, 56; Cf. §125–28, 55.

157. Ibid., §89, 46.

158. *OT*, 2–3. "[S]cience is by no means a business for the individual as such, that it cannot be brought to fruition and fully possessed by one person alone but must be a communal effort."

While holding up autonomous judgment as a virtue, Schleiermacher also recognizes the value of and need for receptivity to different views.[159] Such interchanges between individuals and their communities enable breadth of understanding and creative appropriation of the scientific spirit. Otherwise, one is not a theologian per se, but "a mere carrier of tradition—the lowest rank of all the activities open to a person, and the least significant."[160] The indictment is severe because Schleiermacher takes the office of theologian seriously. One who merely repeats past formulae and doctrines without creative understanding is intellectually sterile. Expectation of individual contribution not only to the edification of and participation in church government but also to church doctrine looms large. There is a real sense in which the vitality of the scholar's inquiry is organically connected to and partly feeds the vitality of polity and doctrine. At the same time, the scientific spirit must resist any tendency toward dogmatism and partiality. Schleiermacher was not blind to the realities of human weakness. Hence there is an emphasis on the community of scholars as a corrective.

Finally, scholarly independence does not simply designate individual judgment. It also includes intellectual freedom—the freedom to inquire, research, and apply scholarly habits of mind to the subject matter at hand. In Schleiermacher's *Occasional Thoughts on Universities in the German Sense*, this point is implicit within his description of the scientific spirit and the university. "The scientific spirit is awakened by philosophical instruction. In addition, it is both strengthened and brought to clarity by getting further perspective, from a higher standpoint, on what has already been learned. By its very nature, then, the scientific spirit must also try out its own powers and exercise them. This it does by moving out from the center more deeply into particulars so as to inquire, to integrate, to produce something of its own and by its correctness to offer proof of the acquired insight into nature and into the connectedness of all knowledge."[161]

---

159. *BO*, §219, 78. "It is to be required of every evangelical student of theology that he be engaged in forming a personal conviction regarding every proper locus of doctrine ... The expression "be engaged in forming a personal conviction" in no way implies a skeptical frame of mind, but rather that inward receptivity to new investigations essential to the spirit of our Church: either to changes in the treatment of the canon, or to the opening up of new sources for dogmatic terminology."

160. Ibid., §19, 24.

161. *OT*, 19.

This spirit informs the mind and stance of the academic, the philosopher, and the theologian in the *Brief Outline*. Consequently, it means that intellectual or academic freedom is fundamental for the theologian. For Schleiermacher, along with nineteenth-century neohumanist educators and idealists generally, intellectual or academic freedom was indispensable.[162] This concept of academic freedom is clear in Schleiermacher's description of the way in which faculty should organize their courses and teach their students.

> [T]he true spirit of the university is that of allowing the greatest freedom possible to prevail within every faculty as well. It is folly to prescribe sequences that lectures must follow or to divide up the whole domain of scholarship into precise individual parts. Not even such a private arrangement of faculty members among themselves would be desirable. The arrangement would be a standing invitation to stagnation. On the other hand, new life comes to any branch of the sciences when it is once more treated by others afresh, especially those who have occupied themselves more with other branches. This is why no teacher should allow one's talent to be so determined and externally bound or should

---

162. For Schleiermacher's discussion of the relationship between state and university, see *OT*, 2–11. It seems that Schleiermacher believed this principle on the basis not only of conviction but also from some personal experience. The historian Fritz Ringer notes that the history of university and state relations concerning academic freedom reached a decisive moment after the promulgation of the Prussian General code in 1794. As all universities and schools fell under state control, the issue of state power over academic affairs, especially given previous interference in the late eighteenth century—censorship of Kant's *Religion within the Limits of Reason Alone* being perhaps the most famous instance—was serious. Intellectuals, philosophers, and academics, the most noteworthy being the German Idealists, Schleiermacher, and Humboldt, protested against state interference and censorship. They argued that university teaching and learning involved much more than professional and technical training: science in the richest sense denoted the pure pursuit of knowledge for its own sake. *Decline of the German Mandarins*, 23–24; 111. Indeed, Lichtenberger notes that Schleiermacher experienced censure at first hand when contributing to a political journal. *History of German Theology in the Nineteenth Century*, 121. Looking back on the nineteenth century, Friedrich Paulsen confidently declares, "Freedom of teaching (*Lehrfreiheit*) is the pride of the German university. It is ultimately connected with the intellectual freedom which constitutes such a marked feature of our national life. When other nations boasted of their power, their dominion, and their free institutions, the German people—whatever great cause it may have had for dissatisfaction in other respects—prided itself upon its intellectual freedom. When it was denied the privilege of free and vigorous action, it found compensation and consolation in independent thought. And this free thought had its seat especially in the universities." Paulsen, *German Universities and University Study*, 227.

oneself so bind it. Industrious and spirited individuals, for whom the enterprise they pursue at the university is precious and honorable, cannot possibly need an external law in this respect; they have in themselves whatever drives them to do as much as they can, and they must themselves be their own law.[163]

There is a deep sense that the fecundity and ability of the scholar resist restriction; that limitation on what can be thought and taught frustrates the aims of theological education and the duties of scholarship. Schleiermacher's comments certainly continue the Enlightenment motif of personal autonomy. But the ecclesial relationship between the theologian and church leadership seems to mitigate the possibility of serious conflict. Intellectual freedom thus ensures the creative life of theology. It is the theologian's noble and heroic obligation to pursue his subject matter. Schleiermacher's phrase "prince of the church" was one expression of this notion among many during the nineteenth century, an epoch that witnessed the apotheosis of the scholar.[164]

---

163. *OT*, 39.

164. The influence of the Romantic notion of the hero can be seen in the first edition of the *Speeches*, 82–83, and *SP*, 135. This question of whether and to what extent Schleiermacher was a "Romantic" is a vexed and complex one lacking consensus. Richard Crouter gives a splendid but brief treatment of the issue in his Introduction to the 1799 edition of the *Speeches*. He argues persuasively that Schleiermacher contributed to and was influenced by the movement. "Far from being a theological interloper among the writers and poets of the romantic movement, Schleiermacher was a full participant whose special contribution was that of a "thinker of finitude." *Speeches*, 38. The motif influencing Schleiermacher's theological ideal, though, was not unique. The Romantic view of the scholar as a hero or great person who stood above the rest of humanity was a well known late eighteenth- and nineteenth-century idea. In 1794, Johann Fichte delivered a series of public lectures characterizing the scholarly vocation as *"the supreme supervision of the actual progress of the human race in general and the unceasing promotion of this progress."* He esteems the scholar as "the *teacher* of the human race," "a priest of truth," and "the *ethically best* man of his time." Eight years later in 1802, Schelling described the scholar as the one who with an "inner, living vision" sees the "universal" and brings his chosen field "into an all-embracing totality." He adds, "The realm of the sciences is not a democracy, still less an ochlocracy, but an aristocracy in the best sense of the word." This high, heroic view of the character and duty of the scholar, however, extends beyond Germany. In 1841, Carlyle could refer to the "Man-of-Letters" as a "Hero" and as someone who "must be regarded as our most important modern person. He, such as he may be, is the soul of all. What he teaches, the whole world will do and make." But it is Emerson who expresses it best. In 1837, Emerson proclaimed with his characteristic intensity, "The office of the scholar is to cheer, to raise, and to guide men by showing them facts amidst appearances. He plies the slow, unhonored, and unpaid task of observation . . . He is to find consolation in exercising

the highest functions of human nature. He is one who raises himself from private considerations, and breathes and lives on public and illustrious thoughts. He is the world's eye. He is the world's heart. He is to resist the vulgar prosperity that retrogrades ever to barbarism, by preserving and communicating heroic sentiments, noble biographies, melodious verse, and the conclusions of history. Whatsoever oracles the human heart in all emergencies, in all solemn hours has uttered as its commentary on the world of actions,—these he shall receive and impart. And whatsoever new verdict Reason from her inviolable seat pronounces on the passing men and events of to-day,—this he shall hear and promulgate." J. G. Fichte, "Some Lectures concerning the Scholar's Vocation," *Early Philosophical Writings*, 172, 174–76. Italics in original. Schelling, *On University Studies*, 24–30. Carlyle, "Hero as Man of Letters," *On Heroes, Hero-Worship, & the Heroic in History*, 134. Emerson, "American Scholar," *Collected Works of Ralph Waldo Emerson*, 62–63.

2

Friedrich Schleiermacher—Theology and Its Place in the University

> The first place in the history of theology of the most recent times belongs and will always belong to Schleiermacher, and he has no rival.
>
> —Karl Barth

ANY EFFORT TO UNDERSTAND why Schleiermacher affirms theology as a university discipline involves more than an elaboration of its possibility as provided in the experience of God. Schleiermacher's view takes this inquiry beyond the limitations of defining the attributes of a positive science. On examination, the location of theology within the university involves a certain tension. On the one hand, theology is essentially ecclesial because it is soteriological knowledge. On the other hand, theology requires the nourishing atmosphere of the other scientific disciplines and the organization provided by a university because it is an intellectual enterprise. The position of theology lies within a nexus of historical circumstances and influential principles: philosophical, pedagogical, professional, and theological. These forces elicit the underlying assumptions of a broader context, namely the relationship of the Reformed church to human knowledge.

Schleiermacher's position on the legitimacy of theology as *wissenschaftliche* can be read as a response to the question: What does the religious have to do with the academic? To answer this question, I will explore the following aspects of the university and its character: 1) the nature of the university and scientific knowledge; 2) the architectonic role of philosophy; 3) the significant features of university faculties and their historical context; 4) theology as ecclesial knowledge within the

Reformed framework of faith and reason; and finally, 5) the scientific aspects and practical functions of theology. Having established these characteristics of university culture, one can then evaluate the place of theology within it. In doing so, I also hope to sketch an important outline of the Reformation's legacy on the role of Christian theology as it bears upon not only the scientific-doctrinal aspects of theology but also on its professional tasks.

THE UNIVERSITY AND SCIENTIFIC KNOWLEDGE

Schleiermacher locates the meaning of the university in relation to other organizations of information and knowledge.[1] True to his hermeneutical method, his approach views the whole range of human scientific knowing before inquiring into one part of it.[2] Knowledge is scientific because it concerns the order and organization of information. Schleiermacher distinguishes three forms of "scientific associations" [*wissenschaftlichen Vereins*].[3] These include the secondary school, the university, and the academy. He defines "the school as the being together of master and apprentices, the university as the being together of master and journeymen, and the academy as the gathering together of masters."[4] The form

---

1. It might be assumed that the university of Berlin and other German universities only educated aristocratic and social elites. The reality is more complex. Certainly, the social elites did receive their training at universities; but demographic records, for example, from the University of Halle, also show students from various backgrounds coming from the middle-class as well. Sons of merchants, artisans, farmers, innkeepers did matriculate, though not in high numbers. Prussia was one of the first European countries to develop a central and government run network of secondary schools. This fact accounts for some social mobility by the middle class. Efforts by progressive and liberal-minded reformers like Baron Karl Stein and Karl August von Hardenburg championed egalitarian social reforms to kindle national unity and realize Idealist educational aims. Cf. Sheehan, *German History, 1770–1866*, 515–16; Levinger, "Prussian Reform Movement and the rise of enlightened nationalism," 266–75.

2. Schleiermacher asserts that "unless all three have been understood it would be difficult to get agreement on the nature and intended structure of the one that we are now attending to." *OT*, 12.

3. Ibid., 2; *KGA* I.6, 21.

4. *OT*, 11. Schleiermacher's understanding virtually mirrors Kant's. Kant maintains, "In addition to these *incorporated* scholars [university], there can also be scholars *at large*, who do not belong to the *university* but simply work on part of the great content of learning, either forming independent organizations, like various workshops (called *academies* or *scientific societies*), or living, so to speak, in a state of nature so far as learning is concerned, each working by himself, as an *amateur* and without public precepts

of scientific knowledge, then, depends partly on composition: that is, the different relationships among teachers and students. Participants relate to the nature of the knowledge judged as belonging to the university and its character as *wissenschaftlich*. But there is another important element—namely the unifying feature of each scientific association.

The secondary school is the basic location of scientific knowledge. General information and skills are transmitted to those who will later pursue university studies—not technical or vocational schools.[5] For Schleiermacher, secondary education must involve "the overall content of what is known in meaningful outlines, so that the talent dormant in each person can feel attracted to its special subject." Again, the dialectic between parts and whole is evident. Schleiermacher continues by saying that "it must also put in relief and treat with special diligence that in which the scientific form of unity and of interconnectedness can be clearly demonstrated at the earliest moment and, on the same basis, whatever serves as a general aid to all other knowing."[6] Two considerations control this underlying distinction: a distinct talent for a specialized field of knowledge and "the systematic spirit of philosophy." Students need both skills if they are "to be culturally formed to any degree of distinction."[7] Consequently, secondary education initiates and fosters the grasp of particular fields as well as alerting the student to their place within the expanse of human knowledge. The disciplines of grammar and mathematics are particularly important at this level of education. For Schleiermacher, these two fields "are justifiably the main subjects in schools." These disciplines, necessary for further study and technical occupations, are the only subjects "in accord with what is characteristic of science."[8] As science reaches toward the whole and universal, so do the skills and methods proper to these two pervasive disciplines. Secondary schools do not generate new knowledge; they prepare students for either practical applications of learning or the cultivation of habits ordered toward systematic thinking. Fundamentally, secondary education is an introduction to human knowledge as information on

---

or rules, at extending and propagating [his field of] learning." *Conflict of the Faculties*, 25.

5. *OT*, 11 ; "*die gelehrten Schulen*," KGA 6:30.
6. *OT*, 13.
7. Ibid., 12.
8. Ibid., 13.

its most basic level. In schools, writes Schleiermacher, "one moves from one particular to another, little concerned about whether each generally fits into some whole."[9] Analogously, one could say that secondary education in Schleiermacher's sense is like learning the elements of bridge; for instance, the cards, the point values, the process of bidding, and so forth, without knowing how bridge partners form units and compete in singular matches. The pupil acquires some elementary information about the game but not the ability to play it successfully. Secondary schools do not cultivate scientific knowing but merely "arouse insight into the nature of knowledge."[10]

In contrast to secondary schools, academies are assemblies of scholars who pursue and increase knowledge within their respective fields collaboratively. The notion that scholarly life and its vocation entail strict isolation contradicts Schleiermacher's vision. "Each member" he writes,

> ... must strive to enter into this joint effort since the talent that one has cultivated would be worth nothing for science without completion by the other members. All form a whole because they feel at one through their lively sense and enthusiasm for knowing, as such, and through their insight into the necessary interconnectedness of all parts of the process of knowing ... As a result, in each individual both participation in the progress of the whole and enthusiasm for one's own special discipline mutually stimulate each other, and in this way the closest community among the different parts of science comes to be most easily sustained in the bosom of the academy.[11]

Scholarship and advanced intellectual inquiry constitute a communal undertaking. Schleiermacher conceives academic cooperation as bringing interdisciplinary exchange and its fruits to bear on research. In their own way, academies foster and advance scientific knowledge through conversation, support, and correction among mature scholars. Academies enjoy an interactive dynamism between the whole of knowledge and specific parts, each giving and receiving from the other. This reciprocity is their distinctive character.

This mutuality also influences the nature and scope of their scholarly products. Schleiermacher writes: "[I]t is expected of any academy

---

9. Ibid., 17.
10. Ibid., 15.
11. Ibid., 14.

that it issue works, not large comprehensive or revolutionary books but collections of essays which shed light on particular subjects previously unexplored, present the author's discoveries, and critique or bring to light new found methods, for it is the business of the academy through many small contributions to advance the sciences, which to a certain extent have already gained scope and reliability."[12]

Specialized and particular research in academies means that Schleiermacher reserves these institutions exclusively for scholars. Academies stand at the zenith of the professional pursuit of science and learning. Membership in an academy in Schleiermacher's usage assumes not only scholarly competence in one's own area of expertise but also the stimulation and cultivation of a "philosophical spirit" (*philosophischem Geist*).[13] Though scholars raise and pursue particular problems to their full resolution, a proper perspective remains essential. That is to say, genuine scientific inquiry presupposes a philosophical spirit aware of and sensitive to the interconnections among all genuine branches of knowledge. In academies, writes Schleiermacher, "everything depends on elaborating the particular in a completely accurate and exact manner, in the domain of all 'real' sciences."[14] Ideally, academies in a nation are few, "one or two at the most," enhancing the possibility of cross-disciplinary influence through centralized locations.[15] Standing in the academy presumes that scholars possess a "perspective on the entire domain of knowledge, at least in its basic features." Lacking this acuity, specialized research easily becomes myopic.[16]

In relation to schools and academies, universities stand "in the middle between the two."[17] Schleiermacher offers two models for consideration: the theoretical or ideal university according to its principles and the real university viewed in its more complex mechanics and limitations. In what follows, I will concentrate primarily on the theoretical

12. Ibid., 15. In the later nineteenth century, one of the more famous French examples was the *Collège de France*. Noteworthy academies included the Royal Academy in London (1663), the Academy of Prague (1770), Munich (1763–68), the *Instituto delle Scienze* in Bologna (1712), and the Academy of Madrid (1735). Müller, "Ecclesiastical Learning in the Eighteenth Century," 543–45. See also Frijhoff, "Patterns," 43–80.

13. *OT*, 16; *KGA* I.6, 35.

14. Ibid., 17.

15. Ibid., 14.

16. Ibid., 24.

17. Ibid., 23.

model in order to uncover Schleiermacher's philosophy of university education. Consequently, several controlling questions need elaboration: What is a university's purpose? Why does it have that purpose? How do its aims occur? Schleiermacher's thinking reaches toward a predictably idealistic vision, given the strong influence of German idealism at the time. Still, his vision never loses its rigorous and logical consistency.

Schleiermacher begins his analysis with the university's "essential character" (*wesentlichen Charakter*), which also reveals its formal aim.[18] In contrast to schools and academies, he maintains:

> The university . . . has to do chiefly with the introduction of a process, with guardianship over its first developments; and this is nothing less than a wholly new intellectual process of life. The business of the university, then, is this: to awaken the idea of science in the more noble youths, who are already supplied with many kinds of information, to aid the idea's holding sway over them in the area of knowledge, to which each chooses to be especially devoted, so that it will become second nature for them to contemplate everything from the viewpoint of science, to perceive nothing for itself alone but only in terms of the scientific connections most relevant to it, and in a broad, cohesive manner bringing it into a continual relation to the unity and totality of knowledge, so that they may learn to become conscious of the basic laws of science in every thought process and precisely in this way gradually develop in themselves the capacity to investigate, to contrive, and to give account.[19]

In other words, the university educates the human scientific spirit by providing a forum in which the student encounters the totality of knowledge, its extent, and its relative implications for all fields of human knowing.[20] It is the place that "has to embrace all knowing and, in the way it looks after each individual branch, it must express its natural internal relation to knowing as a whole, its degree of proximity or distance from the common center."[21] Moreover, one must note that the center of this formative and intellectual process is philosophy.

---

18. Ibid.; *KGA* I.6, 42.
19. *OT*, 16.
20. Ibid., 17.
21. Ibid., 24.

PHILOSOPHY: ARCHITECTONIC DISCIPLINE AND ORGANON OF SCIENCE

If secondary school education introduces pupils to the scientific process and academies advance particular fields of knowledge under the guidance of minds scientifically formed, universities seek to cultivate and form "a definite philosophical mode of thinking" (*philosophische Denkungsart*).[22] Schleiermacher describes the content of this mode of thought. "[O]nly one moment is actually spent at the university, only one act is completed: the idea of knowledge, the highest consciousness of reason, awakens in the person as a regulative principle."[23] This principle is not a "sheer transcendental philosophy," something terribly abstract or unrelated to more empirical or concrete knowledge. It is not, in other words, a form of philosophical idealism disguised as a university education. Schleiermacher speaks contemptuously of any approach lacking this integration: "Unfortunately, many have tried to accomplish this, carrying sundry phantoms and strange concerns into the effort. Probably no more vapid a philosophy is thinkable than one that extracts itself so purely and expects that real knowing, as something lower, should be given or taken from a totally different source."[24] Rather, for Schleiermacher, the scientific spirit integrates the speculative and the empirical because "[o]nly in its lively influence on all knowing does philosophy admit of being presented; only with its body, with 'real' knowing, does its spirit admit of being grasped."[25] This kind of thinking warrants philosophical instruction to include the totality of human knowledge, not simply limited perspectives concerned with abstract thought separated from the natural or practical sciences. In its true identity, the university is the institution in which the "totality of knowledge is to be presented, accounted for."[26] At the university, students learn how to learn and what it means to see knowledge from a systematic standpoint.

Achieving this philosophical mode of thinking requires several important components. Most basically, Schleiermacher contends that

---

22. Ibid., 18; *KGA* I.6, 36.

23. *OT*, 17.

24. Yet it must be noted that Schleiermacher did conceive universities—not the academies—as places where different and conflicting philosophies and their respective schools would clash. Cf. *OT*, 18–19.

25. Ibid., 19.

26. Ibid., 17.

the "encyclopedic perspective," as he calls it, is duly cultivated through ". . . the general overview of the scope and cohesive structure of each area, and makes this the foundation of all instruction. Thus the chief published products of the university, as such, are textbooks, compendia the aim of which is not to give exhaustive or enriched account of science in detail."[27] Systematic interconnections, broad relationships, patterns and perspectives on the whole and the unity of knowledge—textbooks and courses at the university impress these principles on students as the main goal of learning. The faculty and discipline most fitting to guide and shape this scientific spirit, most naturally becomes "philosophy, the intrinsically speculative field."[28] For this reason, the art of philosophy or dialectic is "the organon of all science."[29] What does this privileged position of philosophy mean more specifically? It certainly does not mean that the essence of university education tends to the excessively abstract on the one hand or lacks a foundation in the lived experience of history on the other. Instruction should maintain an equilibrium between the concrete and abstract.[30] Schleiermacher contends that both the empirical and speculative principles underlying all human knowing can take their origin only from the branch of human knowing as comprehensive or "architectonic." He states, "Over the system of coordinated sciences there must be certain principles they share, an architectonic for these principles. However much one is to expect unity in all these principles, unity is just as little available nonetheless, and the diversity among these principles extends its influence over all the other sciences."[31] Philosophy's architectonic nature and ability to integrate—not oppose—speculation and empirical knowing ultimately comprehends both kinds of principles. Schleiermacher maintains, "The supreme and most general elements of knowing . . . and the principles for doing philosophy themselves are the same."[32] All sciences, that is, all forms of human knowing and understanding, can be reduced to the principles with which philosophy is fundamentally concerned. Put differently, this extensive capacity of philosophy holds true because "[i]n relation to the whole of science, it

27. Ibid.
28. Ibid., 30.
29. Schleiermacher, *Dialectic*, 7.
30. *OT*, 23–24.
31. Schleiermacher, *Dialectic*, 1–2.
32. Ibid.,5.

[philosophy] is, as it were, what the given center and farthest periphery is to a sphere. By means of it one can assign to each individual proposition its place and find which organic part of the whole it is."[33] Surpassing any other faculty or discipline, philosophy provides the intellectual formation for students to look further, to investigate, and to grasp the underlying principles and intelligibility of all branches of human knowing. The university's self-understanding and identity at their best flow from its philosophical faculty. The university forms and guides a philosophical and "general scientific spirit" in its students.[34] It follows then quite naturally that the starting point for students in a university curriculum is philosophy. Schleiermacher maintains that "[H]ow university instruction must be formed can easily be recognized in any university ... That is, the most general subject matter is common to all; all begin with this, and only later do they divide themselves within the domain of the particular, as in each person one's distinctive talent is awakened and along with this one's love for that occupation wherein one can especially exercise it. Everything begins, therefore, with philosophy, with pure speculation, and whatever belongs propadeutically to that as a transition from school to university."[35] As the organon of science, philosophy or dialectic forms the rational and scientific ability of students to move from the center of knowledge—its principles—into the particulars of any scientific field.

The development of the systematic standpoint, however, presupposes more than what one discipline or subject matter can realize by itself. Other pedagogical and scientific features must also exist. The process of educating the scientific spirit requires students and professors whose mutual influence occurs within a community.[36] In terms of communication and pedagogical techniques, lectures, seminars, different courses, and faculties serve and advance this intellectual formation toward its term.

---

33. Ibid.,7.

34. *OT*, 20.

35. Ibid., 27. Those subjects or fields "common to all" are rather substantial. All take their direction from "the two great domains of nature and history." These domains include philology, ethics "insofar as it presents the nature of all human being and doing," natural science "of organic and of the inorganic," and "the essence of mathematics, of geography, and of natural philosophy and natural history." Ibid., 27–28.

36. Ibid., 28.

Paramount among these pedagogical elements are the lectures—the university's "sanctuary."[37] Lectures are a critical way to elicit and hone the scientific philosophical spirit. They combine and they reproduce "one's own coming to know, the act itself, so that the listeners are not constantly gathering mere information but are directly perceiving the activity of reason in bringing forth knowledge and are perspicaciously continuing that activity."[38] Done well, lectures exemplify the human intellect's systematic movement toward comprehension and meaning. They seek to direct the development of such reasoning precisely in the listeners—the students. So important is the lecture for Schleiermacher that he calls it "the proper art of the university teacher overall."[39] All these aspects are institutional patterns of cooperation, empowering the presence of different realms of knowledge and information that cultivate the student's ability to see meaningful relations among fields. The presence of the various sciences also increases the opportunity for realizing this intellectual life. For the diverse dispositions and interests of students to be drawn toward science, there must be respective fields capable of arousing "one's special talent."[40] Many students are thus naturally drawn into this intellectual process from different vantage points.

Though different fields of scientific knowledge come together to assist in the formation of the learner's philosophical perspective, Schleiermacher's vision of a university education, especially concerning the place of theology, is not easily grasped. In the previous remarks concerning the essential characteristics of scientific formation, the faculty of theology seems to play no more important a role than the other faculties. Its ambiguous position raises the question: what is the place of theology in the university? The role of theology can be illuminated by consider-

---

37. Ibid., 29.

38. Ibid.

39. Ibid., 30. A philosophical perspective also emerges in the experience of lecturing itself. "Two virtues must be conjoined in it. On the one side, there are vitality and enthusiasm. The reproducing that occurs must be veracious, not a mere game. In the lecturing, whenever one truly looks upon knowledge in its origination, in its existence and having come into existence, whenever the lecturer traces the way from the center to the circumference of science, the lecturer must also make this real. In no true master of science does the situation ever become different from this. For such a scholar, no repetition is possible without some new combination enlivening oneself, without some new discovery drawing one to it. In teaching, one will continually learn, and will always stand before one's audience, in a vital and truly productive fashion."

40. *OT*, 24.

ing it alongside the other main departments of knowledge within the university.

Schleiermacher acknowledges that the university in the nineteenth century took its form during the medieval period. Yet in contrast to the medieval and early modern idea of a university, and along the lines of Kant before him, Schleiermacher argues that "the authentic university, as it would be formed by the scientific union, is contained solely in the philosophical faculty."[41] This privileged place follows from the constitutive position of philosophy as the major component of scientific knowledge and intellectual formation. Positive faculties stand in contrast to the philosophical faculty. In the history of early modern universities, the typical paradigm among the faculties distinguished higher and lower faculties. The higher or positive faculties were law, medicine, and theology. The arts or philosophy faculty took a secondary position under the others.[42] A significant reason for the evolution of the university into the form that Schleiermacher analyzes is its close contact with and determination by state interests. The distinction between higher and lower faculties corresponded to different social functions. The higher faculties were related to the public sphere while the lower ones were "a purely private undertaking."[43] Schleiermacher explains this distinction in his general descriptions of these faculties.

> The "positive" faculties have arisen individually by virtue of the need to provide a sure foundation for absolutely essential practice through theory, through the passing on of information. The legal faculty is immediately based in the instinct for building up the state, in the need to have a situation ruled by law emerge out of an anarchical situation—anarchical because provision of laws had not progressed apace with the culture. This effort was accompanied by the feeling that such could occur only if people sought to attain possession of a system of laws, complete and consistent

---

41. Ibid., 34. Truth in learning is what is essential about a university and its guardian is philosophy. See Kant, *Conflict of the Faculties*, 43–45. See also Howard, *Protestant Theology and the Making of the Modern German University*, 167ff.

42. For a good overview of this development and particular treatments of it, see the essays by Jacques Verger and other scholars in *History of the University in Europe*, vol. 1. For a detailed history of the medieval university, see Ferruolo, *Origins of the University*. Despite the prestige and rhetoric bestowed on philosophy by philosophers, in reality its lower ranking would continue relatively unchanged throughout the eighteenth century. Cf. McClelland, *State, Society, and University in Germany, 1700–1914*, 151–232.

43. *OT*, 34.

with each other, and to attain higher principles that could be used to interpret the laws in ambiguous cases. The theological faculty has been formed in the church in order to maintain the wisdom of the fathers, to separate truth and error in what has gone before so that earlier truths are not lost for the future, and to provide an historical basis, a definite, secure direction and common spirit, for further development of doctrine and of the church. Further, as the state came to be bound more closely with the church, it had also to sanction these institutions and to place them under its care. From earliest times, the medical schools have been based partly on the need to detect and modify the condition of the body, partly in a more or less dim, mysterious presentiment of intimate relations of all the rest of nature to the human body. Hence from the beginning on, they were in part preponderately gymnastic in character, in part magical and mystical. Through the uniting of the two branches these concerns gradually won a more artful look. To the degree that they began to work their way into the various branches of natural science, through observations and inquiries of their own, and thus to need greater external supports, the state had to take them on as well.[44]

Lawyers, clergy, and doctors serve the needs of legal, spiritual, and physical health in modern society—irreplaceable functions for any state government and civil culture. Their nature and term extends from the university to the public and practical realms of life. The positive faculties are thus engaged in an "external enterprise; and they join together what is required for this enterprise out of the various disciplines."[45]

This professional orientation differs considerably from the philosophy or arts faculty concerning the coherence of knowledge. In the positive faculties, "the purely scientific direction has an external and subordinate status."[46] Practical concerns—not the coherence or drive to know the totality and unity of knowledge—determine and measure the degree of their scientific character. Consequently, the positive faculties of law, medicine, and theology are less connected than the philosophy faculty to forming the student's scientific spirit.[47] Moreover, they are not

---

44. Ibid., 34–35.

45. Ibid., 35.

46. Ibid.

47. In an ideal situation, Schleiermacher argues the following: "If a university ever arises through a free uniting of scholars, then what is now conjoined in the philosophical faculty will naturally find the first place, and the institutes that state and church will wish to join to the philosophical faculty will take places subordinate to it." Ibid., 36.

essentially related to the intrinsic nature of what a university means or aims to accomplish. In terms of scientific reach, content and intellectual formation, positive faculties are subordinate to and guided by the philosophical faculty, for "it is the first, and in fact the head of all the others because all members of the university must be rooted in it, no matter to which faculty they belong."[48] Schleiermacher goes even further. All teachers in a university must possess a philosophical training themselves so that in their own disciplines they "will not gradually and increasingly approach a mechanical tradition or perish in an entirely unscientific superficiality." Philosophical formation, its scientific spirit and vision, thus prevents ossification or one-sidedness and invigorates the other branches of knowledge it helps to organize.[49]

There are other reasons for the central position of philosophy. First, only philosophy unites and organizes university knowledge in its essential character. Unlike the positive faculties, the philosophy faculty is not ordered directly to practical training for civil service. Of its essential nature, philosophy as the organon of science along with those it orders pursues science for its own sake, seeking a total view of knowledge and its internal connections.[50] As such, the "entire natural organization of science is thus contained in this one entity alone."[51] Philosophy engages in the highest degree of "speculation," which Schleiermacher defines as "a term we would always use for scientific activities that preponderantly relate to the unity and common form of knowing."[52] Its opposite would be scientific inquiry for the sake of real or empirical information as practically useful. In the university, a certain intellectual and scientific balance is achieved between speculative and real when the systematic perspective confronts and relates the different branches of knowledge as a whole. Therefore, philosophy as the guiding principle in the departments of knowledge counters other considerations about the order and meaning of knowledge that tend toward the pragmatic.[53]

48. Ibid.
49. Ibid., 37.
50. Ibid., 17.
51. Ibid., 35.
52. Ibid., 10.
53. Ibid., 35.

Second, another important reason is philosophy's comparative "autonomy" [*Selbstandigkeit*].[54] The context for Schleiermacher's treatment of disciplinary freedom this was the relationship between the state and university at the time. Autonomy, however, did not imply financial or legal independence. It partly means that unlike the positive faculties, the state does not exercise a "dominating relation" to philosophy as it does to law, medicine, and theology.[55] Rather, autonomy marks the integrity of the philosophy faculty concerning its purpose, which is decidedly more removed from the more practical state concerns of the positive faculties.[56] Since philosophy prescinds from external or practical applications fitted for particular needs and problems, it does not "disintegrate and dissolve into a manifold of heterogeneous parts."[57] What Schleiermacher intends can be understood more clearly after examining a positive faculty like theology.

As noted earlier, theology is positive precisely because it is an "assemblage of scientific elements which belong together not because they form a constituent part of the organization of the sciences, as though by some necessity arising out of the notion of science itself, but only insofar as they are requisite for carrying out a practical task."[58] Yet this 'positive' orientation is immensely problematic for its unity, especially concerning governmental support. The more theology works out its different aspects—philosophical, historical, and practical—the more its external relationships reciprocally influence the trajectory of those pursuits, such as serving Christians and citizens of the state. If this effect occurs, the more the scientific organization of knowledge looks to practical undertakings supported by government funding, the more the integrity of the different branches of this positive science lose their coherence. Not only do external demands and interests—for example, the economic, the ecclesial, and the political—enter into its determinations; but the more the term of theology understands itself principally as practical, it will increasingly sever its contacts with philosophy as the organizing faculty and the other sciences. This principle logically extends to the other positive faculties as well. Nonscientific considerations and values enter into

54. *KGA*, I.6, 56.
55. *OT*, 35.
56. Ibid., 45.
57. Ibid., 36.
58. *BO*, §1, 19.

the evaluations and purposes of other positive sciences in such a way that what scientific culture might seek as possible or constructive is undermined. When accidental and practical interests assume prominence, contact among the branches of science that leads to a comprehensive vision of whole and part withers. Historical reasons, however, are partly responsible for this outcome.

Throughout the eighteenth century, European universities suffered enormous financial strains, unable to pay instructors adequate salaries or control maintenance costs. In part, this problem occurred because, as historian Charles McClelland notes, "eighteenth-century universities were still not thoroughly integrated into the financial existence of the state, or even into the money economy." Financial strain, economic imbalance, and second jobs or teaching positions among university professors were widespread. On the whole, German universities saw costs exceed revenues from endowments and other sources. Given this dire situation, they increasingly relied on state subsidies until the German government assumed economic and administrative control over university finances.[59] McClleland observes: "Turning to the state for salvation from economic perils of the time constitutes one of the most important results of the general university crisis of the eighteenth-century."[60] Reliance on state funding also explains why Schleiermacher discusses at length the relationship between science and the state. Universities were once again thinking through certain reforms that could not now occur apart from the state.

Schleiermacher's view concerning the relationship between the state and the university or science seems to have evolved from one of hopeful promise to uncertain ambiguity. In a work titled *Occasional Thoughts on Universities in the German Sense*, he thinks the university or scientific associations in general ought not to proceed utterly free from the state. Ideally, a cooperative and healthy relationship benefits each institution. It is important that universities enjoy the state's "protection and patronage."[61] In turn, universities benefit the state in several ways, not simply by providing professional training. Universities also instill respect for the pursuit of "true knowledge" in the cultured citizenry. University graduates who later become civil servants experience "a feeling of de-

---

59. McClelland, *State, Society, and University*, 90–91; 80ff.
60. Ibid., 91.
61. *OT*, 5.

pendence" on their universities precisely as places of true knowledge in civic and national life. Their education nurtures their scientific and intellectual vitality, which in turn cultivates an openness to innovation and change that the graduates might bring to their own civil service.[62] For such reasons, Schleiermacher believed that a university's scientific qualities could spread throughout the culture at large, vitalizing it in significant and progressive ways. From this perspective, universities could be agents of scientific enlightenment and social progress.

These views reflect Schleiermacher's thinking around 1808, however. He grew less sanguine about the positive effects of university scientific knowledge pervading the citizenry and German culture. In a later work, Schleiermacher could write, "That the intellectual is cultivated is also in the interest of the state, but it is in no way clear that the government will perceive that the cultivation of the intellectual in the majority of the people is also in the interest of the state."[63] Indeed, even in the earlier work Schleiermacher expressed concerns about certain interests that could threaten scientific culture. The warrant for this anxiety stems from the fact that the state employs the products of the positive faculties for its own ends. In turn, professional position and advancement receive their proper value and term in large part from public, specialized, and professional demands. The greater the external demands, the more nonphilosophical interests enter into the priorities of these faculties and their commitments apart from their organic link to philosophy. More narrow, political, pragmatic, and economic interests assume prominence.[64] From the state's perspective, these concerns and outcomes suit its educational investments. The state funds and supports the universities and the positive faculties. But when the relationship between state and university deteriorates, Schleiermacher describes starkly the virtual end of scientific knowledge.

---

62. Ibid., 26.

63. Schleiermacher, *Die Praktische Theologie*, 685.

64. Schleiermacher considers these dangers to be especially grave when scholars participate in state sponsored "administrative councils" that oversee "public instruction." There, he writes, the "more their relation as servants of the state assumes a greater weight among these civil scholars, which will naturally result, the more readily will they carry this view into their particular spheres of scientific activity, evaluating and dealing with everything according to its immediate effect on the state—and, as experiences also teaches, certainly not the advantage of intellectual improvement." *OT*, 22.

However, a very pernicious misunderstanding is involved when governments here and there begin to view the political aspect of these institutions as the main thing and, whenever there is conflict, to force the genuinely scientific element to wait. Moreover, when they actually intend to be completely spared of the form of the university and to join the special schools for the various departments of state service directly to the general scholarly schools, this is a tragic sign that the value of highest culture for the state is being denied and that mere mechanism is being preferred to life ... there are places where the state has ravaged the universities— the very center, the nursery of all knowledge—and has then sought, as it were, only to dismember scientific endeavors and to tear them away from their vital interconnection. There, it must not be doubted, the design, or the unconscious effect of such an operation at least, is to stifle the highest and freest culture and all scientific spirit; and the unfailing result in all departments is that a mechanistic way of being and a deplorable narrow-mindedness get the upper hand. Those who propose to us that the universities be dispersed and turned into specialized schools are acting thoughtlessly or are infected by a ruinous, non-German spirit.[65]

Political and utilitarian considerations enervate the ends of scientific and philosophical education.[66] The French Revolution and the subse-

65. Ibid., 26–27. It is difficult to determine which universities Schleiermacher had in mind. It is quite possible, however, that he is thinking of the utilitarian reforms carried out in Heidelberg and Landshut. See McClelland, *State, Society, and University*, 106ff.

66. The influence of Napoleon's reforms cannot be underestimated. Thomas Howard describes the emergence of new forms of higher education resulting from the French Revolution's exaltation of modern scientific rationality. "The Napoleonic system sundered the tasks of research and teaching, assigning the former to a number of extra-university institutions rejuvenated during the Revolution, such as the *Collège de France*, and to newly established scientific and professional training centres such as the *École Normale supérieure*. The task of teaching was handed over to a new university apparatus, the *Université impériale*, established by Napoleon in 1808. State-dominated, utilitarian in focus, and having virtually no resemblance to the pre-revolutionary university, the new educational structure was designed to prepare reliable teachers, officials, and other professionals for imperial service." Though the Prussian universities did not ape those of France, Howard notes that many German Protestant and Catholic universities that failed to meet the new Enlightenment expectations were closed. Universities that survived found ways of adapting to the new environment. *Protestant Theology and the Making of the Modern German University*, 134–36. McClelland notes a "very strong utilitarian current was perceptible in the thinking of most 'enlightened' bureaucrats by the 1780s and the drift of their thinking was toward changing or even abolishing the traditional university model in favor of the specialty school." McClelland, *State, Society, and University*, 76.

quent rise of Napoleon toward the end of the eighteenth century initiated precisely the general direction in which states moved concerning universities, esteeming more the benefits of specialized schools and seeing the university primarily in terms of its usefulness to state interests.[67] But utilitarianism is not the only danger. Schleiermacher also warns against the state's taking sides within the competing intellectual positions of universities. Government must refrain from this exercise of power. Promotion and position, catering to state favor, only weaken and undermine genuine philosophical debate for other interests and erode its spirit. Philosophical settlements and positions are not determined by the pursuit of truth or knowledge but by lesser and self-serving interests.[68] This pragmatic tendency was present and understandable at the time. Since the universities relinquished economic and corporate control during the eighteenth century, the state increasingly played a role in determining "appointments, curriculum, regulations for students and faculty, criteria for awarding degrees, discipline, and other areas of university life." In Schleiermacher's view, the danger of philosophy's losing its ability to give intellectual and scientific coherence to the organization of knowledge was real. Professors became less seekers of truth and producers of knowledge than civil servants.[69] The status of civil servants is also what the government would accord to Protestant and Catholic clergy. Nevertheless, given Schleiermacher's view of the university, scientific knowledge, and the role of cultivating the scientific spirit primarily though philosophy, what becomes of theology within this context? How can it achieve legitimate status within an ideal geared far more to science than religious faith? Schleiermacher's response is complex.

THEOLOGY WITHIN THE REFORMED FRAMEWORK OF FAITH AND REASON

A university as such comprehends all branches of human science and knowledge. It is centralized and given orderly coherence through the architectonic function of the philosophy faculty since that faculty alone combines "pure transcendental philosophy and the entire natural and historical science sides of scholarship." The theoretical and the empirical

---

67. Ibid., 93ff.
68. *OT*, 45.
69. McClelland, *State, Society, and University*, 91–2.

are not alienated but harmonized. In this way, the university represents the "inner connectedness of all knowing."[70] Maintenance and development of the philosophical spirit, moreover, permeates the twofold hierarchy of faculty and students. Professors from different disciplines are called to cultivate individual appreciation of fields of study and embody this character by informally consenting to rotate within the network of university sciences. Such collaborative practices foster and develop synthetic perspectives and philosophical sensitivities that can be transmitted to students and permeate individual research.[71] Faculty and students, therefore, can be exposed to the totality of human knowledge. Hence one can argue that Schleiermacher implicitly holds that the theological faculty and theology do have a place within the university by virtue of the principle that all knowledge is vitally interconnected. Viewing and approaching the whole as the realization of a philosophical or scientific spirit presupposes the presence of theology as it does the other positive sciences of law and medicine. The absence of theology or any other science, positive or not, does violence to the aims of the scientific spirit and is therefore antithetical to the nature of the university.

The question remains whether the relationship of theology and the theological faculty to the universe or aggregate of sciences is ultimately directed by the architectonic science of philosophy and based primarily on an implied need for inner connections among the various disciplines. Does Schleiermacher in fact make interconnectedness the strongest argument for the inclusion of theology within the university? The answer depends on considerations of theological principles and internal ecclesial relationships. The understanding of theology as a positive science, especially concerning its influence on other sciences, far more resembles what I call a soteriologically cooptative science—that is, one far more narrowly concerned with church doctrine and life. If this understanding of Schleiermacher is accurate, the question becomes to what degree theology can seriously relate to or influence the universal organization of human knowledge.

Though the positive character of theology defines it within the university as a cooptative science and though it is scientifically arranged, its inner dynamism and supervision manifest an exclusive concern with ministerial practice—not the fulfillment or true meaning of university

70. *OT*, 35.
71. Ibid., 38–39.

or scientific knowledge. Professors and students engaged in Christian theology ultimately contribute to advancing and understanding the Christian faith and the institutional church. Schleiermacher's understanding of theology and what counts as theological knowledge appears to be ordered toward separation and isolation from the other university disciplines. More specifically, Christian theology evidences conflicting dynamics between its subject matter and its scientific form. In considering both, I hope to show that it is foundationally extrinsic to the nature of the university due to its aims on the one hand and because of an operative theological principle derived from the Reformers on the other. This theological principle regards the sacred and the profane as profoundly distinct and separate spheres of knowledge. Schleiermacher's description of the theological faculty is central. He maintains: "The theological faculty has been formed in the church in order to maintain the wisdom of the fathers, to separate truth and error in what has gone before so that earlier truths are not lost for the future, and to provide an historical basis, a definite, secure direction and common spirit, for further development of doctrine and of the church. Further, as the state came to be bound more closely with the church, it had also to sanction these institutions and to place them under its care."[72] This description is part of a brief historical survey of the different positive faculties alongside law and medicine. Schleiermacher's discussion neither repudiates nor modifies this description.[73] Without evidence to the contrary, it seems to be not simply a historical description but a normative statement of the identity of the theological faculty. It is odd, however, that this account omits the difficulties suffered by universities in the eighteenth century that led to state oversight. Though the problems were real and increasing, Schleiermacher indicates nothing, paradoxically, about the dangers of government influence on scientific knowledge that he notes earlier in the same text and elsewhere.[74] Even so, the account is immensely significant.

---

72. *OT*, 34.

73. What Schleiermacher upholds as an important aspect of the theological faculty not clearly indicated here, however, is the productive exchanges between professors and students in the seminar. See *OT*, 40–41.

74. Cf. Ibid., 2–11; 22; 69; *Praktische Theologie*, 685.

Before and after the Napoleonic wars, the state strengthened its interest in German education.[75] As noted earlier, the state took over the ailing universities in the eighteenth century. The various German kingdoms and duchies saw increasing state and administrative control, therefore, over the general sphere of knowledge and learning. In this situation, Schleiermacher recognized that what constitutes the diversity of university knowledge as such fell under a broad category, namely, the "organism of knowledge" (*Organismus des Wissens*). The organization of knowledge (*Organisation des Wissens*) for Schleiermacher embraces human knowledge as a whole, that is, "all public teaching and science," (*aller öffentliche Unterricht und alle Wissenschaft*). It encompasses more than what is simply contained in the university or other educational institutions. What is crucially significant about this concept, however, is how and why Schleiermacher makes an important distinction within it: "This organization consists of two elements: the universally human and the particularly Christian."[76] As Schleiermacher maintains, the origin of the theological faculty and of theology is not, however, the university but the church. What proceeded from the Christian church as a form of human knowledge has over time grown apart from it; that is, it has become a "for-itself existing organism for the purpose of knowledge" that is independent of the church.[77] Ecclesial ties were not eliminated but transformed. In the course of these changes, clergy became not less involved in government but a new kind of civil servant employed by the state.[78] Given these realities, therefore, what kind of influence should the church have on the organization of knowledge? If Schleiermacher maintains the legitimate reality of an organism of knowledge, and if he holds for a distinction within it between the universally human on the one hand and the particularly Christian on the other, how does his position tell upon the place of theology in the university? To answer this question

---

75. See Maynes, *Schooling for the People*, 52ff. By "state" here I refer to the authorities behind and that maintained Prussian cities and participated in the German Confederation of 1815. Germany would not be a single unified "state" in the contemporary sense until much later.

76. "In einem christlichen Volk als solchem, kann es nur eine Organisation des Wissens begen, dennoch besteht sie aus zwei elementen, aus dem allgemein menschlichen und dem eigenthümlich christlichen." *Praktische Theologie*, 681.

77. "Einen für sich bestehenden Organismus zum Behuf des Wissens." *Praktische Theologie*, 680.

78. Sheehan, *German History, 1770–1866*, 517.

adequately, it is critical to understand the deeper issue: the separation of religious and secular knowledge.

Since the sciences found within universities "began in the dependence on the Christian church," they are thus ecclesial products—however tenuous their links to the church later became.[79] In this historical context, Schleiermacher distinguishes the legitimacy of an independent organization of knowledge and the realm of the church as part of one whole but distinct. The latter he calls a "self-contained realm" (*abgeschlossenen Gebiet*).[80] As a concrete example of this distinction, Schleiermacher flatly maintains "*such organizations that deal with the entirety of knowledge as the academy cannot proceed from the church.*"[81] This distinction is important. It implicitly reveals not a political principle of expediency but a deeper theological axiom operative in Schleiermacher's thinking: the sacred and the secular are two different spheres.[82] This principle explains not only how theology figures in a university but also why Schleiermacher separates philosophy and theology in his dogmatics. This principle also offers a way to organize Schleiermacher's somewhat disparate comments characteristically within the Reformed theological tradition.

During the Reformation's theological and social tumult, Martin Luther rejected many of the theological and philosophical principles affirmed by Roman scholastics: the merits of Aristotelian reason, the use of syllogistic form and dialectics, the good will and nature of human beings.[83] Philosophical wisdom and reason had little to do with the most important knowledge of God mediated through Scripture and received in faith by grace.[84] It would be misleading, however, to claim that Luther

---

79. "Angefangen hat der Organismus des Wissens in der Abhängigkeit von der christlichen Kirche." *Praktische Theologie*, 679.

80. *Die Praktische Theologie*, 681.

81. Ibid., 682. Italics in original.

82. Cf., *LU*, 85–87.

83. Luther, *Disputation against Scholastic Theology*, 13–20.

84. The following is the first point, "oratio" in Luther's prescription for "a correct way of studying theology." "Firstly, you should know that the Holy Scriptures constitute a book which turns the wisdom of all other books into foolishness, because not one teaches about eternal life except this one along. Therefore you should straightway despair of your reason and understanding. With them you will not attain eternal life, but, on the contrary, your presumptuousness will plunge you and other with you out of heaven (as happened to Lucifer) into the abyss of hell. But kneel down in your little room [Matt 6:6] and pray to God with real humility and earnestness, that he through his dear Son may give you his Holy Spirit, who will enlighten you, lead you, and give you

always viewed reason negatively. Although his rhetoric sounds extreme at times, he does recognize the good and positive attributes of reason.[85] It is really more a question of emphasis and limitation. Without direction and explicit connection to Christ's life, cross, and resurrection, human wisdom is incomplete at best and dangerously wrongheaded at worst.[86] Human reason did have its own proper autonomous sphere, but according to Brian Gerrish, "it only begins to be called in question when it approaches the boundary-line of the Heavenly Kingdom."[87] A distinction was made between knowledge appropriate and necessary for salvation and knowledge of the world—for example, the arts or sciences—which was either irrelevant at best or obstacles to salvation at worst. While medieval theologians tried to harmonize faith and reason, Luther began to separate them. The split between sacred and secular knowledge began its Protestant history.[88]

Calvin follows Luther in separating matters of faith from those of reason. The famous opening lines of the *Institutes* announce: "Nearly all the wisdom we possess, that is to say, true and sound wisdom, consists of two parts: the knowledge of God and of ourselves." But it is from our own "unhappiness" that we come to "some knowledge of God." Still further, for Calvin it is precisely from our own "depravity and corruption" that we "recognize that the true light of wisdom, sound virtue, full abun-

---

understanding." *Martin Luther's Basic Theological Writings*, "Preface to the Wittenberg Edition of Luther's German Writings," 65–66.

85. See Martin Luther, *Lectures on Jonah*, 1:5, in *Luther's Works*, vol. 19. Speaking of the Gentile sailors on the ship with Jonah, Luther writes: "Let us here also learn from nature and from reason what can be known of God. These people regard God as a being who is able to deliver from every evil. It follows from this that natural reason must concede that all that is good comes from God; for He who can save from every need and misfortune is also able to grant all that is good and that makes for happiness. That is as far as the natural light of reason sheds its rays—it regards God as kind, gracious, merciful, and benevolent." Yet reason possesses "two big defects," nevertheless. It does not know whether God is willing to help us and that although it "knows that there is a God . . . it does not know who or which is the true God" (54–55).

86. Martin Luther, "Heidelberg Disputation," #20: "He deserves to be called a theologian, however, who comprehends the visible and manifest things of God seen through suffering and the cross; #22: "That wisdom which sees the invisible things of God in works as perceived by man is completely puffed up, blinded, and hardened," *Martin Luther's Basic Theological Writings*, 43–45.

87. Gerrish, *Grace and Reason*, 15.

88. For a good synopsis of this split between sacred and secular in relation to other intellectual changes, see Schmidt-Biggeman, "New Structures of Knowledge," 489–530.

dance of every good, and purity of righteousness rest in the Lord alone."[89] Yet what is the procedure for coming to this knowledge that ultimately promises to be salvific? Calvin maintains, "[I]t is certain that man never achieves a clear knowledge of himself unless he has first looked upon God's face, and then descends from contemplating him to scrutinize himself." Theological and procedural priority lies with God's revelation to humanity given in Christ and mediated by Scripture. This was the knowledge, the wisdom essential for human beings to recognize in their fallen state. Calvin's emphasis moves away from what human reason could accomplish independently of God's revelation.[90] His axiom also excludes philosophic reflection on God.[91] Calvin draws a sharp separation between the sacred and the profane when he holds that God cannot be accurately or edifyingly seen in the natural world. The only important kind of knowledge necessary for Christians comes from the Spirit and the Scriptures.[92] Like Luther, Calvin shares a deep pessimism in regard to fallen human reason compared to biblical revelation. This view is illustrated when Calvin juxtaposes philosophy with Scripture:

> Now this power which is peculiar to Scripture is clear from the fact that of human writings however artfully polished, there is none capable of affecting us at all comparably. Read Demosthenes or Cicero; read Plato, Aristotle, and other of that tribe. They will, I admit, allure you, delight you, move you, enrapture you in wonderful measure. But betake yourself from them to this sacred reading. Then, in spite of yourself, so deeply will it affect you,

89. Calvin, *Institutes of the Christian Religion*, vol. 1, I.i, 36–7 [1559].

90. Ibid., 36; I:vi, 69–74.

91. Blasting the different conceptions and arguments reason employs to discover knowledge about God, Calvin contends that "among the philosophers who have tried with reason and learning to penetrate into heaven, how shameful is the diversity! As each was furnished with higher wit, graced with art and knowledge, so did he seem to camouflage his utterances; yet if you look more closely upon all these, you will find them all to be fleeting unrealities." Ibid., I:v, 65.

92. Calvin argues that it is "in vain that so many burning lamps shine for us in the workmanship of the universe to show forth the glory of its Author" and that to see God properly in the workings of creation, of nature, our eyes need to "be illumined by the inner revelation of God through faith." Following this, Calvin maintains that "God bestows the actual knowledge of himself upon us only in the Scriptures." Ibid., I:vi, 69. "[T]hey who strive to build up firm faith in Scripture through disputation are doing things backwards . . . the testimony of the Spirit is more excellent than all reason. For as God alone is a fit witness of himself in his Word, so also the Word will not find acceptance in men's hearts before it is sealed by the inward testimony of the Spirit." Ibid., I:vii, 79.

> so penetrate your heart, so fix itself in your very marrow, that, compared with its deep impression, such vigor as the orators and philosophers have will nearly vanish. Consequently, it is easy to see that the Sacred Scriptures, which so far surpass all gifts and graces of human endeavor, breathe something divine.[93]

God's revelation in Scripture can effect a conversion in mind and heart that makes all other literary knowledge or philosophical wisdom pale. Believers ought to commit themselves to the Bible for truth, meaning, and value. At the same time, however, Calvin acknowledges reason's abilities. Though human nature is corrupt, it still possesses "the many preeminent gifts with which the human mind is endowed" and "proclaim[s] that something divine has been engraved upon it."[94] But this ability of reason is only in its own secular domain. When it comes to divine matters, as Calvin states concerning human reason, we are "extremely reluctant to admit that it [reason] is utterly blind and stupid in divine matters."[95] Calvin distinguishes different spheres in which knowledge of God and knowledge of other things do not meet. He concludes a section on the limits of rationality as follows: "Human reason . . . neither approaches, nor strives toward nor even takes a straight aim at, this truth: to understand who the true God is or what sort of God he wishes to be toward us."[96] Insofar, therefore, as human reason orders those disciplines that do not concern such divine things as the arts and sciences, they are not salvific resources for coming to God.[97]

Schleiermacher stands in the theological tradition of Luther and Calvin. His understanding of theology presupposes the principle of different spheres of knowledge: sacred and secular. One need only refer to his understanding of religion as neither metaphysics nor ethics to see how, like Luther and Calvin, he distinguishes the realm of the sacred from the secular in terms of religion and theology.[98] At the beginning of the *Brief Outline*, he makes this point clearly. Having given the defini-

---

93. Ibid., I:viii, 82.

94. Ibid., I:xv., 184ff.

95. Ibid., II.ii, 278. For an extensive treatment of Calvin's view of the relationship between faith and reason, see Hoitenga, "Faith and Reason in Calvin's Doctrine of the Knowledge of God," 17–39.

96. Calvin, *Institutes* II:ii., 278.

97. Cf. Ibid., I:vii, 79; viii, 82 .

98. See *Speeches*, "Second Speech," 28–41.

tion of theology as a positive science, Schleiermacher states: "Reference is certainly also made to the God of whom we are conscious in the case of "rational theologies" formerly constructed within the organization of sciences. As speculative science, however, *these are entirely different from the theology whose definition we are elaborating here.*"[99] This somewhat implicit distinction between rational and positive in this citation is precisely what Luther and Calvin achieve in their division between matters of faith and those of reason. Speculative and metaphysical considerations were purged from mingling with theological interpretations of biblical revelation.

Schleiermacher's understanding of theology continues this separation by virtue of its nonmetaphysical or speculative character. However, unlike Luther and Calvin, Schleiermacher evinces no outright hostility toward or skepticism of human reason; he simply affirms and continues the sharp distinction between the different spheres of knowledge. The problem then becomes how sacred and secular interact without losing their autonomy. Theology abides not only in the church but also in the university for reasons that can be broadly classed as scientific-doctrinal and practical-professional. If this classification is true, then, how does theology still remain an "organic" member within the universally human organization of knowledge? Paradoxically, Schleiermacher has so defined theology as to make the logic of specialization and professionalism convincing. Theology is oriented away from knowledge that might impede theological development. On the other hand, Schleiermacher recognizes the need for theology to be a part of the university curricula for the sake of its own survival. How can Schleiermacher justify its location within the university? I propose to examine each set of arguments that will demonstrate the place of theology in the university as one of paradox and tension, presupposing the Reformed theological principle in each. First, let me take the scientific-doctrinal reasons.

THEOLOGY: SCIENTIFIC-DOCTRINAL ASPECTS AND PROFESSIONAL FUNCTION

Schleiermacher discusses the topic of the Evangelical church's relationship to science in a section of the *Practical Theology*. It contains a rich statement regarding the scientific-doctrinal issues at stake for theology

---

99. *BO*, §1, 19. Italics mine.

in the university. It also makes one of the most revealing, suggestive, and problematic claims in Schleiermacher's thinking.

> The Protestant church cannot disregard science (*wissenschaft*) ... The Protestant church requires the proportionate role of the philological-historical for the education (*Bildung*) of its intellectual condition ... If we look at the present situation, we discover that the theological faculties operate as organic members of a larger organization. According to their form, these organizations are combined, a situation which arises from its relationship with the state. *It is an essential interest of the Protestant church to preserve the theological educational institutions in unison with the general development of knowledge so that its character does not degenerate into a traditional one.* For if the theological faculties became specialty schools (*Specialschulen*) this would be most dangerous for the Protestant church because the Protestant church desires progress in doctrine (*fortschreiten inn der lehre*), that is only possible when in the intellectual (*geistlichen*) there is a speculative interest and a historical education. And it is obvious that this can be achieved in its totality better in general educational institutions than in specialty schools.[100]

This remarkable statement touches on not only theological organization and science but also on strong reasons for the inclusion of theology within the university. While the first set of reasons concerns the nature of theology, the second set takes up the historical context of theological education. It is especially in the latter field, I believe, that Schleiermacher would have recognized problems regarding the location of Christian theology during the first third of the nineteenth century.

First, Christian theology requires the skills and knowledge of such other disciplines as philology and historical research for its vitality and development. Contact between the theological faculty and other university faculties ensures intellectual fecundity in methodology and interpretation of doctrinal content. For Schleiermacher, the meaning of the "general development of knowledge," therefore, is that theology engages the cultural and intellectual streams of Enlightenment schol-

---

100. *Praktische Theologie*, 687. Italics in original. Specialized schools of various kinds had existed throughout the eighteenth century. The founding of these schools did compete with and challenge related disciplines or fields in the universities. In Germany, some of the specialty schools included: artillery (Mannheim 1754), veterinary medicine (Dresden 1774), commerce (Hamburg 1768), forestry (Berlin 1770), and civil and military engineering (Munich 1780). Frijhoff, "Patterns," 58, 60 (Table 2.1).

arship.[101] Church polity, furthermore, actively benefits from the creative reflection that occurs among the different fields of science, especially when such fields are essential for the proper task of ecclesial knowledge and practice. Subordinate sciences, as part of the positive character of Christian theology, contribute to its aims: linguistics, history, philology, hermeneutics, forms of criticism, and even philosophy.[102] The assistance of these sciences enables Christian doctrine to speak and define itself for the present church. Theological disciplines co-opt useful elements, language, concepts, and insights, from secular sciences for their own purposes—a practice hardly novel in theological history. Nevertheless, only insofar as theologians remain linked to the ongoing life and development of science, can theology adequately sustain its careful balance between the religious and the scientific. Furthermore, theological disciplines are organic members of a larger organization of knowledge and therefore warrant a place within a university based on compositional and disciplinary kinship. Since the nature of theology "is philosophical and philological in its critical character," it rightly belongs in a university because it is *wissenschaftliche*.[103]

Second, like other university disciplines, the practice of Christian theology enjoys the academic freedom to pursue its investigations unimpeded. Theology possesses this freedom in two ways: by virtue of its status as a scientific university discipline and because of its Protestant character. In terms of the university or scientific aspect, Schleiermacher maintains that

> ... the true spirit of the university is that of allowing the greatest freedom possible to prevail within every faculty ... It is folly to prescribe sequences that lectures must follow or to divide up the whole domain of scholarship into precise individual parts. Not even such a private arrangement of faculty members among themselves would be desirable. The arrangement would be a standing invitation to stagnation ... This is why no teacher should allow one's talent to be so determined and externally bound or should oneself so bind it. Industrious and spirited individuals, for whom the enterprise they pursue at the university is precious and

---

101. For instance, Schleiermacher's comments on exegetical theology indicate the importance and validity of the higher biblical criticism and its modern methods developed during the Enlightenment. Cf. *BO*, §111–48, 52–60.

102. *BO*, §69–70; §124–34, §149–50, §214–15; 41, 54–57, 60–61, 77.

103. *Die Praktische Theologie*, 713.

honorable, cannot possibly need an external law in this respect; they have in themselves whatever drives them to do as much as they can, and they must themselves be their own law.[104]

Restrictions on the study and teaching of theology are therefore incompatible with its identity as a scientific discipline.

The principle of scholarly freedom also receives qualified support within the Protestant ecclesiological framework concerning theological studies.[105] Schleiermacher holds that church polity exhibits two elements: the authoritative and the discretionary. The authoritative or binding element aims to preserve doctrinal traditions and ensure the structural integrity of church polity. The "discretionary" element refers to the "'free spiritual power' within the Evangelical Church."[106] Understood theologically, the discretionary element is ecclesial permission granted to theologians to "bring something new into this communal disposition and spirit."[107] But this discretionary element also involves creativity, religious reflection, and risk. Admittedly, discretionary freedom therefore exists in a healthy tension with the authoritative element.[108] The purpose of the authoritative and the discretionary elements, according to Schleiermacher, is "ever more authentically to represent the idea of Christianity within the evangelical Church according to that Church's distinctive conception of it, and to gain increasingly greater support for this idea."[109] Ultimately, theologians take ideas and methods from other

---

104. *OT*, 39.

105. I should note that Schleiermacher's discussion of academic freedom and ecclesiological freedom of inquiry presupposes a distinction between Protestant and Catholic ecclesiology. Schleiermacher is consciously defining certain churchly characteristics over against those he perceives to be present in Catholic ecclesiology. Difficulties arise, he acknowledges, when the Protestant churches deliberate about ways to safeguard doctrine. In these cases, although certain goods might be obtained for the community by appointing an ecclesiastical censor, Schleiermacher holds in the end that such a practice is "superfluous." See his discussion in *Praktische Theologie*, 690–92 ; also *BO*, §304, 104; §310, 105; and §338, 114.

106. *BO*, §328, 111.

107. *BO*, §313, 107.

108. "The condition of a given whole within the Christian church is the more satisfactory the more vitally both sorts of activity affect each other and the more definitely action in both areas is accompanied by a consciousness of the contrast." *BO*, §314, 107.

109. *BO*, §313, 106.

university disciplines and labor for the Protestant church to fulfill its practical mission in caring for souls (*Seelenleitung*).¹¹⁰

The second set of reasons for the inclusion of theology within a university concerns the danger that doctrine might become "completely secluded" (*abgeschlossen*). This concern, I suggest, is tied to Roman Catholicism and clerical education. There is a real danger of allowing theology to "degenerate" into a traditional form.¹¹¹ Schleiermacher defines *traditional* in regard to theological education or training rather broadly.¹¹² He seems to indicate that it entails a rigid and confined interpretation of Scripture that employs "tradition" to defend or attack theological positions outside its purview.¹¹³ If this approach lacks

---

110. Cf. *BO*, §263, 92–93.

111. *Praktische Theologie*, 687. In a section titled "The activity of the academic instructor," [*Die Thätigkeit des akademischen Lehrers*] Schleiermacher describes two misguided and unbalanced approaches to theological advancement. "The first [mistake] is this: that there are times when a tendency towards literalism and intransigency dominate; the second [mistake] is when this attachment is removed and where the application of the historical and critical view proceeds in a contradiction with the results of an earlier period." Ibid., 713.

112. He might have had in mind theological textbooks along the lines of positive or manual theology of the eighteenth century. According to Schleiermacher, one of the "strictest dogmaticians" was the Lutheran Johann Quenstedt (1617–88) whose *Theologia didactico-polemica sive systema theologicum* was reissued five times and considered one of the great textbooks. It proceeds from questions to theses to expositions to antitheses and to confirmation of the theses. For these reasons, it bears the marks of a scholastic text untouched by historical-critical methods. See Quenstedt, *Nature and Character of Theology*. For an explanation of positive theology, see Congar, "Théologie," 426–30. On the Catholic side, Schleiermacher might have had in mind Professor Petro Dens of the University of Louvain (1690–1775). His seven volumes of *Theologia ad usum seminariorum et sacrae theologiae alumnorum* went through ten editions, up to the tenth, published in 1880. Another instance of positive or manual theology, the work is an abridgment of questions, notes, and explanations of Aquinas's *Summa theologiae*. The bulk of Dens's text treats moral theology, sacraments, religious life, and prayer. It is more likely, however, that Schleiermacher is referring to one of the most widely used textbooks in Catholic seminaries of the period, that of Professor Bruno Franz Leopold Liebermann, the *Institutiones theologicae*, first published in Mainz in 1819–27. The manual went through ten editions, the last published in Mainz in 1870. It was one of the most widely used textbooks in seminaries throughout Germany, France, Belgium, and the United States in the nineteenth century. See Lauchert, "Liebermann, Bruno Franz Leopold," 235–36.

113. *Praktische Theologie*, 687. Schleiermacher's target of criticism is Roman Catholicism. He states that Catholic theology "considers doctrine completely secluded (*abgeschlossen*), and holds the interpretation of scripture to be completely given, requiring only tradition."

a critical character, it would be antithetical to legitimate theological diversity—something Schleiermacher contends "is an essential aspect of the Protestant church."[114] The problem, however, is that in some universities of the time in which priests might matriculate, like Tübingen, Munich, and Landshut, creative new forms of Catholic thought were being explored by theologians appropriating modern thought and the Scriptures.[115] Traditional, scholastic, and narrow theological approaches would be less popular and less common in these universities. There is a better explanation.

Schleiermacher criticizes not simply Catholic theological faculties at universities to the extent that their intellectual horizons were narrow. He also attacks by implication the only other schools on the continent of Europe where theology could be isolated from modern theological currents: Catholic seminaries. As the first third of the nineteenth century in Germany saw the rise of new reactionary Catholic movements and ultramontanism, Schleiermacher's criticism of secluded theological education could not have been more apt. It coincides with the description provided by the distinguished church historian Roger Aubert, who wrote: "[T]he nineteenth century was to produce the peak of ghetto mentality within Catholic Church history."[116] Prior to the nineteenth century, the Council of Trent—not the Reformers or their descen-

114. Ibid., 709.

115. There are many examples. In Tübingen, one must mention the groundbreaking work of Johann Sebastian Drey (1777–1853). See especially his *Brief Introduction to the Study of Theology*. Drey's influence would continue and evolve through his student J.A. Möhler. In Landshut, there was the influential work of Johann Michael Sailer (1751–1832), whose *Vorlesungun aus der Pastoraltheologie* went through four editions (Munich 1820, fourth edition). There was also the controversial yet influential Georg Hermes (1775–1831) who taught first in Münster and then in Bonn. His reconciliation of Catholic faith with Enlightenment reason, presented in his *Einleitung in die christkatholische Theologie*, eventually drew ecclesiastical fire and was condemned by the Vatican along with other works in 1835. Finally, there was the work of the layman Johann Joseph Görres (1776–1848) in Munich. For more information, see entries in *The Catholic Encyclopedia*. Cf. Roger Aubert, "Catholic Thought Searching for New Ways," 31–56..

116. Jedin and Dolan, *History of the Church*, vol. 7, 113. Thomas Howard notes the same trend from 1789 to 1815. "While a number of Catholic theological faculties survived the revolutionary onslaught, often proving to be fruitful centres of inquiry and dialogue with their Protestant counterparts, seminaries directed by bishops and religious orders, often tilting toward ultramontanism, began to play a more prominent role in Catholic theology at this time." Howard, *Protestant Theology and the Making of the Modern German University*, 135.

dants—began to move theological and clerical formation of diocesan priests from the universities into diocesan seminaries. Catholic youth aspiring to the priesthood were to be trained in "ecclesiastical learning" [*disciplina ecclesiastica*] expressly to be "ministers of God" [*ministrorum Dei*].[117] This meant, however, that for the most part, the Tridentine seminary reforms in Spain, France, Italy, and Germany up to the nineteenth century—though including dogmatic and systematic theology in many curricula—generated a theological milieu more favorable to moral, catechetical, sacramental, and liturgical exigencies than to dogmatic. What Timothy Tackett maintains for eighteenth-century French seminaries is generally true for seminaries elsewhere in Europe. "[W]hatever the period of seminary preparation, the theology studied was usually quite minimal. Intellectual training focused, for the most part, on the practical skills necessary for the "governing of souls": how to preach, hear confession, or judge the legality of marriage alliances."[118] The practical and functional character of the seminaries and the kind of education envisaged for them was represented by the atmosphere and priority of its teaching. Almost two hundred years after the Council of Trent, Jean Bonnet, the superior general of the Lazarists, could maintain, "The bishops send their ecclesiastics to us not to make teachers of theology out of them, but just curés and vicaires capable of instructing and directing the

---

117. *Decrees of the Ecumenical Councils*, 2, 750–51. For an analysis of the Council of Trent and seminary legislation, see O'Donohoe, *Tridentine Seminary Legislation*.

118. Tackett, *Religion, Revolution, and Regional Culture in Eighteenth-Century France*, 103. For a historical and geographical cross-section, see Deutscher, "Seminaries and the Education of Novarese Parish Priests, 1593–1627," 303–19. Dominique Julia maintains of eighteenth-century seminarians, "La prédominance de la théologie dogmatique et surtout moral une théologie positive pratiquement inexistante est an autre signe d'un enseignement tourné essentiellement vers les exigences du ministère." Julia, "Le prêtre au XVIII ème siècle. La théologie et les institutions," 529. See also Tackett, *Priest & Parish in Eighteenth-Century France*, 78–83 . For an in-depth study of seminary life, culture, and theology in the French seminaries, few studies can match A. Degert, *Histoire des séminaires français jusqu'à la Révolution*, especially vol. II. In Spanish seminaries between 1700 and 1730, theological decay reinforced the pastoral focus. "In this time of decadence, the battles invade the movement in the seminaries and students get lost in the confusion of tendentious minor issues and sterile labyrinths. Abandoning the direct study of the Scriptures, Fathers and councils, they come out with a great mastery of the "therefores" and the "contras", but with a weak preparation to accomplish their mission, alien to the positive sciences, the exact pastorals and even the spiritual formation. They are content with the indispensable knowledge "for ministering well the care of souls." Hernández and Hernández, *Los seminarios españoles en la época de la Ilustración*, 18–19. Translation mine.

faithful."[119] Seminary graduates clearly served a professional role under the bishop.[120] What this professional role meant concretely from diocese to diocese could and did vary tremendously.[121] It was possible therefore for theologians working in different contexts not only to oppose one another but also to sever innovative academic theology from religious practice and ministry.

In the history of German Protestantism from the Reformation up through the early nineteenth century, formal theological training was the preserve of the faculty of theology.[122] Dogmatic or systematic theology was taught and learned in the university. Its aims, however, were not as narrow as one might expect of an academic program in theology today. Theological training for parish clergy also incorporated religious and educational pedagogy beyond the formally theological and pastoral. This practice is not new in the history of universities. Even the medieval university at times educated the young at the secondary or primary level.[123] Moreover, the Council of Trent decreed that even poor churches

---

119. R. Darricau, *La formation des professeurs de séminaire au début du XVIII siècle d'après un directoire de M. Jean Bonnet*, 4–12; quoted in McManners, *Church and Society in Eighteenth-Century France*, 1:205.

120. It is striking to note that ecclesiastical authorities were authorized not only to "compel and oblige ... those occupy lectureships and other to whose office is attached the duty of reading or teaching, to teach those to be instructed in these schools" but also to see that in regard to course content the burden to teach falls primarily "only on doctors or masters or licentiates in holy scripture or canon law and on persons otherwise suitable who can fulfil the duty themselves." Preaching and confession were of utmost concern, not dogmatic theology. Tanner, *Decrees of the Ecumenical Councils*, 2:752–53.

121. For examples of this variety in France, see McManners, *Church and Society*, 198–207.

122. Dorner, *History of Protestant Theology*, vol. 2, 1–23 and 103–9. Exceptions can certainly be admitted; for example, one could argue that Calvin's Academy of Geneva during the seventeenth and eighteenth century was a seminary. Yet its evolution had features far more similar to colleges and universities than Catholic seminaries. The Academy trained students for a variety of professional fields. See Klauber, *Between Reformed Scholasticism and Pan-Protestantism*, 36ff. It is highly probable that young Protestants unable to attend university for formal theological training studied under a pastor at his local church, much like colonial American training for the ministry prior to the separation of theological seminaries from undergraduate colleges after 1820. See Fraser, *Schooling the Preachers*, 3–27.

123. Willem Frijhoff, "Patterns," 53ff. Frijhoff goes on to note that even in the seventeenth century and beyond, "Grammar schools were, of course, still closely associated with the universities (and they continued for a long time to provide elementary teaching in reading and writing). In many university towns the grammar school remained linked

should have a master to teach grammar to "clerial and other poor students."[124] The same held true for Catholic seminarians. In the latter half of the seventeenth century, the seminarians of Saint-Sulpice in Paris "were assigned to the task of instructing the children of the parish, and later, as priests, many also as bishops, introduced into every corner of France the methods which had been so effective at Saint-Sulpice." Such practices continued throughout the eighteenth century.[125] Nineteenth-century Catholicism in Germany, however, was influenced by the rise increased spiritual power of the papacy and stricter forms of piety after the ravages of the French Revolution and the growth of cultural secularization. Catholic revival movements, formed in reaction to absolutist governments and Enlightenment rationalism, not only weakened traditions connected to Gallicanism, Febronianism, and Josephinism, but also drew strength from the new spiritual vigor and increasing leadership of the papacy. Various cultural and religious conditions came together in a detrimental situation made possible by the Tridentine decrees: university and seminary theology in opposition.

There were two major conflicts between ultramontane bishops and their seminaries on the one hand and university theology faculties on the other in the first third of the nineteenth century. The first occurred during Schleiermacher's lifetime, the other shortly after he died. Johann Ludwig Colmar (1760–1818), appointed bishop of Mainz by Napoleon in 1802, founded a seminary on the Tridentine model in 1805 rather than establishing a theological faculty at the university. He opposed theological faculties at the university because thought they were vulnerable to the dangers of secularization and rationalism. The university theology faculties did not have a sufficiently ultramontane mentality. Colmar appointed a strongly conservative priest, Bruno François Leopold Liebermann (1759–1844) to direct the seminary. Against the historical and more progressive theological currents of the time, Liebermann advocated a return to scholasticism. He wrote the *Institutiones theologicae*, which was one of the most widely used theological textbooks throughout German

---

to the university because members of the higher classes of the school were regarded as parts of the arts faculty and so had to matriculate with the university" (55).

124. Tanner, *Decrees of the Ecumenical Councils,* 2: 668.

125. Elwell, *Influence of the Enlightenment on the Catholic Theory of Religious Education in France, 1750–1850,* 230–31.

seminaries.[126] Some twenty-five years later, the Archbishop of Cologne, Clemens August von Droste-Vischering (1773–1845), reacted to ongoing controversy concerning the work of the eminent Catholic theologian Georg Hermes and his students. Roger Aubert critically narrates what happened.

> In his [Droste-Vischering's] youth he had belonged to the circle around the Princess Gallitzin with its mystic and Platonic tendencies. Now, quite unjustly, he suspected the Hermesians of making common cause with the Prussian government in order to secretly undermine Catholicism. The archbishop also intended to destroy the influence of the department of theology at the University of Bonn and to replace it with the diocesan seminary in Cologne. He demanded from the professors an express submission to the papal brief and from all ecclesiastical candidates a sworn agreement with the eighteen theses in which the errors condemned by the Pope [those attributed to Hermes' theological work] were even more sharply formulated; they were in fact very tactlessly phrased.[127]

Schleiermacher's concern about the possibility of theology becoming marginal, stagnant, unscientific, and alienated from the university context makes sense within his historical circumstances. The rupture he foresaw in Catholic seminary education between the religious and the scientific was not about to happen for Christian theology in the Protestant church. Against this hazard, theology must be lodged within the scientific circle of university disciplines.

Aside from the scientific-doctrinal aspect, Schleiermacher presumed that those encouraged to pursue theological studies would possess a "religious interest." The students of theology were believers preparing to carry out some form of church service. The vast majority of those studying theology were in some stream of ministerial education. The fundamental definition of theology as a positive science indicated in the *Brief Outline* links theological study to ecclesial government.[128] Furthermore, according to Schleiermacher theology develops concurrently, as I have argued, with the lived religious experience of God revealed in Christ. As the Christian community grows and reflects on its faith and its

---

126. Lill, "Beginnings of the Catholic Movement in Germany and Switzerland," 216–27.
127. Aubert, "Catholic Thought Searching for New Ways," 33–34.
128. See *BO*, §5–§13, 20–22.

ways of proclaiming and evoking the religious experience of Christ in others, its leadership roles emerge. Church leaders are vital for ongoing church community, polity, service to others, and collective identity. Nowhere is this religious interest more evident than in the character and qualities of religious leaders as theologians. Religious interest presupposes, of course, cognate religious experience as specifically Christian. Such persons are "prince[s] of the Church" and typify the "theological ideal."[129] Ideally, theologians serve primarily as ecclesial representatives and agents who also evince a scientific spirit. This point becomes crucial yet again. Since representatives of the church have the conjunction of religious interest and scientific spirit in the highest degree, it follows that theology cannot be done without explicit ecclesial ties. Schleiermacher states: "When this same knowledge [theology] is acquired and possessed without relation to the "government" of the Church, it ceases to be theological and devolves to those sciences to which it belongs according to its varied content."[130] Theology is not, therefore, carried out in academies but guided by ecclesial leaders who employ secular knowledge for theological development.

As the reform principle separating secular and sacred knowledge already precludes predominantly secular organizations like academies from possessing ecclesial origins or supervision, it becomes increasingly difficult to conceive of lay theologians as somehow integrated or widespread within Schleiermacher's ecclesiological vision. Schleiermacher's comments about the audience of theological writings also seem to confirm this exclusion.[131] Hence, for him theologians are clerics and church leaders.[132] But if service to the church at the highest ecclesial levels re-

129. Ibid., §9, 21.
130. *BO*, §6, 20.

131. See *Praktische Theologie*, 721–22. "Individual authorial products are only written for a small circle . . . there is a false appeal to advance one's views publicly and to emerge with his thought processes [*Gedanken bewegungen*] into the general literary public."

132. The distinction between clergy and laity is a concern in Schleiermacher's thinking, linked to the tension between the authoritative and discretionary elements in the church. He states, "The opposition between clerics and lay people will be seen in the sense that the former educate the latter in that which is the knowledge concerning the Christian church; the latter are those in whom this knowledge is not placed. This opposition (*Gegensatz*) will be developed with and the historical being of the Christian church touches on this. Everywhere this opposition vanishes there also vanishes the participation in the historical being of the church. This opposition can only be main-

quires proportionately the highest degree of theological acumen, it follows that all church leaders will be trained at the universities. Theological faculties have therefore a serious ecclesial function that educates people not only in terms of the theoretical but also the practical exigencies of church government and service. Based on the practical mission of ecclesial leaders, the vitality and openness of the university are essential. For the authoritative and discretionary elements to promote Christian faith, they must work in creative tension; therefore, they cannot be detached from the university context.

In terms of the practical and professional aspect of theology, what Schleiermacher means by organic membership with university knowledge must be viewed against the larger cultural horizon: the Christian ethos and population of Prussia. Theologically trained students who left the university after a course of studies would also be involved in supervising or sometimes teaching, either in a parish or for "the common teaching of the whole people, *the trivial schools* [*Trivialschulen*]."[133] Forerunners of the elementary school, these institutions taught the basic skills of reading and writing to children.[134] Graduates of the theological faculty would also participate in the religious instruction of youth and to some degree in the *Volkschulen*—the popular schools.[135] It was true that in Germany during the late eighteenth and nineteenth century, the church still enjoyed influence, however waning, in the educational sphere. This authority would encompass different levels of education.[136]

In the broader sense, educational training that was not necessarily theological or specifically Christian in nature would have been activities that the theological faculty understood in its student formation. This

---

tained by maintaining the historical knowledge and this tendency must always remain in the Christian church. That we must maintain this (belief) we can see especially in the Protestant (*Evangelische*) church." *Praktische Theologie*, 680; Cf. *BO*, §315, 107.

133. *Die Praktische Theologie*, 683; see also La Vopa, *Prussian Schoolteachers*, 38ff.

134. See "*Trivialschulen*," *Lexicon der Pädagogik*, 4:240.

135. *Praktische Theologie*, 683. It must be remembered that religion was among the dominant subjects in the German *Volkschule* throughout its history and development. See Alexander, *The Prussian Elementary Schools*, 286–303. The influence of theologians in elementary teaching positions in Berlin was so great, in fact, that Christian Wolff is said to have registered this complaint in 1783: "The schools will never do better so long as the schoolmasters are theologians by profession." Vizetelly, *Berlin under the New Empire*, 48.

136. Cf. McClelland, *German Experience of Professionalization*, 43–47; Maynes, *Schooling for the People*, 28–32; LaVopa, *Prussian Schoolteachers*, 53; 98–105.

practical dimension would hold insofar as church government and polity maintained an interest in religious education and literacy among the Christian population. For Schleiermacher, this interest is not only present but serious because of its religious and soteriological implications. Salvation in the Reformed tradition is mediated by the Word proclaimed in Scripture and received in faith. Indeed, he maintains: "The Protestant church rests on the principle that the written divine word must be accessible to all Protestant Christians. This reality is not possible without a certain degree of spiritual development and instruction."[137] This notion of access to God's Word underlines even more the importance of higher learning and education for the responsibilities proper to church government. It also highlights the significance of the broader pedagogical ability of pastors and ministers responsible for religious training as essential to the church's self-understanding and Christian mission. Thus, as theology is an ecclesial knowledge with soteriological characteristics bearing upon its fulfillment in church life, worship, and practice, it must work from a context that can maximize not only its intellectual development and requirements but also its practical tasks. It can do this most effectively and professionally only if it operates from a university.

CONCLUSION

Let me return to my initial question about theology's place in the university: what does the religious have to do with the academic? I have surveyed the characteristics of university life, scientific disciplines, and the function of theology within this pedagogical and scientific complex. In addition, I have examined aspects of theology's orientation toward the scientific, the religious, the practical and the professional. What has emerged is a situation of paradox and tension concerning the location of theology within Schleiermacher's concept of the university. Theology is not the center of university life—philosophy enjoys preeminence. The professional and denominational features of theology, moreover, push it to the periphery of university relevance, as theological study presumes a deep ecclesial commitment. It is a commitment whose orientation divides the realm of knowledge into separate parts and whose influence is not mutual. Historical and political circumstances accidentally bestow upon Christian theology broader cultural responsibilities than it would

---

137. *Praktische Theologie*, 680.

otherwise enjoy according to its native impulses. By definition and internal trajectory, the positive nature of theology dictates a more professional than scientific character. Furthermore, its internal dynamism as ecclesial knowledge insists upon a faith born of distinctively Christian experience. From the tense combination of the religious and the academic, Christian theology seeks to fulfill its duty to doctrinal vitality and relevance; but it delivers true depth and meaning only when the care of souls is its final term. These features represent a scientific discipline that enjoys a special sphere of discourse and meaning because it excludes other forms of knowledge as relevant for salvation.

Scientific knowledge becomes salvifically and doctrinally acceptable only when put at the disposal of the religious intellect and only for religious reasons. Because of this ecclesial and soteriological condition, however, despite Schleiermacher's argument for the warrant of theology's inclusion to be based upon its form, he cannot escape the contradiction that the content of this ecclesial knowledge manifests in relation to other disciplines. The material unity of human knowledge represented in the university clashes with the Reformed principle that regards the realms of faith and reason as distinct and separate. Because of this principle, theological discourse tells little upon how and what theology gives or brings to other disciplines in contrast to what it takes from them. Its audience and culture is not the general public. The audience of theology is specifically and particularly Christian. Theology is interconnected with other scientific disciplines due to its form but its content is strictly theological and ecclesial. Theological unity is not material but one of order. Philosophical, historical, and practical theology co-opt the fruits of science and order them to Christian duties: church service, care of souls, preaching, and elementary teaching. Yet Christian theology gives the trees that bear this fruit little nourishment in return.

Finally, Schleiermacher also argues that theology assumes pedagogical and cultural responsibilities beyond the formally religious or theological. For these reasons, theology must abide within the university. But this justification is weak and determined by particular historical circumstances. Pedagogical and denominational tasks, however so historically intertwined in a largely Christian German culture, are clearly accidental and extrinsic to the purposes of theological reflection. What Schleiermacher claims as necessary for theology to do, namely, serve the church by educating its ministers, already implies a trajectory to a location more akin to a seminary or university-affiliated divinity school than to a university as such. The scientific vitality of theology in the hands of its practitioners need not be restricted to the university. Other arrangements for developing the philosophical spirit, so central to the meaning of university education, could be offered prior or subsequent to formal theological training. For these reasons, the place of Christian theology in the university is one of paradoxical and tense coexistence. Due to the trajectory of this scientific discipline, bound by its Protestant content and professional orientation, it exists fundamentally as a non-reciprocating alien whose similarities to other university disciplines cannot overcome its contradiction to them.

3

John Henry Newman—The Possibility and Nature of Theology

> As determined by his First Principles, such is his religion, his creed, his worship, his political party, his character, except as far as adventitious circumstances interfere with their due and accurate development; they are, in short, the man.
>
> —John Henry Newman

THIS CHAPTER AND THE subsequent one explore Newman's meaning of "theology." In this chapter, I will consider two broad dimensions of the term that provide the background for understanding how theology fits within a university. First, I will examine the conditions that legitimate theology as an academic discipline. In short, this is the "possibility" of theology. Secondly, I will define "theology." The problem in attempting a definition is that Newman was not a systematic thinker. He did not use terms consistently. Consequently, I need to set up the definition by explaining how theology differs from religion. It is precisely after the difference between natural and revealed religion becomes clear that I can demonstrate why theology takes two basic forms: natural theology and revealed theology. The scope of this analysis largely draws upon *The Idea of a University* and *An Essay in Aid of a Grammar of Assent*.[1] As it seeks definition and meaning from Newman's writings, my analysis is not primarily a historical study but a theological inquiry. Before beginning, let me lay out some preliminary principles that dictate the argument's parameters.

---

1. Newman, *Idea of a University*. Cited as *Idea*; *An Essay in Aid of a Grammar of Assent*. Cited as "GA." All references to *Idea* and to *GA* will be from the Ker editions unless indicated otherwise.

In the preface to *The Idea of the University*, Newman maintains that "these Discourses are directed simply to the consideration of the *aims* and *principles* of Education."[2] While they treat theology in some depth, Newman establishes principles that are not theological. He specifies these at the beginning of Discourse I and at the beginning of Discourse IX.[3]

> Let it be observed, then, that the principles on which I would conduct the inquiry are attainable, as I have already implied, by the mere experience of life. They do not come simply of theology; they imply no supernatural discernment; they have no special connexion with Revelation; they almost arise out of the nature of the case; they are dictated even by human prudence and wisdom, though a divine illumination be absent, and they are recognized by common sense, even where self-interest is not present to quicken it; and, therefore, though true, and just, and good in themselves, they imply nothing whatever as to the religious profession of those who maintain them. They may be held by Protestants as well as by Catholics; nay, there is reason to anticipate that in certain times and places they will be more thoroughly investigated, and better understood, and held more firmly by Protestants than by ourselves.[4]

These are some characteristics of his "first principles." They provide the working assumptions or starting points of his argument.[5] As Newman states, these principles are "attainable . . . by the mere experience of life": they are open to "common sense" and to most people "on the grounds of human reason and human wisdom."[6] They purport to be intelligible to the educated person, not only the specialist.

From a higher viewpoint, the principles also accomplish several things. Newman removes any appeal to "special information," religion, or "authority."[7] The assumptions of the Discourses within the *Idea of the*

---

2. *Idea*, 12.

3. "I declared my intention, when I opened the subject, of treating it as a philosophical and practical, rather than as a theological question, with an appeal to common sense, not to ecclesiastical rules; and for this very reason, while my argument has been less ambitious, it has been deprived of the lights and supports which another mode of handling it would have secured." Ibid., 182.

4. Ibid., 21–22.

5. Cf., *GA*, 321.

6. *Idea*, 24.

7. Ibid., 22–23.

University that treat theology "have no special connexion with Revelation." "Revelation," for Newman, means not the natural truths or teachings about God upheld by monotheism but specifically the doctrine of God and the contents of Christian faith set forth authoritatively by Roman Catholicism. Furthermore, the account advances on rational, ecumenical grounds—not ecclesial authority—and it is "the mode," Newman writes, "in which I propose to handle my subject altogether."[8] Though Newman claims not to proceed formally from assumptions based on Christian revelation, his thinking and interpretations are marked by it.[9] Moreover, he maintains on rational grounds not only that his idea of the university is sound, but that the inclusion of theology within the university is true and correct.[10] In essence, Newman builds a rational and public argument about the relation of theology to the university and its claim to truth.

Newman first argues briefly that "universality" distinguishes the university from other institutions of human learning. Newman then asks: "Is it, then logically consistent in a seat of learning to call itself a University, and to exclude Theology from the number of its studies?"[11] In response, he posits a thesis.

> [I]f a University be, from the nature of the case, a place of instruction, where universal knowledge is professed, and if in a certain University, so called, the subject of Religion is excluded, one of two conclusions is inevitable,—either, on the one hand, that the province of Religion is very barren of real knowledge, or, on the other hand, that in such University one special and important branch of knowledge is omitted. I say, the advocate of such an institution must say *this*, or he must say *that*; he must own, either that little or nothing is known about the Supreme Being, or that his seat of learning calls itself what it is not. This is the thesis which I lay down, and on which I shall insist as the subject of this Discourse.[12]

---

8. Ibid., 24.

9. Cf. Ibid., 20. "[T]hough it has been my lot for many years to take a prominent, sometimes a presumptuous, part in theological discussions, yet the natural turn of my mind carries me off to trains of thought like those which I am now about to pen, which, important though they be for Catholic objects, and admitting of a Catholic treatment, are sheltered from the extreme delicacy and peril which attach to disputations directly bearing on the subject matter of Divine Revelation."

10. Cf. Ibid., 24.

11. Ibid., 34.

12. Ibid., 34–35.

Newman is claiming something central for the identity of the university. He ties theology and the university together organically. Both relate to a subject and a location of human knowledge and instruction. If theology is a branch of knowledge, it is not something whose relevance lies outside the university. "I cannot," writes Newman, "so construct my definition of the subject-matter of University Knowledge, and so draw my boundary lines around it, as to include therein the other sciences commonly studied at Universities, and to exclude the science of Religion."[13] From the start, the validity of theology as knowledge and a university's "universal" character are intimately related in Newman's thought.

THE (IM)POSSIBILITY OF THEOLOGY AND (IM)POSSIBILITY OF A UNIVERSITY

Newman argues that the possibility of theology links intrinsically to the idea of a University in several ways. In the beginning of *Discourse II*, Newman poses the problem syllogistically. "A University, I should lay down, by its very name professes to teach universal knowledge: Theology is surely a branch of knowledge, and yet to exclude from the subjects of its teaching one which, to say the least, is as important and as large as any of them? I do not see that either premiss of this argument is open to exception."[14] There is no middle ground. Either theology is not knowledge or the University cannot be a place that teaches universal knowledge. The possibility of theology, therefore, concerns what is included, what is studied, what comprises part of the knowledge and subject matter pursued as what universities achieve. This connection between theology and the university raises, however, a prior question: is theology a legitimate form of knowledge?

If theology is not knowledge but something else, it might be an enterprise of some validity, but it cannot exist within university. The assumption here is that knowledge, in principle, is public and accessible to everyone. Though the sources of theological knowledge can be natural or supernatural, its cognitive status must be secured. It must be a body of facts and relations to cohere as a legitimate academic discipline.[15] Theology must possess a content coordinate with other disciplines. This

---

13. Ibid., 37–38.
14. Ibid., 33.
15. Cf. Ibid., 38–39.

idea is central to Newman's argument. In his explanation, however, he must address ways that theology contradicts academic rigor. Newman elaborates two views of theology incompatible with academic canons. His critique of them figures enormously. These views broaden and sharpen the problem and allow Newman's view of theological knowledge to unfold.

The two basic positions antithetical to theology's possibility that Newman addresses in the *Idea* stem from the Reformation and Deism.[16] The Reformation position is "feeling or sentiment" comprises theological subject matter. Contrariwise, the Deistic view of theology takes nature as evidence for knowledge of God.[17] Implicit in both of these intellectual options, for Newman, is the inherent impossibility of either understanding to deliver adequate theological science. Though both positions have different starting points, each view ultimately terminates in incredulity, thereby stripping theology of any cognitive content. In either case, it is impossible for claims about God to adhere within a monotheistic framework and thus merit consideration as an academic discipline.[18] Let me briefly examine each position.

The first inadequate understanding of theology derives from the Evangelical, Lutheran tradition, though Newman posits that its influence crosses confessional boundaries.[19] Theology came to be understood

16. Ibid., 39–41.
17. Ibid., 39–40.
18. Ibid., 46. Monotheism teaches that: "God is an Individual, Self-dependent, All-perfect, Unchangeable Being; intelligent, living, personal, and present; almighty, all-seeing, all remembering; between whom and His creatures there is an infinite gulf; who has no origin, who is all-sufficient for Himself; who created and upholds the universe; who will judge every one of us, sooner or later, according to that Law of right and wrong which He has written on our hearts. He is One who is sovereign over, operative amidst, independent of, the appointments which He has made; One in whose hands are all things, who has a purpose in every event, and a standard for every deed, and thus has relations of His own towards the subject-matter of each particular science, which the book of knowledge unfolds; who has with an adorable, never-ceasing energy implicated Himself in all the history of creation, the constitution of nature, the course of the world, the origin of society, the fortunes of nations, the action of the human mind; and who thereby necessarily becomes the subject-matter of a science, far wider and more noble than any of those which are included in the circle of secular Education."
19. A brief observation on the term "evangelical" is needed. At the time of Newman's writing, *evangelische* was (and still is) a term commonly used to denote German Lutheranism. However, "Evangelicalism" was a movement that crossed confessional boundaries. Its hallmark was a deeply emotional religious conversion to Christ cen-

as something non-intellectual, as something unrelated in its methods and subject matter to truth, knowledge, or "an acceptance of revealed doctrine." This position shifts the focus away from objective truth and knowledge about the divine to "a feeling, an emotion, an affection, an appetency."[20] When theology is so severed from faith and knowledge, it reduces to a subjective disposition and taste. It then becomes that which supplies the desires, wishes, or psychological needs of the believer rather than a cognitive understanding of what is objectively real and the believer's cognitive apprehension of it.[21] As theology departs from matters of knowledge and truth, when it shifts to the psychological and reductively anthropological, it slides into incredulity. Consequently, it forfeits the claim to knowledge and a place within a university.

What came to be called "Physical Theology" is the second inadequate position. It was a supposedly theological approach that Newman viewed "with the greatest suspicion."[22] He describes it succinctly.

---

tering around personal salvation from sin. In England, one could distinguish between Anglican, Calvinist, Methodist and Lutheran "evangelicals." This plurality is lost in Newman's use of the term. Newman's own religious experience as an Anglican prior to entering the Catholic church, was assisted by Rev. Walter Mayers, an evangelical Calvinist. Mayer was an clergyman who himself underwent a religious conversion. Sheridan Gilley relates that in 1814, "Newman, weakened by illness and domestic calamity, and still lingering at the school after the departure of his contemporaries, was especially receptive to the books which Mayers lent him, 'all of the school of Calvin.' There was a notable English bias in Mayers' list, which was of lasting importance for Newman's intellectual development; he was encouraged to immerse himself in the English Calvinist tradition, rather than in Calvin himself, and in the end he was to weigh Protestantism in the balance and find it wanting by reading its English exponents rather than the theological giants of the continent, like Luther and Calvin himself." Gilley, *Newman and His Age*, 18. It can be argued that Newman is setting forth an idea about the primacy of an emotionally charged religious experience over intellectual content that one might find among evangelical, pietistic Methodists as well as through filtered interpretations he would get about Luther's theology. I am indebted to Dr. Rebecca Frey for this historical distinction.

20. *Idea*, 39–40. Newman flatly states concerning Evangelical Religion that "it had no intellectual basis; no internal idea, no principle of unity, no theology." *Apologia Pro Vita Sua*, 104.

21. This shift in nature of what constitutes theology is similar to that of Ludwig Feuerbach, who in the *Essence of Christianity* wrote that, "Religion is essentially emotion; hence, objectively also, emotion is to it necessarily of a divine nature." The consequences of this understanding, moreover, lead to the same denial of God and the reduction of theology to anthropology that lies at the heart of Feuerbach's argument. Feuerbach, *Essence of Christianity*, 25.

22. *Idea*, 48; 364.

> The school of Physics, from its very drift and method of reasoning, has, as I have said, nothing to do with Religion. However, there is a science which avails itself of the phenomena and laws of the material universe, as exhibited by that school, as a means of establishing the existence of Design in their construction, and thereby the fact of a Creator and Preserver. This science has, in these modern times, at least in England, taken the name of Natural Theology; and, though absolutely distinct from Physics, yet Physical Philosophers, having furnished its most curious and interesting data, are apt to claim it as their own, and to pride themselves upon it accordingly.[23]

Historically, the arguments of Physical Theology were apologetic and used against the claims of unbelief.[24] In varying forms, this kind of argumentation seeks to demonstrate a knowledge and proof of God by moving from effects to a cause, from a seeming design in nature to the source of all intelligibility. For Newman, however, the argument neither persuades nor qualifies as academic theological knowledge. Fundamentally, Physical Theology is not concerned with theological doctrines, evidence, or the knowledge proper to theology.

> Sanctity, omniscience, justice, mercy, faithfulness. What does Physical Theology, what does the Argument from Design, what do fine disquisitions, about final causes, teach us, except very indirectly, faintly, enigmatically, of these transcendently important, these essential portions of the idea of Religion? . . . What does Physical Theology tell us of duty and conscience? of a particular providence? and, coming at length to Christianity, what does it teach us even of the four last things, death, judgment, heaven, hell, the mere elements of Christianity? It cannot tell us anything of Christianity at all.[25]

The essential elements that make Christianity distinctive and contribute to a vital, personal, monotheistic and theological knowledge of God are absent from Physical Theology. This position is not only a theological dead-end but a potential cause of disbelief. Newman was convinced that it also led to a certain idolatry of nature, a way of seeing the world

---

23. Ibid., 362.

24. For a theologically and philosophically sensitive treatment of the argument from design and its relation to physical or natural theology, see Buckley, S.J., *At the Origins of Modern Atheism*, 48–55.

25. *Idea*, 365.

that eventually dispels anything transcendent or supernatural from within its horizon.[26] As such, physical theology reduces to anthropology in the same way that the evangelical view of theology does. Newman rejects both theological positions. In either instance, theology cannot be academically valid knowledge. The burden for Newman is how to show that the subject matter of theology positively coheres as scientific knowledge.

The pursuit of university knowledge must satisfy certain conditions. One condition is the "diffusion and extension" of universal knowledge. Another is the product of this, namely, the existence of human knowledge itself.[27] Newman seeks to integrate theology within both conditions. There is here, in some sense, a prior judgment about what counts as legitimate knowledge that the university ought to pursue as valuable. Newman addresses the position "that there are different kinds or spheres of Knowledge, human, divine, sensible, intellectual, and the like." There are those who argue against the inclusion of theology within the university because it is not serious knowledge. Theology is not a university subject. This view argues against the relevance of God's existence within the sphere of university knowledge. Yet Newman insists that theology is not simply an extracurricular activity, something proper "to the parish priest, the catechism, and the parlour." Newman makes the extraordinary claim that theology is "a condition of general knowledge."[28] Thus, theology cannot be excluded based upon false judgments about the possible divisions of knowledge.[29] To lay out, then, how Newman argues that theology can be considered knowledge, it first becomes necessary to address how he understands the distinctive features of universities themselves and their subjects.

The understanding of knowledge as academic concerns the cognitive status of theology as knowledge. But what does Newman understand as academic "knowledge?" Furthermore, how and why does it take the character of science? These questions and their relationships provide an important entry into Newman's conception of theology.

The aim of all knowledge, for Newman, is "Truth," which comprises "facts and their relations." He explains,

26. Ibid., 365–67; 46–48.
27. Ibid., 5; 36–37.
28. Ibid., 52; 71.
29. Ibid., 36–38.

> All that exists, as contemplated by the human mind, forms one large system or complex fact, and this of course resolves itself into an indefinite number of particular facts, which, as being portions of a whole, have countless relations of every kind, one towards another. Knowledge is the apprehension of these facts, whether in themselves, or in their mutual positions and bearings. And, as all taken together form one integral subject for contemplation, so there are no natural or real limits between part and part; one is ever running into another; all, as viewed by the mind, are combined together, and possess a correlative character one with another...[30]

Knowledge, then, is mentally apprehended as "facts" and "relations."[31] These latter terms encompass an immense field. The mind cannot grasp all possibilities that can be known in an instant. It must order, divide, specify, and categorize the results of knowing into "various partial views or abstractions."[32] These partial views emerge from this "method" of science that proceeds from a particular thing to a general idea. Such knowing concerns realities as general and impersonal. As the realities that science moves towards in apprehension—apprehending the objects of knowledge either as "things" or as "notions"—are common, so their truth must be communicable.

Since the mind cannot grasp all things simultaneously, the process of knowing involves dividing reality into areas of study. Newman calls these areas "sciences." "Science" for Newman means not simply the intelligent process of forming hypotheses, induction, and repeatable experi-

---

30. Ibid., 52. The "unity of truth," a theme in Newman's educational philosophy, was a common one in nineteenth century higher education. While I am drawing out its intellectual dimension, there was also a moral one I do not treat. For a good overview of each in the United States context, see Reuben, *The Making of the Modern University*, 17–32.

31. Newman's use of the word "system" seems to be his own definition. But the word has a long history. Michael J. Buckley notes that "The uses of *system* go back to the works of Plato and Hippocrates, and συστημα always denotes some kind of order achieved within a multiplicity. This sense of the whole organized of many disparate parts, of the one out of the many, found its realization in such vastly divergent and complex organizations as the body of a literary compositions, the constitution of a government, a confederacy of nations, a corps of soldiers, a college of priests or of magistrates, a system constituted according to musical intervals, an accumulation of sediment in medicine, and a union of several *versus nexi* in Greek meter." *At the Origins of Modern Atheism*, 125.

32. *Idea*, 53.

ment, but fields of data that the mind orders coherently. "Sciences are only so many distinct aspects of nature," writes Newman, "sometimes suggested by nature itself, sometimes created by the mind."[33] Partitions allow the mind to handle data with clarity and precision. Universities commonly classify such areas as physical sciences and the humanities. Yet something more important hinges in this ordering than intelligibility. Indeed, scientific advancement and success require the different divisions. Knowledge spreads further into "sciences." Optics, Mental Philosophy, Astronomy, Geology are examples.[34] Variously material phenomena or ideas are implied in such a distribution of the potentially known. The various "science" is the result of abstractions that constitute the specific coordinates, principles, relations—everything one expects from a department of knowledge.

These partial views or abstractions, however, are precisely divisions of a unity of "all that exists."[35] But this statement must be qualified. The unity of 'all that exists' refers to knowledge as it is apprehended by science, and thus, knowledge insofar as it possesses an impersonal character. Sciences deal with the general, the universalizable and more properly with the notional than with real things. Determinate elements, such as this triangle, that letter A or the story of the Quebec Jesuits enjoy a place within academic sciences. But specific sciences and their subject matters serve a larger horizon of coherence. This horizon refers to more generalizable connections and implications between sciences themselves. Put differently, all the human mind can and does know, whether it be a science, a simple fact, or an axiomatic set, relates to other views, other abstractions, other parts of the whole. Precisely because of these connections, what is not a subject of one science helps constitute the determinate identity of something in another. For example, the identity of the color "white" inscribes black within its total meaning and coherence. "Young" carries meaning only in reference to old just as "organic" in relation to artificial. It is this dimension of knowledge's comparative nature that matters. All things and ideas are parts of a comprehensive unity. Hence, sciences only truly make sense within a comprehensive vision of different areas of knowledge.

33. *GA*, 239.
34. *Idea*, 53.
35. Ibid., 52.

What different sciences reveal is simply a "differentiation of consciousness" in various areas.[36] Such differentiations of human knowing are branches of knowledge. Intrinsic to these branches of knowledge are the internal coordinates that combine to form this particular science rather than another. Each science is also characterized by independence, by the possession of its own internal logic and principles that express an integrity proper to its subject matter. Principles proper to astronomy and the warrants that issue sound conclusions in it, for example, are not the same principles that mark poetic beauty. Sciences and their principles cannot be identified. Newman does not reduce the sciences into each other. Still, none of the sciences are so independent that they possess little or nothing in common. This stress on commonality is Newman's contention with an eye to theology. Mathematics bears upon physics; chemistry upon biology and astronomy; biology bears upon medicine and medicine upon ideas of health, and so on. The range of possible relations and connections between sciences and views is potentially unlimited, restricted only by the degree and capacity of human intelligence to see the relationships.

Sciences are not only related to each other, but they also satisfy intellectual inquiry only temporarily. They never reach an end or solve a problem with a comprehensive or final answer. Inevitably, new information raises new questions. Newman maintains that

> they never tell us all that can be said about a thing, even when they tell something, nor do they bring it before us, as the senses do. They arrange and classify facts; they reduce separate phenomena under a common law; they trace effects to a cause. Thus they serve to transfer our knowledge from the custody of memory to the surer and more abiding protection of philosophy, thereby providing it both for its spread and its advance;—for, inasmuch as sciences are forms of knowledge, they enable the intellect to master and increase it; and, inasmuch as they are instruments, to communicate it readily to others.[37]

There is, then, an inherent and irreducible element within all the sciences. Sciences retain their own integrity precisely by being partial

---

36. I borrow this term from Bernard Lonergan, S.J., whose discussion of undifferentiated and differentiated consciousness parallels much of what Newman does. See *Method in Theology*, 138f.

37. *Idea*, 53–54.

views, intrinsically incomplete when seen against the compass of the knowable. But due to this feature, they neither do nor can provide a full view of a subject matter under consideration. By definition, particular views or sciences cannot grasp or apprehend the "whole." They concentrate on portions, aspects, probing ever deeper but seldom synthesizing or relating themselves to principles, coordinates or views external to their own.[38]

Let me return to the relationship between theology and the university. As noted earlier, if the university excludes theology, then the discipline of theology must either be empty of real knowledge and thus inappropriate; or due to theology's subject matter, the university is an unfit location for it. In terms of the latter, the definition of theology's subject matter as "feeling" or "emotion" or "physical theology"—a quasi romantic view of nature—are two definitions Newman rejects among others. Each subject matter ensures theology's incompatibility with university knowledge. The other position, external to the definition of what theology studies, holds that knowledge of God is impossible. What is impossible cannot have a claim upon the other branches of knowledge. Newman describes this view as follows."[I]t is absurd for men in our present state to teach anything positively about the next world, that there is a heaven, or a hell, or a last judgment, or that the soul is immortal, or that there is a God . . . such persuasions are not knowledge, they are not scientific, they cannot become public property."[39] Here, the issue is not the kind of subject matter, but the denial of the very ground—God's existence. In a serious way, however, the exclusion of theology based upon a prejudgment distorts the very idea of an "academic" discipline. Newman maintains that a university "is a place of *teaching* universal *knowledge.*"[40] It is necessary, then, for a university to teach, to pass on its knowledge to others. Likewise, it is requisite for its subject matter to be universal knowledge. Yet the meaning of university does not end there. Its "special function" is to "draw many things into one."[41] For the univer-

---

38. Paradoxically, the restriction to a particular view vital for its success hinders it from acknowledging dependence on or relation to other sciences. It is difficult for one person to achieve impressive results or discoveries in more than one field of knowledge. Conditions for success in one field normally prohibits others necessary for specialized success in others.

39. *Idea*, 315.

40. Ibid., 5. Italics his.

41. Ibid., 369. Newman held that one of the major problems afflicting universities in his day was the absence of anything that might unify them. This contrasted poorly with

sity to be genuine, it must by definition include theology as a branch of knowledge.

Theology does not simply deserve inclusion within a university: it is essential. Theology is "a condition of general knowledge."[42] Put differently, genuine university knowledge is not possible without theology.

First, all knowledge is a connected whole. Different branches, while retaining integrity proper to their methods, fields and advances, necessarily bear upon every other. This influence affects not the internal structures of different academic fields, but their accuracy, procedure, and reality of the particular subject matter in terms of the whole "circle of knowledge."[43] Independently, branches of knowledge yield limited knowledge and thus proportionally limited truth. But when sciences are seen together, it is this drawing of many perspectives into a certain unity that makes for the highest form of knowledge about a subject. This does not mean that such knowledge is irreformable or immune from criticism. It is just the most accurate knowledge at a given time. For Newman, the relations that constitute such sciences internally must also extend to others. In other words, it is the community of sciences that yields real knowledge.[44] Sciences are the results of differentiated consciousness and possess restricted views of the whole. Yet as each science advances into particularity, the broader context of other areas diminishes proportionally. This is what Newman means by unreal. That is to say, one science's connection with other parts of reality are dimmed and thus distorted.[45] It is necessary and unavoidable for branches of knowledge to narrow in their development. But that is precisely why combination and relationality remain vital for real knowledge about any subject. A condition

---

previous understandings of the role and function of the university. In the suppressed Discourse V, Newman wrote, "The majestic vision of the Middle Age, which grew steadily to perfection in the course of centuries, the University of Paris, or Bologna, or Oxford, has almost gone out in night. A philosophical comprehensiveness, an orderly expansiveness, an elastic constructiveness, men have lost them, and cannot make out why. This is why: because they have lost the idea of unity: because they cut off the head of a living thing, and think it is perfect, all but the head." Ibid., 422–23.

42. Ibid., 71.

43. Ibid., 73; 38.

44. Ibid., 54; 62.

45. "Unreal," comments Dwight Culler, was a favorite word of Newman's "which means partly that a set of opinions has no consistency within itself and partly that it has no relation to reality." Culler, *Imperial Intellect*, 197.

of true knowledge, then, means not only the relations of the sciences together but the existence of such sciences together without omission. For Newman, the form of university knowledge is one in which theology plays an integral part. Theology assists the other branches of knowledge to be more real.

Newman is describing a series of integral relationships within a principle of unity. From this principle of unity, particular subject matters become more philosophical. As mentioned earlier, Newman holds that true knowledge and its conditions entail a web of interdependent relationships. As a branch of knowledge, theology stands subject to the same limitations as any other science. It is incomplete and inaccurate without the other sciences correcting it to a more "real" view of a thing.[46] No science, no branch of knowledge, no field of inquiry escapes the limitations inscribed within the economy of partial views and abstractions. That which can be known as a subject matter manifests layers and textures so rich and varied that no one science does justice to it.

Consider an example that Newman uses. A human being can be viewed diversely: physiologically, morally and so forth.[47] At stake, there is the mind's movement towards what is, the real, towards a matrix of relationships. Consideration of a human being in terms of pain and pleasure, for example, can yield certain insights and knowledge about individual or social behavior in different historical contexts. To view a human only from this one perspective, however, proportionally reduces the richness and reality of the person. However sophisticated or accurate such claims may be, if they are taken as in any way complete, the reality of the human being is distorted. Viewing human beings only in terms of pain and pleasure omits other aspects such as self-sacrifice, selfless love, duty. Thus, a particular view taken beyond its limited utility violates the whole. In the same way, Newman argues that theology is a more necessary condition of all university knowledge. Without the presence

---

46. *Idea*, 57–58. "Not even Theology itself, though it comes from heaven, though its truths were given once for all at the first, though they are more certain on account of the Give than those of mathematics, not even Theology, so far as it is relative to us, or is the Science of Religion, do I exclude from the law to which every mental exercise is subject, viz., from that imperfection, which ever must attend the abstract, when it would determine the concrete."

47. Ibid., 54–55.

of theology, Newman will call this knowledge "untrustworthy" because it leads to an incomplete view, a distortion of the real.[48]

If university knowledge is to be grasped as a whole and according to each discipline's limits, then the presence of theology is necessary. These limits refer to the parameters of any subject matter. They might include method, principle, data, and conclusions. When parameters of the sciences respect the others, each develops in a healthy manner. If the boundaries of the sciences blur, the knowledge from each area becomes less consistent and the whole suffers. At issue for Newman is not the existence of branches of knowledge but the action of various fields upon others as they teach their subject matter that embodies an intellectual unity. In practice, how might this occur?

There is a coherence to each branch of knowledge that proceeds upon its own principles, follows a deliberate methodology and yields real knowledge. Yet it is possible for a branch of knowledge to assume the questions and subject matter of another discipline. If sociologists, for instance, take up the fundamentals of poetry and try answering questions proper to poetic statement. If Freudian psychology, for example, assumes responsibility for analyzing and evaluating data proper to constitutional law. What happens in each instance, according to Newman, is not the advancement of knowledge but its "perversion."[49] What results is not poetry, not constitutional law but something else.[50] The

---

48. Ibid., 64.

49. "And now I have said enough to explain the inconvenience which I conceive necessarily to result from a refusal to recognize theological truth in a course of Universal Knowledge;—it is not only the loss of Theology, it is the perversion of other sciences. What it unjustly forfeits, others unjustly seize. They have their own department, and, in going out of it, attempt to do what they really cannot do; and that the more mischievously, because they do teach what in its place is true, though when out of its place, perverted or carried to excess, it is not true." Ibid., 77.

50. An illuminating instance of what Newman means appears in the comments of R. G. Collingwood when he describes how fledgling "new" science of psychology, manifest in William James's attempts to treat religion. "Like every one else who studied that subject in those days, I read William James's *Varieties of Religious Experience* and a lot of other books in which religion was treated from a psychological point of view. If I was profoundly shocked by the *Varieties*, that was not because some of the facts described in it were such as I would rather not hear about. They were, on the whole, amusing. Nor was it because I thought James was doing his work clumsily. I thought he did it very well. It was because the whole thing was a fraud. The book professed to throw light on a certain subject, and threw on it no light whatever. And that because of the method used. It was not because the book was a bad example of psychology, but because

problem is not the legitimate possibility of interdisciplinary collaboration. Moreover, Newman is not addressing the question of voluntary cooperation among different disciplines to consider common problems. Perversion results when sciences take up, analyze, and evaluate data and then derive conclusions from methodologies and principles upon subjects for which they were never intended. This kind of action of one science upon another is an illegitimate encroachment. Though Newman focuses on theology as the subject matter omitted and then encroached upon by other sciences, the rule extends to all branches of knowledge.[51]

Much of Newman's thinking focuses upon respecting disciplinary boundaries in university teaching and knowledge. But he also sees the need for the correction of university knowledge as a whole. If theology is omitted from the circle of university disciplines, its subject matter is not neglected. Instead, the topics proper to theological science become unclaimed and liable to misappropriation. If the subject matter of theology is thus being taken up and investigated by another science, it cannot be treated properly. The methodology and principles proper to theological inquiry vanish. For example, the assumptions theology makes about the transcendent human search for truth and love are not the same principles that guide the science of business. If the first principle of business is the self-interest of human nature to pursue self-gain, it will have difficulty in handling theological topics. In this case, the assumption of theology's subject matter by business contradicts the first principles of theology, according to Newman, by definition.

Another way that one science distorts its own province is to overestimate its own significance. This mistake confers an exaggerated importance to one part of knowledge in relation to the whole. "Many men there are, who, devoted to one particular subject of thought, and making its principles the measure of all things, become enemies to Revealed Religion before they know it ... they have made their own science, whatever it is, Political Economy, or Geology, or Astronomy, to the neglect of Theology, the centre of all truth, and view every part or the chief parts of knowledge as if developed from it, and to be tested and determined

---

it was a good example of psychology, that it left its subject completely unilluminated." *Autobiography*, 93.

51. Cf. *Idea*, 193. "[T]o depress unduly, to encroach upon any science, and much more an important one, is to do an injury to all."

by its principles."[52] This error not only usurps the province of theology but of the other disciplines. In brief, the possibility of such a perversion can affect the whole circle of knowledge, albeit in different modes and degrees. Still, why does Newman believe that another science would encroach upon theology? Would not the field be ignored or abandoned as worthless, as empty of meaning and content? No. The reason is the drive of the human mind.

The dynamism of human mind to understand reality is unlimited. Newman puts it this way.

> This method [of philosophizing] is so natural to us, as I have said, as to be almost spontaneous; and we are impatient when we cannot exercise it, and in consequence we do not always wait to have the means of exercising it aright, but we often put up with insufficient or absurd views or interpretations of what we meet with, rather than have none at all. We refer the various matters which are brought home to us, material or moral, to causes which we happen to know of, or to such as are simply imaginary, sooner than refer them to nothing; and according to the activity of our intellect do we feel a pain and begin to fret, if we are not able to do so. Here we have an explanation of the multitude of off hand sayings, flippant judgments, and shallow generalizations, with which the world abounds. Not from self-will only, nor from malevolence, but from the irritation which suspense occasions, is the mind forced on to pronounce, without sufficient data for pronouncing ... though it is no easy matter to view things correctly, nevertheless the busy mind will ever be viewing.[53]

Philosophical minds synthesize, discern connections, and want answers to all questions. Consequently, issues that concern human life, death, meaning, and purpose would be considered in the university regardless of disciplinary context. Human beings face realities that are the subject matter of theology with an almost existential necessity.

In sum, partial views arise, sciences emerge and knowledge evolves because the human mind necessarily desires coherence, meaning and order. Sciences order areas of study. "They arrange and classify facts; they reduce separate phenomena under a common law; they trace effects to a cause."[54] Commenting on this activity further, Newman gives it a sig-

52. Ibid., 81.
53. Ibid., 75.
54. Ibid., 53.

nificant name. "I suppose Science and Philosophy, their elementary idea, are nothing else but this habit of *viewing*, as it may be called, the objects which sense conveys to the mind, of throwing them into system, and uniting and stamping them with one form . . . We cannot do without a view, and we put up with an illusion, when we cannot get a truth."[55] The ability to perceive interconnections between branches of knowledge rather than amassing details restricted to one science is what Newman understands as "Philosophy." This mental capacity is broader than a particular academic discipline.[56] Newman insists on the capacity to see the whole, perceiving the real in a larger context that naturally corresponds to a "philosophical habit of mind."[57] Synthesis, connection, holism—in many ways these are the *basso continuo* of Newman's thought throughout the *Idea*.

RELIGION AND CONSCIENCE

Having sketched briefly the conditions for its possibility, what does Newman mean by "Theology"? What comprises its subject matter, its method, its function and its status within the university? Aspects of these questions have been discussed. Still, a terminological difficulty persists. In the *Idea of a University*, Newman often employs "theology" and "religion" synonymously, though at other times and in different works, he distinguishes them.[58] Questions that seek definition and determinacy frequently require characteristically systematic answers. Yet Newman was far from being a systematic theologian.[59] His imprecise and often inconsistent use of terms evidence this. Still, an inquiry that seeks pre-

---

55. Ibid., 75.

56. Newman does refer to "philosophy" in this narrower sense in "Literature: A Lecture in the School of Philosophy and Letters," ibid., 226f. In most instances, Newman means the "habit of viewing."

57. Ibid., 57; 371.

58. Newman distinguishes the meaning of "religion" from "theology" clearly in the *Grammar*. However, he seems to blur the distinction in the *Idea*, a work written almost twenty years earlier. Yet, oddly, he notes a difference only three years later in his lecture on "Christianity and Physical Science," in which he says "Religion is more than Theology; it is something relative to us; and it includes our relation towards the Object of it." ibid., 365. But for the most part, in the *Idea*, "religion" and "theology" are used synonymously at times. A prime example occurs in Discourse 2, 38. There, Newman refers to a "science of religion" when he clearly means "theology."

59. See the comments of Sykes, *Identity of Christianity*, 102–22; Cf. Blehl, "Spiritual Roots of Newman's Theology," *John Henry Newman*, 17.

cision and clarity cannot overlook possible similarities or differences between "religion" and "theology." Any attempt to explain the meaning of "theology," therefore, must examine Newman's understanding of "religion." I shall proceed towards a positive understanding of theology by first sorting out what theology is *not*. It is hoped that what "theology" means will become that much clearer. In short, our inquiry needs to purify and distinguish relevant terms. Accordingly, the meaning of religion will be examined in terms of its two main types: natural and revealed.[60]

In the *University Sermons*, Newman broadly defines "Religion" as "the system of relations existing between us and a Supreme Power, claiming our habitual obedience."[61] This definition becomes more specific in the *Grammar of Assent*. There religion is "the knowledge of God, of His Will, and of our duties towards Him."[62] By "system," let me suggest that Newman means a group or an aggregate of things that combine to form a complex whole. While the term "habitual" refers to patterned activity, "obedience" denotes the system as laying a special claim upon the person and the person's disposition towards it. Religion, then, entails at least a cognitive and performative element. There is an assumption of something greater and beyond human experience, on the one hand, and a concrete, lived response to it on the other. Similarly, awareness of this claim or relationship may take one of two modes. Newman distinguishes "religion" as something "natural" and "revealed."[63] By no means, however, is this distinction Newman's invention.

Peter Harrison argues that the career of these terms, "natural" and "revealed" religion, is a complex one and traceable to reflections upon the interconnections between "religion," "reason," and "nature," that extend from the Classical Age up through the Protestant Reformation and Renaissance. These periods were the "chief ideological sources for the seventeenth-century construction of 'religion.'"[64] Natural and revealed religion was a distinction that largely took its form from Protestant the-

---

60. Newman takes up "Natural Religion" and "Revealed Religion" in the second of his Oxford University sermons as well as chapter 10 of *GA*.

61. Newman, *Fifteen Sermons Preached Before the University of Oxford*, Sermon 2, 25–26. Henceforth all references to Newman's sermons shall be taken from this edition and noted *US* unless specified otherwise.

62. *GA*, 251.

63. See *US*, Sermon 2; *GA*, 251f.

64. Peter Harrison, *"Religion" and the Religions in the English Enlightenment*, 7.

ology in reaction to the medieval view which held a positive and harmonious relation between a natural and revealed knowledge of God.[65] But they did not "gain currency until the latter half of the seventh century." Debates between English Protestants on the one hand, and the strange agreement among Catholics and philosophers on the other, concerning the legitimacy of "natural religion"—understood as an implicit or "natural" knowledge of God—enabled the distinction to become commonplace in the Enlightenment.[66] Since its publication in 1736, Newman certainly read, like others, Bishop Butler's enormously influential work *The Analogy of Religion* whose subtitle, not to be overlooked, is *Natural and Revealed*.[67] Newman's distinction was borrowed.

For Newman, the claim of and evidence for natural religion comes from a divine power—not formal revelation. In revealed religion, the claims and form of knowledge are explicitly Christian.[68] The question that underlies both is how human beings experience this claim as real and whether, fundamentally, both forms of religion can be distinguished from theology. As we shall argue, what links and yet distinguishes natural from revealed religion is Newman's understanding of conscience.

Newman argues that natural knowledge of God comes from three different sources or "channels": "our own minds (conscience), the voice of mankind, and the course of the world, that is, human life and human

---

65. "The Protestant theology which came to dominate English thought in the post-Reformation era had a number of important implications. The sharp distinction between two sources of religious truth—revelation and nature—not only provided the ideological basis for the separation of the sacred realm from the secular, but also spawned two discrete species of the newly ideated 'religion'—'natural religion' and 'revealed religion.'" Ibid., 19.

66. Ibid., 185 n. 19. See also Buckley's remarks, "If atheism was unacceptable, superstition and fanaticism were emphatically more so. Voltaire and the Enlightenment with him insisted that the evidence for the reality of god be obtained independently of any religious community. The natural religion of human beings sensitive to the world around and within them was discovered here, and it could provide criteria by which the truth and falsity of confessional doctrines could be sifted." *At the Origins of Modern Atheism*, 38.

67. See Butler, *Analogy of Religion Natural and Revealed*. For the influence of Butler, see Newman, *Apologia Pro Vita Sua*, 22–23. Edward Sillem describes the formative influence of Butler upon Newman as foundational along with Aristotle, "Aristotle had taught Newman to think of the external things we observe and know from experience; Butler taught him how to think of his Creator." Newman, *Philosophical Notebook*, 1:171; 170–81.

68. Cf., *US*, 25–26.

affairs."[69] Each are ways that human beings discern the activity of God independently of Christian revelation. They are "natural." They denote general but concrete warrants or 'Evidences' for the intelligibility and credibility of an original, universal knowledge of God.[70] But it is the first channel, for Newman, the universal experience of conscience that conditions recognizing and interpreting God's activity within the others. "[T]he most authoritative of these three means of knowledge, as being specially our own, is our own mind [conscience], whose informations give us the rule by which we test, interpret, and correct what is presented to us for belief, whether by the universal testimony of mankind, or by the history of society and of the world."[71] He locates, in other words, the center of natural religion within the individual experience of conscience. To expand this principle, various religious practices express a fundamentally inward reality.[72] Indeed, individual self-knowledge and awareness become the controlling elements in natural religion's code and cult.[73] Anthropology, therefore, assumes a crucial role. It would not be an exaggeration to maintain that the experience of God in conscience underlies all human religious expression. In general and variant ways, religious traditions derive their sense of the sacred from this foundational experience and knowledge of God. Because of its centrality, Newman's understanding of conscience deserves careful scrutiny. After examining briefly the other two channels of religious knowledge, we will consider it in some depth.

The second channel of religious knowledge, the "voice of mankind" or "the universal testimony of mankind," concerns the social response of human beings to the divine driven by a universal "sense of sin." What Newman predicates as a universal human condition is the religious and Christian doctrine of original sin. It is not simply a Christian idea

---

69. *GA*, 251.

70. *US*, 181.

71. *GA*, 251.

72. It is important and interesting to note that the topical order in which Newman explains each of these channels is not arbitrary. The order indicates a methodological primacy given to individual human experience concerning natural knowledge of God.

73. "I take our natural perception of right and wrong as the standard for determining the characteristics of Natural Religion, and I use the religious rites and traditions which are actually found in the world, only so far as they agree with our moral sense." *GA*, 269. Also, cf. 270.

but a human truth.[74] Sinfulness or guilt characterizes the experience of God in conscience as "Judge" writ large within the history of religions.[75] Throughout history, religious ideas and customs implicitly or explicitly acknowledge that "man is in a degraded, servile condition, and requires expiation, reconciliation, and some great change of nature."[76] There is a recognition of limitation, of finitude, of human separation from the divine. Religious practices that concern sin disclose this as the severe aspect.[77] At the same time, acknowledgment leads to response. An appropriate "duty and responsibility" to atone for this state of alienation from God then arises. Sin and guilt, in other words, should not be and merit penitential efforts. Newman regards rites and devotions, especially varying religious practices of 'atonement' as confirmation of this situation and how it needs to change.[78] This state, then, of individual and social guilt and recrimination is not simply defined by pessimistic despair but involves the real possibility of conversion, of hope and redemption. These hopeful elements are religion's "blessings"—something we shall discuss momentarily.

The third channel of natural knowledge of God is extensive, incorporating natural religion's severe and positive aspects.[79] For Newman, though sin and guilt mark natural religion, the awareness is not a one-sided. Where sin exists, there is also promise or "blessing."[80] This channel extends farther than the individual experience of conscience and the universal acknowledgment of guilt before the divine socially expressed, though it presupposes both. It involves not primarily the history of certain religious and universal rites proper to it based upon a sense of sin (e.g., atonement rituals, auricular confession, fasting on Yom Kippur).

---

74. *US*, 32–33.

75. This is what Newman is referring to when he states that it is "a necessary point to adjust the religions of the world with the intimations of conscience . . ." *GA*, 254.

76. *GA*, 253.

77. Newman understands natural religion to possess characteristics that remind humanity of its finitude and failure on the one hand, and of the possibility for solace and relief concerning its relationship to the divine. He sometimes refers to these aspects as "severe" and positive or the "blessing." See ibid., 253; 258–59.

78. Ibid., 253.

79. See Ibid., 254f. "Positive" refers to natural religion's "happier side" and "blessings."

80. The echo of Paul is unmistakable: "but where sin increased, grace abounded all the more" (Rom 5:20).

Rather, it regards the discernment of God's providential action in the system of nature and in the course of human affairs opposing the mystery of human evil and suffering.[81] Though the workings of providence may be "faint and fragmentary views of Him" and quite dependent upon conscience as the rule of discernment, Newman views them as valid evidence of a "Good God."[82] Put simply, human beings can naturally discern the ongoing struggle and triumph of good over evil in historical events and, by implication—directly or indirectly—the activity of God.[83] On this, there are several points to note.

First, Newman indicates the subtle influence of God within the broadest context of natural religion: the pervasive reality and historical depth of human pain. This is its severe aspect. The problem and reality of evil he neither dismisses nor anesthetizes. Still, he conjectures from the limited experience of human nature that a better future awaits human struggle. This supposition holds—albeit vaguely—that God works continually to effect beneficial change in humanity. Independently of God, human beings cannot presage hopeful outcomes for several reasons: (1) human beings cannot reach happiness naturally; (2) the affliction accompanying the violation of conscience; and (3) human nature's stubborn resistance to reform.

Nevertheless, Newman maintains that the laws of the world—specifically alluding to the historical affect of evil upon human suffering—suggest an alleviation.[84] But how is a better state discerned? What is its evidence? Again, discernment occurs through "the instinctive power of an educated conscience, that by some secret faculty, and without any intelligible reasoning process, it seems to detect moral truth wherever it lies hid, and feels a conviction of its own accuracy which bystanders cannot account for."[85] Evidence for this alleviation lies in the positive aspects of natural religion's third mode. How one comes to view this as evidence is through implicit reasoning. In this channel, human life's universal elements bespeak or signify a fundamental hope, trust and disclose providential action. They comprise the "blessings" of natural

---

81. "This established order of things, in which we find ourselves, if it has a Creator, must surely speak of His will in its broad outlines and its main issues." *GA*, 255.

82. Ibid., 256–57.

83. Ibid., 257.

84. Cf. Ibid., 258.

85. *US*, 56.

religion. These blessings retain their validity through their universality and their capacity to disclose God within human history.

The virtually universal acceptance of religious beliefs and social institutions (e.g., churches) witnesses to a deep human hope for a happier, future state. Such religious groups and practices provide means to handle human suffering, and thus, reciprocally supply coping mechanisms and expectations. The hope such institutions bring, for Newman, "sweetens all suffering." Second, the physical and social goods of human life are evidences. They "bring home to our experience the fact of a Good God, in spite of the tumult and confusion of the world."[86] Third, if human beings acknowledge and attend to experiences of conscience, Newman contends that "the Hand of an unseen power, directing in mercy or in judgment the physical and moral system" is evident. There is, then, a natural human sensitivity to the sacred and transcendent given in conscience responsive to the complexity, travails and achievements of humanity. His illustrations of this are sweeping.

> In the prominent events of the world, past and contemporary, the fate, evil or happy, of great men, the rise and fall of states, popular revolutions, decisive battles, the migration of races, the replenishing of the earth, earthquakes and pestilences, critical discoveries and inventions, the history of philosophy, the advancement of knowledge, in these the spontaneous piety of the human mind discerns a Divine Supervision. Nay, there is a general feeling, originating directly in the workings of conscience, that a similar governance is extended over the persons of individuals, who thereby both fulfil the purposes and receive the just recompenses of an Omnipotent Providence. Good to the good, and evil to the evil, is instinctively felt to be, even from what we see, amid whatever obscurity and confusion, the universal rule of God's dealing with us.[87]

A personal and a social sensitivity springing from conscience, in some sense, sees the workings of Providence and assures humanity that God's goodness and justice triumphs over despair, confusion and wickedness. Fourth, the predominance of prayer—"the voice of man to God"—within human life is also a blessing because of its capacity to be "a natural relief and solace in all trouble." Such human acts proceed naturally, spontane-

---

86. *GA*, 259.
87. Ibid.

ously and obtain "in various places and times." Fifth, he posits the notion proper to all religions of a revelation from the divine to humanity.[88] This element is one of "the most important effects of Natural Religion."[89] Concretely, Newman cites the doctrine of atonement as a profound expression of the human religious response to the divine and as a witness to the claim of God already operative and manifest within human experience.[90] And finally, there is the blessing of "the doctrine of meritorious intercession" or holiness. People benefit and improve when confronted with goodness made palpable in others, a goodness that mediates the holy and the divine. Through the recognition, activity and experience of holy people, humanity's suffering and pain can be seen against a broader canvass of hope as real and holiness as possible.[91] It is expressly through those persons that the holy can enter and substantially influence the lives of others.

The second and the third channels by which human beings can possess a knowledge of God independently carry their own warrants and remain significant for a natural knowledge of God. But the primary channel is conscience. It is key natural and religious knowledge of God because it serves as the essential relation between the human and the divine. As we shall see, Newman argues that it is an irreducible aspect of human experience, a central condition for a natural knowledge of God and its supremacy as an essential principle of religion.[92]

Though the topic of conscience emerges throughout Newman's writings, my consideration of it draws principally from the *Grammar of Assent*. There Newman considers it principally in two places.[93] He

88. Cf. *US*, 24–25.

89. *GA*, 272.

90. Ibid., 260–61; "This presentiment is founded on our sense, on the one hand, of the infinite goodness of God, and, on the other, of our own extreme misery and need—two doctrines which are the primary constituents of Natural Religion." Ibid., 272.

91. "[E]very religion has had its eminent devotees, exalted above the body of the people, mortified men, brought nearer to the Source of good by austerities, self-inflictions, and prayer, who have influence with Him, and extend a shelter and gain blessings for those who become their clients. A belief like this has been, of course, attended by numberless superstitions; but those superstitions vary with times and places, and the belief itself in the mediatorial power of the good and holy has been one and the same everywhere." Ibid., 262–63; See also, Sermon 5, "Personal Influence: The Means of Propagating the Truth." *US*, 62–77.

92. *US*, 25–26.

93. If Nicholas Lash is right in arguing that Newman's discussion of conscience does not constitute a "stage or element" in the general argument of the *Grammar of Assent*,

examines conscience regarding the relationship between apprehension and assent applied to religion. Taking up the subject of dogmas and what constitutes belief in them, Newman considers "what God is" and "what the mind does, what it contemplates, when it makes an act of faith." Momentarily deferring the issue of the revealed God, he frames the subject of "Belief in One God" as a natural truth. Second, he names conscience as one of three "Evidences" of religion in discussing the relationship between inference and assent in religion. In this section, Newman develops conscience as the "most authoritative" and personal ground of religious belief. As the best and most authoritative means of religious knowledge, it is the "great internal teacher of religion."[94]

The first detailed discussion comprises a phenomenological analysis, showing how "we gain an image of God and give a real assent to the proposition that He exists." At issue in his description is how the process and term of conscience furnishes an "image" of God as the object of a real assent. Newman lists conscience "among our mental acts; as really so, as the action of memory, of reasoning, of imagination, or as the sense of the beautiful." Conscience denotes, therefore, a key operation of mind, exercising what Newman terms "the feeling of conscience." "It is a moral sense, and a sense of duty;" he writes, "a judgment of the reason and a magisterial dictate."[95] In the *Grammar*, Newman does not consider conscience as a "moral sense" or what he calls elsewhere the "rule of Morals."[96] Both aspects—though "indivisible" in act—can be considered

---

I will focus my treatment of it less in terms of its relation to the complex of terms and definitions that comprise the main ideas of the *Grammar*. In this way, I hope to preserve focus and explain conscience, as much as possible, on its own merits. Newman, *Essay in Aid of a Grammar of Assent* (1979), Introduction by Nicholas Lash, 12–13. For a dated but detailed and thorough study of conscience in Newman's thought, see Kaiser, *Concept of Conscience According to John Henry Newman*. For a more narrow and recent study of conscience, see Grave, *Conscience in Newman's Thought*.

94. *GA*, 69–70; 251.

95. Ibid., 73. Lee H. Yearley describes the variation of these aspects: "Newman uses a variety of terms or phrases to specify the two parts: moral sense/sense of duty; judgment of reason/magisterial dictate; moral sense/ commanding dictate; shame/fear; precept/ injunction; critical/judicial; testimony of right and wrong/sanction; remaining within oneself/being carried beyond oneself to another person." *Ideas of Newman*, 11.

96. *US*, 26. For an analysis of the "moral sense" aspect of conscience, see Grave, *Conscience in Newman's Thought*, 30–59; It is interesting to note that some commentators find a strong parallel between Newman's idea of conscience as a "moral sense," and Aristotle's concept of "phronesis" or "practical judgment." See Magill, "Interpreting Moral Doctrine," 10; Powell, "Cardinal Newman on Faith and Doubt," 140–41.

separately. His chief interest concerning conscience in the *Grammar of Assent* is as a "sanction" to right and wrong actions, as "an authoritative monitor bearing upon the details of conduct."[97] People recognize this aspect, he argues, as the ordinary meaning of "conscience."[98] This feature is at issue.

The characteristic "magisterial dictate" arises in the *Grammar of Assent* and in other writings. It marks conscience as something religious, something more than ratiocinative.[99] In the *University Sermons*, Newman contends that, "While Conscience is thus ever the sanction of Natural Religion, it is, when improved, the rule of Morals also. But here is a difference; it is, as such, essentially religious."[100] The *Letter to the Duke of Norfolk*, written after the *Grammar* in 1875, reveals Newman illustrating conscience far less as a moral judgment and more as a "Divine Law" possessing "absolute authority."[101] When Newman describes conscience as a "magisterial dictate," then, the term implies a relation of the self to something beyond the scope of moral acts though obviously encompassing them. A claim upon the person conveying the sense of duty and obligation comprises more than simply a moral discernment of acts to perform or avoid, but something experienced as transcendentally imperative. Newman states, for example, that "conscience does not repose on itself, but vaguely reaches forward to something beyond self, and dimly discerns a sanction higher than self for its decision, as is evidenced in that keen sense of obligation and responsibility which informs them." "Conscience" in this respect, operates beyond individual control

---

97. *GA*, 74. Cf., *US*, 25–26.

98. *GA*, 73–74.

99. Newman's decision not to treat the "moral sense" aspect of conscience in the *Grammar* seems to be due to the difficulty in universalizing the notion of "right and wrong" in different people. Indeed, one discerns something of his hesitation when reading a passage on the difference between the aspects from his earlier "Proof of Theism." "The feeling of conscience is of right and wrong *under* a *special sanction*. And, while the notion of right & wrong varies indefinitely in individuals, & while it is in consequence most difficult to say, or rather impossible to maintain, that there is any idea of moral right or wrong bound up in the primary consciousness which contemplates my existence as reasoning, sensation &c are, the sense of a special sanction remains on & the same in all men. All men know what the feeling of a good or bad conscience is, though they may differ most widely from each other as to *what* conscience injoins." *Philosophical Notebook*, II:49. Italics his.

100. *US*, 26.

101. Newman, *Letter Addressed to His Grace The Duke of Norfolk* (1874), 246.

or manipulation. "Its essence," according to Newman, is precisely in "this prerogative of dictating and commanding."[102]

The treatment of conscience gains greater precision when Newman describes its actions rather than as a power of the mind. Broadly and viewed as a whole, it functions in several ways. First, it influences the emotions; second, it generates an "image" of God that becomes the object for a real assent; and third, conscience "teaches" about God. It thus possesses attributes that are affective, cognitive and pedagogical. "Conscience," writes Newman, "is ever forcing on us by threats and by promises that we must follow the right and avoid the wrong." When one acts in certain instances rightly or wrongly, concomitant with the awareness of the action descends corresponding emotions, positive or negative. One experiences the feeling or sensibility of "reverence," "awe," "hope," "inward peace," "self-approval," "lightness of heart," upon acting rightly; the feeling of shame and "especially fear" upon acting wrongly.[103] These affective states spring from the fundamental experience of conscience's effect as either "pleasant or painful."[104] When conscience acts, therefore, it always bears upon the emotions. Second, Newman maintains that real assent to the proposition that "There is one God, such and such in Nature and Attributes," involves the possibility of having what he calls an "imaginative apprehension of it [the proposition]." Put more simply, Newman explores the question of whether one "can believe as if I saw." The object of this inquiry is to see how one can give the "most perfect and highest" kind of assent to the proposition, which entails not a notional but real one.[105] Since real assents require "things" for their objects and not notions, Newman must show how one can give a real assent to the effects of conscience. He must, more precisely, explain "how we can gain an *image* of God."[106] Of course, it is misleading to think Newman means by "image" pictorial representation or a singular attribute of the divine. This is simplistic and excessively anthropomorphic. Charles Hefling maintains,

---

102. *GA*, 75.

103. Newman lists, as "perturbations of mind," the following emotions: "self-reproach, poignant shame, haunting remorse, chill dismay at the prospect of the future"—all indicative of a "bad conscience," *GA*, 75.

104. *GA*, 73.

105. "An act of assent, it seems, is the most perfect and highest of its kind, when it is exercised on propositions, which are apprehended as experiences and images, that is, which stand for things" *GA*, 33; 71; cf., 73.

106. *GA*, 73. Italics mine.

"'image' means something more than 'picture,' despite the fact (which he notes himself) that most of Newman's examples, like his talk about 'graphic accounts,' 'field of view,' 'gazing on Tiberius,' and so on, involve sight."[107] If Hefling is right and Newman expands the meaning of the term "image" beyond "pictorial representation," what does he mean?

The terms "image," "impression," and "experience"—all of which Newman uses or implies in discussing how conscience evokes emotions in response to living objects—share the aspect of a "personal relation" when employed in the contexts of "conscience" and "real assent." Acknowledgment of the force or impression of another's presence upon us is not simply an act of one or two channels of knowing and affectivity. It is a combination of many. It depends on the formation of the person in his or her environment—past experience, recurrent and variant patterns of behavior, emotion, and so forth. For instance, our consciousness of past or present persons, our knowledge of them and our feelings towards them connect, thus giving us an 'image' and 'experience' of the whole. At the same time, we are to remain simultaneously open to new and ongoing concrete information about them.[108] This is precisely the force of their personality upon us. Newman does argue for the apprehension of mental acts such as "hope, inquiry, effort," and so forth in addition to emotions.[109] A similar kind of apprehension, then, that can become a real assent occurs in really assenting to the image of God generated by the knowledge and emotional effects of conscience. It is qualitatively different in kind and more interior than anything else in human experience. Indeed, Newman holds that "Conscience is nearer to me than any other means of knowledge."[110] With friends and parents, of course, most people adopt pictorial representations joined to a general understanding-affective response. Yet with God this principle, the 'image,' obviously only holds analogously.[111] Newman's point, however, is that it is still capable of the force and vividness required for a real assent—a personal relation of the whole person—to be given it.

---

107. Hefling, "Newman on Apprehension, Notional and Real," 66.
108. See Newman's discussion on image formation, GA, 25–26.
109. Ibid., 24.
110. Ibid., 251.
111. See Newman's comments concerning the term "Personal" regarding the Trinity. Ibid., 86.

> Inanimate things cannot stir our affections; these are correlative with persons. If, as is the case, we feel responsibility, are ashamed, are frightened, at transgressing the voice of conscience, this implies that there is One to whom we are responsible, before whom we are ashamed, whose claims upon us we fear. If, on doing wrong, we feel the same tearful, broken-hearted sorrow which overwhelms us on hurting a mother; if, on doing right, we enjoy the same sunny serenity of mind, the same soothing, satisfactory delight which follows on our receiving praise from a father, we certainly have within us the image of some person, to whom our love and veneration look, in whose smile we find our happiness, for whom we yearn, towards whom we direct our pleadings, in whose anger we are troubled and waste away. These feelings in us are such as require for their exciting cause an intelligent being; we are not affectionate towards a stone, nor do we feel shame before a horse or a dog; we have no remorse or compunction on breaking mere human law: yet, so it is, conscience excites all these painful emotions, confusion, foreboding, self-condemnation; and on the other hand it sheds upon us a deep peace, a sense of security, a resignation, and a hope, which there is no sensible, no earthly object to elicit.[112]

The affect of conscience—always emotional—is always towards *persons*, towards *living things*, that influence us.[113] Notions lack this character of a claim and personal relation. This is, furthermore, the essential difference between "things" and "notions" (or realities).[114] Images, therefore, may or may not be pictures, but they are personal relations expressive of emotion.[115]

Lastly, conscience teaches about God. Newman argues that conscience is "[o]ur great internal teacher of religion." He lists it as "the most authoritative" of the "three main channels" of religious knowledge which "teach us the Being and Attributes of God, our responsibility to Him, our dependence on Him, our prospect of reward or punishment." The idea

112. Ibid., 76.

113. Ibid., 75–76.

114. Newman is not concerned with how one gives a "notional assent" to the proposition, though many people do. See Ibid., 86.

115. I hold these remarks to be somewhat along the lines with Charles Hefling's conclusion concerning the meaning of "image": "Its ground is inward experience; to that experience is joined some notion which, without it, would be only an abstraction; and it is interpersonal inasmuch as it relates the person I am to the Person God is." "Newman on Apprehension, Notional and Real," 71.

of retribution and personal accountability for action figures strongly here and characterizes how Newman's conception of conscience relates us naturally to God. Characteristically, Newman argues that "its most prominent teaching, and its cardinal and distinguishing truth, is that he is our Judge." And God's primary attribute according to conscience "is that of justice—retributive justice." This feature holds universally. It is the aspect of God disclosed by conscience independently of Christian revelation.[116] In turn, the human response to this divine attribute is "that we are personally responsible for what we do, that we have no means of shifting our responsibility, and that dereliction of duty involves punishment."[117] The religious aspect and the moral aspect of conscience, therefore, cannot be neatly disconnected. Still, though the aspects reciprocally imply each other, the religious dominates. At the same time, the command of conscience, our felt duty, is not something divorced from the image and the attribute of the One obligating. Experience of conscience does not become, therefore, a relation to an abstraction or moral principle. Its effects imply something more. Conscience, consequently, teaches not only "that God exists," but also that "I am alienated from Him."[118] What Newman characterizes in this teaching of conscience, Karl Rahner might describe as "man as a being threatened radically by guilt" or Paul Tillich would call "the self-estrangement of our existence."[119] In this way, conscience informs human beings about God perceived naturally.

The revealed system of religion, for Newman, is Christianity—its creed, cult, code, Scriptures.[120] Its various doctrines, liturgical and sac-

---

116. *GA*, 252.

117. Ibid., 254.

118. Ibid., 256.

119. Karl Rahner, *Foundations of Christian Faith*, 91 ; Paul Tillich, *Systematic Theology Volume I*, 49.

120. *GA*, 249–50. In its idea, Newman maintains that Christianity is a "'Revelatio revelata;' it is a definite message from God to man distinctly conveyed by His chosen instruments, and to be received as such a message . . . And the whole tenor of Scripture from beginning to end is to this effect: the matter of revelation is not a mere collection of truths, not a philosophical view, not a religious sentiment or spirit, not a special morality,—poured out upon mankind as a stream might pour itself into the sea, mixing with the world's thought, modifying, purifying, invigorating it;—but an authoritative teaching, which bears witness to itself and keeps itself together as one, in contrast to the assemblage of opinions on all sides of it, and speaks to all men, as being ever and everywhere one and the same, and claiming to be received intelligently, by all whom it addresses, as one doctrine, discipline, and devotion directly given from above." Cf., *Idea*,

ramental rites, ecclesial structures and ideals of conduct constitute it as the ongoing life of the Church. It is important to note, however, that when Newman treats the elements of Christianity as such, seldom does he catalog or list or organize them systematically. When he lists the central doctrines, they seem more or less elements of the creed in an unsorted form.[121] His treatments look nothing like Calvin's *Institutes of the Christian Religion* or Karl Rahner's *Foundations of Christian Faith*. As such, that Newman presents no unified form of revealed religion in either the *Oxford University Sermons*, the *Idea of a University*, or the *Grammar of Assent*, is unsurprising. His purpose, when discussing revealed religion is not logical rigor, but comparative and explanatory meaning. Newman desires to relate two different ways that human beings know God and show how one does not negate the other, but satisfies it. He clearly states that revealed religion "is simply an addition to it [natural religion]; it does not supersede or contradict it."[122] Moreover, revealed religion is intrinsically connected to natural religion as its "result and completion."[123] It suggests the classical medieval position between nature and grace, reason and faith. Thus the key issue in comparing revealed religion and natural hinges less on cataloging Christianity's elements and more on exploring a multi-part question: What does revealed religion "add" to natural religion, how does revealed religion complete the natural and why is their difference significant?[124] Clarifying these questions helps lay the groundwork for understanding the contrast between religion and theology more definitively. In what follows, let me address some of revealed religion's characteristics.

Perhaps the most important point to notice is context. Newman's understanding of revealed religion as it concerns conscience and natural knowledge of God is not theoretical but practical.[125] His remarks in the

---

158–59; "Christianity is Dogmatical, Devotional, Practical All at Once." Newman, *Essay on the Development of Christian Doctrine* (1989) 36.

121. See *Essays Critical and Historical*, vol. 1, 45.

122. *GA*, 250.

123. *US*, 33.

124. For many of the elements covered in revealed religion, see Newman, *Essay on the Development of Christian Doctrine*.

125. In *US*, Newman states the kind of context in which he will compare natural with revealed. He will "compare the two together in point of *practical efficacy*." 24. Italics mine.

Idea concerning the relationship of knowledge and religious duty illuminate how revealed religion relates to natural.

> [W]hen I speak of Catholicism ... I am contemplating Catholicism chiefly as a system of pastoral instruction and moral duty; and I have to do with its doctrines mainly as they are subservient to its direction of the conscience and the conduct. I speak of it, for instance, as teaching the ruined state of man; his utter inability to gain Heaven by any thing he can do himself; the moral certainty of his losing his soul if left to himself; the simple absence of all rights and claims on the part of the creature in the presence of the Creator; the illimitable claims of the Creator on the service of the creature; the imperative and obligatory force of the voice of conscience; and the inconceivable evil of sensuality.[126]

He frames this understanding of revealed religion in terms of lived experience. And here, though Newman does not reduce revealed truth to morality, it manifestly assumes a significant posture insofar as conscience is the essence of natural religion.[127] The human condition comprises alienation from God that carries the lived effects of sin and guilt. The redemption of human beings confronted by the experience of their own limitations indicates something different from speculation upon dogma or ecclesiology or the pursuit of abstract questions.[128] For how one comes to know and respond to God is something inextricably linked to morality as the internalization and expression of what is held true. Put differently, it is a lived and appropriated religious knowledge. The framework, then, for understanding the relation between natural and revealed is precisely how revealed communications of God influence human life within the condition of sin and guilt.

---

126. *Idea*, 159.

127. See *US*, 25f. Prefacing the discussion of natural and revealed religion in the *Grammar*, Newman clearly states the moral context of the discussion: "I begin with expressing a sentiment, which is habitually in my thoughts, whenever they are turned to the *subject of mental or moral science*, and which I am as willing to apply here to the Evidences of Religion as it properly applies to Metaphysics or Ethics, viz. that in these provinces of inquiry egotism is true modesty." 248. Italics mine. Also, see *US*, 31–32; 55–56. "Revealed Religion . . . is one comprehensive moral fact." It should be stressed, however, that the center of Christianity for Newman is not a moral principle or scheme, but the Incarnation. He states this quite clearly in the *Essay on the Development of Christian Doctrine*, 36. Cited hereafter as *Essay on Development*.

128. See *GA*, 312–13.

If the context of Newman's discussion is moral, natural religion ultimately becomes something—for all of its evidences, promptings, and blessings—that is an inadequate system of experience and evidence for a religious knowledge of God and morality.[129] Reasons for this inadequacy reach the center of Newman's view. Though Newman gives several, let us consider two. First, though natural religion expressed and experienced in human conscience can recognize and feel an objective state of alienation from God, conscience cannot overcome it. It cannot, in other words, remove sin. "Natural religion is based upon the sense of sin," Newman writes, "it recognizes the disease, but it cannot find, it does but look out for the remedy. That remedy, both for guilt and for moral impotence, is found in the central doctrine of Revelation, the Mediation of Christ."[130] Certainly, natural religion testifies and manifests grounds of alienation, such as the stark impressions of judgment and anticipations of eternal loss. Nor can it be objected that because natural religion encompasses and evokes hopes for a better state it overcomes the problem. The hope of natural religion may express a desire, a longing, but it cannot fulfill or satisfy it on its own. Natural hope remains too obscure, too vague, to sustain human lives over time. It does not, therefore, alleviate the alienation. Guilt remains. Second, as one increasingly adheres to conscience's dictates and grows progressively more virtuous, the more one tends toward self-adoration and idolatry. It is the classic problem of moral (or spiritual) pride. "A mind, habitually and honestly conforming itself to its own full sense of duty, will at length enjoin or forbid with an authority second only to an inspired oracle."[131] The standards and claims of a fallible conscience, though noble, begin to assume a primacy disproportionate to its nature and function. Newman cites Aristotle's virtuous man as an example.

129. Though the claim of conscience possesses a unique and absolute power, it cannot settle the restlessness and skepticism prone to minds unformed and untouched by Christian revelation. Thus Newman maintains that "No thought is more likely to come across and haunt the mind, and slacken its efforts under Natural Religion, than that after all we may be following a vain shadow, and disquieting ourselves without cause, while we are giving up our hearts to the noblest instincts and aspirations of our nature." *US*, 30–31. Any abstract system, intellectual or moral, cannot continually challenge the human heart to conversion. And for Newman, only God revealed in Christ can work this change within the concrete lives of human beings. It is the concrete, "practical efficacy" of natural and revealed religion that matters. Cf. *US*, 24, 30–32.

130. *GA*, 313.

131. *US*, 26–27.

> An incidental and unstudied greatness of mind is said by him to mark the highest moral excellence, and truly; but the genuine nobleness of the virtuous mind, as shown in a superiority to common temptations, forbearance, generosity, self-respect, calm high-minded composure, is deformed by an arrogant contempt of others, a disregard of their feelings, and a harshness and repulsiveness of external manner. That is, the philosopher saw clearly the tendencies of the moral system, the constitution of the human soul, and the ways leading to the perfection of our nature; but when he attempted to delineate the ultimate complete consistent image of the virtuous man, how could he be expected to do this great thing, who had never seen Angel or Prophet, much less the Son of God manifested in the flesh?[132]

Abstract moral standards of natural religion fail to curb moral pride or contempt for others. What ennobles and inspires on a human level of conduct cannot redeem.[133] It is here that revealed religion enters. Revealed accomplishes what natural religion *per se* cannot.

This does not mean, however, that the truths of natural religion change or disappear. All the evidences and experiences associated with discerning God in the dictates of conscience, in the universal religious experiences of sin and atonement, and in the course of human affairs—alienation and blessing—remain valid and necessary. Yet revealed religion adds something radically different and new. Revealed religion differs from natural because it manifests an awareness or experience of God as personal. It expresses God's intimacy with human beings. God's self-disclosure does not mean a relationship to an abstract, infinite power or a reductively rational moral principle. In the Christian moral life, the experience of God entails not an obscure, commanding force bearing down upon human beings, judging and dispensing punishment. A personal knowledge of being in relation to Christ transforms the meaning and experiences of the elements proper to natural religion into something evocative of human identity and destiny. There is a radical difference in the meaning bestowed upon individual life. It is not so much that the information of conscience and adherents to the precepts of right and wrong change. Human self-understanding and motivation

---

132. Ibid., 32.
133. Cf. Ibid., 29.

for acting do. In scholastic terminology, the agent gains an utterly new formal object.[134] Newman explains:

> While, then, Natural Religion was not without provision for all the deepest and truest religious feelings, yet presenting no tangible history of the Deity, no points of His personal character (if we may so speak without irreverence), it wanted that most efficient incentive to all action, a starting or rallying point,—an object on which the affections could be placed, and the energies concentrated. Common experience in life shows how the most popular and interesting cause languishes, if its head be removed; and how political power is often vested in individuals, merely for the sake of the definiteness of the practical impression which a personal presence produces. How, then, should the beauty of virtue move the heart, while it was an abstraction?[135]

Personal knowledge of God thus transforms moral duty.[136] Consequently, the teachings of natural religion reach their completion and satisfaction only in the system of revealed religion.[137] Still, what does personal relation mean specifically? What is its context?

Though natural religion is a necessary propaedeutic foundation, revelation supplies a knowledge of God's personality.[138] What natural religion points to as "highest principle," revealed religion manifests as "person." It is knowledge of God's activity for human beings. Elements of Christian faith, such as Jesus Christ's life, death, resurrection and commissioning of the church possess this character.[139] The evidences and the effects of conscience are thus built upon, clarified, and directed towards God's revelation in Christ as their aspiration and true fulfilment.[140] Jesus changes and qualifies the knowledge, action and worship of the Christian.

---

134. See Aquinas, *ST* I, Q. 1, art. 3.

135. *US*, 28–29.

136. Cf. ibid., 32–33.

137. Ibid., 24–33.

138. Ibid., 27–29. "Natural religion teaches, it is true, the infinite power and majesty, the wisdom and goodness, the presence, the moral governance, and, in one sense, the unity of the Deity; but it gives little or no information respecting what may be called His *Personality*." Newman qualifies this statement noting it is somewhat overstated, but it is nonetheless generally correct. Also, cf. ibid., 28.

139. *GA*, 313.

140. Ibid., 276–77.

> Here, then, Revelation meets us with simple and distinct *facts* and *actions*, not with painful inductions from existing phenomena, not with generalized laws or metaphysical conjectures, but with *Jesus and the Resurrection*; and '*if Christ be not risen*' (it confesses plainly), "then is our preaching vain, and your faith is also vain." Facts such as this are not simply evidence of the truth of the revelation, but the media of its impressiveness. The life of Christ brings together and concentrates truths concerning the chief good and the laws of our being, which wander idle and forlorn over the surface of the moral world, and often appear to diverge from each other.[141]

It is precisely from the encounter with Christ's person as an exemplar that generates a religious understanding and an appropriation of what natural religion discloses through conscience. Natural religion, for Newman, lacks this impressive power because "it does not urge and illustrate virtue in the Name and by the example of our blessed Lord."[142] Newman calls this approach to understanding Christian revelation a "method of personation," and extends its logic to theological topics like the Holy Spirit, original sin and ecclesiology.[143]

Let me return to the initial question of this comparison: how and why does revealed religion add to or complete natural religion? For Newman the reason is literally and theologically personal. Directed by conscience, human beings possess a natural knowledge of God as moral law that revealed religion discloses as a person. Knowledge or awareness of being in a personal relationship transforms the meaning of natural knowledge from something incapable of preventing alienation to something salvific.

The foundational awareness and knowledge of God obtained in the human experience of conscience is ultimately directed towards and in relation to something living, concrete, personal—a God who enfleshes human history. The vagueness and ambiguity in natural religion becomes definite, realizing God's continuing self-revelation. For Newman, the claim and experience of a personal relationship is something that

---

141. *US*, 31. Italics his.

142. Ibid., 35.

143. Ibid., 32–33. John Coulson mentions Newman's "method of personation" but brings out very different meaning than Newman's use of the term here. For Coulson, "method of person" concerns Newman's first-person appeal as part of a theological methodology directly observed in *Apologia Pro Vita Sua* and the *Grammar*, 145–47.

bears profoundly upon minds and hearts. Revealed religion, in other words, possesses "facts and actions" that powerfully confront and challenge human beings with the image of the redemptive, personal and loving God. Conscience aids in virtue, but its presentiments and hopes point towards the unsure, the abstract and ultimately the unredemptive. But the knowledge and experience of conscience informed and touched by a personal, loving God transforms the information and claims of nature into something that transcends human judgment and calls human action to a supernatural standard. And it is precisely this standard, this exemplar, this model of behavior that inspires, supports and gives conscience a direction coordinate with self-denial. Obedience to conscience in revealed religion leads beyond virtue to a redemptive holiness patterned on Jesus.

SPECIFYING THE NATURE OF THEOLOGY

Thus far, our inquiry has shown what distinguishes natural and religious knowledge of God. Their divergence concerns not only the different kinds of knowledge involved, but a fundamentally different quality of relationship to the divine. But just as there is a parallel, a distinction, and an overlap between natural and revealed religion, there is also a corresponding one between religion and theology. In the *Idea of a University*, Newman writes, "Religion is more than Theology; it is something relative to us; and it includes our relation towards the Object of it."[144] If religion comprises a lived and appropriated knowledge of God which can be this impersonal or personal "more," how does theology differ from it? But an even prior and pressing questions arise, made more difficult because Newman does not employ consistent vocabulary: (1) what does Newman mean by the term 'theology'? (2) what elements comprise and eventually reach an adequate definition? and (3) how does its subject matter, method, and setting diverge from religion? Though overlap in subject matter is inevitable when the issue concerns knowledge of God, the nature and quality of religious knowledge differs from theological. This section, accordingly, proposes to explore and answer these questions.

    Elements of what Newman means by "theology" can be considered in two fundamental ways. Similar to his understanding of religion as something natural and something revealed, it will be shown that he un-

---

144. *Idea*, 365.

derstands theology in two forms: natural and revealed (or dogmatic). Newman himself defines the meaning of "Theology" in the *Idea* as "Natural Theology," and in the *Grammar* clearly describes it as "Revealed" or "Dogmatic Theology."[145] This distinction, however, needs to be viewed as heuristic. It must allow for similarities and overlap between the subject matter and procedure proper to each form. Prior, then, to exploring the issues of subject matter, method, and setting, let us begin with definition.

Newman's succinct definition of natural theology largely coordinates with a subject matter characterized as a university science. "[B]y Theology, I simply mean the Science of God, or the truths we know about God put into system; just as we have a science of the stars, and call it astronomy, or of the crust of the earth, and call it geology."[146] Initially, this definition seems overly general; yet it articulates four distinct and crucial elements of Newman's conception that show it to be aligned with a serious academic endeavor. First, the subject matter of natural theology is God; second, it involves an exercise of reason that is science; third, the kind of knowledge thus described is termed "truth" and denote the determinations and judgments of reason upon certain evidence or warrants; and finally, natural theology entails a "system" that means and requires an intellectual form or coherent organization of knowledge. Moreover, this system shares characteristics normally associated with secular sciences such as astronomy or geology. Further, if truth, as Newman contends, means 'facts and their relations,' then the system of truths about God that is the science of Theology will also demonstrate a level of interconnection and relation. The truths about God, in other words, bear upon and influence each other reciprocally without contradiction. Doctrines or truths about God also possess a logical coherence and an order.[147] Subject matter, science, truths, system—these elements are critical to Newman's understanding of natural theology. I propose,

---

145. Ibid., 71; "I have been insisting simply on Natural Theology."

146. Ibid., 65.

147. Of these doctrines, Newman contends, "I am not throwing together discordant doctrines; I am not merging belief, opinion, persuasion, of whatever kind, into a shapeless aggregate, by the help of ambiguous words, and dignifying this medley by the name of Theology." Ibid., 69. It should be stressed, however, that Newman suspects systems while simultaneously arguing for them. The doctrines proper to natural theology do comprise a system, but are foundationally, nevertheless, incapable of being limited to them. Doctrines are fundamentally mysteries. Cf. ibid., 66.

however, to explore them within two broad categories: subject matter and method.

Newman discusses natural theology in brief but illuminating detail throughout discourses two to four of the *Idea*, but specifically in discourse three. There the issue of its definition is closely tied to the nature of its subject matter and an initial problem. It is one that should be set against its larger historical context. The Enlightenment assault on aspects of Christianity had left Christian theologians defensively entrenched. Polemical refutations and counter-positions were advanced with "proofs" or "evidences" for God and Christianity. Defenders sought to defend the legitimacy and intelligibility of revelation. Gradually through the seventeenth and eighteenth centuries, Protestant and Catholic theologians moved away from the traditional sources of evidence proper to theology, assuming principles and methods eventually incompatible with the subject matter of theological reflection and argument.[148] When Newman elaborates natural theology's subject matter in the third discourse, he sets it against a historical and contemporary context whose province remains confused and problematic. He recognizes how vulnerable any discussion of 'natural theology' is to misunderstanding given the current state of Christian apologetics and polemics. Newman cannot, therefore, proceed directly to an elaboration of theology without purifying the terms and ideas that characterize the discordant conceptions of theology and its subject matter. In addition, unlike other Christian thinkers, Newman does not seek to "prove" God's existence in defining theology. He assumes it.[149] With God as first principle, five interpretations of natural theology and its putative subject matter are rejected.

First, Newman does not assume the truths of Catholicism in the definition of natural theology. In the second through fourth discourses,

---

148. Michael J. Buckley argues that, "By the heady age of the Enlightenment, the tensions and contradictions within the various forms of natural theology had reached such a point that the next stage of dialectical development was inevitable. As theology generated apologetic philosophy and philosophy generated Universal Mathematics and Universal Mechanics, and as these in their turn co-opted theology to become the foundations of theistic assertions, theology itself became a *disciplina otiosa* in the justification or establishment of its own subject-matter." *At the Origins of Modern Atheism*, 358f.; 38; 97–99. Max Wildiers attributes the effort to found Christian apologetics upon the appeal of emerging new sciences as evidence of the role played by deism and its promise of discerning "order" in the cosmos. This view would help explain the appeal of Physical Theology in Newman's context. *Theologian and His Universe*, 153–54.

149. *Idea*, 62.

"Theology" does not denote the dogmatic or something exclusively reliant upon formal, Christian revelation. It should be noted, there, that Newman's point concerning natural theology's independence from a determinate religious tradition coheres with his initial assumptions concerning *The Idea of a University* as a whole. Its principles are rational and accessible to all reasonable inquirers including the definition of natural theology. This condition, however, does not pertain to the lectures. In the second part of the *Idea* ("University Subjects), Newman describes theology as "revealed" or "dogmatic." But the occasion and matter of the lecture in which he does identify "theology" with "revealed" differs from that of the discourses. Again, this is consistent with the thrust of his argument's principles. Especially in 'Christianity and Physical Science,' Newman expounds explicitly "Catholic theology" and presumes revelation.[150]

Second, Newman considers natural theology in relation to what arose as "Physical Theology." They are not identical.[151] But the terms of this description are part of the history of terminological confusion and the intellectual option of using philosophical or non-Christian evidence as grounds for theological assertions. The figure Newman cites as the proponent of physical theology is William Paley. "I am not . . . arguing from the works of man to the works of God, which Paley has done, which Hume has protested against . . . Physical Theology is a most jejune study, considered as a science, and really is no science at all, for it is ordinarily nothing more than a series of pious or polemical remarks upon the physical world viewed religiously, whereas the word 'Natural' properly comprehends man and society, and all that is involved therein."[152] Nature and the physical order are not the primary subject matter of natural theology. Exemplified in the writings of Christian apologists like

---

150. Ibid., 346; "Catholic Theology has nothing to fear from the progress of Physical Science, even independently of the divinity of its doctrines." Ibid., 354.

151. In the lecture "Christianity and Physical Science," Newman equates Physical Religion and Natural Theology since the two had become synonymous. "This science has, in these modern times, at least in England, taken the name of Natural Theology; and, though absolutely distinct from Physics, yet Physical Philosophers, having furnished its most curious and interesting data, are apt to claim it as their own, and to pride themselves upon it accordingly." But he makes clear that there is an older and different sense of 'natural theology.' Newman writes in a footnote, "I use the word, not in the sense of 'Naturalis Theologia,' but, in the sense in which Paley uses it in the work which he has so entitled." Ibid., 362. It is precisely this sense of the term that he considers in the third discourse.

152. Ibid., 62–65. See Paley, *Natural Theology*. For the criticisms of David Hume, see *Dialogues and Natural History of Religion*.

Paley, physical theology excludes what should be integral to Christian reflection—"man and society." The subject of humanity figures importantly in any discussion of theology for Newman as it did for many eighteenth century conceptions of "natural religion and theology."[153] What dooms physical theology is its methodology—its use of inferential reasoning upon data or information too abstract and remote from the nearest source of human knowledge of God, namely, conscience. In this respect, Newman doubts the utility of the classical argument from design which could be included within the teachings of physical theology. "[W]hat ... are those special Attributes, which are the immediate correlatives of religious sentiment? Sanctity, omniscience, justice, mercy, faithfulness. What does Physical Theology, what does the Argument from Design, what do fine disquisitions about final causes, teach us, except very indirectly, faintly, enigmatically, of these transcendentally important, these essential portions of the idea of Religion?"[154] Characteristically human and personal elements—informations of conscience given in the channels of natural religion—do not figure convincingly in physical theology. Its subject matter is, therefore, inadequate for natural theology.

Third, Newman argues that natural theology is not "polemics of any kind." In particular, he means "'the Evidences of Religion.'" There are two senses of the term "evidences," namely, external and internal. Newman intends a narrow understanding of evidence that can mean something much broader. This distinction corresponds to reason conceived as working or exercising itself in one of two ways: "explicit" or "implicit."[155] Evidences, then, can derive from implicit or explicit reason. More specifically, they either reason to a conclusion without external argumentation and logical form—implicit reasoning—or they can be rational argument as proof, e.g., a syllogism—the form of explicit reasoning. In the *Oxford Sermons*, Newman presumes the validity of both senses when describing the relationship of evidence to religion.

> By the Evidences of Religion I mean the systematic analysis of all the grounds on which we believe Christianity to be true. I say "all," because the word Evidence is often restricted to denote only such arguments as arise out of the thing itself which is to be proved; or, to speak more definitely, facts and circumstances

---

153. See Welch, *Protestant Thought in the Nineteenth-Century*, 32–34.
154. *Idea*, 365.
155. See *US*, 173–89.

which presuppose the point under inquiry as a condition for their existence, and which are weaker or stronger arguments, according as that point approaches more or less closely to be a necessary condition of them. Thus blood on the clothes is an evidence of a murderer, just so far as a deed of violence is necessary to the fact of the stains, or alone accounts for them. Such are the Evidences as drawn out by Paley and other writers; and though only a secondary part, they are popularly considered the whole of the Evidences, because they can be exhibited and studied with far greater ease than antecedent considerations, presumptions, and analogies, which, vague and abstruse as they are, still are more truly the grounds on which religious men receive the Gospel.[156]

In the broadest sense, "evidences" can mean all the various ways in which one grounds belief in Christianity's divine veracity. In the third discourse, Newman does not refer to the general sense of evidence quoted above or repeat his criticism of physical theology. He restricts the meaning of the term "evidence" to clarify his understanding not of revealed but natural theology. In the restricted sense, therefore, Newman refers to "Christian evidences" or "polemics" as "rather answers to objections than direct arguments for Revelation."[157] He writes: "Such is Origen's great work against Celsus; and Tertullian's Apology; such some of the controversial treatises of Eusebius and Theodoret; or St. Augustine's City of God; or the tract of Vincentius Lirinensis. And I confess that I should not even object to portions of Bellarmine's Controversies, or to the work of Suarez on laws, or to Melchior Canus's treatises on the Loci Theologici."[158] In essence, they are the "exercises of Reason in proof of its divinity."[159] For Newman, these works are needed in the broader context of Christian thought but only secondarily, only as "a science supplemental to Theology."[160] They are a necessary but twice removed, so to speak, from natural theology. The works do not directly concern themselves with the true subject matter of theology. In some way, they presuppose it. From that assumption, their work defends religion and revelation.

Fourth, Newman does not mean by natural theology "'Christianity' or 'our common Christianity,' or 'Christianity the law of the land.'" Far

156. Ibid., 181.
157. Ibid., 55.
158. *Idea*, 309.
159. *US*, 55 n. 11.
160. *Idea*, 65.

from possessing anything like definition or intellectual coherence, what Newman refers to is less intellectual reflection and more characteristic of cultural and social assumptions. The effort to specify them remains risky since Newman himself offers no elaboration. Still, they seem to mean a mélange of explicit or implicit moral or customary forms of etiquette that, in some vague and nebulous way, comprise the "Christian ethos" of a region. For instance, it would be those ill-defined "givens" and practices anyone would encounter when born into a Christian country with an established Church.

Fifth, Newman excludes Scriptural exegesis or spiritual reading from the province of natural theology. "I do not understand by Theology," writes Newman, "acquaintance with the Scriptures; for, though no person of religious feelings can read Scripture but he will find those feelings roused, and gain much knowledge of history into the bargain, yet historical reading and religious feeling are not science."[161] In a different ways, Scripture has traditionally been used to incite religious devotion and stir the emotions. The *Spiritual Exercises* of St. Ignatius would be an example. Citing the Scriptures in support of different positions or values classically means "proof-texting." But the problem is that this exegesis lacks a scientific character. And if to science belongs, in the broad sense, the task of organizing doctrines or truths or propositions relevant to the subject matter of theology, Scripture does not accomplish this of itself. Doctrines and their propositional expression need to be extracted, shaped, determined and so forth by the community of faith. For Newman, these tasks belong to theology and not to the plurality of biblical interpretations and devotional uses.

To sum up, Newman lists five different definitions and subject matters antithetical to natural theology. It is neither inductive reasoning applied to the physical world seeking evidence nor reasoning from evidence intended for apologetic or polemical purposes. Thus the proper subject matter concerns not the rational warrants for belief in God or Christianity. Newman does not engage in adducing the *praeambula fidei* in the strict sense.[162] The subject matter is neither vague ethical assumptions nor cultural sentiments leading to religious knowledge. Cultural sentiment cannot be construed as the subject matter for statements

---

161. Ibid.

162. For the definition and history of this term, see "Faith. IV. Preambles of Faith," *Encyclopedia of Theology: The Concise Sacramentum Mundi*, 512–14.

about the divine. Lastly, natural theology differs from biblical exegesis. Though historical information can stimulate religious investigations or kindle piety, neither pertain to Newman's understanding. Some of these may be related to theology but only secondarily. All of these definitions and subject matters describe, therefore, what natural theology cannot be. The question now is how does Newman positively define it?

A good place to begin concerns what natural theology teaches positively. Its fundamental tenet is the following: "I mean, for this is the main point, that, as in the human frame there is a living principle, acting upon it and through it by means of volition, so, behind the veil of the visible universe, there is an invisible, intelligent Being, acting on and through it, as and when He will. Further, I mean that this invisible Agent is in no sense a soul of the world, after the analogy of human nature, but, on the contrary, is absolutely distinct from the world, as being its Creator, Upholder, Governor, and Sovereign Lord."[163] God is an invisible 'living principle,' and 'intelligent Being.' This is not the God of Deism or of the philosophers. For Newman, natural theology teaches those numerous ideas and doctrines associated within a general and classical understanding of God.[164] It thus teaches the doctrine of God as its center. Doctrines proper to God are the classical attributes (e.g., omnipotence, omnipresence) that can be discussed but not ultimately comprehended since they are mysteries. What Newman maintains as fundamental teaching about the divine attributes is scarcely new. It abounds in numerous texts and various ways throughout philosophical and theological history. But he also holds conscience as the privileged point of contact with and natural knowledge of God. This means that the subject matter of natural theology encompasses not simply an abstract doctrine of God, but God in relation to creation. There is more. Though the subject matter is properly God, he draws relationships between God and creation: different beings, substances, laws, principles, the physical world derived from God. Newman maintains that God has so implicated Godself within created reality that everything can be viewed in relation to its ultimate source. The subject matter of natural theology thus specifies God and everything in relation to God.[165]

---

163. *Idea*, 65.

164. See Ibid., 65–66.

165. Ibid., 67–68. "[I]n the intellectual, moral, social and political world. Man, with his motives and works, his languages, his propagation, his diffusion is from Him . . . All

The issue of Newman's own theological method or specific kind of theological argumentation will not be addressed for two reasons. First, this topic has been treated by others. Secondly, this question differs altogether from what Newman held as the method proper to natural theology.[166]

Inquiry into what Newman means by the method of natural theology from the *Idea* confronts two problems. One is the aforesaid lack of theological precision regarding vocabulary and definition. This characteristic is not restricted to the *Idea*. It marks most of his theological work. Indeed, given Newman's ambivalence about systems and systematizing, it is unsurprising that detailed descriptions and definitions of technical vocabulary concerning his understanding of theology—let alone natural theology—are few and broad.[167] Secondly, there is the issue of genre. The *Idea* is not systematic treatise but a collection of public lectures delivered at different times. Furthermore, the lectures and essays are not scholarly works concerned with technical precision. Discourses on the theory of university education form the first part. Newman delivered the first five in Dublin over a period of weeks from May 10 to June 7 of 1852. Discourses six to nine were never "publicly delivered" and nine was finished at the end of November of the same year.[168] Part two comprises disparate lectures and essays spread over four years with "some of them being written for public delivery, others with the privileged freedom of anonymous compositions." They concern literature, university preaching and the relation between "Christianity and Medical Science."[169] Newman's theological style and the genre of the work, therefore, presents

---

that is good, all that is true, all that is beautiful, all that is beneficent, be it great or small, be it perfect or fragmentary, natural as well as supernatural, moral as well as material, comes from Him." Newman's understanding here of natural theology remarkably parallels what Aquinas argues is the subject matter of *Sacra doctrina*: "Omnia autem pertractantur in sacra doctrina sub ratione Dei, vel quia sunt ipse Deus; vel quia habent ordinem ad Deum, ut ad principium et finem." *ST* I, Q. 1, art. 7. The difference, however, is that for Aquinas, sacra doctrina includes natural and revealed theology within itself.

166. See Norris, *Newman and His Theological Method*.

167. Ker, *Achievement of John Henry Newman*, 118. On Newman's ambivalence towards "system," see the comments of Sykes, *Identity of Christianity*, 102–22, and Merrigan, *Clear Heads and Holy Hearts*, 131–68.

168. *Idea*, "Editor's Introduction," xiv–xvii.

169. Ibid., 207–9.

an initial challenge to discerning evidence of detailed and technical definition in writings more popular than scholarly.

Despite these *prima facie* difficulties, it is possible to construct an accurate meaning of the method proper to natural theology. Abstractly, it would entail a description and explanation of intelligent pattern or movement from one idea to the next that seeks coherence and intelligibility. The question concerns the notion of procedure, how reason moves upon and handles its subject matter. To this end, the examination of several key elements of Newman's thought that figure in his descriptive statements is crucial. Taken together, these implicit and operative elements provide a framework in which natural theology's method can be adequately grasped. They are: (1) the form of reasoning as deductive formal inference; (2) the notional nature of theological propositions; and (3) its scientific character.

What kind of reasoning does natural theology employ? Referring to it, Newman maintains, "I speak of one idea unfolded in its just proportions, carried out upon an intelligible method, and issuing in necessary and immutable results."[170] This statement follows Newman's account and critique of definitions antithetical to the subject matter of natural theology. These inadequate definitions of theology, furthermore, employ inductive reasoning. So if induction is implied in the antithetical definitions, its role within the method of natural theology seems problematic.[171] Though embedded within the opposing definitions of theology, one of Newman's clearest descriptions of induction comes from the rational operation of physical science. He contrasts the inductive reasoning of physical science with that of theology as follows:

> The argumentative method of Theology is that of a strict science, such as Geometry, or deductive; the method of Physics, at least on starting, is that of an empirical pursuit, or inductive. This

---

170. Ibid., 69.

171. In Newman's lecture, "Christianity and Physical Science," he contrasts physical science with revealed—not natural theology. It is noteworthy how unambiguous he wants to make the method of revealed theology by showing how if revealed theology proceeds according to induction, the phenomena would shift from God to other subjects, e.g., Scripture, historical events, natural phenomena. After adducing this evidence, he claims that "it was nothing more than huge mistake to introduce the method of research and of induction into the study of Theology at all." *Idea*, 360–61. Whether Newman succeeds in eliminating inductive reasoning from the method of natural theology is another question.

> peculiarity on either side arises from the nature of the case. In Physics a vast and omnigenous mass of information lies before the inquirer, all in a confused litter, and needing arrangement and analysis. In Theology such varied phenomena are wanting, and Revelation presents itself instead. What is known in Christianity is just that which is revealed, and nothing more; certain truths, communicated directly from above, are committed to the keeping of the faithful, and to the very last nothing can really be added to those truths. From the time of the Apostles to the end of the world no strictly new truth can be added to the theological information which the apostles were inspired to deliver. It is possible of course to make numberless deductions from the original doctrines; but, as the conclusion is ever in its premises, such deductions are not, strictly speaking, an addition; and, though experience may variously guide and modify those deductions, still, on the whole, Theology retains the severe character of a science, advancing syllogistically from premises to conclusions. The method of Physics is just the reverse of this: it has hardly any principles or truths to start with, externally delivered and already ascertained. It has to commence with sight and touch; it has to handle, weigh, and measure its own exuberant *sylva* of phenomena, and from these to advance to new truths,—truths, that is, which are beyond and distinct from the phenomena from which they originate.[172]

The reasoning proper to the account of theology is deductive. But whether natural theology is restricted to deduction is not so clear. For the kind of theology Newman intends in this citation is clearly revealed.[173] In any case, if natural theology proceeds according to deductive reasoning, then the form of reasoning proper to natural theology is formal inference.

Among other things, formal inference means that reasoning assumes an explicit, public form of argumentation. By "inference" Newman means the "conditional acceptance of a proposition."[174] "Formal" denotes that reasoning proceeds by way of propositions logically linked from premise to conclusion. The archetype of this is the logical syllogism, but it can extend further. Newman explains.

> The first step in the inferential method is to throw the question to be decided into the form of a proposition; then to throw the proof itself into propositions, the force of the proof in the com-

---

172. *Idea*, 356.
173. *Idea*, 190.
174. *GA*, 169.

parison of these propositions with each other. When the analysis is carried out fully and put into form, it becomes the Aristotelic syllogism. However, an inference need not be expressed thus technically; an enthymeme fulfils the requirements of what I have called Inference. So does any other form of words with the mere grammatical expressions, "for," "therefore," "supposing," "so that," "similarly," and the like. Verbal reasoning, of whatever kind, as opposed to mental, is what I mean by inference, which differs from logic only inasmuch as logic is its scientific form.[175]

Formal inference, then, according to Newman's description, applies equally to induction and deduction. It does not matter whether reasoning begins by working upon disparate phenomena, struggling towards synthesis on the one hand, or moving from first principles by which multiple implications can be deduced on the other. Deduction assumes a first principle, a necessary premise from which other propositions then follow leading to a conclusion. Implications of the principle can then relate to different topics or subject matters depending on the range and depth of the principle assumed. For instance, to expand Newman's reference to geometry, all internal angles of a triangle always total 180°. It necessarily follows that no matter whether a triangle is right-angled or scalene or obtuse, however three straight lines are connected that produce three angles, the total will always be 180°. In this case, the principle is more than implied in the conclusion. Or consider a more theological example. If God creates, creation is the work of God. Any work, then, will show or disclose the handiwork of the creator. It follows, then, that God's imprint can be discerned in the meditation of any created reality, from the simple to the most complex structures. However imperfect or imprecise these analogies may be, they demonstrate an instance of deduction as formal inference. In either case, premises conditionally stand and logically cohere. The conditions Newman sets forth are therefore satisfied in either mode. Such is the kind of reasoning proper to natural theology.[176] But there is more.

The manner of reasoning tells upon the kinds of propositions involved. The issue of the kinds of propositions concerned in exercises of formal inference returns our inquiry to one of the essential differences between religion and theology: the difference between notional

175. Ibid., 171–72.
176. Cf. *Idea*, 191.

and real apprehension. "Apprehension," writes Newman, "is simply an intelligent acceptance of the idea, or of the fact which a proposition enunciates." It has "two subject-matters," namely, "things external to us, or our own thoughts, so is apprehension real or notional."[177] Notional and real apprehension are the two main ways of holding propositions. In practice, however, this distinction is not always so simple or consistent. It is possible that "the same proposition is to one man an image, to another a notion." One could have, in other words, a real apprehension of the proposition as referring to a concrete "thing" or an "image" and another as simply referring to an abstract idea or a notion not necessarily abstract but lacking the character of a real apprehension. Here lies the critical difference between theology and religion. Propositions can be real, notional or even both simultaneously depending upon the disposition of the person apprehending. Newman gives this example. "When Virgil says 'Varium et mutablile semper fœmina,' he both sets before his reader what he means to be a general truth, and at the same time applies it individually to the instance of Dido. He expresses at once a notion and a fact."[178] The statements of natural theology, similarly, can be appropriated in two ways: theologically or religiously. If religiously interpreted, recalling the operation and influence of conscience, propositions will possess a personal meaning and force irrespective of the idea's apparent vagueness or abstraction. But Newman is explicit concerning theology. "Theology," writes Newman, "properly and directly, deals with notional apprehension; religion with imaginative."[179] If propositions or statements involved in deductive reasoning, either as assumptions or conclusions, refer to "things" or "realities," real apprehension of the proposition is possible. Depending, therefore, upon the one following the argumentation of formal inference, the apprehension of propositions—even ones quite notional—can, on the whole, if appropriated and understood with a personal meaning, be subject legitimately to a real and religious apprehension. This is so because they refer to a reality already experienced and appropriated.[180] Newman maintains: "'There is a God', when really

---

177. GA, 20.

178. Ibid., 14.

179. Ibid., 82. "Imaginative" is another way Newman denotes "real."

180. There are, however, certain technical notions or, in a particular case, the whole complex of propositions of that denote the Trinity that Newman claims cannot be "the formal object of religious apprehension and assent; but as it is a number of propositions, taken one by one. That complex whole also is the object of assent, but it is the

apprehended, is the object of a strong energetic adhesion, which works a revolution in the mind; but when held merely as a notion, it requires but a cold and ineffective acceptance, though it be held ever so unconditionally. Such in its character is the assent of thousands, whose imaginations are not at all kindled, nor their hearts inflamed, nor their conduct affected, by the most august of all conceivable truths."[181] Abstract statements about God, in other words, can be apprehended by some as real if they convey an impressive force, work upon and through the conscience, and evoke a deep, individual, personal relation to God.[182] With the exception of complex wholes of abstract terms or propositions, it is not the character of the proposition taken singularly, such as "God is good," however that evokes the form of apprehension as real or notional. It is the prior experience and antecedent probabilities of the person *already* in relation to God. If this was not true, liturgical statements and creedal affirmations could only remain at the notional level and never become expressive of saving religious truth.[183] Such is the main difference between theology and religion more broadly and natural theology more narrowly.

In short, natural theology deals with apprehending notional propositions and religion with real. Because natural theology's method proceeds according to formal inference and deductive reasoning, theo-

---

notional object; and when presented to religious minds, it is received by them notionally." Ibid., 88. The issue becomes even more complicated, requiring further nuance. Not only can complex wholes not be the object of real assent or apprehension, but certain technical terms. This is because they are abstract terms such as "substance, essence, existence, form, subsistence, notion, circumincession; and, though these are far easier to understand than might at first sight be thought, still they are doubtless addressed to the intellect, and can only command a notional assent." Ibid., 87. In Newman's discussion of belief in the Trinity, however, a real assent is possible because the words "... Three, One, He, God, Father, Son, Spirit,—are none of them words peculiar to theology, have all a popular meaning, and are used according to that obvious and popular meaning, when introduced into the Catholic dogma ... There are then no terms in the foregoing exposition which do not admit of a plain sense, and they are there used in that sense; and, moreover, that sense is what I have called real, for the words in their ordinary use stand for things. The words, Father, Son, Spirit, He, One, and the rest, are not abstract terms, but concrete, and adapted to excite images." Ibid., 86–87.

181. Ibid., 86.

182. And here the effort to probe the real apprehension its possibility for theological statements means to move, at this point, into spiritual theology or what is commonly understood as "spirituality." An obvious instance of this is the Ignatian approach to biblical texts which invites the reader to discern God through reflective meditation and discernment of God within the person's emotional interiority.

183. Cf., Ibid., 90.

logical statements possess characteristics of notional propositions and, accordingly, correspond to the manner of their apprehension. These differences, in turn, would render certain theological propositions both real and notional simultaneously. These elements build to a third.

If deductive reasoning and the notional character of propositions are proper to natural theology, then taken together, its method is scientific. Certain conditions, put differently, requisite for Newman's understanding of a subject matter to be a science are fulfilled. And indeed, in the *Idea*, Newman describes natural theology as the "Science of God" or "science of religion" or simply as "science."[184] The question of how sciences can be considered in their relational character as abstractions or partial views and relate to knowledge has been considered already.[185] But how science operates specifically needs elaboration. The effort to understand something of the movement of science will disclose the general character of natural theology. Let us, then, repeat Newman's description of sciences and their functions. "They arrange and classify facts; they reduce separate phenomena under a common law; they trace effects to a cause. Thus they serve to transfer our knowledge from the custody of memory to the surer and more abiding protection of philosophy, thereby providing both for its spread and its advance:—for, inasmuch as sciences are forms of knowledge, they enable the intellect to master and increase it; and, inasmuch as they are instruments, to communicate it readily to others."[186] The activity and method corresponds to the method and character of natural theology outlined thus far. This can be illustrated by referring briefly to the previous discussion of natural religion.

Natural religion certainly arranges and classifies three different ways that human beings naturally know God. It also brings the different channels—conscience, the voice of mankind and the course of the world—under the common law of conscience. And finally, Newman shows how all the effects in each channel are ultimately traced to the operation of God within conscience. If this is true, what has been illustrated is not simply the scientific character of natural theology, but an instance of where Newman *performs* natural theology. The employment

---

184. *Idea*, 65; 33–34; 38; 50; 57; 58; 69–70; 91–92; See also the suppressed Discourse 5 of 1852, 419. As we shall see, Newman explicitly refers to dogmatic theology as "theological science." GA, 98f.

185. See above, pp. 111–16.

186. *Idea*, 53–54.

of deductive reasoning, the primacy of notional propositions, and the character of scientific method all mark Newman's discussion of natural religion. Such a discussion is, therefore, a concrete instance of natural theology and its method as Newman employs it in argument. Though the subject is religion, all of the conditions are satisfied that mark it as the "science of religion," and thus, natural theology. The discussion of religious topics in this manner, then, is also part of what distinguishes theology from religion.

There is no question that Newman includes dogmatic theology in the work of a Catholic University and as a legitimate academic discipline.[187] Yet several problems immediately confront its exposition in the context of university culture given in the *Idea*. Although Catholicism informs his interpretation, his formal consideration of university education prescinds from it. The subject matter, he insists repeatedly, develops philosophically and rationally. Further, unlike this exposition of natural theology in the *Idea*, Newman does not provide a clear, satisfactory account of dogmatic. This stems partly from his first principles but also because his "undertaking . . . has been of a preliminary nature." Consequently, "the characteristics of a University which is Catholic" are not developed.[188] How dogmatics relates to issues like the unity of science, university teaching and liberal knowledge as a whole, therefore, is not addressed in any detail. Insofar as intersections exist between them, they figure in the final discourse on university teaching.[189] There, Newman considers the issue of "Catholicity" in relation to university identity. Unfortunately, the content of this discourse is even more exploratory and ambiguously excursive. Its framework suggests but its fine points are few. Given these complications, therefore, I will clarify characteristics of dogmatic theology, its relation to the Church, and its joint influence within Newman's understanding of university education in a limited way. Issues pertaining to course instruction in theology and dogmatics shall be considered in a later section.

---

187. Newman wrote Archbishop Cullen about a list of professors. In this list, he mentions "dogmatic theology" among the disciplines. Newman to Archbishop Cullen, June 23, 1854. *Letters and Diaries of John Henry Newman*, 16:173. Cited hereafter *L&D*.

188. *Idea*, 183. For broad characteristics as to what a "Catholic University" might include, see Newman to Dalgarins 23 July 1852 and Newman to David Moriarty July 23, 1852, *L&D*, 15:129–37.

189. *Idea*, "Duties of the Church Toward Knowledge," 182–202.

Recalling the important contrast between religion and theology, Newman argues that religion regards a lived, felt relation to God. It "enlightens, terrifies, subdues; it gives faith, it inflicts remorse, it inspires resolutions, it draws tears, it inflames devotion."[190] The heart and mind, will and intellect, find integration in religious apprehension absent from the notional character of theologizing. Theology does not make this unique and existential claim upon the entire person, her thoughts, decisions or course of life. A correlative cluster of its characteristics include: deductive, rational, technical, notional, necessary, systematic, scientific and ecclesial. Since many already characterize natural theology, they do not bear repeating. But in its subject matter, practitioners and purpose, it evinces different and overlapping characteristics from those of natural theology.

First, what dogmatic professors do differs from teachers of natural theology. In speaking of the "duty of intellect" towards revelation, Newman illustrates not simply key elements of the discipline, but the theological method and activity of the dogmatic mind.

> It is ever active, inquisitive, penetrating; it examines doctrine and doctrine; it compares, contrasts, and forms them into a science; that science is theology. Now theological science, being thus the exercise of the intellect upon the *credenda* of revelation, is, though not directly devotional, at once natural, excellent, and necessary. It is natural, because the intellect is one of our highest faculties; excellent, because it is our duty to use our faculties to the full; necessary, because unless we apply our intellect to revealed truth rightly, others will exercise their minds upon it wrongly. Accordingly, the Catholic intellect makes a survey and a catalogue of the doctrines contained in the *depositum* of revelation, as committed to the Church's keeping; it locates, adjusts, defines them each, and brings them together into a whole. Moreover, it takes particular aspects or portions of them; it analyzes them, whether into first principles really such, or into hypotheses of an illustrated character. It forms generalizations, and gives names to them. All these deductions are true, if rightly deduced, because they are deduced from what is true; and therefore in one sense they are a portion of the *depositum* of faith or *credenda*, while in another sense they are additions to it; however, additions or not,

---

190. *Idea*, 160; see also 365; 413–14.

they have, I readily grant, the characteristic disadvantage of being abstract and notional statements.[191]

A short definition of dogmatic theology, then, is "the exercise of the intellect upon the *credenda* of revelation." One could abbreviate its method as to a "scientific analysis of all revealed truth."[192] In it, several aspects command attention. The philosophical and theological activity of the theologian employs rational operations when organizing and eliciting coherence from the revealed body of propositions. While not the sum total of her province, the accent lies on research, investigation, active inquiry, ecclesial commitments. Dogmatic theology, as we shall see, is actually the custodian of the *depositum* within the Church by virtue of its office.

Little in the foregoing description, however, tells how revealed doctrines in a dogmatic system bear upon other sciences. This is puzzling since Newman insists dogmatics and universities mutually implicate each other. For instance, in the ninth discourse, Newman binds Catholic identity and university together in a comprehensive description.

> If the Catholic Faith is true, a University cannot exist externally to the Catholic pale, for it cannot teach Universal Knowledge if it does not teach Catholic theology. This is certain; but still, though it had ever so many theological Chairs, that would not suffice to make it a Catholic University; for theology would be included in its teaching only as a branch of knowledge, only as one out of many constituent portions, however an important one, of what I have called Philosophy. Hence *a direct and active jurisdiction of the Church over it and in it is necessary*, lest it should become the rival of the Church with the community at large in *those theological matters which to the Church are exclusively committed*—acting as the representative of the intellect, as the Church is the representative of the religious principle.[193]

Unlike natural theology, the subject matter of dogmatics seems strictly doctrinal and ecclesial. Although Newman maintains only a preliminary and therefore general view of a Catholic university, it seems plain that dogmatic theology's work is ordered to the "the church's keeping."[194]

---

191. GA, 98–99.
192. *Essay on Development*, 336.
193. *Idea*, 184. Italics mine.
194. GA, 99.

Indeed, it requires safeguards of "a direct and active jurisdiction of the Church."[195] At the very minimum, Newman seems to view vertical and clerical oversight as welcome and necessary beyond the university rector's authority. This point is critical because "it is no sufficient security for the Catholicity of a University, even that the whole of Catholic theology should be professed in it, unless the church breathes her own pure and unearthly spirit into it, and fashions and moulds its organization, and watches over its teaching, and knits together its pupils, and superintends its action."[196] University science, however, falls outside this particular charge. Indeed, Newman asserts, "the Church has no call to watch over and protect Science."[197] Why? Perhaps the reason lies in dogmatic theology's responsibility for revealed truth. Not only is dogmatic theology by definition an ecclesial preserve, but it is also a discipline highly at risk that needs more than intellectual defenses. As he states, "the Church, as in duty bound, protects the sacred treasure which is in jeopardy."[198] This is precisely why Newman wants built-in checks against reason's tendency to rationalize and reduce.[199] "Ecclesiastical authority," not reason, writes Newman, is "its sole sanction."[200] The concern has merit. University education does incline the intellect to a certain egoism and idolatry, thereby making submission or obedience to higher truths of revelation problematic.[201]

THEOLOGY AND ECCLESIAL AUTHORITY

Yet these statements from 1852 suggest theology as something comfortably secured under juridical authority or at the behest of papal prerogative. But this is not what Newman thought a short time later. Indeed, it is misleading and erroneous to hold that Newman saw dogmatic theology

---

195. *Idea*, 184. It is interesting to note that Newman does not seem to involve the laity or the faculty in these matters concerning university theology. Only a few years later, he judged lay participation in the development of doctrine something quite important. See John Henry Newman, *On Consulting the Faithful in Matters of Doctrine*.

196. *Idea*, 185.

197. Ibid., 193.

198. Ibid., 187.

199. See Ibid., 185–87.

200. Ibid., 190.

201. "A University, as such, involves, as one of its necessary conditions, a risk to the faith of these or those members of it." John Henry Newman to J. Spencer Northcote, February 27, 1872, *L&D*, 26:34.

as inferior to ecclesiastical power or that papal authority enjoys privilege over individual conviction given in conscience.[202] These ideas, unfortunately, are not conveyed in Newman's statements above. Even so, though the intellect errs, obedience to conscience remains paramount.[203] As for theology, it actually shares jurisdiction with the juridical office in the church to which it is actually *superior*. Let us take it as the example.

Between *The Idea of the University* (1852) and his most mature ecclesiological work, the *Preface to the Third Edition* of the *Via Media* (1877), Newman's grew disillusioned about Roman juridical and papal power. His thinking builds to a different view than the one taken in the *Idea*.[204] In the *Preface to the Third Edition*, he posits "the doctrine of the triple of office of the Church" as prophetical, regal and sacerdotal.[205] Offices or functions are distinct and proper to each one. Each

202. For comments on the issue of conscience and papal or magisterial authority, see Newman, *Certain Difficulties Felt by Anglicans in Catholic Teaching*, 2:246–61. Cited as "*Diff.*"

203. Newman writes that "did the Pope speak against Conscience in the true sense of word, he would commit a suicidal act. He would be cutting the ground from under his feet." *Diff*, 2: 252.

204. It is not surprising that Newman changed his mind about the political influence of the Catholic hierarchy on theology and theologians. His experience with the Irish hierarchy during the period of the Catholic University in Ireland and his treatment by the English hierarchy over "The Rambler" controversy certainly paved the way for a sober assessment compared to a recent convert's enthusiasm for all things hierarchical. For the episode with the Irish hierarchy, see the "Memorandum about My Connection with the Catholic University," *Autobiographical Writings*, 280–333; 327; See also, Newman to James Hope-Scott, August 29, 1864, *L&D*, 21:212. For his involvement with "The Rambler," see Newman to Mrs. T. W. Allies January 20, 1864, *L&D*, 21:23 ; Newman to Miss E. Bowles May 19, 1863. Ward, 1:586–90. The famous last sentence of *On Consulting the Faithful in Matters of Doctrine* reads, "I think certainly that the *Ecclesia Docens* is more happy when she has such enthusiastic partisans about her as are here represented, than when she cuts off the faithful from the study of her divine doctrines and the sympathy of her divine contemplations, and requires from them a *fides implicita* in her word, which in the educated classes will terminate in indifference, and in the poorer in superstition." 106. Commenting on this passage, Sheridan Gilley gives further testimony to Newman's change of mind. "The concluding sentence was a brutal hit at the actual state of the Church in Latin countries for combining aristocratic indifference with popular superstition. Having been the champion of the revival of church authority, Newman sought to blunt the edge of Ultramontane hyper-clericalism, and as in the Church of England, he was to find himself the victim of the very authority which he had been exalting." *Newman and His Age*, 314. See also Ker, *John Henry Newman: A Biography*, 480–83.

205. "Christianity, then, is at once a philosophy, a political power, and a religious rite: as a religion, it is Holy; as a philosophy, it is Apostolic; as a political power, it is

enjoys relative autonomy and influence upon the others.[206] In a certain sense, together they serve as a mutual system of checks and balances.[207] "Truth," writes Newman, "is the guiding principle of theology and theological inquiries; devotion and edification, of worship, and of government, expedience."[208] Theologians hold the prophetical office—not the pope or bishops. Newman notes that in the course of church history "the Regal function of the Church, as represented by the Pope, seems to be trampling on the theological, as represented by Scripture and Antiquity." Indeed, in a backhanded praise of theologians and implicit swipe at ecclesiastical authority, he remarks that "ambition, craft, cruelty, and superstition are not commonly the characteristic of theologians . . ."[209] This is part of Newman's defense and attestation of the vital role of Theology and "the Schools of theology," what he refers to elsewhere as the "Schola Theologorum."[210] Much of Newman's reversal since writing the *Idea*, evidenced in the *Preface to the Third Edition*, can be seen in perhaps its most stunning passage.

> I say, then, Theology is the fundamental and regulating principle of the whole Church system. It is commensurate with Revelation, and Revelation is the initial and essential idea of Christianity. It is the subject-matter, the formal cause, the expression, of the Prophetical Office, and, as being such, has created both the Regal Office and the Sacerdotal. And it has in a certain sense a power of jurisdiction over those offices, as being its own creations, theologians being ever in request and in employment in keeping within bounds both the political and popular elements in the

---

imperial, that is, One and Catholic. As a religion, its special centre of action is pastor and flock; as a philosophy, the Schools; as a rule, the Papacy and its Curia." *VM*, 25.

206. "Each of the three has its separate scope and direction; each has its own interests to promote and further; each has to find room for the claims of the other two; and each will find its own line of action influenced and modified by the others; nay, sometimes in a particular case the necessity of the others converted into a rule of duty for itself." *VM*, 26.

207. Newman to Lord Blachford February 5, 1876, Ward, *Life of John Henry Cardinal Newman*, 2:374.

208. *VM*, 25.

209. Ibid., 29.

210. Ibid., 29; see also, Newman to Mr. Brownlow November 1, 1863, "By the Schola Theologorum is meant the teaching of theologians. It applies to all times, as the Fathers to the early times. We speak of the *consensus Patrum*—and so I spoke of the *unanimous* decision of the Schola." Ward, *The Life of John Henry Cardinal Newman*, 1: 653.

Church's constitution,—elements which are far more congenial than itself to the human mind, are far more liable to excess and corruption, and are ever struggling to liberate themselves from those restraints which are in truth necessary for their well-being. On the one hand Popes, such as Liberius, Vigilius, Boniface VIII, and Sixtus V, under secular inducements of the moment, seem from time to time to have been wishing, though unsuccessfully, to venture beyond the lines of theology; and on the other hand, private men of an intemperate devotion are from time to time forming associations, or predicting events, or imagining miracles, so unadvisedly as to call for the interference of the Index or Holy Office.[211]

This statement comes as a necessary re-affirmation and corrective to the excess of papal and curial influence.[212] Furthermore, the idea of a corrective is Newman's.[213] Just above this passage he states that "theology, so far from encouraging them [corruptions], has restrained and corrected such extravagances as have been committed, through human infirmity, in the exercise of the regal and sacerdotal powers; nor is religion ever in

---

211. *VM*, 29–30.

212. Critics of Newman's sweeping statement on theology often note that in the next paragraph Newman waters down his earlier statement. "Yet theology cannot always have its own way; it is too hard, too intellectual, too exact, to be always equitable, or to be always compassionate; and it sometimes has a conflict or overthrow, or has to consent to a truce or a compromise, in consequence of the rival force of religious sentiment or ecclesiastical interests; and that, sometimes in great matters, sometimes in unimportant." *VM*, 30. But Newman did not retract his comments about theology's "power of jurisdiction over those offices, as being its own creations." He simply maintains that for various external and pragmatic reasons, pastoral judgments of ecclesiastical authority or ministry sometimes need more weight. He does not deny but merely qualifies in the concrete instance what he lays down.

213. Explaining how the schools of theology carry out their work, Newman distinguishes different dimensions of the infallibility proper to the church. "Some power then is needed to determine the general sense of authoritative words—to determine their direction, drift, limits, and comprehension, to hinder gross perversions. This power is virtually the *passive infallibility* of the whole body of the Catholic people. The active infallibility lies in the Pope and Bishops—the passive in the 'universitas' of the faithful ... Here on the one hand I observe that a *local* sense of a doctrine, held in this or that country, is not a 'sensus universitatis,' and on the other hand the schola theologorum is one chief portion of that universitas—and it acts with great force both in correcting popular misapprehensions and narrow views of the teaching of the active infallibilitas, and, by the intellectual investigations and disputes which are its very life, it keeps the distinction clear between theological truth and theological opinion, and is the antagonist of dogmatism." Italics his. Newman to Miss Froude July 28, 1875. *L&D* 26:337–38.

greater danger than when in consequence of national or international troubles, the Schools of theology have been broken up and ceased to be."[214] In his judgment, this is what had happened—theology had been weakened.[215] Three years earlier, Newman remarked: "Just now, as I suppose at many other times the devotional sentiment, and the political embarrass the philosophical instinct—however, she [the church] has been prospered and has made way, in spite of this, for 1800 years and will still."[216] In this respect, the inclusion of the popes is deliberate. One year prior to writing the Preface, Newman soberly observed the lack of theological competence in Pius IX.[217] Here, even though in the *Idea* Newman held that juridical authority was theology's "sole sanction," he changed his mind. The prophetical office of Theology does not really refer to the pope or the bishops whose proper office in the church concerns governance, rule, polity—the regal or kingly function.[218] In fact, in his fine study of Newman and papal primacy, Paul Misner observes: "It

---

214. *VM*, 29.

215. "This age of the Church is peculiar,—in former times, primitive or medieval, there was not the extreme centralization which now is in use. If a private theologian said anything free, another answered him. If the controversy grew, then it went to a Bishop, a theological faculty, or to some foreign University. The Holy See was but the court of ultimate appeal. *Now*, if I, as a private priest, put anything into print, *Propaganda* answers me at once. How can I fight with such a chain on my arm? It is like the Persians driven to fight *under the lash*. There was true private judgment in the primitive and medieval schools,—there are no schools now, no private judgment (in the *religious sense* of the phrase), no freedom, that is, of opinion. That is, no exercise of intellect." Newman to Miss E. Bowles May 19, 1863. *L&D*, 20:447.

216. Newman to Lord Blachford June 3, 1874. *L&D*, 27:70.

217. "I think, when you were here last, I said to you our great want just now was theological schools, which the great French Revolution has destroyed. This had been the occasion of our late and present internal troubles. Where would Ward have been, if there had been theological schools in England? Again, the Archbishop is not a theologian, and, what is worse, the Pope is not a theologian, and so theology has gone out of fashion." Newman to Lord Blachford February 5, 1876, cited in Ward, 2:374. Six years earlier we find even more evidence of Newman's dissatisfaction with the "Regal office." He had this to say about the pope and infallibility: "I have no hesitation in saying that, to all appearance, Pius IX wished to say a great deal more, (that is that the Council should say a great deal more) than it did, but a greater Power hindered it. A pope is not *inspired*; he has no inherent gift of divine knowledge, but when he speaks ex Cathedrâ, he may say little or much, but he is simply protected from saying what is untrue. I know you will find flatterers and partizani, such as those whom St. Francis de Sales calls 'the Pope's lackies,' who say much more than this, but they may enjoy their own opinion, they cannot bind the faith of Catholics." Newman to Mrs. Froude, March 5, 1871, *L&D* 25:299.

218. *VM*, 25.

is striking how Newman consistently aligns the prophetical or teaching office with "the schools," or "theology," and not with the official *magisterium* of the pope and bishops."[219] Theology's "prophetical office" and prerogative fall to theologians, the very people who, in large part, would be university teachers.

In light of his later thinking, then, Newman charges the work of dogmatics, those responsible for the *depositum fidei*, to a specialized group of theologians who interpret it.[220] An interesting insight into the character of this comes from a description of reason in dogmatic reflection. It reveals an adaptation of Anselm's famous theological definition of "*fides quaerens intellectum.*" "Reason . . . is subservient to faith, as handling, examining, explaining, recording, cataloguing, defending, the truths which faith, not reason, has gained for us, as providing an intellectual expression of supernatural facts, eliciting what is implicit, comparing, measuring, connecting each with each, and forming one and all into a theological system."[221] Here is yet another complexity. This description of reason exceeds catechetical exposition. Its practice and goal press beyond what passes for a university field of knowledge whose character, unlike those of academies or seminaries, is "the diffusion and extension of knowledge rather than the advancement."[222] Dogmatic, rational reflection, quite the contrary, highlights precisely its advancement. It seems to be a graduate and research field.

This task, however, demands satisfaction of certain conditions. In some sense, the mysteries themselves move and affect the apprehension of the dogmatic theologian, assisting in the interpretation and exposition of dogmatic meaning.[223] Those engaged in dogmatic theology possess graced vocations to the work and religious, ecclesial commitments. Another important condition is an advanced understanding of doctrine that, in turn, entails a solid grasp of heresy. For Newman, this means that

---

219. Paul Misner, *Papacy and Development*, 165.

220. In his letter to Norfolk, Newman writes that "theology is a science, and a science of a special kind; its reasoning, its method, its modes of expression, and its language are all its own. Every science must be in the hands of a comparatively few persons—that is, of those who have made it a study . . . young theologians, and still more those who are none, are sure to mistake in matters of detail; indeed a really first-rate theologian is rarely to be found." *Diff*, 2:294.

221. *Essay on Development*, 336.

222. *Idea*, 5.

223. *GA*, 87.

dogmatics presumes familiarity with forms of argumentation ancillary to theological reflection itself—polemics. Polemics helps establish doctrinal meaning and content. It is an integral component to the dogmatic enterprise because "the disavowal of error is far more fruitful in additions than the enforcement of truth."[224] Arguments and issues raised by propositions contradicting accepted, revealed dogmas force theological reasoning to probe the *credenda* of revelation more deeply as it refutes errors. And refutation of error is an object of faith—the rejection of falsehood.[225] Newman recognizes the possibility of fallible minds to err while affirming the right and duty of theologians to employ necessary, salutary correctives. In an important sense, then, heresy comprises part of the natural development of doctrine and theological inquiry. This is part of what Newman means by "additions."

Positively, a good example of "additions" concerns the acceptance of the scientific term "Consubstantial" into the Nicene Creed. At the time of the Council, since it lacked exact scriptural parallel and religious precedent, its insertion occasioned doubt and dispute. The term, according to Newman, "means nothing more than 'really one with the Father.'"[226] As such, the technical word found its way into the *credenda* of revelation because the Council desired to refute the Arian attack on Christ's divinity. Though alien to "rudimental facts of Christianity," it gained acceptance because it did not contradict but gave precision to revealed meaning.[227] Thus "Consubstantial," for Newman, remains part of "a large and ever-increasing collection of propositions, abstract notions, not concrete truths" that "become, by the successive definitions of Councils, a portion of the *credenda*, and have an imperative claim upon the faith of every Catholic."[228]

For Newman, the deductions and comparisons of doctrinal propositions, for example those of the Trinity, also manifest a certain reverence and responsibility absent from natural theology. One could call it the dogmatic disposition. It is the desire to understand divine truth. Newman indicates, however, that this desire differs greatly from intellectual excellence that marks, for example, liberally educated minds (topics

---

224. Ibid., 99; see also *US*, 54–55.
225. *GA*, 100.
226. Ibid., 97.
227. Ibid.
228. Ibid.

we will explore subsequently). "The first step in theology is investigation, an investigation arising out of the lively interest and devout welcome which the matters investigated claim of us; and, if Scripture teaches us the duty of faith, it teaches quite as distinctly that loving inquisitiveness which is the life of the *Schola*."[229] This remark suggests a specialized and professional undertaking. Intellectual gifts alone are inadequate for dogmatic theology. This "loving inquisitiveness," a faithful and believing disposition alive to God's presence, binds the intellect and will together in ways strict intellectual excellence does not.[230] An affective-intellectual disposition, therefore, conditions dogmatic pursuits despite the notional character of theological reflection. Of instructors and students, therefore, dogmatics demands a prior assent of faith.

Regarding the serious content of dogmatics, its audience does not seem to be students engaged in cultivating philosophical habits of mind. Despite decisions concerning course content in undergraduate liberal education, Newman holds that dogmatics is a field of propositional statements and thought "more or less unintelligible to the ordinary Catholic."[231] This raises a question: what precisely are doctrinal or dogmatic propositions inaccessible to the "ordinary Catholic"? Newman states:

> Theological dogmas are propositions expressive of the judgments which the mind forms, or the impressions which it receives, of Revealed Truth. Revelation sets before it certain supernatural facts and actions, beings and principles; these make a certain impression of image upon it; and this impression spontaneously, or even necessarily, becomes the subject of reflection on the part of the mind itself, which proceeds to investigate it, and to draw it forth in successive and distinct sentences. Thus the Catholic doctrine of Original Sin, or of Sin after Baptism, or of the Eucharist, or of Justification, is but the expression of the inward belief of Catholics on these several points, formed upon an analysis of that belief.[232]

The subject matter of dogmatic theology is creedal statements as revealed and accepted. These are appropriated by theologians, given technical

---

229. *Essay on Development*, 337.

230. For the modern estrangement between mind and heart, see Newman's sermon, "Intellect, The Instrument of Religious Training," *Sermons Preached on Various Occasions*, 1–14.

231. *GA*, 99.

232. *US*, 216.

precision and largely adumbrated in catechisms since most Catholics do not read dogmatic tracts.[233] Since dogmatics abides in a university setting, one wonders whether its content extends beyond catechetical treatment. To answer this more fully, however, we must address the issue of theology's place in a university.

---

233. Cf., *GA*, 87.

4

John Henry Newman—Theology in the University

> ... only when one begins to ask about asking itself, and to think about thinking itself, only when one turns his attention to the scope of knowledge and not only to the objects of knowledge, to transcendence and not only to what is understood categorically in time and space within this transcendence, only then is one just on the threshold of becoming a religious person.
>
> —Karl Rahner

I HAVE EXPLORED NEWMAN's understanding of theology as a science and knowledge in terms of its possibility and nature. Primarily internal, these aspects designate theology as a legitimate, serious intellectual discipline. The aspects of possibility and nature also mark theology's method and subject matter. The question of setting or place, however, extends the inquiry beyond simply elemental coordinates. Location poses the problem of purpose and meaning pertaining to liberal education or, more generally, university education. Newman's idea of liberal knowledge incorporates theology as essential. It is not the whole, but a component. Context accounts not simply for the characteristics of theology as such within an academic environment, but also tells upon the nature and purpose of what universities accomplish. This is critically important.

The arguments advanced to understand theology's place in the university run along parallel lines. Hitherto, I have considered Newman's argument for theology as an academic endeavor. A university must profess it in order to be what it claims, namely, a teacher of universal knowledge. For this, Newman proposes several factors that concern the relation of theology to other sciences and how different sciences bear upon or influence theology. But another set of reasons obtain for theology's inclusion. These reasons diverge from questions about its status as academically legitimate or its authority to exclusively interpret its subject matter. These reasons concern how theology fits into Newman's theory of university learning and knowledge, how it actually informs and determines the general aim of university education. Consider the context from which theology takes its character.

> Among the objects of human enterprise ... none higher or nobler can be named than that which is contemplated in the erection of a University ... it professes to teach whatever has to be taught in any whatever department of human knowledge, and it embraces in its scope the loftiest subjects of human thought, and the richest fields of human inquiry. Nothing is too vast, nothing too subtle, nothing too distant, nothing too minute, nothing too discursive, nothing to exact, to engage its attention ... My reason for speaking of a University in the terms on which I have ventured is, not that it occupies the whole territory of knowledge merely, but that it is the very realm; that it professes much more than to take in and to lodge as in a caravanserai all art and science, all history and philosophy. In truth, it professes to assign to each study, which it receives, its own proper place and its just boundaries; to define the rights, to establish the mutual relations, and to effect the intercommunion of one and all; to keep in check the ambitious and encroaching, and to succour and maintain those which from time to time are succumbing under the more popular or the more fortunately circumstanced; to keep the peace between them all, and to convert their mutual differences and contrarieties into the common good ... Thus to draw many things into one, is its special function; and it learns to do it, not by rules reducible to writing, but by sagacity, wisdom, forbearance, acting upon a profound insight into the subject-matter of knowledge, and by a vigilant repression of aggression or bigotry in any quarter.[1]

It would be difficult to find a richer, more suggestive illustration regarding the character and responsibility a university upholds towards scientific knowledge. This view of the university also determines the meaning of theology in a distinct way—how it issues and influences the formation of what it means to possess an "imperial intellect."[2] This is the formative, ideal target at which liberal arts aim. But theology serves a vital role in the philosophical formation of the intellect. In Newman's conception of a university, it must not be conflated, then, with a research discipline, a

---

1. *Idea*, 368–69.
2. Ibid., 371.

quantity of "learning," or set a of mental techniques. It surpasses each. Theology's university character differs from the one it may take in other institutions like Academies.³ At the same time, theology is something eminently teachable and capable of contributing to the "realm" of knowledge. Ultimately, it aids and influences the intellect's trajectory toward a kind of transcendence.

It is not, however, a transcendence that occurs in a Christian apostolate or a mission or a catechesis. It does not radiate those attributes particular to what passes for theology in monasteries or retreat centers. Similarly, one finds it not precisely in the occupations of the world, those of the servile arts and labor. Finally and perhaps most significantly, this specific transcendence remains external—though not inimical—to the seminary.⁴ All have their proper contexts and particular dynamics that qualify transcendence, and thus, differ from that of the university. For if universities are not seminaries—despite however close and important their ecclesial ties may be—the way theology teaches, the perspective in which students hold its subject matter, and the manner in which they pose essential questions will also differ. Let me turn, then, to key presuppositions and ideas concerning theology's academic context. The grasp of Newman's view, then, requires an investigation of three areas: (1) the nature of liberal knowledge as philosophical; (2) theology as servant and type of contemplation; and (3) the character of theology within a curriculum of studies.

LIBERAL (PHILOSOPHICAL) KNOWLEDGE: TOWARDS INTELLECTUAL CONTEMPLATION

Abstractly for Newman, knowledge can be viewed from two perspectives, philosophically or mechanically: "the end of the one is to be philosophical, of the other to be mechanical." One means liberal, the other "useful."⁵ Moreover, the philosophical concerns "neither moral impression nor

---

3. Cf. ibid., 6–8.

4. On the difference between universities and seminaries, Newman could not be more emphatic. "No two institutions are more distinct from each other in character, than Universities and Seminaries; and their very difference might seem a pledge that they would not come into collision with each other. Seminaries are for the education of the clergy; Universities for the education of laymen. They are for separate purposes, and they act in separate spheres; yet, such is human infirmity, perhaps they ever will be rivals in their actual working." Newman, *Historical Sketches*, 3: 240; Cf., *Idea*, 197; 248.

5. *Idea*, 104–5.

mechanical production." Put differently, liberal knowledge comprises neither "art" nor "duty."[6] University education may contribute or relate to these but the liberal knowledge it seeks to cultivate in its students prescinds from them. In other words, for Newman, liberal knowledge does not understand the meaning of enlargement of mind as a precondition for simply professional application or "acquirement." This knowledge is not concerned with orienting students toward practical pursuits or teaching information as if their minds are capacious depositories.

As liberal knowledge does not concern professional training or applied skills, neither does it directly involve "duty."[7] Beginning the discourses, Newman plainly states that the university's object is "not moral."[8] Knowledge does not generate virtue.[9] While certainly not hostile to morality, universities are still not its prime teachers or instruments. "I consider," writes Newman, "that intrinsically excellent and noble as are scientific pursuits, and worthy of a place in a liberal education, and fruitful in temporal benefits to the community, still they are not, and cannot be, *the instrument* of an ethical training."[10] Moral formation is not the university's direct charge. Newman insists that department lies elsewhere as the purpose of the college. Newman states:

> [A] College is the scene of order, of obedience, of modest and persevering diligence, of conscientious fulfilment of duty, of mutual private services, and deep and lasting attachments . . . and . . . for the catechetical lecture. The University is for theology, law, and medicine, for natural history, for physical science, and for the sciences generally and their promulgation; the College is for the formation of character, intellectual and moral, for the cultivation of the mind, for the improvement of the individual, for the study of literature, for the classics, and those rudimental sciences which strengthen and sharpen the intellect.[11]

6. Ibid., 114.

7. For more on Newman's understanding of "duty," see *GA*, 73–74; *US*, 101–13.

8. *Idea*, 5.

9. See especially, "Tamworth Reading Room," 254–305. Cited hereafter as *TR*.

10. *TR*, 304. Italics his.

11. Newman, *Rise and Progress of Universities* in *Historical Sketches*, 3:228–29. See also Newman's Sermon "Intellect, the Instrument of Religious Training," *Sermons Preached On Various Occasions*, 1–14. Newman distinguishes the university proper and its object from that of the college but they certainly form part of the larger educational enterprise. For the Catholic University of Ireland, according to Colin Barr, Newman took Oxford's colleges as the model for student residential life. *Paul Cullen, John Henry Newman, and the Catholic University of Ireland, 1845–1865*, 146.

The object of the college differs in kind from that of the university that concerns the formation of "intellect" and its "philosophical reach of mind."[12]

In many ways, the discourses treating of knowledge and its character represent the heart of Newman's argument for liberal education. The aspect under which Newman examines it—and theology by implication—is "utility."[13] When Newman disclaims utility in matters of liberal knowledge, he does not mean "without use." He elevates the level of inquiry and its subject matter beyond the realm of reason as instrument to reason as intellect or power. The intellect's most proper term embraces utility but, as we shall see, transcends it in the form of "enjoyment." Intellectual activity and its possession of the known already imply a more profound relationship. For what liberal knowledge achieves insofar as receptive students allow, and before an explicit relationship with revelation, is both a cultivated talent and an activity. It is both a mental state and a rational operation. These realities are subsumed by the term "philosophical habit."[14] Yet, what does this mean?

Newman inscribes his view of liberal knowledge with an axiom: "the end cannot be divided from that knowledge itself." Philosophical habit reaches completion in its end, in knowledge. Put differently, "knowledge . . . is its own reward." The principle applies to particular sciences but also to the more general object of liberal knowledge and the meaning of "university" in its profound richness. Liberal knowledge entails not simply an intellectual enjoyment of the particular, although this ought to occur, rather, it is "a comprehensive view of truth in all its branches, of the relations of science to science, of their mutual bearings, and their respective values."[15] This grasp of the whole comprises the rational activity of comparing, seeing connections, noting relative drifts and implications of meaning. Neither the intellects' activity nor its attendant delight signifies

---

12. Newman holds that "intellect, too, I repeat has its beauty, and it has those who aim at it. To open the mind, to correct it, to refine it, to enable it to know, and to digest, master, rule, and use its knowledge, to give it power over its own faculties, application, flexibility, method, critical exactness, sagacity, resource, address, eloquent expression, is an object as intelligible . . . I say, an object as intelligible as the cultivation of virtue, while, at the same time, it is absolutely distinct from it." *Idea*, 112, 135.

13. Ibid., 96.

14. Ibid.

15. Ibid., 97.

a static experience.[16] Further, philosophical habit by definition indicates the ability to repeat and expand intellectual activity as it assimilates new knowledge.[17] The experience must be recurrent. It also encompasses a certain sensitivity and openness to change, to flux, to alternation. Still, why is it necessary? Newman points to the trajectory of human nature.

> That further advantages accrue to us and redound to others by its possession, over and above what it is in itself, I am very far indeed from denying; but, independent of these, we are satisfying a direct need of our nature in its very acquisition; and, whereas our nature, unlike that of the inferior creation, does not at once reach its perfection but depends, in order to it, on a number of external aids and appliances, Knowledge, as one of the principal of these, is valuable for what its very presence in us does for us after the manner of a habit, even though it be turned to no further account, nor subserve any direct end.[18]

Liberal knowledge, then, indicates neither a decorative quality nor a symbol of social status quasi-caricatured as a gentleman's qualities.[19] It is more. Knowledge as an end helps direct human beings to a more profound understanding of their identity. The impulse of human nature toward it involves a transformation, an enlargement of mind that develops the habit. In pursuing liberal knowledge, levels of the human condition are disclosed in and through these philosophical habits. If Newman's position is true, what sort of need underlies it?

First, human nature supplies the need, not convention or artifice. Paraphrasing Cicero, Newman maintains "Knowledge" is "the very first object to which we are attracted, after the supply of our physical wants."

---

16. Examples Newman employs to illustrate an "enlargement of mind" show otherwise. Also, see ibid., 118f.

17. "For instance, let a person, whose experience has hitherto been confined to the more calm and unpretending scenery of these islands, whether here or in England, go for the first time into parts where physical nature puts on her wilder and more awful forms, whether at home or abroad, as into mountainous districts; or let one, who has ever lived in a quiet village, go for the first time to a great metropolis,—then I suppose he will have a sensation which perhaps he never had before. He has a feeling not in addition or increase of former feelings, but of something different in its nature. He will perhaps be borne forward, and find for a time that he has lost his bearings. He has made a certain progress, and he has a consciousness of mental enlargement; he does not stand where he did, he has a new centre, and a range of thoughts to which he was before a stranger." Ibid., 118.

18. Ibid., 97–98.

19. Ibid., 6.

This manifests a natural, intellectual drive, precisely "the search after truth." This is because "as soon as we escape from the pressure of necessary cares, forthwith we desire to see, to hear, and to learn; and consider the knowledge of what is hidden or is wonderful a condition of our happiness."[20] Liberal knowledge, in short, contributes to and constitutes to a large degree the content of a life well lived—the happy life. In the context of liberal education, Newman draws attention to how human intelligence contributes to its attainment.

One necessary condition for forming the philosophical habit in relation to the character of theology is the quality and nature of time spent. Newman describes not a practical or servile time, nor posits an artistic or an athletic time. It is an older and richer understanding. As Josef Pieper reminds us, "The Greek word for leisure (σκολη) is the origin of the Latin *scola*, German *Schule*, English *school*. The name for the institutions of education and learning mean "leisure"."[21] Enlargement of mind and leisure enjoy a long relationship. If we interpret the previous citation of Cicero seriously, Newman holds leisure as a critical condition of genuine philosophizing or enlargement. This principle, however, operates implicitly in Newman's understanding of university culture. Its clearest emergence occurs when he distinguishes two kinds of education.

> [I]f I must determine which of the two courses was the more successful in training, moulding, enlarging the mind, which sent out men the more fitted for their secular duties, which produced better public men, men of the world, men whose names would descend to posterity, I have no hesitation in giving the preference to that University which did nothing, over that which exacted of its members an acquaintance with every science under the sun ... How is this to be explained? ... When a multitude of young men, keen, open-hearted, sympathetic, and observant, as young men are, come together and freely mix with each other, they are sure to learn one from another, even if there be no one to teach them; the conversation of all is a series of lectures to each, and they gain for themselves new ideas and views, fresh matter of thought, and distinct principles for judging and acting, day by day.[22]

20. Ibid., 98.
21. Pieper, *Leisure: The Basis of Culture*, 3–4.
22. *Idea*, 129–30. Here there is, in some way, a striking parallel between what Newman proposes as a possibility and Augustine attempted in practice: a group of people living together for contemplative leisure. Though Augustine's project failed, his

The essential condition of leisure as a time of serious reflection, growth, and enlargement of mind figures importantly. So also, as noted in this excerpt, is the importance of dialectic. Though embracing moments of solitary reflection and study, leisure as a quality of time is not defined by it—conversation, the exchange of ideas, communication is. Moreover, the effort to bring students or young adults together evinces a distinct, elevated endeavor.[23] Leisure differs in kind and degree from entertainment, labor, and especially from "recreations." Newman writes: "Recreations are not education; accomplishments are not education. Do not say, the people must be educated, when, after all, you only mean, amused, refreshed, soothed, put into good spirits and good humour, or kept from vicious excesses ... Stuffing birds or playing stringed instruments is an elegant pastime, and a resource to the idle, but it is not education; it does not form or cultivate the intellect."[24] Leisure enables genuine education and counters the unreflective. It serves to engage and attune the person to a deeper sense and appreciation of reality. Leisure is an earnest time for the mind "to grasp things as they are."[25] It represents and discloses a deeper meaning to "rest," to study, to reason. Its principle and purpose aims at something more individual and philosophic. Leisure, then, conditions a duration of enjoying knowledge, reasoning upon it, synthesizing its dissonant and coordinate features, defining meaningful categories and terms.

Though Newman privileges priority of mind, of enlargement and how university sciences form it, he does not mean, in the stricter sense, this illumination as somehow essentially quantitative. In his judgment, this view was "the practical error of the last twenty years" in British university education. The problem is "not to load the memory of the student with a mass of undigested knowledge, but to force upon him so much that he has rejected all. It has been the error of distracting and enfeebling the mind by an unmeaning profusion of subjects; of implying that a smattering in a dozen branches of study is not shallowness, which

---

remarks strikingly parallel Newman's. "Among our group of friends we had had animated discussions of a project: talking with one another we expressed detestation for the storms and troubles of human life, and had almost decided on withdrawing from the crowds and living a life of contemplation. This contemplative leisure we proposed to organize in the following way ..." *Confessions*, 108.

23. Cf. *Idea*, 149.
24. Ibid., 128.
25. Ibid., 400.

it really is, but enlargement, which it is not."[26] Expansion of mind is not plenitude but empowerment.

Newman addresses empowerment when he refers to the meaning of learning as "acquirements."[27] He states, "this notion is, I conceive, a mistake . . . the end of a Liberal Education is not mere knowledge, or knowledge considered in its *matter*."[28] Earnest and attentive conversation by itself can effect and develop illuminative reasoning. It is true, however, that enlargement presupposes possession of some content. But the university sciences: geology, history, physics, music, chemistry—all of these and more are, for Newman, viewed by students in their "great outlines of knowledge, the principles on which it rests, the scale of its parts, its lights and its shades, its great points and its little."[29] Form figures more than detail. Furthermore, content really "is not the whole of the process."

> The enlargement consists, not merely in the passive reception into the mind of a number of ideas hitherto unknown to it, but *the mind's energetic and simultaneous action upon and towards and among those new ideas, which are rushing in upon it. It is the action of a formative power, reducing to order and meaning the matter of our acquirements*; it is a making the objects of our knowledge subjectively our own, or, to use a familiar word, it is a digestion of what we receive, into the substance of our previous state of thought; and without this no enlargement is said to follow.[30]

---

26. Ibid., 127. The parallel here with Nietzsche is striking. Nietzsche similarly disparaged the deleterious excess of historical knowledge upon life, German culture, and especially its youth. "The education of German youth, however, proceeds precisely from this false and unfruitful concept of culture: its aim, quite purely and loftily conceived, is not at all the liberally educated man but the scholar, the scientific man, namely, the scientific man who will be useful as soon as possible, who takes a position outside of life in order to know it quite clearly; its result, viewed in a mean empirical way, is the historico-aesthetic cultural Philistine, the precocious newly wise chatter box on matters of state, church and art, the sensorium of thousands of sensations, the insatiable stomach which yet does not know what honest hunger and thirst are." *On the Advantage and Disadvantage of History for Life*, 59–60.

27. Cf. *Idea*, 115–16.

28. Ibid., 117.

29. Ibid., 96.

30. Ibid., 120. Italics mine.

Newman describes not only a state of mind but also a habit, an activity, a "philosophical process" upon the subjects that engage it.[31] A coincidence of taking and receiving, a vigorous dialectic—analogous to conversation—means that the mind's illumination from liberal knowledge cannot be sterile or superficial if it is genuinely liberal.[32] The known and the knower are, to expand the implications of Newman's physical metaphor, becoming something together—transforming data or material or information through a power to change the being of the knower. "When, then, we speak of the communication of Knowledge as being Education, we thereby really imply that the Knowledge is a state or condition of mind."[33] The faculties, the capacities of knowing and reasoning are more important than the content. "There is no enlargement," states Newman, "unless there be a comparison of ideas with one another, as they come before the mind, and a systematizing of them. We feel our minds to be growing and expanding *then*, when we not only learn, but refer what we learn to what we know already."[34] Intellectual illumination does not simply develop reason—it transforms the knower.

Something more, however difficult to describe concretely, changes and guides a cultivated intellect. Cultivated rational powers possess qualities and tendencies, for example, the ability to view relationships between subjects or contrast conclusions and principles to a greater degree than illiberal ones. A businessman liberally educated, for instance, not only sees the implications of fiscal policy proper to his own specialty, but enjoys the capacity to see its implications in the spheres of earth science, sociology, perhaps even the fine arts. In other words, such a person "is above" her knowledge. This principle also affects academic and professional knowledge. For each area, in its own way, tends to contract and oppose precisely the "special illumination and largeness of mind and freedom and self-possession" that liberal knowledge effects.[35]

---

31. Ibid., 104.

32. "[K]nowledge," states Newman, "is something more than a sort of passive reception of scraps and details; it is a something, and it does a something." Ibid., 131.

33. Ibid., 105.

34. Ibid., 120–21. Italics his. "I readily grant, that the cultivation of the 'understanding,' of a 'talent for speculation and original inquiry,' and of 'the habit of pushing things up to their first principles,' is a principal portion of a *good* or *liberal* education" (143).

35. *Idea*, 146.

Minds so developed and thereafter employed in particular pursuits perform better because, qualitatively, they are better. For Newman, this is true because "general culture of mind is the best aid to professional and scientific studies, and educated men can do what illiterate cannot." Though general cultivation fits no one exactly for one specific occupation, nonetheless, it "will be placed in that state of intellect in which he can take up any of the science or callings I have referred to, or any other for which he has a taste or special talent, with an ease, a grace, a versatility, and a success, to which another is a stranger."[36] An enlarged mind sees more, compares more, judges relations with superior insight. The liberally educated are more apt to be people of vision and of leadership, ultimately either to virtue or vice.

Philosophical habit fosters powers of discrimination and comparison. Judgment, then, as principle and activity helps shape, determine, and estimate genuine meaning and value, truth and falsity, beauty, goodness. It augments the meaning of an "imperial intellect" significantly.[37] That the building blocks of such a liberally educated mind presuppose it, that contemplation elevates it, and that living hones it, allows Newman's understanding to evoke a certain intellectual transcendence and religiosity concerning it.

Newman furnishes a modified argument about the nature and aims of liberal education as the contemplative life—the life of excellence. Since the Pre-Socratic philosophers, the term "contemplation" has enjoyed a depth and range of meaning in philosophy, theology, mysticism and spirituality. Etymologically, the Latin term "*contemplatio*" derives from *tempus* marking a sacred space and time for a seer to observe omens and make divinations. It is interesting to note that the Greek origin of the word "contemplation" is the term, *theoria*, meaning to see, inspect, meditate, philosophize. Its roots join God (θεό) and sight (θέα) together. "Theory" and "theoretical" are common derivatives.[38] Newman does not elaborate a theory of contemplation. He implies a type. On this

36. Ibid., 145.

37. For two fine studies on this notion, see Culler, *Imperial Intellect*; Vargish, *Newman: The Contemplation of Mind*.

38. See "Contemplation," *Dictionnaire de spiritualité ascétique et mystique*, 2:1643–2193, but especially "*Contemplation Chez Les Grecs Et Autres Orientaux Chrétiens*," by J. Lemaitre, 1762–871; J. Aumann, "Contemplation," *New Catholic Encyclopedia*, 4:258–63; see also, McGinn, *Foundations of Mysticism*, 23–61 ; C. Jones et al., *Study of Spirituality*.

point, a remarkable passage in *The Idea of a University* repays attention. Recapitulating ideas on liberal education, he states:

> All that I have been now saying is summed up in a few characteristic words of the great Philosopher. "Of possessions," he says, "those rather are useful, which bear fruit; those *liberal, which tend to enjoyment*. By fruitful, I mean, which yield revenue; by enjoyable, where *nothing accrues of consequence beyond the using*." ... While the world lasts, will Aristotle's doctrine on these matters last, for he is the oracle of nature and of truth. While we are men, we cannot help, to a great extent, being Aristotelians, for the great Master does but analyze the thoughts, feelings, views, and opinions of human kind. He has told us the meaning of our own words and ideas, before we were born. In many subject matters, to think correctly, is to think like Aristotle; and we are his disciples whether we will or no, though we may not know it.[39]

This reverent affirmation is more than epideictic rhetoric. Aristotle furnishes the deeper, philosophical reservoir of Newman's first principles concerning reason, liberal knowledge, and the profound aim of a university considered theoretically: to cultivate the human mind towards a "philosophy of mind" or "imperial intellect." Aristotle's ideas also permeate Newman's eclectic and implicit understanding of contemplation.

In the *Nichomachean Ethics*, Aristotle argues a teleological view of human nature. Human beings move toward an end that reflects purpose and meaning. This goal, that for sake of which everything is done, is happiness—the highest good and final end. Happiness remains an activity sought for its own sake and, thus, it lacks nothing—it is complete in itself. Its achievement satisfies human beings. But it is not a notion that admits deeply divergent and subjective preferences concerning basic principles. Aristotle's view of happiness excludes elements commonly thought fundamental to living well such as "amusements," or diversions—forms of pleasure—power, wealth, honor. He rejects these in part because they fail to realize in the highest degree what constitutes the human "function," namely, "an activity of the soul conforming with

---

39. *Idea*, 102. Italics his. Also, cf. 219. The basic distinction between use and enjoyment in terms of knowledge was a theme treated by Augustine. "So, then, there are some things which are meant to be enjoyed, others which are meant to be used, yet other which do both the enjoying and the using. Things that are to be enjoyed make us happy; things which are to be used help us on our way to happiness, providing us, so to say, with crutches and props for reaching the things that will make us happy, and enabling us to keep them." *Teaching Christianity*, 107.

a rational principle."[40] As reason and intellect manifest the soul's highest and most divine constituents, so also do they frame its fullest and highest activity. But what kind of life does this denote? Of the three "most notable kinds of life" regarding the issue of happiness and the life of excellence—the pursuit of pleasure, politics, and contemplation—Aristotle judges the latter superior.[41]

> For this activity is the best (since not only is intellect the best thing in us, but the objects of intellect are the best of knowable objects); and, secondly, it is the most continuous, since we can contemplate truth more continuously than we can *do* anything. And we think happiness has pleasure mingled with it, but the activity of wisdom is admittedly the pleasantest of excellent activities; at all events philosophy is thought to offer pleasures marvellous for their purity and their enduringness, and it is to be expected that those who know will pass their time more pleasantly than those who inquire. And the self-sufficiency that is spoken of must belong most to the contemplative activity... So if among excellent actions political and military are distinguished by nobility and greatness, and these are unleisurely and aim at an end and are not desirable for their own sake, but the activity of intellect, which is contemplative, seems both to be superior in worth and to aim at no end beyond itself, and to have its pleasure proper to itself (and this augments the activity), and the self-sufficiency, leisureliness, unweariedness (so far as this is possible for man), and all the other attributes ascribed to the blessed man are evidently those connected with this activity, it follows that this will be the complete happiness of man, if it be allowed a complete term of life (for none of the attributes of happiness is *in*complete).[42]

Aristotle acknowledges that this description denotes an ideal, something towards which one thinks and acts. Though it is the fullest expression of the happy life, the contemplative form is not the only kind. Still, anything less does not signify a genuine intellectual life, that which is proper for human beings. For Aristotle, contemplation represents the zenith of human happiness because its activity is "most akin" to the divine.[43]

40. *Nichomachean Ethics* 1098a14; 1176b; 1177a1–20.

41. Ibid., 1095b15–19.

42. Ibid., 1177a20–1178a1.

43. Ibid., 1178b20–23; It is also true because, for Aristotle, God's self-contemplation or a "thinking on thinking" is "the most excellent of things." *Metaphysics*, L, 1074b30–35.

Terms that Aristotle associates with and uses to describe contemplation include: wise, philosophy, self-sufficient, pleasant, leisurely, enjoyable for its own sake, happiness, unpractical, intellectual activity. These characteristics suffuse Newman's understanding of "liberal knowledge" and satisfy the conditions for an Aristotelian inspired account of contemplation. This interpretation of contemplation differs from authors in the Platonic and Plotinian traditions, and thus, the long history of Christian mystical reflection and spirituality.[44] This is important because Newman carefully distinguishes the religious and moral from the philosophical just as Aristotle differentiates moral virtues from the intellectual.[45] What he intends foremost is not something instrumental, moral, or practical but an activity or state of mind evocative of the ontological—the being and formation of mind.[46]

Contemplation is a kind of transcendence, that is, an extension or enlargement of mind proper to its ability and which elevates it above the particular to see the whole. "Transcendence" need not denote the super-rational, the mystical, or the superhuman. Newman does not imply this meaning in the *Idea*.[47] Liberal or philosophical contemplation mirrors what constitutes the essence of a university, namely, drawing things together into a unity—a unity to be contemplated by the intellect. For Newman, cultivation of intellect mirrors in a special, profound way the high view of the university as that which "draws many things into one."[48] In so uniting diverse sciences, this educated intellect will, writes Newman, "reach out towards truth, and to grasp it."[49]

---

44. See especially, McGinn, "The Greek Contemplative Ideal," *Foundations of Mysticism*, 23–61.

45. *Nichomachean Ethics* 1103a1–10.

46. Newman's concern and argument regards more the higher levels of mind, reason, "intellectual illumination," than simply knowledge as a *techne* or skill, a means to some further end. "Surely it is very intelligible to say, and that is what I say here, that Liberal Education, viewed in itself, is simply the cultivation of the intellect, as such, and its object is nothing more or less than intellectual excellence." *Idea*, 111; 115.

47. For the different meanings of "transcendence," see *Oxford English Dictionary*, 28:389.

48. For a concrete example of this in terms of "worship," see *Idea*, 424–25.

49. Ibid., 114. The pliant language of *Idea of a University* frustrates efforts to secure meaning and define terms consistently. Newman frequently employs words without consistent definitions. This characteristic explains his varied use of the term "contemplation."

THEOLOGY: SERVANT AND TYPE OF CONTEMPLATION

Theology's purpose precisely in the university as opposed to other contexts emerges more clearly when seen as effecting excellence in individual minds. If theology is a legitimate academic discipline whose subject matter justifies inclusion, and if this liberal education illumines, enlarges minds striving toward "that form of Universal Knowledge" which is intellectual contemplation, then theology figures in this academic context insofar as it assists the individual intellect's contemplative activity.[50] The manner of expression, however, invites various designations of this intellectual process as Newman acknowledges. Theology's deeper purpose, I am arguing, is to be, as Newman asserts, "cultivated as a contemplation."[51]

Though Newman recognizes and insists that intellectual excellence and moral virtue are not causally linked, he desires their integration. Although this occurs, for Newman, most explicitly in terms of the college—an institution different from the university per se—in the *Idea*, where mention of ecclesiastical oversight and religious devotion seldom arises with any specificity, "contemplation," provides an indirect orientation and coherent foundation for this reunification.[52] This is so because it focuses attention away from the demands of the pragmatic. Theology as a sub-type of intellectual contemplation helps enrich the enlargement of mind not only through its content as such but also through the way it habituates ways of seeing and raising questions of ultimacy.

Specifically, theology as a contemplation enters into the formation of a liberally educated mind by achieving two implicit goals. First, as the liberally trained mind learns to see the form of knowledge philosophically, it is possible to perceive a matrix of relationships metaphysically rich and beautiful. Secondly, it sensitizes individual minds to view the whole of knowledge with aesthetic enjoyment. These broad, subtle aims directly serve the formation of a philosophical and university culture. The possibility exists for honing human reason to perceive an ontological depth to knowing and knowledge.[53] Precisely as they act and reason,

---

50. Ibid., 123.

51. Ibid., 101.

52. Newman to J. D. Dalgairns July 21, 1852. *L&D*, 15:129–32; Newman to J.D. Dalgairns July 23, 1852. *L&D*, 15:133–35; Newman to David Moriarty July 23, 1852. *L&D*, 15:135–37.

53. Cf., *Idea*, 52f.

students' philosophical habits can be brought before religious moment and influence more tangibly.

The harmony theology as contemplation brings to the student's philosophical reach, extends to a certain appreciation of the metaphysical and the beautiful. The two aspects are not sequential stages of reasoning but moments whose conscious realization is probably as particular and unique as the apprehending intellect. "All that is good," Newman maintains, "all that is true, all that is beautiful, all that is beneficent, be it great or small, be it perfect or fragmentary, natural as well as supernatural, moral as well as material, comes from Him."[54] If we interpret this comprehensive, sacramental principle seriously and allow it to form a key assumption within the process of liberal education, then the possibility of understanding contemplation's relation to the transcendent increases significantly. Topics proper to theological reflection naturally complement and enhance the contemplation. Moreover Newman's statement resonates with certain tenets of medieval theology, particularly that of Aquinas. Some of Aquinas' principles provide explicit insight into the metaphysical and aesthetic dimensions that Newman's thought implicitly affirms. Aquinas maintains that "Good and being are really the same, and differ only according to reason...The essence of good consists in this, that it is in some way desirable. Hence the Philosopher says "The good is what all desire." Now it is clear that a thing is desirable only in so far as it is perfect; for all desire their own perfection. But everything is perfect so far as it is in act. Therefore it is clear that a thing is good so far as it is being."[55] The contemplative knowledge of the imperial intellect concerns what exists, not only the particular content of a given science and its principles, but also the expanse of university knowledge. As it does so, it engages goodness, being. This means the intellect configures to reality in a particular intellectual way that possesses its own perfection, its own integrity. Now, if the mind is brought before the expanse of knowledge as a good in itself, not to be used or manipulated by a reason inappropriately instrumental, then it can and does contact the real. It sees knowledge differently. By extension, the mind can discipline its perception to see its world and its myriad parts differently. Contemplation initially points the way towards and, in some sense, establishes possibilities of intellectual transformation.

54. Ibid., 68.
55. *ST* I, Q. 5, art. 1.

For Newman, an important way this occurs follows from and relates to the metaphysical ideas just noted. To perceive a branch of knowledge in itself and in relation to others involves not only a grasp of it as good, as real, but also as something beautiful. Aesthetic qualities are elicited before the intellect's contemplation. Why is this true? Again, let me rely on Aquinas to expand upon the link between existence and beauty. He states:

> Beauty and good in a subject are the same, for they are based upon the same thing, namely, the form; and consequently good is praised as beauty. But they differ logically, for good properly relates to the appetite (good being what all things desire), and therefore it has the aspect of an end (for the appetite is a kind of movement towards a thing). On the other hand, beauty relates to the knowing power, for beautiful things are those which please when seen. Hence beauty consists in due proportion, for the senses delight in things duly proportioned, as in what is after their own kind—because even sense is a sort of reason, just as is every knowing power.[56]

What is crucial to notice within the two passages of Aquinas just cited is that Newman echoes these metaphysical notions concerning the philosophical intellect's apprehension of the form of knowledge given in universities. Newman maintains: "Truth has two attributes beauty and power; and while Useful Knowledge is the possession of truth as powerful, Liberal Knowledge is the apprehension of it as beautiful. Pursue it, either as beauty or as power, to its furthest extent and its true limit, and you are led by either road to the Eternal and Infinite, to the intimations of conscience and the announcements of the Church."[57] He is describing intellectual pleasure and satisfaction in knowing aspects of reality. Philosophical habits cultivate modes or ways of perceiving that enable students to enjoy, take pleasure in the objects they behold and know. Consequently, a richer and subtler understanding of reality becomes disclosed that approaches forms of religious reflection. Indeed, such metaphysical apprehension of the circle of the known inevitably leads to a deeper contemplation of the divine, of ultimacy.

Knowledge so perceived can be "rested in" as something beautiful. This intellectual experience is somewhat analogous to the aesthetic

56. *ST* I, Q. 5, art. 4 ad. 1.
57. *Idea*, 185.

transports found in painting, sculpture, or music. The mind's perception of the beautiful differs radically from its need for the practical or the profitable. The end is the beholding, the possession that is an enjoying—what Aquinas calls "delight" [*delectatur*].[58] But this delight and beholding, as Newman has described, involves an active reasoning, comparing, discriminating. The contemplation is anything but static. Ideas mix and intermingle; forms and drifts and implications of varied meaning pulse through the experience. It is rationally reflexive self-consciousness, the passive and active dialectically cooperating. Precisely when students are brought before the branches of knowledge and are trained to "a comprehensive view of truth in all its branches, of the relations of science to science, of their mutual bearings, and their respective values" does theology attain its proper place.

For this reason, Newman holds the intellectual and the religious as intrinsically but indirectly related. An operative assumption throughout the *Idea*, especially in terms of theology as a contemplation of truth and of the beautiful, again finds clear expression in Aquinas. "All things, by desiring their own perfection, desire God Himself, since the perfections of all things are so many likenesses of the divine being . . . And so of those things which desire God, some know Him as He is Himself, and this is proper to the rational creature; others know some participation of His goodness, and this extends even to sensible knowledge; others have a natural desire without knowledge, as being directed to their ends by a higher intelligence."[59] The comprehensive view of the truth (as an ideal!), for Newman, is the movement, the activity of mind seeking its own perfection, and thus, engaging in something beyond itself, higher than itself, a transcendence.

> If . . . Theology, instead of being cultivated as a contemplation, be limited to the purposes of the pulpit or be represented by the catechism, it loses,—not its usefulness, not its divine character, not its meritoriousness (rather it gains a claim upon these titles by such charitable condescension),—but it does lose the particular attribute which I am illustrating; just as a face worn by tears and fasting loses its beauty, or a laborer's hand loses its delicateness;—

---

58. Jacques Maritain maintains that such natural contemplation "can, nevertheless, be joined to a natural love of the object contemplated and to a heartfelt complacency in it." *Degrees of Knowledge*, 285.

59. *ST* I, Q. 6, art. 1. ad. 2.

for Theology thus exercised is not simple knowledge, but rather is an art or a business making use of Theology.[60]

I have argued that, for Newman, theology assists the education of students' minds toward a type of contemplation. The reasoning mind so shaped by liberal education overcomes the constraints of pragmatic and utilitarian views, moving towards the philosophical. As it does so, the form of knowledge thus known in university education nurtures intellectual habits of attending to and appreciating a richness and beauty not simply tied to the specific subject matters of science, but seeing in them a relation to a divine source and mystery from which they come and to which they refer that effects an intellectual transformation. This transformation that the subject matter of natural theology assists in shaping (the philosophical habit of mind) is a subtler yet rich grasp of human knowledge and its organic relations as mysterious, as something intimately connected to God. It is this "simple knowledge," both power and object, that relates and assists intellectual apprehension to deeper questions and issues of religious, spiritual meaning. The type of transcendence that Newman holds as constitutive of and ordered by university teaching concerns viewing liberal knowledge and theology together as assisting the human mind's contemplation of knowledge as metaphysical and aesthetic encounter. This rich and suggestive function of theology for the contemporary Christian university offers more to students than simply the value of interdisciplinary education or augmenting calls for a university's "catholicity." It offers them a way to organize and contemplate the process and possession of knowledge as something profoundly valuable in itself beyond pragmatic considerations. Knowledge does not simply remain as a narrow "specialty field" that truncates the process and ends of university knowing.[61] Theology as a servant and type of contemplation brings students into contact with the mystery of their own minds, leading them ever so perceptively upwards toward the mind of God that becomes ever more sacramentally present to human intelligence. This is a type of contemplation implicitly present in Newman's thought that helps sustain a real transcendence or enlargement of mind.

60. *Idea*, 101.
61. For a penetrating criticism of the university specialty field, see Farley, *FK*, 29–55.

THEOLOGY IN A CURRICULUM OF STUDIES

At the time that Newman delivered the *Discourses* in Dublin during May of 1852, Christianity was an integral part of the British university system. Most undergraduates intended clerical careers, attended chapel, and subscribed to the Anglican Thirty-Nine Articles of the English church.[62] Such were accepted practices, however customarily practiced or tepidly observed they eventually became. In what we have described, one can discern a concrete meaning of this by examining Newman's ideas concerning "General Religious Knowledge." In an important section titled "Elementary Studies," Newman indicates, at least in terms of the more fundamental form theology assumes in its subject matter, how it could proceed.

> But now as to Theology itself. To meet the apprehended danger [theological error or conceit], I would exclude the teaching *in extenso* of pure dogma from the secular schools, and content myself with enforcing such a broad knowledge of doctrinal subjects as is contained in the catechisms of the Church, or the actual writings of her laity. I would have students apply their minds to such religious topics as layman do treat, and are thought praiseworthy in treating. Certainly I admit that, when a lawyer or physician, or statesmen or merchant, or soldier sets about discussing theological points, he is likely to succeed as ill as an ecclesiastic who meddles with law, or medicine, or the exchange. But I am professing to contemplate Christian Knowledge in what may be called its secular aspect, as it is practically useful in the intercourse of life and in general conversation; and I would encourage it so far as it bears upon the history, the literature, and the philosophy of Christianity.[63]

Though not a specified and approved course, the conjectural nature of these comments discloses critical ideas. First, they cursorily suggest two points about the nature of religious instruction: (1) "the matter to be introduced" and (2) "how much." But they do more—Newman clarifies the general kind or quality of theology he intends. Here university theology differs from that of the seminary or the specialty school. The accent rests on a qualitatively different type of theological knowledge than the dogmatic or particularly clerical. As a profile, it seems more congruent with

62. David Bebbington, "The Secularization of British Universities since the Mid-Nineteenth Century," in *Secularization of the Academy*, 259.

63. *Idea*, 306–7.

an introductory course on Christianity, and in particular, of a section on Monotheism or a philosophy of religion. Other sections or possible courses might attend to church history and biblical literature.[64] Indeed, Newman claims nothing for the teaching of theology other than its scientific dignity as serious and important knowledge. Its audience is lay. Yet one must recognize the argument's consistency. It should be recalled that the arguments made in the discourses that concern "Theology" specifically are not dogmatic or particularly doctrinal in nature. They regard less a systematic examination of creedal affirmations such as the Incarnation, Holy Spirit, Resurrection, Communion of Saints, and so forth, than a general doctrine of God proper, in some sense, to philosophical reflection.

What stands out, at least in this discussion written from 1854–1856, some four years after the discourses, is how ordinary and unexceptional the subject matter remains as far as theological courses go. Newman desires a balanced, well-rounded, educated knowledge of Christianity in his students. He says as much. "I should desire, then" writes Newman, "to encourage in our students an intelligent apprehension of the relations, as I may call them, between the Church and Society at large; for instance, the difference between the Church and a religious sect; the respective prerogatives of the Church and the civil power; what the Church claims of necessity, what it cannot dispense with, what it can; what it can grant, what it cannot."

Such information comprises the general points and facts of Catholicity. It presumes neither theological sophistication nor high academic achievement. The formation of a liberally educated mind whose powers of discrimination, perception, and judgment tell more significantly upon its purpose. One could add that this also describes the cultivation of intellect proper to persons attending the evening classes.[65] Still, Newman reveals far more about what kind of theology suits students' liberal education in a university as opposed to seminary instruction.

Near the end of "Elementary Studies," Newman somewhat casually draws an enormously important distinction. Commenting on the

64. Ibid., 305–6.

65. Such people, for Newman, comprise "a body of men . . . not disputatious, contentious, loquacious, presumptuous . . . but gravely and solidly educated in Catholic knowledge, intelligent, acute, versed in their religion, sensitive of its beauty and majesty, alive to the arguments in its behalf, and aware both of its difficulties and of the mode of treating them." Ibid., 392.

propriety of secular knowledge serving Christianity in general, and immodestly championing Catholics as its stewards, he remarks: "As secular power, influence, or resources are never more suitably placed than when they are in the hands of Catholics, so secular knowledge and secular gifts are then best employed when they minister to Divine Revelation. Theologians inculcate the matter, and determine the details of that Revelation; they view it from within; philosophers view it from without, and this external view may be called the Philosophy of Religion, and the office of delineating it externally is most gracefully performed by laymen."[66] Who, however, is primarily teaching theology in the university? Laymen. Where are they teaching it? The Faculty of Philosophy and Letters. What sorts of texts are they reading? For Newman, in addition to the "broad knowledge of doctrinal subjects as is contained in the catechisms of the Church, or the actual writings of her laity," students study lay authors on apologetics and polemics.[67] However, Newman came to think that students should read classical and authoritative texts, preferably by deceased. "In all teaching," Newman writes, "we take *standard* books. To take the books of the *day*, instead of such as have stood the test of time, is a great mistake ... I should like to lay down the rule, that no work of living authors should be a class book."[68]

What is crucial in these statements, however, is not what they say but what they preclude. Newman distinguishes an internal and external aspect and methodology to theology. The "internal," one can reasonably infer, considers "the teaching *in extenso* of pure dogma"; whereas the "external" comprises an eclectic assemblage of catechetical, historical, biblical, apologetical and polemical information.[69] Newman omits dog-

66. Ibid., 308.
67. Ibid., 306–7.
68. Newman to William Monsell, February 21, 1873, *L&D*, 26:257.
69. One of Ker's editorial notes to this section of the *Idea* points to the type of theology course Newman had in mind. It concerned the thirty-nine articles. *Ideas*, 646. Newman provides an initial overview of this in his first novel. "It was a capital lecture so far as this, that the tutor who gave it had got up his subject completely. He knew the whole history of the Articles, how they grew into their present shape, with what fortunes, what had been added, and when, and what omitted. With this, of course, was joined an explanation of the text, as deduced, as far as could be, from the historical account thus given. Not only the British, but the foreign Reformers were introduced; and nothing was wanting, at least in the intention of the lecturer, for fortifying the young inquirer in the doctrine and discipline of the Church of England." *Loss and Gain*, 89.

matic or serious doctrinal reflection from theological teaching. Detailed reasons as to why are not offered. He acknowledges common concerns about the "risk of theological error" and " the effects of theological conceit" as having merit because they "are so mischievous."[70] What these terms mean remains open to conjecture. Since Newman never saw the fruition of the Catholic University of Ireland but became a champion of the laity in all matters ecclesial, especially in its education, one can only think he would not have prevented the study of revealed alongside natural theology. Unfortunately, we shall never know what he would have done concretely.

CONCLUSION

For Newman, theology takes two main forms, natural and revealed. Natural theology encompasses the teaching and doctrines proper to the classical doctrine of God, God's relationship to creation, and the information human beings have innately from conscience. The subjects proper to religion and natural theology are the same; the difference lies in their apprehension. Intellectual or theological reflection does not mean a "personal relation" or existential engagement in a lived manner with the subjects of study. Religion does. Theology accents notional apprehension; religion denotes real. Revealed or dogmatic theology, at least for the *Discourses*, does not find a comfortable place within the larger, liberal aims to cultivate intellect. By "dogmatic theology" he means serious dogmatic tracts or theological controversy. These are not what students study. Subjects students actually learn come from church history, scripture and catechetical knowledge or lay writings. Newman did not obviously have in mind a graduate seminar in Christology or current upper level undergraduate courses. At the time, he sought "general religious knowledge."[71] And this is not what one might find in seminaries but simply considered in its "secular aspect" and taught in the faculty of letters by lay professors.[72] This view also excludes, supposing students were exposed to the

---

70. *Idea*, 305.

71. "I should desire, then, to encourage in our students an intelligent apprehension of the relations, as I may call them, between the Church and Society at large; for instance, the difference between the Church and a religious sect; the respective prerogatives of the Church and the civil power; what the Church claims of necessity, what it cannot dispense with, what it can; what it can grant, what it cannot." Ibid., 307.

72. Ibid., 308.

basics of the biblical commandments and moral prohibitions, texts on moral theology.[73] Whether theology became something "religious" for the student in the course of study really does depend upon the nature of apprehension—something that cannot be coerced but only evoked. For some, theological knowledge remains an intellectual topic; for others it becomes religious knowledge and moves them toward God.

Besides the direct content or matter of theology in a university, whether natural or revealed, it is necessary as a condition of general knowledge in a liberal education. It provides coherence to the reality of the sciences and subjects studied and also offers a necessary corrective to the claims of exaggeration or unjust usurpation. Theology aids and assists the mind toward a philosophical view of the world that refines perception, judgment, and the natural trajectory toward truth. This circle of knowledge or unity of truth is not concerned primarily with the pragmatic and the professional affairs of the world. As I have argued, Newman believes the academic and the religious are intrinsically related. A liberally trained mind moves towards the contemplation of the metaphysical and aesthetic aspects of the known. Theology as a subject matter assists the minds movement towards it through purification and a transcendental elevation. To this end, theology's place in the university helps the mind achieve a kind of transcendence in learning and appreciating created reality. In doing so, it implies and evokes questions that are inchoatively religious and reach toward the divine.[74]

---

73. "It is quite correct to say," writes Newman, "that books on Moral Theology are guides to the Priests, and not to Penitents; still, they are put into the hands of Priests *for the sake of* their Penitents." Newman to Lady Chatterton, June 30, 1864, *L&D*, 21:140.

74. Cf., Newman to Edmund S. Ffoulkes, August 31, 1863, *L&D*, 20:515.

5

Avery Cardinal Dulles—Ecclesial-Transformative Theology and the University

> In faith there is enough light for those who want to believe and enough shadows to blind those who don't.
>
> —Blaise Pascal

SCHLEIERMACHER AND NEWMAN'S' THOUGHT on the place and nature of theology in the university does not find an empty silence in contemporary theological reflection. They still remain challenging topics, especially so for Catholics since the publication and ongoing implementation of John Paul II's apostolic constitution *Ex corde ecclesiae*.[1] Current treatment reflects continuities and differences from Schleiermacher and Newman that can be fruitfully clarified by examining the work of two modern theologians: Avery Cardinal Dulles (d. 2008) and Edward Farley. Both university professors, their selection seeks to indicate something of the different trajectories and characteristics proper to the historical settlements derived from the Catholic and Protestant theological traditions. In some sense, then, they not only disclose individual perspectives but also represent two different types. In particular, how each theologian diagnoses the problem and the issues involved necessarily contributes to the characterization of the theological task. I suggest that these aspects affect its academic context, aims and identity.

Raised to the College of Cardinals in the Roman Catholic Church in 2001, Avery Cardinal Dulles (d. 2008) was an internationally recognized theologian who wrote extensively on ecclesiology, ecumenism, revelation and theology. The examination of his understanding of Catholic

1. For the full English version and important, related documents, see *Catholic International*, 107–15.

theology and its place in the university draws primarily from select monographs, articles and reviews. My attempt seeks accuracy rather than exhaustive examination. For these reasons, the following presentation is conditional. Granting this limitation, my investigation focuses on four related areas representative of his theological position: problematic situation, methodology, content, and context.

PROBLEMATIC SITUATION

Dulles' argument concerning the contours of theology and its academic meaning needs to be viewed as a serious response to a pressing set of problems. The problematic situation constitutes a set of philosophical, ecclesial and methodological coordinates that frame key positions about the state of Catholic theology. The contemporary context in which theologians and theology find themselves, for Dulles, militates against constructive conditions and common criteria whose absence impedes the theological enterprise. Aside from disagreements within the field, the discipline itself works within a larger culture whose "prevailing intellectual climate" is one "deeply infected by relativism and agnosticism."[2] Consequently, it can seem that all aspects of the theological enterprise are changeable and negotiable. Some of these elements pertain necessarily to theology's proper existence while others concern theological competence. Dulles explains:

> The different theological schools have drifted so far apart that what seems false and dangerous to one school seems almost self-evident to another. Theologians lack a common language, common goals, and common norms. Civil argument has ceased to function, and in its absence opposing parties seek to discredit one another by impugning the motives or competence of their adversaries. In any field of learning such radical diversity would be debilitating. History would not be taken seriously if historians had no agreed method of resolving disputes about whether some past event had actually occurred. Medical experts are supposed to have commonly accepted norms about the signs of health and disease and about methods of curing diverse ailments. Even if the agreement is not universal, there is at least a prevalent and normative methodology. Members of the profession share a common vision of what they are about. The same can hardly be

2. *Craft*, 191.

said of theology today, even within a single ecclesial body, such as the Catholic Church.³

The absence of professional collegiality, methodology and unified purpose helps explain the hostility between theologians selecting oppositional first principles. If this analysis illustrates the difficulties proper to the context of theological activity, Dulles also offers a balanced approach to resolving most of the obstacles. In an interview just weeks after becoming a cardinal, Dulles described the function of the contemporary theologian.

> The theologian is always trying to see how the tradition of the church can be adapted to speak to contemporary culture. But speaking to the culture does not necessarily mean embracing the dominant presumptions of the culture. These presumptions have to be scrutinized, accepting what is good and rejecting what is bad . . . The task of the theologian is to be very critical, to use in some cases what St. Ignatius would call *agere contra*. Where one sees a tendency to move in a certain direction that is contrary to the Gospel, Ignatius would say, move in the opposite direction. Throughout my career I have tended to be critical of what I saw as the principal dangers of the day. Sometimes the danger was to be insufficiently open and to adhere too strongly to past traditions, forms and ways of behaving. The opposite danger confronts us today in thinking that everything is up for grabs.⁴

Part diagnosis and part lament, he again stresses the significance of integrated discourse, unified methodology and judicious discernment for theological reflection. In turn, one of theology's main aims becomes clearer: the ability to speak to contemporary culture. Still, while Dulles will accept a certain kind of intellectual pluralism, the project of Catholic theology still lacks a common vision.⁵ He also notes problems beyond disciplinary and scientific procedure, namely, the character or

---

3. Ibid., x.

4. "Reason, Faith, and Theology: An Interview with Cardinal Avery Dulles, S.J.," 10–11.

5. Dulles has characterized this more forcefully. "Lacking a common language, common goals, and common norms, theology seems to be in a state of chaos." Dulles, "Theological Education in the Catholic Tradition," *Theological Education in the Catholic Tradition*, 18; See also Dulles' comments about the state of Catholic theologians as a professional society in "How Catholic Is the CTSA? Three Views," Dulles et al., *Commonweal*, 13–14.

disposition of the theologian and excessive intellectual accommodation to reigning cultural values. Yet the more profound influence that affects the project of Catholic theology, as I will argue, is what Dulles criticizes as a "rampant secularism." It generally denotes that the culture at large "recognizes no higher sovereignty than the human will and rejects in the name of autonomy the very idea of a divine intervention in the world."[6] In his view, therefore, not only does there need to be a change in fundamental theological thinking concerning norms and methodology, but also a shift in the behavior and formation of those conducting it. In Dulles' judgment, they are inseparably linked. Accordingly, a new integration should align with salutary measures that affirm ecclesial identity. "For the better health of theology," he argues, "I believe that its ecclesial character needs to be more clearly recognized. Theology must serve the church and be accountable to it. While theology needs to have a measure of autonomy in order to perform its distinctive service, it loses its identity if it ceases to be a reflection on the faith of the Church."[7]

As a positive step to address both, Dulles proposes a "post-critical theology." This post-critical theology establishes the kinds of theological criteria needed to restore order to a perceived "chaos" in terms of methodology, vision, aim and identity. In the process, it is important to note that Dulles is not assailing all other theological solutions to the problematic situation. He differentiates between "the kind of pluralism that heals and unifies" and "a pluralism that divides and destroys."[8] Post-critical theology, for Dulles, will indirectly indicate what each type of pluralism means and their implications for doing theology in a university context.

THEOLOGY AS POST-CRITICAL AND ECCLESIAL TRANSFORMATIVE

To begin, let me start with a definition. Over his career, Dulles provides numerous and complementary meanings of theology.[9] Let me take a recent description as normative. "[T]heology is *fides quarens intellectum*,

---

6. Dulles, "Principles of Catholic Theology," 82.
7. *Craft*, x–xi.
8. Dulles, *Models of the Church*, 13.
9. See Dulles, "Theology Education in the Catholic Tradition," *Theological Education in the Catholic Tradition*, 11; *Church To Believe In*, 125; *Models of the Church*, 22; "Evangelizing Theology," 28; "Knowledge, Wisdom, and Theology," 270–71.

a disciplined reflection on faith. Taking its departure from the word of God (*theo-logia*), theology explores the content and implication of divine revelation. This reflection is carried on, at least normally, from within a stance of faith (*fides qua creditur*), which in the case of a Catholic means personal adherence to a definite body of beliefs (*fides quae creditur*)."[10] This Anselmian understanding is classical and firmly scholastic. It describes a personal relationship to a set of realities expressed as an intelligible and positive content. This understanding also indicates theological rationality's ecclesial orientation as it proceeds from faith and moves towards a deeper explanation of faith's content. But Dulles' understanding of it methodologically, while evincing continuity with this traditional view, also displays "post-critical" characteristics. One comes from the influence of Lutheran theologian, George Lindbeck.

In his book *The Nature of Doctrine*, Lindbeck introduces a different way to classify approaches to how doctrines operate and what they signify based upon the findings of philosophy and social science.[11] The types are cognitive-propositional, experiential-expressive and cultural-linguistic. The first approach emphasizes, "the ways in which church doctrines function as informative propositions or truth claims about objective realities." Propositions are affirmed as corresponding to reality, and hence the truth of such a statement endures over time. This means that "if a doctrine is once true, it is always true, and if it is once false, it is always false."[12] The second classification of Lindbeck's typology, "experiential-expressive," concerns the application of and interest in human experience as it relates to doctrine. At root, it signifies that underlying all human religious experience is a core unity of experience that provides a foundation of likeness between faiths and their representation of the divine.[13] It covers not one kind but different accents that characterize similar forms within a category. In contrast to the propositionalist, "religiously significant meanings can vary while doctrines remain the same, and conversely, doctrines can alter without change of meaning."[14] Yet Lindbeck proposes an alternative view of doctrine—the cultural-linguistic. One way to understand it is to recognize that its meaning is

10. Dulles, "Principles of Catholic Theology," 73.
11. Lindbeck, *Nature of Doctrine*.
12. Ibid., 16.
13. Ibid., 31–32.
14. Ibid., 17.

not limited to simply rethinking methodological approaches to doctrine but "extends to the notion of religion itself."[15] Lindbeck's view of religion goes beyond how doctrines mutually relate.

> Stated more technically, a religion can be viewed as a kind of cultural and/or linguistic framework or medium that shapes the entirety of life and thought. It functions somewhat like a Kantian a priori, although in this case the a priori is a set of acquired skills that could be different. It is not primarily an array of beliefs about the true and the good (though it may involve these), or a symbolism expressive of basic attitudes, feelings, or sentiments (though these will be generated). Rather, it is similar to an idiom that makes possible the description of realities, the formulation of beliefs, and the experiencing of inner attitudes, feelings, and sentiments. Like a culture or language, it is a communal phenomenon that shapes the subjectivities of individuals rather than being primarily a manifestation of those subjectivities. It comprises a vocabulary of discursive and nondiscursive symbols together with a distinctive logic or grammar in terms of which this vocabulary can be meaningfully deployed. Lastly, just as a language (or "language game," to use Wittgenstein's phrase) is correlated with a form of life, and just as a culture has both cognitive and behavioral dimensions, so it is also in the case of a religious tradition. Its doctrines, cosmic stories or myths, and ethical directives are integrally related to the rituals it practices, the sentiments or experiences it evokes, the actions it recommends, and the institutional forms it develops. All this is involved in comparing a religion to a cultural-linguistic system.[16]

This conceptual matrix as "cultural-linguistic" serves as a kind of meta-category within which other theological disciplines, such as fundamental, systematic or practical theology can be grasped.

The reason for citing Lindbeck at length is because Dulles appropriates aspects of his theological proposal for a cultural-linguistic approach that he differentiates as "ecclesial transformative."[17] With Lindbeck, Dulles prefers a different way to view theological subjects than the

---

15. Ibid., 7.
16. Ibid., 33.
17. It seems doubtful that Dulles would completely agree with Lindbeck's understanding of religious truth as more "intrasystematic" than "propositional." See *Nature of Doctrine*, 65–69. Furthermore, Dulles does not endorse that theology "retain the narrative mode," in manners advocated by "narrative theology." This is because it [theology] "cannot content itself with describing or redescribing the biblical story." *Craft*, 83.

propositionalist or the experiential-expressivist. Moreover, the description of this approach as "ecclesial-transformative" indicates intellectual and faith commitments that influence his examination of traditional theological topics and resources. Among its more important presuppositions, however, is pessimism of the ecclesial-transformative approach concerning the use of contemporary experience as a theological source.[18] Lindbeck's proposals are useful, since they seek to overcome what Dulles perceives as an overly "subjectivist" stance in contemporary theology.[19] In part, Dulles argues that, "Christian faith . . . cannot be justified by public criteria offered in common human experience."[20] Like Lindbeck, then, Dulles rejects the modern "turn to the subject" and its implications for contemporary theological reflection. This judgment, which underlies much of the post-critical approach, can be traced some twenty years earlier to a review of David Tracy. "I do not understand why there could not be certain uncommon experiences from which one could perceive more about the ultimate nature of reality than is given in ordinary experience. If this were true, it would seem that theology would have at its disposal another very important source: the special experiences given at certain privileged times, and perhaps only to certain particular individuals and groups."[21] What helps establish the cultural-linguistic approach to doctrine and religion for Lindbeck becomes an important, singular premise for Dulles. Pushed into a larger context, what Dulles borrows eclectically from Lindbeck is a way to secure and grasp the religious identity of the theological enterprise as well as its practitioners.[22] Specifically, this premise concerns the relationship between religion and experience. There is a certain dynamic between the formation of Christian faith and life on the one hand, and the mechanics of its emergence and development through Christian symbols on the other.

Though his proposal claims to differ sufficiently from Lindbeck's thought, the principles Dulles appropriates in establishing his post-

18. See Dulles, *Testimonial*, 127.
19. *Testimonial*, 126–27. See also, Dulles, Review of *Revelation and Theology*, 170.
20. *Craft*, 54.
21. Dulles, "Method in Fundamental Theology," 304–16; 307–8.
22. One of the chief flaws of contemporary theology, for Dulles, is and has been what he regards as being "too accommodating" towards secular culture. He maintains that Christian theology is under "enormous pressure from the media and from secular academia to conform to the spirit of the times." *Testimonial*, 127–28.

critical theology are important.²³ They figure especially in what Dulles calls "symbolic realism" and in his understanding of "symbolic communication." To clarify these ideas adequately, let me examine Dulles' views on the relationship between religion, symbol, authority and theological reflection. Together, these topics help ground the notion of theology as more of a craft or an art than "a science learned out of books alone."²⁴ Additionally, it will indicate why the appropriation and receptivity to symbols require definite conditions of personal commitment.

For Dulles, understanding religion and its diverse elements requires a serious grasp of its symbols. He states: "[R]eligions are predominantly characterized by their symbols. The Christian religion is a set of relationships with God mediated by the Christian symbols. These symbols are imbedded in the Bible and in the living tradition of the Christian community. The symbols do not operate in isolation; they mutually condition and illuminate one another."²⁵ Employing Rahner's ontological understanding of symbol, Dulles argues that realities express themselves in the other to attain their being or realize their nature. "[A] symbol," he maintains, "is a perceptible sign that evokes a realization of that which surpasses ordinary objective cognition." As a "sign pregnant with a plenitude of meaning," it is more precise to hold that their power lies in evoking rather than stating.²⁶ Hence, human beings act symbolically when expressing themselves to the other communicatively. Bodily nature reflects or symbolizes spiritual nature, for example, since human beings are a composite of body and soul, spiritual meaning is expressed in bodily gestures, acts, and other ways.²⁷ Human beings come to realize and understand their identity, their nature, this way.²⁸

Linguistic statement or proposition tends to limit and contract the richness of the meaning expressed, whereas symbols evoke significance in ways that give it more revelatory power. This idea lies behind the pro-

---

23. I do not want to collapse important distinctions between the two theologians. Unlike Lindbeck, Dulles affirms the importance of viewing doctrines as truth claims. See *Craft*, 14; 191–92.

24. Ibid., 8.

25. Ibid., 19.

26. Dulles, *Models of Revelation*, 132.

27. *Craft*, 20.

28. Ibid.

verbial saying that "a picture is worth a thousand words."[29] What this implies, therefore, is that symbols provoke and stir the imagination more deeply than assertions. This principle also holds true in religion. Religious symbols embrace a vision of interconnecting relationships whose sources can range from religious practices to traditions to texts. In other words, symbols proper to religious traditions exceed what ordinary human experience normally grasps.[30] This knowing is "tacit," silent, unthematized. The symbols, furthermore, operate within a living community that continually reinterprets them—something intrinsic to religion. Indeed, the function and reality of symbols closely mirrors important aspects of revelation. For Dulles, four general characteristics obtain. First, symbols concern participatory knowing more than speculative. Symbols are not the kinds of signs one examines in a detached, impersonal way. Secondly, symbols transform the person engaged in such knowing. Accepted symbols make evocative claims upon human self-understanding, drawing one into degrees of self-examination. Thirdly, symbols concretely effect "commitments and behavior." Upon self-examination, they challenge participants to personal change or conversion. Finally, symbols "introduce us into realms of awareness not normally accessible to discursive thought."[31] As Newman would put it, symbolic communications involve more than a notional assent of the mind. They require a real assent of the whole person drawn into something mysterious, beyond what reason can apprehend or control.[32]

From an ecclesial-transformative perspective, human experience does not become a religious experience independently of symbols and their power. It depends upon them. The lived experience from within the universe of symbolic meaning that is precisely "self-involving," therefore, becomes the essential criterion for doctrinal interpretation, judgment and ecclesial participation. In other words, it gives a unifying framework of meaning and identity to the myriad aspects of a religion. According to

---

29. It is also why Robert Frost insists upon an intimacy between poetry and symbol. "Every single poem written regular is a symbol small or great of the way the will has to pitch into commitments deeper and deeper to a rounded conclusion and then be judged for whether any original intention it had has been strongly spent or weakly lost; be it in art, politics, school, church, business, love, or marriage—in a piece of work or in a career. Strongly spent is synonymous with kept." *Selected Prose of Robert Frost*, 24.

30. *Craft*, 18.

31. Dulles, *Models of Revelation*, 136–37.

32. Cf., Dulles, "Evangelizing Theology," 28.

a passage of Lindbeck that Dulles quotes, to be "religious," therefore, "is to interiorize a set of skills by practice and training. One learns how to feel, act, and think in conformity with a religious tradition that is, in its inner structure, far richer and more subtle than can be explicitly articulated."[33] And for Dulles, when applied to Christian life, symbols become essential for a specific "experience." As he states, "By 'Christian experience' I mean experience that is intrinsically qualified by the Christian symbols through which it is communicated and expressed."[34]

In large part, Christian symbols—no less than other kinds—operate in ways that transcend conscious awareness or, influenced by Michael Polanyi's philosophy, what Dulles calls "tacit powers of apprehension" or "tacit knowledge."[35] As I have indicated, the depth of meaning that symbolic realities express exceeds intellectual articulation and limits. When human beings meet others, for example, they actually apprehend more about the other, various details, nuances, and subtleties than they can express in words. Applied to theologians, access to tacit or unthematic knowledge and understanding comes not from simply conceptual ability and symbolic imagination. Theology presupposes that theologians possess a "subjective sense of faith." Again, this is not, for Dulles, an existential mode of the human condition. He admits that there is a more generic, anthropological understanding of "faith" proper to it. This concerns the trustworthiness of what people learn and believe in ordinary experience, from books to news reports and sense reliability. But it remains simply "philosophical" faith, not "divine" or "theological."[36] "Faith," Dulles asserts, "is not simply the acceptance of an inner orientation of the human spirit to some kind of absolute transcendence."[37] On the contrary, faith is something more specific and distinctive, marking an open disposition as already committed to the symbols in faith. "[T[heology," he writes, "is the kind of inquiry that takes place from within a religious commitment."[38] This remains an essential condition for and criterion of genuine theological reflection. Further styles, concepts, methodologies or resources may serve the theological enterprise with varying degrees of adequacy.

33. Lindbeck, *Nature of Doctrine*, 35 ; quoted in *Craft*, 18.
34. Dulles, "Method in Fundamental Theology," 308 n. 3.
35. *Craft*, 19; 14. See also Polanyi, *Personal Knowledge*.
36. Dulles, *Assurance of Things Hoped For*, 274.
37. Dulles, "Evangelizing Theology," 29.
38. *Craft*, 7.

Nevertheless, there must be a personal engagement with "the contents of faith" behind the reflective intent.[39] There should be, as Dulles implies, an ongoing conversion of the inquirer precisely because the challenge to change is taken seriously by one who thinks deeply about symbolic meanings.[40]

As conditions and resources for religious commitment and knowledge, it naturally follows that liturgy, ritual and prayer figure importantly in what a post-critical, ecclesial-transformative theology means. These dimensions of ecclesial dedication develop and express the theologian's affirmation of the realities that symbols evoke. They possess an altogether different claim upon one as living within a community of believers than intellectual apprehension or assent.[41] Dulles maintains: "Through indwelling in the community of faith one acquires a kind of connaturality or connoisseurship that enables one to judge what is or is not consonant with revelation. In applying this sense of the faith one apprehends the clues in a subsidiary or tacit manner and concentrates on their joint meaning."[42] Participation in the ecclesial community generates a sophisticated sensitivity to and permits a richer supply of tacit knowledge for doing theology. Again, this is why Dulles likens it more to a craftsmen's knowledge gained through apprenticeship than data drawn from empirical observation. Distinctively formed habits of personally acting and thinking in accordance with the claims of the Christian symbols as true yield special skills of interpretation. "Participation in the religious way of life," Dulles maintains, "is demanded of anyone who would wish to assess the force and value of the Christian claims."[43] Consequently, a theological resource for acquiring important tacit knowledge like ritual liturgy figures significantly. "Ritual," Dulles maintains, "is a symbolic or mythic narrative in action. It dramatically renews the sacred events which it recalls. By participation in the ritual the worshipper is able to discern ultimate meaning, to integrate the negative elements of existence, and to experience the power of the scared."[44] Living the Christian vision of

---

39. *Craft*, 8.

40. Dulles has discussed various aspects of religious faith extensively. See *Assurance Of Things Hoped For*, 274f.

41. *Craft*, 8–9.

42. Ibid., 9.

43. Dulles, Review of *The Possibility of Religious Knowledge*, 147–48.

44. Dulles, *Models of Revelation*, 134.

reality as articulated primarily in and through the dominant symbols parallels language acquisition, whose meanings, grammar and expressions remain unmastered until one achieves oral and literate fluency. It is the key religious and theological criterion.

Participation also means that theology and theologians possess specific relationships to the community of believers who receive and modify the realities that Christian symbols communicate. It is not simply then, a question of learning a language, but a shared conversation in the vision that the symbols denote and a distinctive experience of what they concretely realize. Additionally, ecclesial resources must be of primary value and meaning for theological reflection since the primary subject matter remains, as we shall see, Christocentric and ecclesially mediated. Dulles seeks to hold both the subject matter and the communal dimension together as prerequisites for doing theology. It follows, therefore, that theology is essentially an inquiry undertaken by and for believers: it belongs to the believing community. "Theology is . . . an ecclesial discipline. It is done in the Church because the Church is the primary bearer of faith."[45] The relationship between active participation, thought, and the central symbols of Christianity are common to the experiences, articulations and variances of a large community. The signposts of texts and traditions—creedal, ethical, pastoral, spiritual, theological—that shape their self-understanding, accordingly, must figure enormously in a theologian's judgments and interests. To a great extent, the theologian engages a project of Christian self-description.

Precisely what this process of Christian self-description means can assume distinct forms. In Christian intellectual life, for instance, Dulles judges pluralism in thought and method positively.[46] Indeed, he pays tribute to the value of different approaches in ecclesiology and revelation by employing typologies in his own work.[47] He would judge this type of pluralism healthy and, ultimately, one that effects unity. At the same time, he is concerned about a kind of pluralism that impedes a common theological vision. Besides a faith informed by participating in symbolic

---

45. *Craft*, 8.

46. Concerning variant methodological proposals and applications of scripture within theological work, he states: "The coexistence of different styles or models is healthy and desirable. Different methodologies may be useful, depending on the precise questions being asked." *Craft*, 85.

47. See Dulles, *Models of Revelation*; *Models of the Church*.

realities, there is a presumption of unifying criteria regarding both what the subject matter is and the existential stance one exhibits towards that subject matter—religious faith. He recognizes the need for symbolic communication to be faithful to divine revelation and to the community that abides by its accepted, authoritative claims. In turn, as the topic of unifying criteria elevates the relationship of symbolic understanding and participation to the foreground, so it also calls the relationship between the official teaching authority of the Church and the work of theologians into question. As Dulles argued years earlier, this is because "these two classes are inseparably united, reciprocally dependent, but really and irreducibly distinct."[48] As members of the believing community trying to understand divine revelation and employing various intellectual means to do so, what does it mean to say the classes are unified but distinct? In what sense does this concretely occur?

The underlying conception of unity, as the quotation asserts, is not a uniformity of composition but a unity of order. As such, the aims and methods of official teaching and the diverse forms of theological expression interpenetrate and mutually inform. For Dulles, this point is historically true and doctrinally legitimate.[49] Yet as their proximate aims differ from their distant goal, namely, Christian evangelization, their orientations proceed by different methods.[50] Hence, balance needs to be constructed between the symphony of different ecclesial instruments and the piece each instrument aims to play.

Especially for Dulles, a Catholic theologian, the dynamics between ecclesial authority and theological interpretation are critical because authoritative theological interpretation belongs to the magisterium. This differentiation of function is reflected in the Second Vatican Council's teaching in *Dei Verbum*. "The task of authentically interpreting the word of God, whether in its written form or in that of tradition, has been entrusted only to the living magisterium of the Church, whose authority is exercised in the name of Jesus Christ. (DV, 10)."[51] The ordinary magisterium pertains to the pope and the bishops—not to Catholic theolo-

---

48. Dulles, "Two Magisteria: An Interim Reflection," 155.

49. Cf., *Craft*, 107f.

50. Dulles concurs with Pope John Paul II who called evangelization "the deepest identity of the Church." Dulles, "Evangelizing Theology," 27–32; 27.

51. *Craft*, 105; For text of Vatican II documents, see *Decrees of the Ecumenical Councils*, vol. 2: *Trent to Vatican II*.

gians per se.[52] The magisterium comprises the "authentic" and "official" interpreters of God's revelation mediated by Christian symbols for the Catholic community. Yet the scope of hierarchical officials such as popes and bishops to teach authoritatively for the global church on issues of universal concern such as war, peace, social justice in light of the Gospel is inversely proportional to their actual influence in educating the broader church. For, in fact, the transmission of the Christian symbols in the lives of believers largely occurs beyond the direct, pedagogical reach of the magisterium as such. To be more precise, Christian faith's transmission involves teaching; and this teaching is, in varying ways, "Christian education."[53] Hence it embraces all forms of education and theological disciplines. Passing on the faith occurs in different settings such as grammar schools, preparatory schools, colleges, universities, seminaries, and adult faith formation programs. Instructors of theological education, for the most part, come from programs and institutions of higher learning—divinity schools, colleges, universities, and seminaries. Dulles recognizes this explicitly when he maintains, "the hierarchical office-holders are not the sole agents by whom the Church teaches."[54] Why is this the case? The theological justification for the claim that the office-holders are not the only way by which the Church teaches goes beyond decisions of practical logistics (the problem of sheer numbers) or the grace bestowed to ecclesiastical office holders. The reason derives from the very participation and adherence of those Christians living out the vision to which the Christian symbols call. Echoing a Newmanian insight, he posits that "[e]very believer who seeks to acquire or impart an understanding of the faith may be called, at least in a rudimentary way, a theologian or teacher of theology."[55] But how does the university setting and the distinction between official and unofficial teachers influence the relationship between the non-authoritatively academic and the authoritatively ecclesial?

Academically and in terms of rigorous scientific method, theology enjoys a certain "relative autonomy" like any other specialized discipline. Its ecclesial character does not hinder this. Indeed, Dulles cites magiste-

52. *Craft*, 106.
53. Ibid., 167.
54. Ibid.
55. Ibid. Newman maintained that "every religious man is to a certain extent a theologian." *GA*, 69.

rial documents to argue that the "official teachers and the theologians use different methods and have different goals."[56] More specifically, he contends that "[w]ithin its particular sphere of competence theology is free to reach whatever conclusions are indicated by a proper application of its own method."[57] But by "method," he does not mean an isolated or infallible procedure, lacking accountability. Like other sciences, theology also encompasses norms, canons and first principles that apply in its arguments and conclusions which, if denied or ignored, contradict the inquiry.[58] Yet the norms and principles do not derive from the academy or unofficial teachers but precisely from revealed truth as authoritatively passed down and interpreted. Its principles are fundamentally those of the church.

In fact, Dulles argues not only that such principles exist for Catholic theology, but he also identifies ten as essential. These "aspects of a synthetic vision," however, denote and reinforce the identity of theology as "Catholic" in addition to its post-critical view of symbols and human experience. The principles display a certain historical continuity with beliefs, judgments and practices that mark theological reflection and the lived experience of the Catholic church. They provide disciplinary coherence that shapes theology's identity.

Dulles's cursory treatment places the meaning of these Catholic principles within the academic setting, despite their obvious influence in other spheres of ecclesial life.[59] The first tenet is the "esteem for the natural." In others words, there is no "opposition" between the orders of redemption and creation. Nature is created good and must be stewarded sensitively so it remains "a reflection of the divine." The second principle is humanism. It posits the *imago dei* of humankind, the "essential goodness of human nature," and the obligation of Christianity to affirm and defend all things human "with special attention to the unborn, the aged, the weak, and the marginalized." Third, Dulles maintains a "respect for reason" that acknowledges no real opposition to faith but

---

56. *Craft*, 107.
57. Ibid., 169.
58. Ibid., 168.
59. See Dulles, "Principles of Catholic Theology," 73. He lays these out in part because, as he states: "When theological societies, journals, and faculties designate themselves as "Catholic," one does not always know what to expect."

complementarity and mutual assistance.[60] Fourth, he introduces "universalism." This principle endorses God's universally salvific message for all human beings and calls for sensitivity to the "evidences of grace in all religions and cultures." The fifth is "mediation," and is for Dulles, "the Catholic principle par excellence." It concerns the "self-mediation of the divine," supremely given in the Incarnation but also more generally a "sense of the holy—that is to say, the numinous presence of the divine in visible places, persons, actions, and institutions." The fullness of this principle manifests most approximately in the visible church because it "has received through Christ the fullness of revelation and the fullness of the means of grace." The next three principles flow from the fifth—dogmatic, sacramental and hierarchical. The "dogmatic principle" simply means that since dogma makes truth claims about what is real and binding upon the faithful, it obliges a believer's full assent and confidence in it. The seventh principle, the sacramental, broadly affirms the activity of God in the world at large but also specifies ecclesial signs and means of God's grace in historically determinate ways "through a material and visible medium"—Baptism, Confirmation, Eucharist, etc. The hierarchical principle embraces both the necessity of a "sacred ministry" perpetuating the church's apostolicity but also the need for "a living authority that has power from Christ to oversee their teaching." The ninth is consensus. It holds the entire body of the faithful "possess a kind of instinct for discerning what is and is not in accord with the faith." Moreover, consensus points to the Holy Spirit's guidance and sustenance in the church at large. Finally, Dulles advances a "doxological principle." Prayer, ritual, liturgy—such performative elements must play a critical role in the understanding and development of doctrines, beliefs and the symbols of revelation. As such, they are real and efficacious means of uniting with God.[61]

These ten principles tend not to dictate a discursive procedure but act as points on a compass or, as the root meaning indicates, function as "sources." As theological and ecclesial principles, none are particularly innovative. All can be easily discovered and affirmed within the Catholic theological tradition. Moreover, their meanings are not mutually exclusive but overlap. The first, fifth and seventh principle speak

---

60. For a fuller treatment of this topic, see Dulles, "Reason, Philosophy, and the Grounding of Faith," 479–90.

61. Dulles, "Principles of Catholic Theology," 75–82.

of God's presence in the world and are substantially the same. Their accents simply differ. In any case, these principles operate as theological premises and attempt to fix the "identity" coordinates of theology in the most general way.

However, unlike other academic disciplines, theology's principles and relation to the ecclesial magisterium do affect what it can and cannot do. Precisely because theology emanates from the church and is accountable to it, as Dulles maintains, "[s]ome restrictions on the freedom of theologians may be acceptable in order to prevent the authentic teaching of the Church from being ignored or obscured."[62] The magisterium cannot be, in other words, "infinitely permissive" towards theological activity. The obligation is theirs to impose limitations upon "what may be held and taught in the Church."[63] If true, then, the question of limiting theologians extends naturally to the content of theological teaching, and therefore, bears upon the issue of methodology in terms of its *effects*—not its internal operations. "Popes and bishops," he writes, "have no mandate to tell the theologian how to do theology, beyond the negative mandate of seeing to it that theology does not undermine the life of faith itself."[64] It is not, then, that reasoned argument and logical procedure in one of the different theological fields and schools becomes *a priori* illegitimate. Rather, theologians cannot approach their work and draw conclusions without injury to the theological enterprise if they ignore the ecclesial "responsibility of theology to the community of faith and the mandate of the ecclesiastical magisterium to assure the doctrinal soundness of theology."[65] This requirement exists because the subject matter and topics of theology are common to the church universal and treated in non-academic settings such as parishes, lay associations, monasteries, etc. The academic along with these other forums embrace the same, fundamental content: Christian revelation. The theological differs from the academic because it is not occasionally or frequently but *always* accountable to people and groups beyond university or scholarly limits. Ecclesial-transformative theologians, furthermore, never relinquish ecclesial ties. Indeed, Dulles frames this forcefully as an issue of ecclesial identity and intellectual vocation. "The Catholic theologian who wishes to remain a

62. *Craft*, 116.
63. Ibid., 118.
64. Ibid., 169.
65. Ibid., 177.

Catholic is bound to accept the definitive ("irreformable") teaching of the magisterium and must be favorably disposed to accept whatever the magisterium puts forth as obligatory doctrine."[66] In an important sense, therefore, the exercise of negative vigilance by magisterial authority does not distinguish the content or subject matter of what theologians in the academy treat and what the church lives by as salvific doctrine.

In due course, then, ecclesial-transformative methodology offers measured plurality in reflective style and in theological principle.[67] Yet conclusions reached by theologians who, by definition, operate from within an essentially ecclesial discipline differ from other scholars. Theological or religious conclusions stand accountable to the community of faith and the magisterium. As such, they cannot deliberately corrupt or distort the subject matter of theology—Christian revelation. Ultimately, this is because, for Dulles, not only does theological reflection never disavow its ecclesial character, but its *catechetical* character as well. "Religious instruction on the elementary level is called catechesis; on higher levels it takes the form of advanced courses in Christian doctrine and theology. The entire process of Christian education takes place under the supervision of the hierarchical magisterium."[68] In other words, ecclesial-transformative theology never ceases to be, in various ways, religious education or instruction. This idea extends particularly to the university context, Dulles writes:

> On the college level, courses in the basic doctrines of the Church should be offered and highly recommended for Catholic students. Such courses should be taught from a Catholic point of view—the sacraments explained as divinely instituted means of grace, the sacrificial character of the Mass and the real and substantial presence of Christ in the Eucharist—in spite of the many objections I have mentioned. Measures should be taken to ensure that Catholic college students are familiarized with the essential teachings of Catholic faith and morals and that they gain some idea of why the Church teaches what she does. Students should be equipped to answer common objections to the faith, perhaps through courses in apologetics. They should take introductory courses in holy Scripture and Church history, so as not to be ignorant of Christian origins and development. The philosophy

---

66. Ibid., 168.
67. Cf., Ibid., 85. See also, Dulles, "Hermeneutical Theology," 36–37.
68. *Craft*, 167.

department should offer courses, preferably required, that convey a realist theory of knowledge and a sound metaphysics. In this way, our graduates could be somewhat prepared to stand up against the agnosticism and relativism of the day.[69]

Indeed, what theologians actually do in the classroom satisfies a prime definition of "catechize," namely "to give systematic oral instruction."[70] Teachers of theology who employ methods or principles that result in conflicting positions with revealed doctrine, therefore, cast doubt upon the legitimacy of their work as "theological" from the start. Dulles flatly holds that "the most basic reference point for theology is the faith itself, authoritatively set forth in normative documents."[71] The viability of the methods or principles the arguments employ can then become problematic. Though intellectual options can differ, though forums and settings may shift, Dulles seems to seriously hold that theology inhabits a living continuum of beliefs, practices, and normative sources precisely as a form of religious instruction. Though its proximate end in research or investigation pursues the plurality of Christian thought and practice, both catechesis and theology ultimately seek to disclose the self-communication of God for evangelization and the salvation of souls. Thus, post-critical theology, for Dulles, is not genuine if it loses its soteriological character.

ECCLESIAL-TRANSFORMATIVE THEOLOGY AND REVELATION

It is necessary to recall that Dulles seeks to overcome not only the problems of radical diversity in aims and norms but also the problem of attenuated identity concerning the theological enterprise as a whole that such diversity causes. It is imperative for a post-critical critical theology to manifest a real relationship to "revelation" because "theology cannot maintain its identity and vigor if it overlooks this foundational category." Hence he goes on to maintain that, "[m]any functional specializations can arise, but all must contribute to a common enterprise."[72] Dulles attempts to order anew the intellectual and religious priorities of

---

69. Dulles, "Catholicism 101: Challenges To A Theological Education," 303–8; 308.
70. *Oxford English Dictionary*, 2:979.
71. *Craft*, 168. See also Dulles, "Catholicism 101," 304–5.
72. Dulles, *Models of Revelation*, ix; *Craft*, xi.

the theological task. A re-orientation to the revelation of God in Christ, therefore, is a key part of this, especially concerning content.

Having briefly examined what essentially characterizes post-critical theology in terms of method and principles, I must consider briefly its subject matter: Christian revelation.[73] The range of possible topics covered by this term is vast and to do the subject justice would require an extensive treatment of Dulles' major work, *Models of Revelation*. Since this lies beyond the scope of this inquiry, my concern here is not to investigate all, some or even one topic in any depth, but simply to indicate why revelation must be the focal norm or principle in any theological inquiry.

As the source of the Christian symbols, revelation is "a real and efficacious self-communication of God, the transcendent mystery, to the believing community."[74] Revelation's centrality and the insistence upon symbolic communication as its hermeneutic lens for theological understanding build to what Dulles judges as the "primary subject matter of theology," namely, "the saving self-communication of God through the symbolic events and words of Scripture, especially in Jesus Christ as the 'mediator and fullness of all revelation.'"[75] Jesus, the central symbol of the Christian tradition, orders and brings coherence to how all other symbols relate and evoke meaning.[76] Though not the only subject of theology, Christ stands central to Christian faith's varied content.[77]

Christian revelation is historically mediated in and through believers, the church, the primary locus and bearer of the symbols. Revelation is not only given in the written form of God's revealed word. In the Catholic tradition, scripture and tradition constitute—citing Vatican II

---

73. Dulles proposes more generally, that God is theology's "formal object and its principal theme." He adds further: "Theology is true to its nature when it focuses its attention on God and does so in the light of God's self-revelation." "Wisdom as the Source of Unity for Theology," 68.

74. *Craft*, 18.

75. Ibid., 19. It must be noted that in another chapter, Dulles holds that God is the "primary subject matter" since the "theologian, by vocation, deals with mystery." Ibid., 47. This position, however, does not fit well with the ecclesial-transformative approach because it lacks the kind of specificity of form and content Dulles seeks to maintain.

76. Dulles also identifies "the three great mysteries"—the Trinity, the Incarnation and divinization by the Holy Spirit—as theology's "central concern." Ibid., 21.

77. Cf., Ibid., 26.

—the "single deposit of the word of God."[78] Deeply concerned with the revelation of God in Christ, these two forms provide ecclesial-transformative theology with the fundamental symbols, religious practices, codes and realities that religious intelligence seeks to apprehend. Of course, this is not to say theology's focus limits to God's revelation given in its two fundamental dimensions.[79] It also addresses "universal human questions" as well.[80] "Within this ecclesial framework," Dulles writes, "it is proper that there be a variety of theological schools. Different theologians can concentrate on different sets of problems, work with different presuppositions, consider different bodies of data, and address different publics." Revelation is the primary subject matter but not the only one.

The meaning of Christian faith emerges, in part, through the normative texts that comprise the Bible. Scriptural revelation concerns foundational doctrines, historical claims, symbolic events, stories, and the drama of human life in relationship to the triune God. It carries divine authority and import.[81] Theology's data and information, therefore, rely heavily upon the texts the community of faith judges revelatory. Scripture's information about faith's content can be grasped in many ways, just as it has been recognized Scripture contains different levels of meaning. Dulles examines these specifically using models: doctrinal, historical, experiential, dialectical, consciousness and the symbolic.[82] Though not an exhaustive description of theological approaches to biblical statement, it does confirm that he refrains from imposing a monolithic or singular understanding of what "biblical revelation" entails. Nonetheless, all approaches agree upon the centrality of the bible as an indispensable source of Christian faith. It can therefore be taken as a principle of unity.

The issue of biblical revelation naturally generates questions of interpretation, doctrine and application. Such questions are raised and explored by the community who judges the scriptures as divinely authoritative. In the Catholic faith, the ways of thinking and living out the meaning of Jesus concomitantly reflecting upon the canon of Scripture become tradition, "a divinely authoritative norm, on a par with Scripture

78. Ibid., 105.
79. Cf. ibid., 83.
80. Ibid., 180.
81. See *Models of Revelation*, 205–10.
82. Ibid., 193–210.

itself."[83] Furthermore, as it relates to scripture, "[tradition] is temporally antecedent to, concomitant with, and subsequent to Scripture. But it falls short of Scripture insofar as it is not available in inspired and canonical texts."[84] Yet by "tradition," what does Dulles mean? To a great extent, the reality and historical importance of tradition means that the Scriptures alone cannot sustain the life of Christianity.[85] Drawing upon the teaching of Vatican II, Dulles holds that "tradition is needed for a sufficient grasp of the word of God, even though it be assumed that all revelation is somehow contained in Scripture."[86]

What Dulles proposes as the meaning of "tradition" seems to be Vatican II's characterization with additional nuance. In its more formal component, tradition comprises "the transmission of the basic Christian message, contained in the Scriptures and the ancient creeds."[87] Existentially, tradition entails the life of the believer within an ongoing, historical community of faith. Tradition also signifies a certain kind of discernment and is a "fluid reality."[88] It is more than "a matter of handing on what has been thought and said, but also a matter of sifting out the truth of the Christian witness from the distortions of human blindness and ignorance. It has a corrective as well as an interpretative function."[89] This function of tradition, moreover, encompasses—insofar as possible—a comprehensive vision. Dulles, states that "it takes the form of a global consciousness enveloping the total life of the Church and enabling her to apprehend the deeper meaning of Scripture herself."[90] Tradition also possesses divine authority, enjoying the guidance of the Holy Spirit "who remains continuously active in the Church."[91] The assurance of God's presence deepens the attention to the realities embodied by the forms of revealed truth. Hence this divine assurance can be a criterion of reli-

---

83. *Craft*, 87.

84. Ibid., 103–4.

85. Dulles, "Tradition: Authentic and Unauthentic," 380. Cf. *Dei Verbum* # 9 in *Decrees of the Ecumenical Councils,* 974–75. Also see Dulles, *Reshaping of Catholicism,* 75–92.

86. *Craft*, 97.

87. Ibid., 98.

88. Dulles, "Tradition: Authentic and Unauthentic," 380.

89. Dulles, *Catholicity of the Church*, 103–4.

90. Dulles, "Tradition: Authentic and Unauthentic," 380.

91. *Craft*, 99.

gious discernment and judgment as to what belongs or remains foreign to the life of faith. For instance, tradition encompasses both "tacit" and "explicit" elements—knowledge that unites deep commitment, performative behavior, and symbolic formation to normative documents and revelatory texts. Dulles admires the views of Maurice Blondel for precisely this emphasis on the tacit dimension within tradition. "He [Blondel] maintained that tradition is the bearer of tacit knowledge. It preserves the living reality of the past, including elements that cannot be stated in propositions. Tradition is not essential for the transmission of particular items of information but rather for imparting a point of view, a perspective, from which to interpret the data. It instills in the faithful a certain skill or habit of mind, enabling them to be docile to the Holy Spirit in their thoughts, words, and actions."[92] In a significant sense, this tacit dimension of faith also means that tradition is marked by creativity, an indication of its ongoing life and ecclesial relevance. "Like the artist and poet," asserts Dulles, "the theologian must seek to extend the tradition and thereby contribute to it."[93] As such, Dulles can maintain that "[t]radition is 'divine' insofar as it is aroused and sustained by God; it is 'apostolic' insofar as it originates with the apostles; it is 'living' insofar as it remains contemporary with every generation."[94]

What I have described thus far as "tradition" comprises the essential creeds, cults and codes that the Christian community believes that God wills for the ongoing life of the Christian church that is not scripture. However, these facets are not independent or alien to Scripture. Concrete and particular expressions of worship, ethical judgments, styles of prayer, worship and so on, derive from and remain continuous with the written word of God. Dulles summarizes this stating that, "the essential and primary function of Christian tradition is not to transmit explicit knowledge, which can better be done by written documents, nor simply to provide a method of discovery, but to impart a tacit, lived awareness of the God to whom the Christian Scriptures and symbols point. Christian tradition is marked by a deep reverence for its own content, which it

---

92. Dulles, "Tradition: Authentic and Unauthentic," 379. Elsewhere, Dulles interprets the thought of Maritain and Möhler in a vein consistent with the cited passage: "Tradition . . . expresses itself primarily by life and action and only secondarily by explicit statements." Dulles, "Tradition and Creativity: A Theological Approach," 319.

93. Dulles, "Tradition and Creativity: A Theological Approach," 321.

94. *Craft*, 103.

strives to protect against any dilution or distortion. The tradition is not a mere method of investigation and discovery."[95] What Dulles indicates in this description of tradition becomes something radically existential. It is the vision of believers as they live out their Christian identity. It is the ongoing, vital guidance by the Spirit towards the Incarnate mystery of God.

This understanding of formal revelation and its historical recipients has important ramifications. Revelation as symbolic communication is not something given to everyone through a "universal religious experience," or "common experience," that then gets expressed as a secondary effect manifest in a particular religious tradition. For Dulles and Lindbeck, symbols are not products of a "transformed consciousness," but precisely the means by which, in large part and with God's grace, consciousness transforms. This process mirrors the way the vocabulary of a given language constructs social and cultural identity. In this view, what one wishes to say is determined beforehand by the words and definitions offered by the particular language.[96] Similarly, cognitive and temporal priority rests with revelation, with the extant, ongoing and vivifying language of God's self-communication. What is given within the mediums of Scripture and Tradition, however, is the graced possibility of religious faith that can transform human experience into a distinctive religious commitment and ecclesial identity.[97] Consequently, full and true access to the transforming power of those symbols—an accurate understanding of revelation—comes from learning and appropriating them already at work upon human subjectivity. All of this remains quite consistent with the doctrine of tradition given in *Dei Verbum*.[98] Indeed, what Dulles

---

95. Dulles, *Reshaping of Catholicism*, 86.

96. See *Craft*, 78.

97. This style of theology is called "epiphanic," a description he credits to Joseph Komonchak. The opposite position would be those theologians who discern "some other norm in addition to revelation as mediated by the Church." These are commonly known as "correlationists" such as Paul Tillich. Dulles, "Theological Education in the Catholic Tradition," 18–19.

98. Dulles also offers a criteriology concerning how to differentiate genuine from spurious "traditions." The four criteria principally concern continuity, upbuilding, reception, and magisterial judgment: (1) "Without necessarily being explicitly taught either in Scripture or in early tradition, any revealed truth must have roots in these sources"; (2) "No doctrine that truly belongs to the deposit of faith will undermine the faith and devotion of those who profess it"; (3) "The teaching in question, if it truly pertains to the deposit of faith, will be received as such by the People of God, especially

maintains differs very little from the teaching of *Dei Verbum*, provided one substitute "post-critical" for "sacred" to prefix theology.

> Sacred theology takes its stand on the written word of God, together with tradition, as its permanent foundation. By this word it is made firm and strong, and constantly renews its youth, as it investigates, by the light of faith, all the truth that is stored up in the mystery of Christ. The holy scriptures contain the word of God and, since they are inspired, really *are* the word of God; therefore the study of the "sacred page" ought to be the very soul of theology. The same word of scripture is the source of healthy nourishment and holy vitality for the ministry of the word—pastoral preaching, catechetics and all forms of Christian instruction, among which the liturgical homily should have the highest place.[99]

Symbolic communication, religious-ecclesial commitment, use of normative sources and fidelity to the magisterium comprise essential elements that mark theology as—to put it briefly—"the understanding of faith."[100] Dulles holds that these elements do not oppose moderate pluralism in methodology and content. How such the pluralism proper to ecclesial-transformative theology works in the university now requires explanation.

ECCLESIAL-TRANSFORMATIVE THEOLOGY IN THE UNIVERSITY

Ecclesial-transformative theology operates within the different spheres of Christian life, such as "the monastery, the pulpit, the chancery, the base community, and the seminary."[101] Such areas specify the tone and style of certain theological disciplines. Dulles classifies some of them along a familiar division: fundamental, practical, and systematic theology. If revelation remains the prime subject matter, then theology can

---

be those manifestly committed to the following of Christ, even at the cost of sacrifice"; (4) "The final element, capable of resolving any remaining doubt on the part of committed Catholics, will be the judgment by the magisterium, which according to Catholic belief enjoys the special assistance of the Holy Spirit to keep the Church from falling away from the gospel." "Tradition: Authentic and Unauthentic," 383–84.

99. *Dei Verbum*, # 24 in Tanner, *Decrees of the Ecumenical Councils*.
100. *Craft*, 7.
101. Dulles, "Place of Theology in a Catholic University," 63 .

employ different ways to discern and apply its content.[102] "It seeks the intelligibility of the revelation ... through positive theology that probes the sources; through apologetics that seeks to establish credibility; through systematics that concerns itself with the inner coherence of the whole scheme of revelation; and through practical theology that ponders the implications of the revealed message for human conduct."[103] As the subject matter narrows, theology specializes to accommodate differences in accent and audience. Yet even within different specializations and settings, Dulles insists upon the presence of the Catholic principles that ensure theology's disciplinary integrity and ecclesial identity. This point underlies statements such as the following: "No sharp opposition can be drawn between theology done at the university and that done in other forums, but theology does tend to take on different hues depending on the environment in which it is practiced."[104] Still, if the context in which theology appears is not the parish, seminary, monastery or retreat center but the university, what kind of "hue" does theology display that differs from the other settings? Furthermore, as an academic discipline, what does Catholic theology accomplish and how can its aims realize its ecclesial identity?

Regrettably, Dulles does not offer a theory of liberal arts education that would enrich the analysis, especially concerning undergraduates.[105] Yet he does describe certain themes that influence academic theology in the church's mission and that, consequently, tell upon how the academic and theological relate. To understand these dynamics, three areas require clarification: (1) the intellectual currents and premises of the academy; (2) academic theology as evangelical and sapiential; and finally (3) the aims of academic theology.

Dulles argues that certain ideological views influence universities no less than their parent culture.[106] The primary current is the ongoing "secularization" and "secular pluralism" present within teaching and research. In terms of scholarly research, secular pluralism fosters the value of "autonomous reason" as the only valid criterion that conclusions re-

102. Cf., *Craft*, 195. "Christian theology must always keep its primary focus on God and on Jesus Christ as the great revelation of God."

103. Ibid., 169.

104. Ibid., 150.

105. Dulles, "Place of Theology in a Catholic University," 65. It is noteworthy that when describing a university, he draws principally upon Newman.

106. Dulles, "Theological Education in the Catholic Tradition," 16–17.

quire for soundness.[107] In terms of teaching, universities that traditionally originated from religious foundations, including Catholic universities, have become or are becoming institutions increasingly characterized by the absence of denominational or religious affiliation.[108] For Dulles and others, secularization as the attenuating of religious identity and doctrinal conviction has transformed some theology faculties into confessionally neutral departments of religious studies.[109] For a large number of previously religiously affiliated schools this dwindling of religious identity effectively eliminated theology as a scholarly discipline.[110] Secular pluralism also fosters an undue "privatization of religion." Religion does not become a public or serious source of knowledge about human culture and value, but is relegated to personal opinion. When this shift happens, the intellectual atmosphere tends towards "historical relativism," a perspective "which treats truth itself as a function of transitory cultural conditions."[111] This secular view results from a culture that favors an ideology of personal freedom, that is, "the ability to choose whatever one pleases."[112] Since the display of personal faith can become an instrument of proselytism and division, it is better that individual religious commitments remain a private matter of freedom and choice, so the personal freedom of all is left unimpeded.[113] Another consequence closely related to the privatization of religion in university contexts is consumerism. Ideas and knowledge can be viewed within a cultural climate that seems to reduce everything to mechanics of production and consumption. Besides the right to enjoy individual freedom, there seems to be little that enjoys an authoritatively privileged place in the academy.

For Dulles, these currents become particularly significant and worrisome, however, when the locus is a Catholic university. In an academic context, these elements of secularization affect not simply philosophical

107. Ibid., 14. For a view of autonomous reason critiqued, see Dulles, "Can Philosophy Be Christian?" 24–29; 26f.

108. Dulles, "Place of Theology in a Catholic University," 61. See also Dulles, "Catholicism 101."

109. Scholars who have written about the current problem of religious identity at universities include George Marsden, James T. Burtchaell, Michael J. Buckley, S.J. and James Turner.

110. *Craft*, 160–61.

111. Dulles, "Principles of Catholic Theology," 83.

112. Dulles, "Evangelizing Theology," 31.

113. Ibid.

and political convictions but filter into the courses students take. Though admittedly limited, one source of evidence he introduces on several occasions to sustain this claim is the research of Frank D. Schubert on secularization and Catholic universities. After analyzing the attributes of course descriptions from three Catholic universities over a thirty-year period, dividing them in ten-year increments, Schubert concludes his study by commenting on the final decade 1975–1985.

> It is clear, then, that in this final period little trace remains of the very specific sacred order of Roman Catholicism presupposed and promulgated in the first period of our study [1955–1965], and questioned in the second. Not only do offerings which reflect a period of uncertainty and doubt continue well into the curricula of this period, there is also a move within this period to include within the religious curricula a range of courses framing their investigations primarily within secular disciplines as they apply to the study of religion, and at the extreme, courses not based in, nor having reference to, any particular sacred order at all.[114]

Schubert's study maintains that according to patterns in titles of theology courses, the presentation and content of these courses shows a marked decline in confessional perspective or what he calls "the sacred order." For Schubert, "the most documentable change within the curricula of the entire period of our study [1955–1985] is the move from theology (the study of religion from *within* a particular sacred order) to religion (the study of *all* sacred orders)."[115] But this change precisely attenuates the bond between ecclesial authority and academic inquiry. For Dulles, there is a disciplinary liability when Catholic theology comes to be regarded or understands itself as an "objective science independent of faith and ecclesiastical authority."[116] This point touches the core concern: the shift threatens theology's intellectual existence and ecclesial legitimacy.

Specific dangers to theology particularly concern elements native to intellectual scholarship and university teaching, namely, academic freedom and "inclusivist pluralism"[117]—the very milieu that generates Schubert's analysis of theology courses. For example, the secularizing

---

114. Schubert, *Sociological Study of Secularization Trends in the American Catholic University*, 128.

115. Ibid.

116. *Craft*, 156.

117. Dulles, "Principles of Catholic Theology," 77.

shift in course offerings and approaches makes it quite possible "that the courses could be taught by agnostics as well as by believers."[118] He focuses upon these topics primarily because they contradict fundamental principles of the discipline, would dissipate theology's character as ecclesial–transformative, and hasten theology's demise.[119] The value of plurality becomes privileged over that of serious conviction about the truth of one position vis-à-vis others.[120] As a consequence of these secondary currents, whatever a theologian might claim to be "Catholic theology" is so, simply by virtue of individual intent and academic designation. Moreover, secularization seems intimately related with the right of scholars to inquire, research and publish—usually understood as "academic freedom." Even here there are problems, however. Dulles contends that since, "no official or uncontested definition of academic freedom" exists, the accepted meaning proceeds by convention. "In current usage, at least in the United States, the term generally denotes the freedom of professionally qualified teachers, first, to pursue their scholarly investigations without interference; second, to publish the results of their research and reflection; and, third, to teach according to their own convictions, provided that they remain in the area of their competence and present the alternative positions with sufficient attention and fairness."[121] Other criteria, such as objective norms of scholarship and institutional autonomy receive more support and esteem than particular religious confessions or historically formative ideals.[122] Consonant with scholarly, disciplinary and implicitly legal standards, scholars are free to research, propose and criticize ideas. This aspect of university culture, for Dulles, resists gestures of limitation and control. He explains why. "Authority is perceived as the willful self-assertion of a dominant elite and as an unwarranted intrusion on the right of individuals to follow

---

118. Dulles, "Theological Education in the Catholic Tradition," 13 .

119. See *Craft*, 157–58. Concerning academic freedom, Dulles asserts: "If academic freedom meant that theologians were entitled to teach as true whatever seemed to them to be suggested by purely rational methods of inquiry, without any deference to Scripture, tradition, or ecclesiastical authority, theology would sacrifice its status as a reflection on the corporate faith of the Church and would cease to render the kind of service that the church expects from it." Also see Dulles, "Place of Theology in a Catholic University," 61–63 .

120. Cf., Dulles, "Evangelizing Theology," 30.

121. *Craft*, 171.

122. Dulles, "Place of Theology in a Catholic University," 61 .

their own judgment. In universities the principle of academic freedom is sometimes formulated in a way that would exempt theological research and teaching from the surveillance of the magisterium."[123] More nuance, however, is needed about the kind of academic freedom at stake. Although universities are arenas for disciplined reflection, consistent methodology, collegial criticism and reasoning, Dulles insists that academic freedom is not "absolute." "It is limited by moral principles, by civil law, by the common good, and by the norms proper to a particular discipline."[124] Concerning theology, academic freedom exists in tension with the official teaching authority, the magisterium. Before considering more deeply Catholic theology's relationship to academic freedom, and as they both relate to authoritative "surveillance," however, a prior question must be addressed. Given the contemporary currents that influence academic life, what does theology *accomplish* specifically within a university that requires magisterial oversight in the first place?

In Cardinal Dulles's more recent thinking on the nature of Catholic theology in the university, he develops two important areas. First, he offers more specific reflections about higher education within the framework of Christian evangelization. For Dulles, education is a process of socialization to culture. This socialization would form students to "rise above merely material concerns, profit from the achievements of their forebears, live in communion with their fellows, pass on what they have received, and perhaps contribute to further progress."[125] These aims, however, are minimum requirements. Dulles maintains further that in terms of university education, those who graduate "are expected to be men and women of more than ordinary culture."[126] While secular universities should achieve the minimum requirements of living for more than material gain and to become good citizens, Catholic universities must do more. Catholic universities should be forming students to be carriers of Christian culture and as "instruments in the Christianization of the world."[127] Theology within the Catholic university directly con-

---

123. Dulles, "Principles of Catholic Theology," 84. Dulles seems to have the "Land O'Lakes Statement" in mind here. For the document, see O'Keefe, *Catholic Education at the Turn of the New Century*, 119–24.

124. Dulles, "Place of Theology in a Catholic University," 67.

125. Dulles, "Evangelization of Culture and the Catholic University," 2.

126. Ibid.

127. Ibid., 4.

tributes to the evangelizing of culture through its evangelizing influence upon students who will then shape the broader secular culture. Christian evangelization, for Dulles, occurs at three general stages and can take a narrow and broad meaning.

> In the narrowest sense it refers to the proclamation of the gospel to those who do not yet believe. But this activity, sometimes called a first evangelization, is only one stage of a larger process. Prior to conversion people can often be prepared to hear the word by a process known as pre-evangelization, and after conversion they are expected to submit to continued evangelization in order to achieve Christian maturity. At times, having fallen away from the gospel, Christians are in need of re-evangelization. Evangelization in its full sense of the word includes all three stages: the announcement of the gospel to those who have not yet heard it credibly proclaimed, the pastoral care and religious maturation of believers, and the rekindling of faith in those who have fallen away.[128]

The context of the university may include all three stages of evangelization and thus give some indication of what theology might achieve. Dulles distinguishes these levels more precisely by naming them "primary evangelization, catechesis, and theology."[129] Insofar as theology is intrinsically linked to proclamation of the gospel, it can interest people to consider seriously the claims made by Christian revelation. Next, theology may deepen the revelation that has been accepted in faith. Finally, theology can reclaim former believers from non-Christian principles and values.

Dulles's second point is the need to recover a sapiential dimension to theology. The sapiential or "wisdom" dimension relates to theology's ecclesial function and its origin as the fruit of specific, Christian experience. Historically, the source of wisdom can be reason or it can be faith. In the traditional sense, philosophical wisdom pursues "questions such as the existence and nature of God, the creation of contingent beings, the dignity of the human person, the immortality of the soul, the relationship between soul and body, and innumerable other questions of this kind."[130] However, it is the drive of human intelligence towards full co-

---

128. Ibid., 4–5.
129. Dulles, "Catholicism 101," 303–8; 303.
130. Dulles, "Evangelization of Culture and the Catholic University," 9.

herence of the reality as such that lies behind the topics of philosophical inquiry. Dulles writes that "[W]isdom in the full and unrestricted sense of the word belongs to those who can discourse about reality in general, seeing all things in their mutual interrelationships, and assigning to each its proper place within an intelligible whole. To be able to perceive the similarities and differences, the mutual dependences and orientations of a vast multitude of distinct realities is a superlative exercise of the intellectual power."[131] This description and vocabulary of this philosophical sense of wisdom relies on Newman.[132] What builds upon philosophical wisdom is divine revelation. Here he distinguishes two types of theological wisdom.

In laying out the first meaning of theological wisdom, Dulles continues to rely on Newman and incorporates Aquinas. Faith must have a cognitive, rational component that does "provide a synthesis or causal account of its own contents."[133] Revelation is accepted on faith and provides the basic principles from which theological reasoning and argument proceed. These principles cannot be demonstrated rationally but must be accepted as true. The status of a theology which accepts principles but cannot prove them as self-evident in themselves but upon the authority of a higher knowledge is as a "sub-altern" science.[134] Theology as wisdom seeks to harmonize and order the different revealed truths since they do not come to human beings as a system. The means by which revealed truths are constructed systematically are to use "the analogy of objects of natural knowledge; to discern the interconnections among the various revealed mysteries; and to see how these mysteries help us to fulfill our inbuilt drive toward our ultimate end."[135] The latter strategies are the teaching of Vatican I.[136] What results from this view of theological wisdom is a discipline that seeks inner coherence among various Christian doctrines but uses reason and human experience to furnish concepts and language that allow the doctrines to retain their truth in vital expressions.

131. See Dulles, "Wisdom as the Source of Unity for Theology," 61 n. 4.
132. See the note citing Newman, "Wisdom as the Source of Unity for Theology," 61 n. 4.
133. Dulles, "Wisdom as the Source of Unity for Theology," 63.
134. Ibid., 65.
135. Ibid., 66.
136. Ibid.

The other meaning of theological wisdom is that of infused wisdom or as the gift of the Holy Spirit. Dulles distinguishes this form of knowledge about the divine from philosophical and theological wisdom because it involves an experiential "intimate familiarity with God."[137] The view of infused wisdom here is that of Aquinas. There is a special grace that comes to those engaged in theological reflection by having a love affair with God. This love affair with God yields a "connaturality with the divine" that enables one to know God more deeply. This deeper, experiential knowledge of God means that "wisdom involves having a taste for the things of God, so that we delight in them."[138] Certainly, Dulles is picking up upon the contemplative dimension of prayer and worship inscribed within Aquinas's rich understanding of infused knowledge. The benefit of this infused wisdom goes beyond what "is lacking to mere academicians in the field. They know the divine not only through the discipline acquired by study but more directly through the gift of the Holy Spirit."[139] Moreover, persons or theologians who possess this infused wisdom, according to Dulles, have "an interior sense of the divine" that "will greatly help the theologian to judge rightly concerning the things of God." So not only does this gift configure the theologian's affectivity and longings to God but also directs the intelligence better as to what is authentically of revelation and in conformity with it. The prime examples of infused wisdom in the concrete life of the church are the "Fathers and Doctors of the church" who have been saints.[140]

Much of Dulles' recent work concerns the thought of Pope John Paul II.[141] This is especially evident regarding the relationship between Catholic theology and university. He cites the pope's apostolic constitution *Ex Corde Ecclesiae* to furnish basic tenets for his own position regarding the function of academic theology. Along with philosophy, theology generally assists a Catholic university "to determine the relative place and meaning of each of the various disciplines within the context

---

137. Ibid., 67.
138. Ibid.
139. Ibid.
140. Ibid.
141. Some of his recent publications include: "Reason, Philosophy, and the Grounding of Faith," 479–90; *Splendor of Faith*; "Evangelizing Theology," 27–32.

of a vision of the human person and the world that is enlightened by the Gospel."[142] More specifically, he cites John Paul II again.

> Theology plays a particularly important role in the search for a synthesis of knowledge as well as in the dialogue between faith and reason. It serves all other disciplines in their search for meaning, not only by helping them to investigate how their discoveries will affect individuals and society, but also by bringing a perspective and an orientation not contained within their own methodologies. In turn, interaction with these other disciplines and their discoveries enriches theology, offering it a better understanding of the world today and making theological research more relevant to current needs. Because of its specific importance among the academic disciplines, every Catholic university should have a faculty, or at least a chair, of theology.[143]

In theory, theology is synthetic insofar as it helps unify human knowledge; judicial because it evaluates the moral effects of knowledge upon human society and culture; assimilative and contemporary for it renews itself by letting the truths of human knowledge change it and, thereby, enable it to meet "current needs."

Historically, university theology assisted the church in formulating, expressing, even helping to sanction what became normative doctrine and ecclesiastical policy. It also produced scholarly works and addressed "social and moral problems."[144] On occasion, as Dulles indicates, university theology could also help settle problems of secular politics.[145] From the end of the middle ages onwards, however, theology suffered a recession in cultural and intellectual vigor on the whole. Painting with a wide brush, Dulles posits that subsequent to historical-secular movements in Europe—nationalism, religious toleration, Enlightenment criticism—church and theology defined themselves more by opposition to the modern world than by engagement. This introspective orientation continued until the Second Vatican Council. Subsequently, renewed theological reflection has shifted to university life and culture. For Dulles, university theology now fulfils its function—in addition to

---

142. John Paul II, *Ex Corde Ecclesiae*, 269 as cited in Dulles, "Place of Theology in a Catholic University," 59.

143. John Paul II, *Ex Corde Ecclesiae*, 269–70 as cited in *Craft*, 149–50.

144. *Craft*, 105–52.

145. Ibid., 152.

Ex corde ecclesiae's ideals—insofar as it, in a scholarly manner, helps explore, transmit and maintain Christian revelation. But its role is more complex. It encompasses different orientations and vectors within the overarching character of the Church's soteriological mission. The reason for university theology's soteriological character is because theology emanates from the church. Theology's aims must also consider other important factors such as diverse audiences, course content, ecclesiastical oversight and the free character of scholarly inquiry. But what does this soteriological aim mean more concretely?

First, it is not the case—to distinguish university from seminary theology—that academic theology's purpose concerning doctrine is simple repetition or transmission. Dulles does not simply repeat or affirm the notion of theology found in *Humani Generis*—though he thinks parts of it can be defended.[146] Scripture and tradition work as resources to address problems "not explicitly answered in the sources themselves."[147] Properly speaking, to realize its identity as a scientific discipline academic theology is "oriented more heavily toward research ... it maintains, or should maintain, close contact with other disciplines, such as history, literary critics, sociology, psychology, and philosophy."[148] It is necessary for theological research to draw upon the assistance of other disciplines in developing new strategies, views and solutions. Indeed, the more theology dialogues and interacts with "the human and natural sciences," the more it "can be invigorated and purified."[149] What Dulles implies here is the advance and horizon of knowledge not only modifies and refines other disciplines, such as sociology, psychology and philosophy, but also helps keep theology's orientation and voice relevant to contemporary concerns. Dulles writes, "In the contemporary situation it is necessary for Catholic intellectuals to take account of the variety of religions and enter into respectful dialogue with them as well

---

146. See ibid., 128. The sense of "theology" is an internal, an ecclesiastical procedure that uses deductive reasoning from the sources of revelation, Scripture and Tradition to show a connection between present teaching and historical continuity. It cites and affirms the teaching of "Our Predecessor of immortal memory, Pius IX" who held that "the most noble office of theology is to show how a doctrine defined by the Church is contained in the sources of revelation." *Humani Generis*, #21, as cited in Carlen, *Papal Encyclicals 1939–1958*, 175–84.

147. *Craft*, 169.

148. Ibid., 155.

149. Ibid., 159.

as with secular sciences."[150] The achievements and difficulties of human life combined with efforts to enrich human culture are addressed by the range of secular disciplines that theology must confront. Theology's contribution, then, expresses deep engagement with and promotion of genuine human culture that flow from Vatican II's mandate.[151] This aim also emerges from the principle of "humanism" that characterizes the Catholic intellectual tradition and post-critical theology.[152]

Particularly in this effort, academic theology must be unrestricted. Catholic theology can "possess a certain freedom over against even the hierarchical magisterium."[153] As the academic context involves different disciplines and audiences, so theology must adopt methods that move beyond appeal to authority and involve criticism. Non-infallible magisterial teaching, for example, can be critically questioned and challenged by theological inquiry. It may, consequently, generate dissent.[154] Nevertheless, though dissent "should be rare, respectful and reluctant" it can be salutary for theology and the church.[155] In fact, this is and has been true throughout church history. Serious dissent has led to doctrinal change that benefited the church. Acceptance of critical-historical methodologies for the Bible, ecumenism, the possibility of salvation outside formal ecclesial structures and religious freedom were theological positions that moved from being dissent to official teaching. Indeed, such positions constitute part of Vatican II's achievement.[156] More particularly, however, the question arises anew: how do the ecclesial and the post-critical relate? The primary relation is the domain and responsibility of doctrine.

Because every ecclesial doctrine develops and because theology requires academic freedom for its integrative vitality, it exists and func-

150. Dulles, "Evangelization of Culture and the Catholic University," 10.

151. *Craft*, 155.

152. Dulles, "Principles of Catholic Theology," 76.

153. *Craft*, 169.

154. Ibid., 169. Dulles distinguishes "four categories of magisterial statement" in term of authoritative weight: (1) definitively revealed truth; (2) "definitive declarations of nonrevealed truths closely connected with revelation and the Christian life"; (3) "non-definitive but obligatory teaching"; and (4) "prudential admonitions or applications of Christian doctrine in a particular time or place." *Craft*, 108–9. Objects of theological dissent to which Dulles refers seem to be in the second category.

155. Paulson, "Cardinal's Path to faith began simply," B2.

156. Dulles, "Theologian And The Magisterium," 240.

tions within a broader context than merely that of academic teaching and research. "A Catholic college or university," Dulles contends, "is not purely and simply an academy in the secular meaning of the term. It seeks to discharge a service toward the Church and toward the religious development of its students, especially those who are Catholics."[157] Here, Catholic theology's intellectual responsibility and ecclesial accountability exceeds that of other university disciplines and distinguishes it. In part, this is because the work of sustaining and transmitting the content of a living, religious tradition is not solely the effort of university theology, however crucial its role in it. When key components of a religious tradition concern authoritative claims embodied as dogmatic teaching, the problem becomes even more pointed, since it then concerns theological content.[158] To illustrate the relationship between content and context that further differentiates Catholic theology, Dulles adopts key principles from Newman. Insofar as theology pursues its subject matter in the university setting, he transposes limitations upon it judged consonant with its scholarly character. Academic theology should, he states: "not collide with dogma; it must not issue pronouncements on religious matters in competition with the official magisterium of the Church; it must not indulge in brilliant paradoxes but rather propound serious views; it must take care to avoid shocking the popular mind or unsettling the weak."[159] These directives pertain not simply to parochial, spiritual or monastic contexts but also to the academic. The university context is where magisterial authority, the content of faith and the academic approach to disciplined reflection seem to clash most acutely.

Another difference seems to affect directly the content of theological instruction and bear upon classroom pedagogy. Dulles agrees with Walter Burghardt who maintains that Catholic students at Catholic universities are "utterly ignorant of their rich tradition."[160] As a real and pressing problem, therefore, it has a claim upon Catholic theologians and theology. Because there is a deprivation of ecclesial knowledge, and because Catholic universities participate in the larger church, he

157. *Craft*, 172.

158. Ibid., 177. "The dogmas of faith do not have the same status in theology as currently accepted theories have for secular science."

159. Ibid., 159.

160. Burghardt, "Intellectual and Catholic? Or Catholic Intellectual?" 424, as cited in Dulles, "Theological Education in the Catholic Tradition," 21.

insists that Catholic theology shoulders a religious duty marked by its ecclesial character. "Without exposure to university theology," he claims, "many students would never unite their faith with rigorous intellectual discipline."[161] Catholic theology must address religious and doctrinal illiteracy and support intellectual formation. It has a remedial mission. "In a university which is Catholic by tradition and has a large proportion of Catholic students, courses should be offered in theology from a Catholic point of view. A Catholic university would fall short of its mission if it failed to present its students with the possibility of gaining a mature and sophisticated understanding of their faith, developed in proportion to the general state of their intellectual culture."[162] Access to orthodox teaching via Catholic theology in a university, for Dulles, is a "fundamental educational right."[163] Theologians teaching Christian doctrine in classrooms as part of theology courses, therefore, should propound official Catholic doctrine whose catechetical dimension and character is present. On the other hand, the presence of a catechetical dimension does not reduce the teaching of theology to the catechism—an idea Dulles judges as "not necessarily suitable for actual religious instruction."[164] Yet precisely due to its catechetical character, neither should it be taught as speculative or scholarly opinion. This is because theologians function as unofficial or quasi-magisterial teachers of the church.[165] But when this occurs, the parameters of discourse and teaching authority must be different than those of secular disciplines. Indeed, "theologians cannot simply disregard the teaching of the pastors. They cannot responsibly substitute their own opinions for the official teaching."[166] The theologian who then teaches not Catholic doctrine but what is held by the church at the time to be dissenting, different or erroneous opinion, based on individual conviction or popular sentiment, "forfeits any title to be called a Catholic theologian."[167] Yet why would theologians do this? What elements mitigate orthodoxy in the classroom? Dulles advances specific reasons for each.

161. *Craft*, 162.
162. Ibid., 162.
163. Ibid., 172.
164. Dulles, "Church and the Universal Catechism," 201.
165. See *Craft*, 165–67; 171.
166. Ibid., 158.
167. Ibid., 175.

> Under pressure from the modern "turn to the subject," Catholic theologians are often reluctant to speak of sacraments as conferring grace. Some shy away from the very term *ex opere operato* as a vestige of magical thinking. But the principle behind this terminology is one on which Catholics cannot yield. If they allow the efficacy of sacraments to be thrown into doubt, as though the subjective attitude of faith were all that mattered, they will soon find that the whole system of mediation, including the doctrine of the incarnation, begins to crumble . . . Under the pervasive influence of a secularism that denies God's action in the world, theologians are tempted to cast doubt on the biblical account of God's mighty deeds on behalf of his people, including his coming in the flesh. The Christology of the ancient councils is embattled. Claiming to correct the Monophysitism of the past, some fall into a crypto-Nestorianism that treats Christ, at least for practical purposes, as a human person vaguely linked with the divine. The uniqueness of Christ as universal Savior is frequently dismissed as a kind of confessional arrogance.[168]

In this case, such tendencies toward sacramental theology and Christology, undermine crucial communications of theological content that directly affect the religious faith of the ecclesial community.[169] In the particular university setting, a significant representation of the community includes Catholic parents and students. Dulles argues that they expect "the Catholic faith will be faithfully explored and defended in a Catholic university."[170] When this does not occur, the theologian's views directly contradict not only the magisterial expectation and respect for authority inherent in the nature of their task, but abrogate their ecclesial commitments. To avoid this, therefore, theologians must consciously recognize magisterial sway. "In the interests of their own profession, theologians should support the magisterium as it seeks to safeguard the apostolic heritage, whether by way of positively encouraging sound developments or by way of administering, on occasion, a word of caution or correction. The rights of the theologian as an academician become real only when situated in this ecclesial framework."[171] In the end, theologians as teachers transmit, propose, maintain and critically evaluate Christian

---

168. Dulles, "Principles of Catholic Theology," 83.

169. For more of Dulles' criticism concerning sacramental theology, see "Disputed Questions: How Catholic is the CTSA?" 13–14.

170. Dulles, "Place of Theology in a Catholic University," 63.

171. *Craft*, 175–76.

doctrine—but they do not make or establish official teaching.[172] This responsibility is left for the ecclesial authorities, the magisterium.

CONCLUSION

Cardinal Dulles offers an interpretation of Catholic theology as "ecclesial-transformative" for the church and university. It can overcome pervasive tendencies that emerge from the situation of secular pluralism that challenge essential principles of Catholic theological method and proficiency. The secularity of this context, loosely defined as the dismissal of divine activity in the world, spawns an intellectual climate of cultural relativism, privatization of religious discourse, and pedagogical negligence in terms of doctrinal instruction. Its type of "pluralism," one that "divides and destroys," engenders radically different and contradictory principles that severely diminish the possibility of a common language, common norms and common goals.[173] Secular pluralism becomes particularly acute in the university setting, where radical diversity, academic freedom, and a consumerist mentality resist authoritative gestures of control and scorn the truth claims of religious discourse. Consequently, these influences threaten Catholic theology because they tempt it to forfeit features that make it theological and forsake its ecclesial identity.

Ecclesial-transformative theology seeks to address the lack of integrating and identifying principles that must characterize theological research and teaching. At the same time, it tries to restore the requisite pneumatological and ecclesial conditions for its scholarly existence within a Catholic university. Its common norms in pursuing its subject matter comprise scripture, tradition, and deference to the ecclesial magisterium. Towards a common language and vision, Dulles advocates "ten principles" that distinguish and affirm Catholic theology's distinctive identity from other academic disciplines. As common goals, they insist that theological reflection concentrate upon the revelation of God in Jesus to the church and the broader culture as well as creative development of doctrine and genuine transmission of official teaching. In all these elements, Catholic theology presupposes belief in the truth of its

---

172. Dulles cites the example of biblical exegetes. He quotes *Dei Verbum* that holds the exegetes are "subject finally to the judgment of the Church, which carries out the divine commission and ministry of guarding and interpreting the word of God." Dulles, "Tradition: Authentic and Unauthentic," 382–83.

173. Dulles, *Models of the Church*, 13.

content and faithful participation in the symbolic realities that inculcate the formative habits and skills necessary for theological deliberation.

The purpose of ecclesial-transformative theology in higher education becomes clearer when its pedagogical function unites with elements that characterize it as ecclesial. In part, this involves resisting the secular currents in contemporary and academic culture that undermine either the subject matter of the discipline or the theological aptitude. Both remain vital. There is an ecclesial imperative upon the academic teaching of Catholic theology that differs in kind from theological or historical investigation that might lead to doctrinal or otherwise specialized development. Lay Catholics, parents and students, possess legitimate claims to and expectations of theologians as quasi-official teachers of doctrine that do not apply to other faculty or secular disciplines. To satisfy these legitimate claims, ecclesial-transformative theology should define itself, not exclusively, but in the university setting, primarily according to elements and religious conditions that mark seminary theology, namely, the transmission of "safe and established doctrine." For seminary theology generally, as he describes, "[p]roof frequently takes the form of an appeal to authoritative texts, such as Scripture, the councils, and papal utterances."[174] Dulles' more recent insistence on the need to recover an integrated sapiential dimension of theology is a development of this direction. Provided that this type of teaching allowed for measured criticism proper to the scholarly character of theology that may, in some cases, lead to legitimate dissent, it achieves a balance between "inclusivist pluralism" and "sectarian narrowness."[175] This would indeed offset the secularist trend Schubert maintains concerning theological course offerings. The content of faith would then be presented from the unequivocal perspective of authentically Christian religious commitment and scholarly rigor. At the same time, the symbolic grasp and communication of faith would be likewise secured, for the subject matter requires religious dimensions and assent beyond any standard of "autonomous reason." Hence, aside from the goals of scholarly research, evangelization, and ecclesial consultation, educating generations of Catholics in the university is, then, a part of what ecclesial-transformative theology accomplishes and defines its character. The identity of university theology as "faith seeking understanding," therefore, joins doctrinal instruction, ecclesial

174. *Craft*, 154–55.
175. Dulles, "Principles of Catholic Theology," 77–78.

confession and academic standards of intelligibility. The place and value of university theology, then, remains imperative for the ongoing evangelization of the church and the broader secular culture.

6

Edward Farley—Theology as Sapiential Hermeneutic in the University

> The best theology is rather a divine life than a divine knowledge.
> —Jeremy Taylor

A SECOND CONTEMPORARY FORMULATION of theology and its place within the university comes from another distinguished theologian: Edward Farley. Denominationally Presbyterian, Farley's approach to the question, identification of problems and tentative solutions contrasts significantly with those of Dulles. Perhaps the most significant difference, however, is Farley's ecumenical style. While each theologian offers descriptions of theology, its methods, characteristics and meaning within an academic context, Dulles' treatment of the issues manifests a marked confessional commitment. Dulles appeals to Scripture, tradition, the magisterium as authoritative norms but Farley will not. Indeed, Farley considers precisely such elements as part of the "house" or "way of authority." This model of theological criteria and normativity has been and is part of the problem concerning contemporary Christian theology's methodology, pedagogy, public relevance and vitality beyond confessional boundaries. His approach to theological method in general and theology's meaning in the university in particular, consequently, reflects this radical departure from traditional Christian argumentation. He introduces an alternative.

As with Dulles, my inquiry concerns central features or characteristics of Farley's conception of theology and its activities. Due to considerations of space, the analysis cannot be exhaustive. This chapter will identify and describe four main issues divided into two main parts. First, the historical-structural origin of theology, namely, the "ecclesia" will be explained. Farley insists his work is theological repeatedly and therefore grounded in the pre-given realities of Christian faith. Hence, inquiry demands some grasp of what the corporate matrix means especially in terms of images, concepts, symbols that are theological in nature. Second, my analysis explores the problematic situation of doing theology in two aspects: how and why the "legacy of theological method" called the "house" or "way of authority" obscures theology's focus on reality and truth, and an examination of two different genres of etymological meaning associated with the career of "theology." In the second part, we shall trace Farley's recovery of an older and more comprehensive definition of theology as a habitus, a personal and reflective wisdom of the believer and show its superiority to more modern meanings, namely, the "clerical paradigm." Finally, the relationship between the different ideas will converge in understanding ecclesial reflection as specific, hermeneutic modes or ways of seeing in the university.

THE FACTICITY OF REDEMPTION: ECCLESIA AND THEOLOGICAL REFLECTION

The forms, structures, texts, events, activities of Christian faith's historical communities are, for Farley, theologically and practically misunderstood without first grasping the facticity of redemption or, put differently, "how God comes forth as God into the language and experience of the religious community."[1] The present, determinate, redemptive activity of God is Farley's cognitive point of departure. In this sense, it differs from classical apologetics. It is not an attempt to "prove" God's existence or forms of divine activity to those "outside the specific situations of religious communities and their symbolics" but rather "to answer the question why participants in religious communities have such convictions."[2] Understanding a second-order reflective enterprise like theology, then, largely depends upon examining and describing the community and experience of God as redemptive. Why is this true? For Farley, "the way God is God, the very meaning of "God" in actual religious communities, is connected to some sort of experienced redemption."[3] The dynamics of faith as apprehending God's redeeming work effect and sustain that

---

1. Farley, *DE*, 21.
2. Ibid., 74.
3. Ibid., 20.

which emerges into historically reflective consciousness, such as authorities, texts and symbolics.[4] Where such redeeming activity occurs, Farley will not apodictically restrict to the Christian community.[5] But efforts to bypass what he calls "the matrix of redemptive (individual) existence" or "ecclesia" would abstract theology from its subject matter, leaving it prey to philosophical, social scientific, or merely historical interpretation—modes of discourse it may engage and appropriate, but intellectual endeavors to which it remains irreducible.[6] And this irreducibility expresses not a cognitive attribute primarily, but precisely the experience of divine activity as redemption. Hence the entry into Farley's thought must proceed through redemptive experience as such, that is, into the ecclesia in order to discern the reality and significance of what theology means. Indeed, a recent characterization of theology validates this approach: "I am persuaded that theology's first moment is not a specific doctrinal theme but a very compact and multisided state of affairs, the actuality of redemption. Gathered into the fact of redemption—always already there so to speak—are all of faith's specific motifs: human evil, Spirit, creation, divine image, grace, God, Christology, ecclesia."[7] The aim here is not, however, to elaborate fully his ecclesiology but to expose essential features of this "religious community" that condition the character and trajectory of theological reflection.

Deep correspondence and connection obtains between the redemptive experience of God and immediately apprehending the realities of faith. But describing precisely "what happens" in the immediate experience of redemption is notoriously difficult. The effort inevitably involves reductive and idolatrous tendencies to quantify or isolate the divine. Farley frames the issue negatively when he remarks that "our thesis is that God is apprehended neither at the transcendental levels of the religious a priori, nor in and through a trusted authority, nor by means of the intellective acts of which the "proofs" are examples. God being what

---

4. Ibid., 21; 94. Farley maintains that "if reality-apprehensions occur in the mode of presence and appresence at the depth levels of ecclesia, this means that authorities (Scripture, tradition) are not *principia* in the Aristotelian sense of Protestant scholasticism, the first and immediate starting point from which everything else is constructed. Historically speaking, the authorities did not produce but grew out of a social and redemptive existence which preceded them." Farley, *EM*, 232.

5. *DE*, 74–75.

6. Ibid., 24–25; *EM*, 209.

7. Farley, *Faith and Beauty*, viii.

he is, there appears to be no way of really "accounting" for how he is present, or why the reality of God is irreducible. Such accounts themselves invariably reduce him."[8] Pinpointing or detailing the workings of the divine in a particular moment or experience, therefore, is not a task we shall pursue deeply, even though Farley treats it extensively elsewhere.[9] Suffice to say, however, that the apprehensions of faith are "largely preconscious" and thus precede hearing, believing, learning, and being emotionally affected by the tradition's language and symbols.[10] In other words, "faith's apprehensions do not occur as products of theological ratiocination but as concomitants of a largely unconscious shaping of the consciousness."[11] Yet Farley eschews designating God's coming forth in individual and social life as "religious experience." What redemptive experience means does not rely on evidence external to the Christian paradigm of meaning, such as might be offered by William James.[12]

The facticity of redemption is a determinate, historical, intersubjective reality. Farley does not argue to it from the outside on philosophical or a priori grounds.[13] He explains.

> In early Christian literature Jesus' titles and names involve a vocabulary of redemption (redeemer, Lord, saviour, Messiah, Son of Man); the metaphors describing his ministry and work are metaphors of redemption; and the portraits of ecclesia and human life in ecclesia are portraits of redemptive existence (love, freedom, justification, spirit, and life). Participation in ecclesia means, therefore, a modification of human existence toward redemption. This is the most general way of expressing it, and the term *modification* is not used here to exclude more specific descriptions such as justification. We use the expression *toward redemption* to indicate the incompleteness and therefore the eschatological dimension of redemption in ecclesia.[14]

---

8. *EM*, 223.
9. See all of *EM*; *DE*, 62–75; 94–110.
10. *DE*, 68; *EM*, 212–13.
11. *EM*, 232.
12. Ibid., 208.
13. More technically speaking, the "principle of positivity" controls the description of both individual and collective redemptive existence in ecclesia. Farley begins and ends not in universal ontology, but the historically specific actuality of a specific people and their experience. Consequently, problems and issues of "knowledge, evidence, meaning, and verification" cannot be settled or fixed by "merely universal terms." *EM*, 207.
14. Ibid., 127–28.

The constellation of images and terms that orient the human toward the divine, then, Farley subsumes under the term "redemption." However, there are distinctive features. Ecclesial existence and ecclesiality as such is not reducible to a single philosophical position or general ontology.[15]

Descriptions of what intersubjective redemptive existence signifies in Farley's work are formal, abstract and often cast in philosophical terminology. His own account features language cognate with phenomenology and Heideggerian ontology.[16] Yet he insists that the realities under consideration and their description refers to both the personal sphere of human existence and figure in the ongoing community of faith. An important theme and example of this is the "dynamics of idolatry" in relation to redemptive existence. It illumines something significant about the human condition and that which redemption radically alters.[17]

> On the negative side, redemption means the reduction of the need and inclination of the human being to secure itself, to obtain the foundation of its own meaning and telos by absolutizing attachments to worldly entities valued as the eternal. It is clear that anxiety, fear, and enmity of various sorts attend this self-world relation since that entity which the human being regards as the eternal exists in a perilous, worldly environment and thus is as relative and vulnerable as the human being itself. Relating to worldly entities in these anxious modes of guardianship and protection, the human being is not free toward them. On the positive side, redemption alters the idolatrous ways of being-in-the-world. The world and its contents are grasped as not-the-eternal and dependent-on-the-eternal. Replacing enmity and fear are wonder, awe, and concern toward worldly entities, an empathetic, emotive appreciation of them, as part of the network of created being. Universalism is involved here because all worldly entities (persons, nations, possessions, nature, beautiful objects) are relativized and at the same time are manifest and available in their value, usefulness, importance, and beauty. Insofar as such a redemption has been operative, it effects a singular kind of

---

15. For the necessity and value of philosophical pluralism in theology, see Farley's "Thinking Toward The World," 51–63.

16. Farley's coins the phrase "reflective ontology" to define his own particular cognitive style, which he maintains stands in continuity with other thinkers such as Augustine, Schleiermacher, Buber, and Tillich. For more, see Farley, *Good and Evil*, 1–26, Cited as *GE*.

17. Idolatry is one theme, but not the only theme Farley might select to illustrate important features of redemption. See *EM*, 142.

cointentionality between human beings. They "mean" each other not simply through the story and symbols of redemption, but as sharing the new being-in-the-world, as beings who universally have the world in empathetic wonder, awe and concern (that is, in agape).[18]

Redemption concerns three aspects of human being. First there is the facticity of such redemption, that is, God's transforming of idolatrous passions toward self-securing. Second, this transformation regards a human being already caught up in a network of worldly relations influenced by evil and the tragic dimensions of human life.[19] Third, what sin disrupts and redemption transforms does pertain to human existence as such, that is, "an *ontological* pattern, the pattern of what is distinctively and properly human."[20] This empathetic, non-idolatrous, and agapic cointentionality is profoundly Christian, taking its inspiration and meaning from the stories, myths and imagery that comprise it. Presupposed in this redemptive experience, of course, are theological and ontological notions about human self-transcendence defined by a fundamental rupture (sin), and thus, as desiring fulfillment despite pervasive anxiety.[21] Consonant with his philosophical or theological anthropology, redemptive existence orients human beings toward genuine freedom and obligation.[22]

The idolatrous, however, is overcome in the social, intersubjective sphere of ecclesia. Indeed, how people intend and see each other within the ecclesia as faithful participants is unique precisely because the "cointentionalities . . . are possible only within the imagery, the shaped consciousness of this redemptive existence."[23] It is not only a change in human "perspective" but also a real transformation of human being

---

18. *ER*, 229.

19. *GE*, 121f. For more on "tragic," see ibid., 119–38.

20. *EM*, 212.

21. *DE*, 62f; *EM*, 211f. Much of Farley's sophisticated theological anthropology is summarized in chapter five, but it is also meticulously detailed in both *Ecclesial Man* and *Good and Evil*. He situates himself within the "Augustinian tradition" concerning the symmetry between human nature and redemptive activity, called "the religious a priori" but also concerning the human condition as such. That is to say, human beings are ontologically characterized as *inquietus*, suggesting the driving, insatiable nature of historical existence." *EM*, 130; 132.

22. For a fuller account of freedom and obligation, see *EM*, 146–49. See also, *Deep Symbols*, 42–54. Cited hereafter *DS*.

23. *EM*, 158–59.

and meaning.²⁴ This intersubjectivity comprises faith's social matrix concretely and thereby resists attempts to individualize or privatize the meaning of Jesus of Nazareth to a historical entity that would, intentionally or unintentionally, restrict the universally redemptive activity of God. Put differently, Farley maintains that "this through-which of historical redemption (at least for the Christian movement) is the new community, the new corporate reality with its intersubjectivity, traditions, narratives, and symbolics. But whence comes the new community? What is its through-which? The answer is the figure and activity of Jesus, the resolution of which is the beginning of the new community."²⁵ As communal participation is requisite for the formation of intersubjective cointentionality to occur, so institutionalization is necessary for its social duration in history. This naturally raises the question of the social dimension of redemption, namely, the ecclesia.

"Ecclesia" originates with the new community formed from the person, work, and death of Jesus Christ.²⁶ Jesus Christ is the abiding, normative event for the redemptive community of the ecclesia.²⁷ Yet Farley's understanding of this community in some sense transcends confessional lines. He refuses to adjudicate—albeit recognizing—between rival Christian denomination's claims to be definitive, authentic, and the sole carriers of Christian faith's existence as historical and social. Ecclesia denotes the reality of idolatrous responses to reality becoming true freedoms and a historical persistence of this experience that is comprehensive—one might almost say "catholic." "[W]e are adopting Emil Brunner's convention, using ecclesia to mean the distinctive, corporate existence characterized by the presence of Jesus Christ, and church as our inclusive term. Although ecclesia means a distinctive form of corporate existence, it is not easily identified with any one form of human sociality. It is not an exclusive form of social organization such as a nation or tribe, a determinate social world, a "finite province of meaning," a sub-culture, or even a local face-to-face community."²⁸ The reality of "ecclesia," then, cannot be restricted to or contained by any social-historical form, period, ethnicity, political structure, culture. This is why Farley avoids the

24. Ibid., 214–15.
25. *DE*, 256.
26. Ibid., 253.
27. Cf. *ER*, 221–25.
28. *EM*, 152.

word "church" to designate it and also because "church" brings with it "so much dogmatic and confessional baggage."[29] At the same time, however, ecclesia possesses determinate content. It forms a "specific community" with a collective memory, kerygma, and relative forms of institutionality.[30] Historical institutionalizations that spawn forms of socially redemptive mediation, leadership and action function to promote ecclesiality. This encompasses classical expressions of religious life and thought such as tradition, proclamation, literature, sacraments, worship, etc. Farley admits that the closest traditional symbol to what ecclesiality means is not a specific space or time but an unfolding reality, the "kingdom of God."[31] Furthermore, ecclesiality mediated through the institutionalization and its historical career resides more in the "deep levels of symbols and images than at the levels of religious language."[32]

On the other hand, determinacy entails historical expression. "*Ecclesia* or ecclesial community is the church or some aspect thereof insofar as it carries ecclesiality. It, too, is a partly actual, partly ideal and teleological notion."[33] Concerning human intentionality, ecclesia designates a process and reality of determinate intersubjectivity which, precisely because it transcends provincial religious communities, cultures, periods and structures "is part of the mystery of ecclesia and it accounts for the difficulty of locating and identifying it."[34] Yet this is not what distinguishes ecclesia as such from other historical religions or faiths. Institutionality and its vehicles of social duration and identity, such as texts, kerygmas, leaders, rituals, operative symbolics, and fields of interpretation subordinates to the experience of redemptive existence as such. In a deeper, theological sense, "ecclesia" points to *this*. It means, orients, and historically realizes a way of existence, of being, of intentionality and reciprocity between human beings that can be universally redemptive and, therefore, transformative.

More precisely, what does intersubjectivity mean? For Farley, it is sociality's "meaning" and intentional dimension. Fundamentally, inter-

---

29. Ibid., 107.

30. Ibid., 175.

31. *ER*, 250.

32. Ibid., 213. For a recent treatment of some of these in relation to the current postmodern situation and influence, see *DS*.

33. *ER*, 205.

34. *EM*, 171.

subjectivity comprises "the *meanings* which attend those reciprocal intentions that are determinative of the community's distinctive sociality."[35] In the language of social phenomenology which Farley deploys throughout his explanation of ecclesia and its conceptual apparatus, "determinate intersubjectivity" comprises "the largely pre-conscious co-intentions in which each one constitutes the other as "with him" in this community. This view differs from typifications in that typifications guide our behavior toward another's behavior, and thus are tied to specific acts. Determinate intersubjectivity expresses the inter-human structure characteristic of the community as such, hence correlates with the *telos* of that community, its story, and its constitutive imagery."[36] To understand ecclesia, it is necessary to understand its essential determinate intersubjectivity precisely as redemptive existence. All other forms of social, intellectual, symbolic, historical and institutional mediation target this as ecclesia's goal and *raison d'être*.[37] Indeed, the "intended imagery of faith and the nature of ecclesia are simply not understandable apart from the redemptive alteration of existence."[38] This is because ecclesia's historical continuity, collective memory and experience of redemption are distinctive and determinate. The self-understanding and intended meanings of ecclesial individuals and communities, therefore, advance and retain the originating events and person of Jesus Christ as part of their historical and existential structure.[39]

More essential to ecclesial existence than its transitory, institutional structures are its behaviors. This is a central issue for Farley. The activities as part of historical, ongoing ecclesial process manifest far more the redemptive presence of God in the lives of believers than the mediating, institutional vehicles themselves. Three types of behavior characterize ecclesia's institutionality, namely, "*proclamatory* activities (preaching, teaching, writing), *sacramental* activities (communion, baptism, marriage, confirmation), and *caring* activities (political liberation, indi-

---

35. *ER*, 213.

36. *EM*, 153. Borrowing from phenomenologist Alfred Schutz, who Farley quotes extensively, "typification" means how human beings intend one another in daily life.

37. "Since Jesus Christ is the redeemer, ecclesia is both his instrument of redemption and the extension of his redemptive presence." *EM*, 127.

38. Ibid., 149.

39. Ibid., 176.

vidual welfare)."[40] These operations function universally, transcending geographic or cultural limitations. Proclamation involves interpreting past tradition to assist the realization of present possibilities for redemptive activity. Paradigms of ecclesia's symbols, imagery, myths, and doctrines operate within its sphere. The sacramental expresses "a dramatic activity, a bodily acting out which synthesizes the remembered tradition and the present." Members of the ecclesial community are visibly incorporated through this as their intersubjectivity forms, deepens, and even "incorporate into some worldly region (marriage, blessings and prayers of various sorts, dedications, and so on)."[41] Finally, the principle of caring as an ecclesial activity "is that salvific transformation" which effects "human well-being and an alteration of the conditions which assault that well-being."[42] Incarnations of redemptive intersubjectivity, diminishment of idolatrous attachments and re-orientation to agapic freedoms and obligations mediating God occur through and in these realities of Christian existence.

PROBLEMATIC SITUATION: THEOLOGY BEYOND THE "HOUSE OF AUTHORITY"

Ecclesiality persists, paradoxically, as a universal reality with determinate, historically continuous yet changing features. Farley understands and affirms it outside the way or "house" of authority. Its meaning and essence dispenses with the traditional, classical loci of authoritative norms, namely, scripture, dogma, and magisterium. The abandonment of this framework, not simply a discrete part of it—a doctrine, practice or text—and its justification is Farley's critique of historical Christianity which is "more or less identical" to the "house of authority." The parting from the classical authorities also explains the ecumenical character of his reflection.[43] It cannot be located within a single denominational scheme if that scheme (Protestant or Catholic) adopts some or many of the presuppositions that establish the way of authority. Since Farley's view of theology stands and operates outside this framework of authority, to develop its contours requires clarifying the rejected paradigm's

---

40. *ER*, 253.
41. Ibid., 254.
42. Ibid., 255.
43. Ibid., xvii.

essential features. In what follows, we shall advance toward theology's positive meaning by understanding what it is not. For this, we must explain two foundational presuppositions that constitute the house of authority, namely, salvation history and the principle of identity. They also characterize and pervade the different trajectories (Catholic and Protestant) of historical Christianity.[44] Subsequently, four essential areas of Farley's critique will be explored in relation to those presuppositions.

Salvation history as a "foundational presupposition" represents a "comprehensive interpretative framework." Carried over from the faith of Israel into Christianity, its key features comprise a nation or people, a teleological view of its events and history, and a transcendent, governing "divine agent" whose will causally directs the identity and history of a people. These elements characterize Israel and Christianity. Yet as followers of the Jesus movement separated from Judaism in the transition to Christianity, the ethnicity of a people no longer remained decisive for a relationship with God. Redemption became universally available, unrestricted by territory or determinate historical identities. Furthermore, Farley stresses that within this framework God is viewed as a king who governs by causally intervening in the historical events of his people and whose ultimate will cannot be frustrated.[45] These features and the principle itself comprise, for Farley, "an immanent feature of early Christianity."[46]

The other major presupposition operative in early Christianity and throughout its history is the principle of identity. Fundamentally, this presupposition "affirms an identity between what God wills to communicate and what is brought to language in the interpretative act of a human individual or community." The principle of identity sustains theological commonplaces as "divine truths, the divine law, the holy church, the divine Jesus, the sacred Scriptures, and the sacred dogmas."[47] At issue here are acts of meaning which are authoritatively regarded as coming from God. In particular, it embraces four main elements. First, there is a relationship between God and the medium of God's representation. The medium becomes an "ersatz presence of God himself." The second element involves a meaning-act "which has the character of a

44. Ibid., 108.
45. Ibid., 28–29.
46. Ibid., 30.
47. Ibid., 35.

synthesizing of two things ... God's willed or intended communication and the particular interpretation of the representative."[48] For example, Moses' speech from Sinai or the words of John's Gospel are interpretations of God's will in different forms that can be commands, narratives, meditations, etc. Third, this "divine-human synthesis is explained, accounted for, as causally effected by God." Not only is the medium of the writings of John a divine-human synthesis, but God causes them to exist *as such*. The fourth element narrows the scope of what is meant precisely by "identity."

> Predicated of the creaturely act or some aspect thereof is "divinity," something shared with God himself ... This suggests that the synthesized identity is a cognitive identity, a truth or reality known by God and, resulting from an act of communication, now known by human beings ... A cognitive identity shared by God and humanity does not require that God and human being grasp that content in the same cognitive mode. God knows things as God—timelessly, comprehensively, pan-relationally, essentially. Human beings know things through their finite mode of world participation and in postures pervaded by sin ... That the unknown author of the Fourth Gospel asserted that in Jesus the Logos was made flesh is a historical-exegetical assertion. The principle of identity is applied when that assertion takes on the predicate of truth initially known and then communicated by God. Such truths are "divine" not as predicates of God's very being but as contents of his actual knowledge.[49]

This feature enables the medium or representative of the divine communication to predicate that the assertion is infallible and inerrant. These attributes logically and necessarily follow from the other elements that form the principle of identity.

Important implications of this principle further illustrate the structures of the house of authority. Farley calls them "middle axioms" since they extend the principle of identity into vehicles of temporal duration and ecclesial unity. These axioms are secondary representation, leveling, and immutability. Secondary representatives ensure continuity between a living one and subsequent leaders, transitions from oral to written deposits, changes from written sources to "definitive commentary" and finally "the emergence of an institution whose role is to maintain, protect,

---

48. Ibid., 37–38.
49. Ibid., 38–39.

and purify the tradition and its ongoing interpretation."[50] Such elements carry forward the time and event of authoritative divine revelation into forms of tradition. The axiom of leveling differs from secondary representation in that the focus of communication shifts "from the content of the original identity to the vehicle itself." The vehicle's function (doctrine or text) must transcend geographical or provincial limits and thus be fully "trustworthy and valid" to everyone everywhere. For example, "If the vehicle is a written work, the tendency is to attribute divinity, the identity, to the words, even syllables and vowel points. If it is a doctrinal settlement, divinity is attributed to the propositions which comprise it."[51] What this means, then, is that divine revelation, divine truth gets equally distributed throughout every part of the vehicle, be it a doctrine or a text. "The logic which drives this extension of identity to the parts of the vehicle is simply that the vehicle will not be qualified as a location of divine communication if some parts are relative and errant." [52] The very words, the mechanics of the vehicle's medium, therefore, also become divine truths. A third axiom follows from secondary representation and leveling: immutability. "The axiom of immutability attends the axiom of leveling and goes beyond it. The vehicle in which divine communication is deposited is not just a provisional bearer of valid divine truths; it is an *immutably* valid bearer for the total future preeschatological time of the church. The axiom of immutability is thus the following: *the bearers which give social persistence to the divinely communicated content* are, in their *detailed parts, valid and true for all time*."[53] For example, the creeds, statements of the fathers, scriptural teachings are unchanging, a priori givens for establishing and preserving whatever is essential for ecclesial or Christian meaning, identity and historical survival. Truths, commands, laws, precepts judged divinely communicated not only are fixed by the principle of salvation history, but also by the attending principle of identity and its auxiliary implications. These presuppositions establish normative symbols, texts, governing forms, and so forth.

These axiomatic presuppositions remain implicit in most dimensions of Christianity's historical career and Farley's account of them is deliberately formal and ahistorical. So what does "house of authority"

50. Ibid., 41.
51. Ibid., 43.
52. Ibid., 43–44.
53. Ibid., 45. His italics.

mean more concretely and how does the classical criteriology determine theological activity? Given the founding axioms of salvation history and the principle of identity as latently operative, it refers to a certain structure. It comprises a certain priority and order of theological understanding and judgment concerning givens or standards for discerning and practicing the meaning of Jesus Christ. In terms of methodology, however, this developed as a static, deductive procedure.

> In the classical criteriology *the principium* is revelation, but this means specifically (because of the various underlying presuppositional strata of the criteriology) human-historical deposits of revelation: Scripture, dogma, tradition. Accordingly, the theologies, historical recollections, pastoral advice, and editings by known and unknown authors of Scripture as well as of the Fathers and Councils are not seen as relative historical and human attempts to interpret the faith but as principles, unrevisable and undemonstrable starting points of theology. These historical efforts become the theological givens from which theology works and to which theology goes for evidence.[54]

The established loci of divine-human identities are the *sine qua non* for theology to be theology.[55] If this is so, then the "genre" which theology becomes cannot be that of an open-ended, critical inquiry but is rather a sophisticated type of citation. Put differently, theology is eminently a deductive, interpretative, and expository form of reasoning. It is not, then, "scientific" in the modern sense. It is a way of authority. Disputes, differences, questions, doubts—all of these cognitive possibilities that occur in the classical criteriology are settled by authoritative interpretation justified by appeal.

> Scripture and dogma are not simply that through which the religious community retains its continuity with the past and remembers its period of origins; they are locations of evidence for judgments about God and his communications. *And this is the very essence of the way of authority. The vehicles of social persistence thus displace the sphere of immediate evidence, the sphere*

---

54. Ibid., 111.

55. Farley is not maintaining, it must be recognized, that first principles are formally unique to theology and unknown to science, philosophy, and other intellectual endeavours. His point is simply that such principles function to give theological thinking less the form of science and inquiry than exposition, interpretation, and citation—since its principles do not historically change. See ibid., 110–11.

of reality presentation. This is what the authority refers to in the way of authority. What better expression is there for the way of authority than the words of the children's song, "Jesus loves me, this I know, for the Bible tells me so."[56]

Theological or ecclesial reflection in the way of authority privileges, therefore, authorities over the historical and existential apprehension of realities given in faith itself—what we have described above as intersubjective redemptive experience. Each referent of divine-human social and cognitive identity relates and coheres within the framework of authority. The living experience of redemption and its modes of presence to human beings in determinate intersubjectivities is not the focus, and hence, not merited as an authoritative location of God's historical redemption. Those realities as interpreted must configure and cohere with the authoritative norms already established in the locations of divine-human identity, namely, the house of authority.

There is another aspect to theological reflection within the classical criteriology besides its fixed first principles, namely, its distinctive approach to truth claims. Settlements and judgments formed from within its structure and principles extend the basic presuppositions of salvation history and the principle of identity through the locations of scripture, dogma and church. For Farley, theological reflection within the house of authority can, to a significant degree, be subsumed under the heading of "hermeneutics" rather than inquiries ordered to truth. It is not that authority theology plays down or ignores matters of truth. On the contrary, it works to proclaim the relevance and veracity of divine revelation for humanity. But the issue is "how the truth question is present" in its structure given its criteria for judgment.[57] In Farley's view, the classical criteriology leaves unassessed and unquestioned the validity of its first principles. It simply advances them in the form of the received truth towards the adjudication of disputes, polemics or exposition. These "truths" cannot change because the presuppositions of salvation history and principle of identity remain intact. As such, evidence is already apparent for authority theology. Its approach to truth, therefore, evinces a distinctive character.[58] Understanding not critical discovery or

---

56. Ibid., 111. Italics mine.

57. Ibid., 114.

58. Ibid., 116. [T]he kinds of activities which characterize it are: (1) citation (*Do the Scriptures and the father affirm that the Logos assumed flesh?*); (2) exposition (What

assessment dominates the paradigm of truth in the house of authority. It thus involves a sophisticated hermeneutics of meaning and coherence but never assesses the criteria by which its interpretation proceeds. Norms and principles become shielded from criticisms not legitimized by the established divine-human locations of evidence. Consequently, to undertake theology differently or outside its authoritative structures becomes a priori heterodox.[59]

Farley locates scripture, church (institution) and dogma as the authorities of the visible "house." A good metaphorical characterization of the house's circularity of question and answer runs as follows.

> If we ask why Ezra's words are true, we are told they are a divine communication. If we ask how they are given that status, we are told that they occur in a permanent record of a divinely authored work, the canonical Scriptures. If we ask why this collection of human writings is to be regarded as divinely authored, we are told that the *act of canonizing* on the part of the church is divinely authored. If we ask why (how we know) this particular set of events in history is divinely authored, we are told that the church has declared it so and its declarations are divinely authored. If we ask how it is that the church's declarations are divinely authored, we are told that such are *necessary* to the certainty needed for salvation and its historical perpetuation. If we ask why (how we know) such "necessity" is actually operative and not just a logical ideality, we are referred to salvation history and the logic of triumph. If we ask why we are to regard the logic of triumph and its attended notions as an unquestionable criterion, something which is both a priori to Christianity itself and true, we are told that the church has never questioned it. So the circle, a vicious one, is complete. The questioner has been referred from one room to another in the house of authority only to find himself or herself back in the original room.[60]

---

does 'the Logos assumed flesh' mean?); (3) harmonizing (Is the Logos as incarnate consistent with the immutability and impassibility of God?); and (4) rational grounding (Is there any way that the Logos assuming flesh is necessitated by the nature of the human predicament as creature and sinner or the nature of God's relation to the world?). What is not pursued is the question whether the Logos as incarnate is itself a true doctrine. This is because the theological, doctrinal accomplishment itself has been given the status of criterion, given, and evidence."

59. Cf, ibid., 117.

60. Ibid., 166. Italics his. For an oversimplified but helpful illustration, see Hefling, *Why Doctrines?* 74.

The reciprocal and interrelated authorities establish the classical criteriology for all theological or ecclesial doctrine and practice. Self-referential coordinates characterize the criteria for Christian theology. The structure of dogma, church, and scripture are self-contained and immutable to influence from the outside. All legitimate and valid claims originate and terminate within the house for propositions, ideas, beliefs and practices to have any authority. It is a closed and insular framework.

The house of authority refers, then, not only to the classical loci of divine revelation given in scripture, dogma, and church but also to underlying axioms, presuppositions, and theological argumentation. This cognitive structure remained fairly intact until developments from the Reformation through the modern period began challenging many or all of its aspects. Farley's description covers a comprehensive way of thinking and reasoning that is the common element underlying divergences in historical Christianity irrespective of denomination.[61] But Farley sees fatal flaws within it. Four areas of his criticism merit attention: problems of historical evidence, structure, salvation history and the principle of identity.

The first problem with the classical criteriology concerns its claims to ahistorical veracity when confronted by modern historical consciousness and its effects.[62] The issue becomes acute when the classical criteriology upholds the entire content of scripture, for example, as inerrant. Biblical propositions about the earth, historical events, and other details that directly contradict the results of modern historical research, science, and cosmology lead not only to doubt about a particular passage but call into question the authoritative view of inerrancy, the axiom of leveling and divine inspiration.[63] The application of historical-critical method thus discredits a literalistic approach to the Bible concerning authorship

---

61. *ER*, xiv–xv; 107–8.

62. According to Farley, "historical consciousness does not mean some particular philosophical understanding of causality, such as determinism; it is essentially the understanding of any entity, including the human being, as occurring in a very complex network of influences that operate without and even from within (e.g., body chemistry) that being. The entity may exercise some responsiveness to these influences and even transcend them in creative activity. Nevertheless, every entity occurs in an ever-changing situation and is itself, whatever the nature of its self-identity, an ever-changing situation. This view, assumed by all modern cognitive efforts from physics to history to contemporary philosophies, is the very heart of historical consciousness." Ibid., 138.

63. Ibid., 138–39.

of writings (Mosaic authorship), events (Genesis 1&2), and even doctrines supporting institutions (donation of Constantine). Instead, it insists upon the influence of historically relative, situational and changing circumstances at work in biblical literature's development.[64] According to Farley, historical consciousness seriously undermines the idea that the entire writing of scripture was divinely caused and infallible because there are many text-world contradictions associated with the literalistic interpretation.

The second issue regards the relationship between scripture as a vehicle of duration and the identity of ecclesiality as such. Here Farley employs key ideas from "social phenomenology" that frame his argument. As an intellectual field and task, it "refers to the attempt to apprehend the ideal elements, structures, and interrelations within a social phenomenon. It investigates some actual type of human sociality on the assumption that the very act of "meaning" that type, of "having it in mind," involves grasping its distinguishing essential features."[65] The essential features of ecclesial existence, fundamentally, do not correspond to the essential features of social Judaism, and therefore, conflict with the very vehicle of duration, identity, and authority which sustains Jewish life and thought: the Old Testament. His analysis considers the way scripture functions within the community as a location of divine-human authority and its correspondence to characteristics of redemptive existence that define ecclesia. The early Christian movement retained the scripture principle from Judaism because its story was a "fulfillment of the story recorded" in the Old Testament. As it did so, however, the received writings also enjoyed the status of authoritative loci alongside the new literature produced by Christians. This means that the canon of Scripture, both Old and New Testament, share the authority of "divine authorship, inspiration, and identity" but function within very different communities of belief and practice.[66]

> A glance at any stage of the Christian movement reveals that the Judaic solution to the problem of social survival and identity has been abandoned. That is, after the Gentile mission, the new Christian congregations were ethnically pluralistic and the maintaining of their unity and identity was not primarily by

64. Ibid., 135–38.
65. Ibid., 142.
66. Ibid., 140–41.

means of *halakic* regulations but by an experience of a salvation that was a foretaste of the completed salvation of the end-time. Characteristic of the new sect was not the "study of the Torah" but "hearing the message of salvation." Characteristic of the activities of the leaders of the new sect was testifying to the inauguration of the new age, which in their language meant preaching Jesus as the Messiah, as the Lord, and preaching the Gospel of salvation through faith in him. It would be incorrect to say that the new sect had no concern at all for Torah or community regulations. But Gospel not Torah characterized the group's self-identity and self-understanding. Since the new sect as a universal community abandoned the attempt to formulate the conditions of salvation as participation in an ethnic community, this renders superfluous *halakic* regulations functioning to preserve ethnicity. If that is the case, there is no required set of writings whose function is to ground the regulations and no commentary in the sense of a perpetual device to mediate the units of authority to culture. In other words, atomistic, leveled authority of texts is superfluous for the new nonethnic and nonhalakic community. The actual use of the Jewish Scriptures in the early Christian movement confirms this. They were used not to regulate the Christian Gentile communities but to show that these communities were the inheritors of the ancient faith of Israel.[67]

Christianity retained the Old Testament upon grounds extrinsic to ecclesial redemptive existence but instead for reasons of apologetics and historical continuity. The proof, for Farley, is that much of the Old Testament is not and has never been viewed as authoritative for Christian life and practice, especially teachings concerning laws that safeguard ethnic identity. Therefore, the vehicle of social duration, the scripture principle and its axiomatic implications contradict the historical reality of universally unrestricted redemptive participation. Consequently, this inconsistency affects how authority theology operates. The mode of authority then engages an acrobatic hermeneutics privileging some texts and passages over others, thereby practically repudiating the principle that truth is distributed evenly and entirely within the scriptures. How can all of scripture be judged divinely inerrant and inspired if authority theology denies it in its procedures? Confusion and theological incoherence result.[68]

67. Ibid., 148.
68. Cf. ibid., 150–52.

A third criticism targets central features of the salvation history framework, specifically the nature of God's will in history. The view of God and God's activity as willing outcomes and events that determine and govern history toward a final state of affairs is at issue. Classically considered, such a view logically follows from the metaphor of God as "monarch" or "king" meaning a will that can be frustrated but finally triumphs. But this raises the thorny problem of God's causality, specifically regarding historical acts and events claimed, at least from house of authority, as directly determined by God. Farley holds there is a serious problem with this framework in terms of "determinism and indeterminism, and the scope of God's salvific work as universal or provincial."[69] One can view God's activity from two stances: deterministic causality or influence. If the former, then the divine will and the divine outcomes agree and harmonize in history. If the latter, then God can and does act, but historical forces, contingencies, and human choice make a direct one-to-one correspondence difficult or impossible to affirm. The first alternative, that is, God's willing as monarchical, cannot reconcile divine goodness with culpability for historical, human evil. For if all historical events are causally determined by God, dictated by a metaphor of a king, then human autonomy, freedom and the messiness of human response and contingency lose their importance.

> If we assume that God's way of working is an exercise of deterministic causality, the outcome of his activity and the projects of his will coincide. Accordingly, the book of 2 Kings, the sinlessness of Jesus, the crucifixion, and the papacy are effects of God's causal agency, and they amount to no more and no less than what he willed. This causality is exercised either toward one selected strand of history, such as the history of Israel or a line of events within Israel's history, or it is exercised on all history. If the royal metaphor of God's relation to the world is retained (which it is in salvation history), then the first alternative involves a willful nonsalvific presence in most of human history. But if the royal metaphor is retained and the other alternative is chosen, namely, that the scope of God's will and action are universal, this means that all the horrors of human history have the same relation to God's causality as salvific events. Needless to say, both alternatives break up on the reefs of theodicy considerations, for they involve admitting either that God can but does not will to operate

69. Ibid., 156.

salvifically in all his creation or that he can and does determine all his creation and is thus the determiner of good and evil.[70]

Either form of the deterministic causality perspective faces a serious problem theologically in justifying the divine goodness, God's love and affirming human freedom. Whether God's determinate causal agency is limited in salvific reach or universal, it makes no difference: historical evils fall under God's governance.

If God's monarchical power is really to be considered deterministic, God becomes responsible for the chain of events which sometimes involve misery, suffering, slaughter and genocide. Contrariwise, it is possible to view God's activity not as causally determinate but as influencing and working through "mixtures of divine act and creaturely response." This view softens the hard identity between divine will and a specific event, text, practice, leaving it vulnerable to later interpretation and change. This means, in turn, that "the church cannot look back from its actualized existence and claim that the book of 2 Timothy and the Council of Chalcedon are necessary events in an overall plan. It cannot claim that they are required by the coincidence of God's projected action and what actually occurs." In other words, "necessary" and divinely authoritative events have a historical and far more relative and contingent character, subordinate to the more essential elements that mark ecclesial redemptive existence. Farley concludes that God's divine goodness, love, and human freedom are, therefore, better understood and preserved when salvation history is dropped as a guiding principle.[71]

The last major criticism, like salvation history, focuses internally on the principle of identity. For Farley, "the first and most basic meaning of the principle of identity" like salvation history, concerns "causal efficacy." Identity obtains between God's will and actual historical events. It is not an ontological identity, but a causal identity "personally and teleologically." When it comes to expressions or forms, the principle incarnates differently.

> When it takes a primarily social and moral form as in prophetic, social criticism, individual and social ethics, church polity, and canon law, the identity is between a projected will of God in the sense of a commanded ideality and a human individual or social

---

70. Ibid., 156.
71. Ibid., 157.

behavior and course of action. Thus there is claimed identity between God's will and the Crusades, the Inquisition, specific forms of ecclesiastical organization (congregational, episcopalian, presbyterian), a specific fund-raising campaign of a congregation, a genre of church music, and an individual's decision to be a minister (though rarely between God's will and such occupations as journalism, landscape architecture, or accounting). When it takes a primarily cognitive form, as we find it in the classical criteriology, the identity is between the determination of God to disclose a truth and the linguistically formulated interpretation of an individual or institution. Both forms presuppose God's causal efficacy, his successful actualization of his will in human and historical events.[72]

But this claim of divine-human identity is not only as problematic as salvation history but it also displays fissures within the principle itself. Farley holds that, in the end, "it is a literalized myth." It is a way of conceiving divine intervention in the world which takes over elements of "pre-Christian, pre-Israelite mode of thought" and claims them as actual fact.[73] This cosmology presumes a being, carrying forward older mythological ideas, who manifests anthropomorphic attributes of thought and action, directly involving himself in wars, catastrophes, specific illnesses, deaths, and so forth. To the extent that Christianity and the house of authority implicitly or explicitly adopt this cosmology and understanding of the God-world relationship, this framework becomes incoherent precisely because it opposes "contemporary modes of thought informed by scientific and historical consciousness."[74]

Furthermore, the kind of causality intended by this agential model, for Farley, occurs on a level analogous to human intentionality and meaning.[75] The problem is, even in human experience, it becomes virtually impossible to predicate identical sameness in acts of willing and realizing, that is, a synthetic act of meaning, from one event to the other. The desire and will to take a walk and the act of walking, for example, can recur. There is an identity here at "a very synthetic and global level" meaning that future occurrences will share "essential elements" present in the previous willing and act. But the second event, a later occurrence,

---

72. Ibid., 159–60.
73. Ibid., 160.
74. Ibid., 161.
75. For a more detailed explanation of "meaning," see *DE*, 97f.

cannot be strictly identical. The circumstances and network of relationships that influence another willing and another walking always involve differences, such as weather, mood, speed, time, etc. One can only predicate identity at the most general level. Claims to "sameness" break down the more specific and particular comparison becomes. When applied to divine causality "in history and nature" in terms of "direct causal control," however, the result is that "what happens is literally what God wills."[76] According to Farley, "The trouble with this position is that it simply cannot be maintained without admitting that all freedom and self-initiation in creatures is illusory and that, given the actual content of history, God is an incompetent bungler or some sort of sadist."[77] Interconnected networks and different sources and kinds of relationships, therefore, influence and shape occurrences, historical events, determinate accomplishments like the emergence of the scriptures. So if God's direct causal determinism becomes modified to allow creaturely freedom, then the positing of an identity between God's willing and realizing a specific event becomes more difficult to assert with certainty given the network of relationships necessarily open and changing that realize it. Consequently, "characteristics of truth, inerrancy, and immutability" cannot be applied to a specific act, text, rite, and so forth because such a divine-human identity cannot be justified in a synthetic meaning-act. To know God's will in this sense requires unfettered access to God's intentionality which, as finite beings, we lack. Openness and similarity but not authoritative location of identity is all that can be claimed as a result. To claim more than this, as Farley again holds, would affirm a violation of creaturely autonomy.[78]

Thus far, this examination has sketched aspects of individual and communal realities of faith as part of ecclesial redemptive existence. It has also described essential aspects of the classical framework that developed in response to the event of Jesus Christ. This scheme of interpretation, judgment, and authoritative location of divine-human meaning dictates a certain ordering of life and thought for early Christianity's self-understanding and future orientation. Ultimately, Farley's criticism judges this classical criteriology as theologically idolatrous and whose claims become incoherent under the interrogation of historical-

76. *ER*, 162–63.
77. Ibid., 163.
78. Ibid., 164–65.

critical method.[79] Consistent with the criticism, his own proposals for theological reflection are not offered as definitive, uncritical or insular. Theological reflection acknowledges historical relativity in both selection of evidence and ideas in formulating current reality apprehensions of faith as redemptive. In a broad way, Farley articulates three "dimensions" or "moments" that comprise what the cognitive task of theology entails as well as clarifying the differences between his proposal and authority theology.

At the outset, it is necessary to indicate that theology is not restricted in its fundamental meaning to an academic specialty or esoteric pursuit, though it has and can take these forms. We shall examine this point more deeply later. But at present, for Farley, theology can also be "a concomitant of the Christian life." It denotes rather a way of understanding being-in-the-world transformed by the intersubjective participation in ecclesial existence. The dimensions or shape of ecclesial reflection holds true for each of them.[80] Common to both, moreover, are the changed dynamics concerning what grounds and establishes theological investigation, namely, the criteria and genre of theology. Outside the house of authority, criteria are not ahistorical, unchanging, and infallible locations or deposits of a priori truth given in scripture, tradition and the magisterium. What theology must appropriate, however, are the givens of apprehended, pre-reflective realities of faith judged not as ahistorically absolute and sanctioned deposits but evocative norms in the ongoing, developing life of the ecclesia. In this, however, Farley does not abolish historical determinacy or deny continuity with the Christian past. Yet he insists rigorously for its situationality and fallibility in mediating the divine presence.[81] Interpretation stands accountable to its context and correlates with limited methodologies. Yet the criteria for theological understanding and judgment is not "experience" which can be subjectively inaccessible but a matrix of relationality, meaning, and history; in other words, the criteria for theological reflection form a "field of evidence."

> It is not incorrect to say that theological judgments are grounded in experience. In a certain sense, all judgments are. But as it stands, the statement is elusive, and it is utterly misleading if it is

79. Cf. ibid., 173.
80. Ibid., 191.
81. Ibid., 173–74.

> taken to mean that experience is that to which theology appeals to justify a judgment as true. The reason is the one just given. If theology is able to make true judgments at all, it must have some field of evidence to which it refers. That is, it must have some manifested activity, behavior, and structure disclosing itself through experience.[82]

Put differently, an individual's act of faith is directed toward God as referent not toward theological reflection. But this means the act of faith is oriented to transcendence, to mystery, to fundamental incomprehensibility and displays limited analogical predication. Thus authorities such as doctrines, texts, decrees, and so forth are not the primary criteria of evidence for theological understanding and judgment—the historical matrix of redemptively diminishing idolatrous passions informed and shaped by the Christian story, images and ideas is. That is, the "field" of ecclesial realities becomes not absolutized or reduced, but normative for reflection to then move to coherent formulation of why an evidential claim is true. Approaches within the first moment of theological reflection vary depending upon the proximity to the "paramount reality" that the act of faith presupposes as real. One is more historical-critical, more scholarly and distant while the other more restricted and confessional. In each case, what reflective inquiry seeks is the description and understanding of what "ecclesiality" means.[83]

The second moment of reflective inquiry attempts to engage "fields of evidence that are wider than ecclesial existence." Here, the evidential claims and judgments of the first moment are not shielded from rational or philosophical or scientific accounts of the world but brings its assertions into conversation with them. It even subjects its own criteria to rational criticism and norms concomitant with what passes for serious knowledge outside confessional boundaries. Farley holds that this moment, in some sense, the move to the universal, must transpire since the claims of ecclesial existence are not provincially true or valid only for Christians, but are, in some sense, legitimate for the world as well. Ecclesiality, therefore, does make universal truth claims. "Evil and redemption as motifs in the Adam-Gospel story are intended as being in some way universal. And this is what propels ecclesial reflection to a second step, not just because of general world affirmation, but because

---

82. Ibid., 176.
83. Ibid., 186–87.

the realities are experienced as themselves *universal* realities. That is, they have to do with human being as such, not simply with a certain race, nation, epoch, or subculture."[84] This type of universality Farley posits as "*existential* or *determinate universality*." It need not presuppose a priori cognitive features, a correlate of scientific predication or "ontological schemes." Put abstractly: "The human experience of itself and its situation is the mode in which this universality is present."[85] The danger, of course, is simple translation of ecclesial realities that originate in historically determinate events and experiences to universal ontological structures which, at some point, would not require the specificity of determinate experience for support or validation. To do so would deny the distinctive claims about the features of redemptive existence and thus abrogate the normativity proper to such symbols, experiences and traditions that mediate these realities. "Denied its historical matrix and its contemporary function," Farley writes, "theology becomes speculative and academic in the pejorative sense."[86]

Finally, the third moment of theological reflection moves back from its universality in human experience to present, determinate circumstances. Here, the evidence comes partly from what manifests in the particularity of the context and situation, be it "the idolatrous foundations of a particular system of social oppression" or political and other individual events.[87] The other dimensions bring insight to this dimension in terms of symbolic and historical continuity, critical evaluation and measured resolution to particular problems and issues that arise. The distinguishing feature of this moment remains the concrete, individual situation which can differ widely from preceding ones. The effort remains to grasp "reality dimensions" within the particular and then, to some degree, adapt the insights of other dimensions to it. Interpretation, in some sense, bears upon concrete, practical actions.[88]

The significance of Farley's proposal, let me suggest, does not concern the specific details of how its particular methodology proceeds

---

84. Ibid., 188. Italics his.
85. Ibid. Italics his.
86. Ibid., 190–91.
87. Ibid., 189.

88. Indeed, Farley holds that existing theological forms correlate with his threefold classification: historical and biblical inquiry for the first, philosophical and systematic for the second and practical types of theology for the third. Ibid., 190.

towards universal and historically determinate theological description, evaluation and judgment. Its importance lies in the argument over what theology's "genre" is and, accordingly, the unity and form of theological reflection it then embodies. Farley proposes an interdependent and dialectical dynamic of theological activity related to hermeneutical orientations in contemporary theology. Its description presupposes an understanding of theology's genre long lost through a series of historical decisions and shifts in the course of theological education—how theology was conceived, transformed and maintained in certain contexts. This account not only questions the prevailing paradigm of what comprises current opinion concerning theology and theological study, but retrieves a meaning of theological understanding judged necessary to overcome prevalent problems in clergy, church, and university settings. For our analysis, however, the focus rests on the academic.

The loss of *theologia* as a personal and reflective wisdom of the believer is precisely responsible, according to Farley, for the lack of unity, coherence, and subject matter in contemporary theology, theological education and its various specialty fields. As an entry into this criticism, consider one summary definition of theological reflection: "It is a bringing to formulation of prereflective realities apprehended in the intersubjective participation in ecclesial existence by means of the interrogation of ecclesial, universal, and concrete fields of evidence."[89] What this signifies, however, is that theological understanding evinces the same structure in the lives of ecclesial members as it does in its leadership or in "professional" theologian-scholars.[90] "Theological understanding," therefore, is not something "esoteric" but a way of seeing and reflecting upon God's ongoing redemptive activity. This signifies an older conception of theology as a *habitus*. Indeed, ecclesial reflection is not, therefore,

---

89. Ibid., 191.

90. Unfortunately, the history of theology reveals a "narrowing" of theologia from wisdom to other functions, even for ecclesial congregations and its ministers. Writing of contemporary ministry, Farley holds that "[t]his happened when Protestant churches began to define ministry as a cluster of distinctive activities of trained professionals. A minister is a minister by way of such professional skills as counseling, preaching, administering, and educating . . . Theology, accordingly, became functionally obsolete. The minister can be a minister without it." This also means as theology became less relevant for ministers, so also would it spill over into believers and congregations. Farley, *Practicing Gospel*, 5.

"a mere aggregate of special disciplines" but a "transformative illumination of everyday social and individual life."[91]

The typological view of theology Farley develops does not abandon academic rigor or careful thinking. But inscribed within this conception, however, is an insistence that "theology" is not primarily the exclusive property of different groups—academic or ministerial—working for specialized ends. Unfortunately, when theological exclusivity occurs, the older meaning concerning its material unity and aims not only diminishes but relinquishes a theological rationale. This rationale, ideally, should obtain for theological reflection proper to any specific context. That this dispersion has become commonplace is due in large part to a problematic situation involving both the historically ambiguous meaning of "theology" as a genre but also its purposes within the life of the ecclesial community and broader culture. In other words, the problematic situation that frames Farley's retrieval of "theologia" as a correlative of Greek *paideia* is precisely the loss of this meaning.[92] The changes and developments in the historical academic teaching of theology and ministerial pedagogy specifically concern the different settings of theology. What one finds in both spheres is what Farley describes as the dominant theological model responsible for current fragmentation of subjects and exclusive application, namely, the clerical paradigm. To clarify this model, let me briefly encapsulate Farley's overview of the term "theology" in its semantic and contextual development.

AMBIGUITY OF "THEOLOGY" AS TERM AND ACTIVITY

Examining the word's historical career, Farley maintains that "*theology* is fundamentally ambiguous . . . the term refers to things of entirely different genres." The genesis of the genres can be traced to two meanings that inhabit the "premodern" (Early Christianity to Middle Ages) period. "First, theology is a term for an actual, individual cognition of God and things related to God, a cognition which in most treatments attends faith and has eternal happiness as its final goal. Second, theology is a term of a discipline, a self-conscious scholarly enterprise of understanding. In the former sense theology is a habit (*habitus*) of the human soul. In the

---

91. *ER*, 191.

92. For a thorough if dated account, see Jaeger, *Paideia: The Ideals of Greek Culture*, vol. 1.

latter it is a discipline, usually occurring in some sort of pedagogical setting." Further differentiation was introduced by the Greek term *episteme*. Carried by the entrance of Aristotelian thought to the West, it can mean knowledge or "science" in the sense of a discipline generative of knowledge.[93] Furthermore, as inquiries selected "different sorts of things, types of *sciences* can arise." The Latin translation *scientia* retained this double meaning of habit of soul and reflection or inquiry producing knowledge during the rise of universities and theology's development as an academic discipline.[94] Consequently, the history of "theology" cannot be linear because what one references by theology can mean one of two general realities and patterns of meaning. Instead, Farley traces each meaning through three different historical periods defined by "institutional setting" rather than by "conventional epochs of church history." Admittedly, the effort is more about seeking "concepts and presuppositions" of the term's major strata of meaning than marshaling details about particular historical accounts.[95]

Theology as a Sapiential Knowledge, a Habitus

The meaning of "theology" as "a salvifically oriented knowledge of divine being" figures prominently during the patristic period and in the early Christian communities. Yet Farley maintains that it did not go by the term. Later thinkers in the early middle ages considered theology to be a divine illumination, a working of grace, leading to the salvation of the individual (Pseudo-Dionysius). At the same time during this period, the term "theology" received nuance and modification from Greek conceptions, particularly the notion of "episteme, knowledge" as "a *hexis*" or a virtue. This meant that *theologia* could be attributed to not simply a "knowing" but also to a "structural feature of the human soul" not judged accidental. Thinkers in this period, therefore, "portrayed knowledge (*scientia*) as a habit, an enduring orientation and dexterity of the soul, a knowledge of God and what God reveals." But debates ensued about the kind of habit this was. Farley indicates that consensus seems to view this habit as a "practical" more than a "theoretical" one. This type of definition normally attends theologians in the monastic

93. *TH*, 31.
94. Ibid., 32.
95. Ibid., 30. To this extent, Farley characterizes his approach with terms appropriated from Michel Foucault, stating that it is an "archaeology of the theological school."

mold "who see it more as a directly infused gift of God, tied directly with faith, prayer, virtues, and yearning for God."[96] This view survives into pietism and connects intimately with ideas of Christian living, training, and the "Augustinian-monastic view of theology." Study and practically oriented tasks furthering salvation combine during this second period. Farley writes that "theology may be (in the one sense) wisdom, but it is a wisdom which can be promoted, deepened, and extended by human study and argument."[97] It is precisely this sense of theology that relocates from universities to seminaries from the Enlightenment to the present. And the setting of theology within seminaries alters the meaning further. For the salvific knowledge of God gets connected to the practical knowledge and tasks of ministry which necessarily involve not one thing but a plurality in an educational context. In the final period, "roughly the seventeenth century to the present," Farley holds that, "[t]heology as a personal quality continues (though not usually under the term *theology*), not as a salvation-disposed wisdom, but as the practical know-how necessary to ministerial work."[98] Even though in Protestant circles the original meaning of theology was connected to learning and educational institutions, the study of theology for practical application moves to seminaries for specific clerical training. When this happens, "theology as a disposition of the soul toward God simply drops out of 'the study of theology.' Furthermore, there is no unitary science but an aggregate of disciplines whose unity is their pertinence to the tasks of ministry."[99] In other words, the significance of theology as a salvifically oriented wisdom of the believer does not vanish. It disperses into aspects of clerical formation such as efforts to make all areas of study personally relevant or establishing a part of theological education as "formation" or locating it in a *ratio studiorum*. The latter, especially for Farley, has come to be the more pervasive option. Here, the meaning of "theologia" shifts to the varied elements ministers must know. Consequently, when one or all of these options concerning the integration of the personal experience of faith to the study of theology occurs, the knowledge obtained acquires a "strategic, technical character" and not one of individual dis-

---

96. Ibid., 35–36.
97. Ibid., 36.
98. Ibid., 39.
99. Ibid., 42–43.

position.[100] Put differently, the sense of a personal, sapiential and salvific knowledge of God and the things of God have become, in this trajectory, a technology of ministry.[101]

Theology as a Cognitive Enterprise

Like the other sense of theology, let me chart Farley's account of the "disciplinary" sense through the same threefold periodization. Early Christianity to the Middle Ages possessed "theology" in the sense of ordered, rational investigation but "it did not go by the name 'theology.'" Sometimes it passed for Christian "philosophy." But when classical learning was appropriated to help Christians discern the meaning of revelation in Scriptural commentary, polemical and instructional texts, there is "theology" at work. "This effort had primarily the character of exposition, the interpretation of the received text from Scripture or council. The truth of the revealed texts could be assumed, hence the task was to discern and properly formulate its meaning."[102] The second period saw this meaning of theology become more disciplined and rigorous as it became lodged within university education, specifically as the meaning of "scientia" becomes associated with methods of rational demonstrations and conclusions. Though this sense of theology prior to the rise of universities was present in the development of commentaries, treatises on Christian doctrine, and theological controversy, this period sees "theology" as a specific "faculty in a university and some ordered procedures which yield knowledge. It was not simply the direct cognitive vision of something given to it, a cognitive *habitus* of the soul, but a deliberate and methodical undertaking whose end was knowledge. Promoted especially by Thomas Aquinas and the schoolmen, theology in this sense became a discipline."[103] In the university context, the development of the *lectio* and the *quaestio* further shaped the practice of dialectic. Soon other works began rationally sequencing and ordering questions, linking "articles of the faith in relation to each other." In due course, the discipline of theology developed principles, relations to other sciences and becomes more distanced from other aspects of the church such as bishops. Hence, writes

---

100. Ibid., 62–63.
101. Ibid., 43.
102. Ibid., 33–34.
103. Ibid., 37.

Farley, "[t]heology as Aristotelian science continued throughout what I am calling the second period, from the thirteenth to the eighteenth century, and in both Catholic and Protestant universities and schools."[104] In the last period, what radically alters theology in this second sense is its unitary focus and dispersion into a plurality of technical, specialized enterprises. Farley regards pietism and the Enlightenment as the two major forces of this change.

Continental pietism was a movement devoted to restoring spiritual integration into a perceived "scholastic-scientific approach" that seemed to lack it. Theology as scholastic had already been conceived as a cognitive enterprise using reason for demonstrations and particular methods. What the pietists accomplished, however, since they sought "to correct any notion of the minister as primarily a knower" was to stress "preparation and training for specific tasks of ministry."[105] Consequently, along with spiritual formation the "training for ministerial activities" becomes a "second telos of the study of theology."[106] Once this training happens, it disperses the study of theology into a "plurality of studies preparatory for such activities." Indeed, Farley argues that this is no surprise because the pietists "Spener and Francke are the very first to speak of theological *sciences*."[107]

If pietism stands responsible for understanding theology as a series of particular studies proper and attached to practical ministry, the Enlightenment accounts for the modern change of "human and historical sciences into disciplines (science) in a new sense." Critical rationality, ideals of independent and autonomous scholarship, historical consciousness: these elements became the "canons" for justifying evidential claims and further specialize the departments of "theology" into discrete areas.

> A science was a cognitive enterprise working on some discrete region of objects under universal and critical principles. One result of this revolution was that new sciences, new bodies of data, and new methods were available to theology: philology, history, hermeneutics. In the mid-eighteenth century, Ernesti and Semler appropriated these for biblical interpretation. And once this happened it became apparent that the Bible itself could be the object

104. Ibid., 38.
105. Ibid., 41.
106. Ibid.
107. Ibid.

of a "science," a collection to which critical, autonomous methods of interpretation could be applied. It was only a short step to realize the same thing was true about church history, about preaching, about dogmatic theology.[108]

The medieval notion of theology as a "discipline," that is, one cognitive *habitus* directed in various ways to something or its different aspects that can be the subject of inquiry, was not a division into separate disciplines or sciences up to the eighteenth century.[109] But both pietism's shift toward *theologia* not as a disposition but as a content applicable for ministerial skills and the Enlightenment's understanding of specialized, discrete inquiries and fields helped to alter the meaning of "theology as a single science (discipline)" into "an aggregate term for a family of scholarly pursuits."[110]

The idea of theology as a unitary discipline with a single subject matter considered under different aspects, consequently, is lost. Today the unity of theology is gained accidentally, lacking any formal support in systems of clerical training or university instruction. This "fourfold pattern" of Bible, church history, dogmatics, and practical (moral) theology "became virtually universal for Protestant schools throughout the nineteenth century and for theological education in Europe and America."[111] It is this fourfold pattern that is the "clerical paradigm," a way of organizing and conceiving theology and theological education that took hold and continues to influence religious education, seminaries and graduate schools in the twentieth century.[112]

THEOLOGICAL UNDERSTANDING AND THE FRAGMENTED SITUATION OF UNIVERSITY KNOWLEDGE

Before examining theology's relevance and inclusion in university education, a few preliminaries are in order. First, Farley's argument is avowedly "idealizing and futuristic because the study of theology has not yet taken

---

108. Ibid., 41–42.

109. Ibid., 40–41; "Distinctions within the one science (or *habitus*) of theology are common from the Middle Ages to the eighteenth century . . . These distinctions refer back to the one habit, theology, the knowledge of God and the things of God. They do not refer to different 'sciences,' each with its own method." Ibid., 77.

110. Ibid., 42; 61.

111. Ibid., 101.

112. See Farley's discussion of this in the American context. *TH*, 110–16.

hold" in the university as yet.[113] To a great extent, the presentation is visionary, setting forth an idea of what theology in the university might and should be. Secondly, the kind of university at issue is not Christian but secular. The contention attempts, in some sense, to embrace not just religious higher education but the setting of higher education itself. Farley insists theology has an important role within the academy, not just ecclesial institutions. Third, since its setting extends beyond confessional limits, the argument proceeds on two parallel lines. While his criticism of the clerical paradigm as responsible for displacing theological understanding as the central feature and end of theological education on the whole is a theological argument, arguments made for theology's inclusion in the university context are not necessarily restricted to a Christian reading or intrinsically Christian criteria. The warrants can stand, to some degree, as humanistic or philosophical—strikingly similar to Newman's. Especially concerning the function of the "Christian mythos" as third critical principle, Farley admits that "there are forms of it in other faiths."[114] That is to say, there are valid criticisms of culture from within a religious tradition's intellectual and ethical resources. Indeed, his case hinges on the conviction that theological interpretation is an important reflective mode required for adequately understanding and knowing reality as such. And this latter point introduces the broader problem of why the Enlightenment, empiricist paradigm of knowledge and its related correctives can distort university knowledge and impoverish higher education.

The "business," "remuneration," and "responsibility" of the university is knowledge.[115] "Knowledge," Farley writes, "is the experience of being laid hold of by evidencing realities."[116] In the university context, its status and even nature is not secure. Knowledge persists within the effects of historical change, power struggles and the possibility of cor-

---

113. Farley, *FK*, xi.

114. Ibid., 21.

115. It must be noted that Farley subsumes various levels of higher education into the term "university" such as undergraduate, graduate and professional. "University" functions as a cluster term. Ibid., 4.

116. Ibid., 3. The term "realities" here invites misinterpretation since Farley does not explain it sufficiently. I suggest it means that which human being consciously, direct intuit and that which is socially mediated by meanings. In other words, those normal, everyday subjects or thoughts that have reasons or warrants for their acceptance or rejection. For a detailed analysis, see *EM*, 186–205.

ruption by various internal and external forces.[117] It neither stands still nor remains immune from pressures. For these reasons, it is "fragile" because "it is more a responsive activity than a precious possession."[118] But the responsive activity dominant since the Enlightenment has been critical knowledge, that is, "[p]resent knowledge occurs in continued and relentless criticism of past knowledge, a pressing for the establishment of the basis, evidence, and assumptions of any claim." The activity of human reasoning that is knowledge not only must withstand rigorous questioning but abide, grow or perish under future correction. This view presupposed a new understanding of rationality calling for "the primacy of experienced data, and the instrument of empirical inquiry."[119] The "evidencing realities," defined by the empirical paradigm gained and sustained great purchase upon western culture due to its progressive successes and because "almost all of our military, economic, industrial, and even leisure and aesthetic activities depend on it."[120] Still, despite its deep, successful entrenchment, this "empirical paradigm" represents one among others in rightly establishing what passes for "evidencing realities" or "knowledge." "I am talking about a paradigm, a model of knowledge that works better for some sciences than others but that has expanded to most of the specialty fields constituting the social sciences and humanistic scholarship. According to this model, understanding occurs as the result of concentrating research upon a very specific aspect of something."[121] Unfortunately, Farley contends, this model's logic and procedures unduly influence the other areas and ways of knowing that might offer necessary modification and correction. In other words, the empirical model of knowing and understanding is not a "comprehensive metaphysic," a totalizing explanation for what, how, and why human beings understand reality. Its strength comes from its narrow, abstracting, and concentrated methodology that inevitably overlooks other dimen-

---

117. A good and timely example in the United States regards the influence of business corporations upon academic research. For a provocative account, see Press and Washburn, "Kept University," 39–54.

118. *FK*, 3.

119. Ibid., 6. Farley is thinking of Francis Bacon and Isaac Newton as fathers of this type of reasoning and this "paradigm of knowledge and reality." Ibid., 11.

120. Ibid., 11.

121. Ibid.

sions proper to data no less meaningful or bereft of truth.[122] Taken by itself as the carrier of truth, this way of understanding reality becomes reductive, and distorts the very meaning, the complexity of the subject considered.

University knowledge and the understanding that occurs in its setting needs more than scientific rationality delivers. It requires vital and necessary correctives, different activities of interpretation. The reason concerns the nature of knowing itself.

> [K]nowledge has a hermeneutic character: to grasp reality in its complexity involves *interpretive* activities. Of course, knowledge has also to do with reason, explanation, and therefore, attention to evidence and argument. But these always occur in connection with ways of construing what we are trying to know, ways of meaning it, of setting it against its context, of grasping its dimensional complexity. Anything that is actual has different dimensions that call for different kinds of interpretive responses. The various correctives in the Enlightenment tradition are, at the same time, different interpretive perspectives. Accordingly, when knowledge is deprived of any one of them, the very complexity and dimensionality of reality are obscured.[123]

Farley posits three hermeneutical perspectives that predominate: romantic (intuitive-imaginative), theological (tradition), and the political (praxis).[124] These "correctives" might be more clearly grasped as "interpretive activities." Since they originate as critical reactions to the Enlightenment paradigm of empirical rationality, they stand within the Enlightenment legacy thus filling out the posture of "critical reason" more adequately than the empirical view of reason taken alone.[125] Each is necessary because each conveys some true insight or interpretation of knowledge and reality. By "romantic," Farley draws out the intuitive, imaginative aspect of human knowing and understanding, pointing to something's "[m]ystery, felt intuition, nature, concreteness, totalities."[126] The concentrated abstraction of the empirical hermeneutic, according to this corrective, denies these other aspects and dimensions necessary

---

122. Ibid., 7.
123. Ibid., 12.
124. Ibid., 6.
125. Ibid., 12.
126. Ibid., 7.

for knowledge to avoid distortion. The same principle holds for the other two in different respects. The theological or tradition corrective refutes empirical reason's claim "that tradition cannot be a bearer of truth is arbitrary." Positively, it contends that "the corporate experience of past ages and peoples can produce a wisdom that is illuminating and pertinent beyond the past."[127] In the case of the romantic and the theological, both do not adjust the methodology of the empirical paradigm: they simply insist upon its "insufficiency" as an account of reality. This "insufficiency" principle also holds for the third corrective, the political. With roots in Marx and various liberation movements, Farley describes it as follows: "There is no pure reason, only cognitive endeavors in service of whatever is in power in the society. By forgetting this, the institutions of pure reason—the sciences, scholarship, the universities—hide from themselves their complicity in societal agendas of power. Reason thus remains uncritical about its own complicity in the unjust society. It follows that the primary perspective and starting point of a genuine critical principle cannot be innocent reason but must be praxis."[128] Reason, in other words, cannot ignore the limitations of human beings when it comes to the motivations behind knowing and effects of power such knowledge realizes. Farley's description of these correctives is woefully schematic, but their brevity does not weaken the key insight, namely, the progression and identity of knowledge and human understanding is necessarily dialectical. The desire for knowledge cannot simply relax in one cognitive paradigm of interpretation to the exclusion of others. If this occurs, knowledge becomes "corrupt." One way of seeing will pervert the very object or thing under consideration. Therefore, all of the dimensions as "correctives" necessarily critique, modify, and advance the others insofar as they abide in constant interchange. Together, they provide a more adequate account of interpretive experience and knowledge. Denial of dialectical interdependence among the empirical paradigm and its correctives, therefore, affirms forms of rational reductionism and the distortion of knowledge's complexity.[129] In short, two critical principles of Enlightenment reason have been surveyed. If the Enlightenment's first "critical principle" acknowledges the changing forces involved in knowing something as inevitably "temporal and relative," represented by the

127. Ibid., 8.
128. Ibid., 8–9.
129. Ibid., 12.

empirical paradigm, the correctives of intuitive imagination, tradition, and praxis offer its "second principle" of criticism, bringing the first to greater coherence. This second principle maintains that "all actual things are multidimensional" and, therefore, not limited to one paradigm of reasoning, argument or knowing.[130]

Unfortunately, the correctives hitherto discussed are marginalized in the university compared to the support enjoyed by the empirical paradigm. Moreover, the validity of the different perspectives do not guarantee any necessary cohesion to function as a unitary corrective. The ingrained problem, paradoxically generated by the human passion to know, is partly the measure of scientific and technological success: the university specialty field. Several reasons obtain. First, the correctives are interpretive activities, so they do not define specific sciences like econometrics. Second, the ethos of university research repays specialized work, making it increasingly difficult for scholars who might be working in the field embraced by the interpretive activity of praxis to speak with semiotic scholars concerned about ancient languages and texts. Thus, the culture of university research fosters greater isolation not collaboration. Third, the very corrective that the romantic, theological, and political can bring to the empirical risks overestimating and absolutizing its own subject matter and value. It can fall victim to the same narrow understanding of reality expressed in the empirical paradigm.[131] Despite the problem that the correctives cannot fulfill their duty, Farley maintains the need for something beyond what even they cannot provide, namely, a "third critical principle," the "Christian mythos." At issue is what the Christian mythos brings to bear upon university knowledge and the situation of human striving in the form of a "general posture" concerning two fundamental ideas: "an orientation to and seriousness about reality" on the one hand, and "a vision of corruption and redemption" on the other. Both inhabit the term "Christian mythos" borrowed from Bernard Meland: "the pattern of meaning which arises from the structured experience of a people and having to do with the ultimate nature and destiny of human being."[132] The problem is that the Enlightenment correctives fail to grasp the situation of human beings' restless striving to secure themselves by pursuing knowledge idolatrously—how reason

130. Ibid., 21.
131. Ibid., 11–12.
132. Ibid., 22.

"corrupts."¹³³ This Christian mythos discloses a deeper insight about human beings within all paradigms.

> The corruption of human reason is a frequent theme in Western thought from Plato to Michel Foucault and the Frankfurt School. For Plato, the corruption behind all corruptions is the turning aside of the cognitive eros or striving from its proper object, the good, which is to say the real. And the Enlightenment traced the root of human corruption to the reign of uncritical authority over reason, the antidote for which was criticism and objective evidence. These notions of a corrupted cognitive eros and reason threatened by authority seem quaint to many moderns and postmoderns. Sciences and philosophies of science have convinced us of the fragile status of all cognitive claims. Humanistic sciences and hermeneutics have intensified our awareness of knowledge's paradigmatic and metaphorical character. But the theme of corrupted knowledge is not at the center of a technological and therapeutic society's corporate consciousness.¹³⁴

The critical posture of the Christian mythos actually provides a penetrating account of the matrix of human knowledge and desire. Indeed, it serves as an implicit, explanatory and operative theological anthropology. Since it enhances contact with reality, it provides insight to university education. Though elements within intellectual culture are not "entirely unaware" of how knowing and knowledge misses the real when contracted, the Christian mythos intensifies awareness of the corruption caused by a "technocratic world-view," and provides cogent reasons for what he calls "reality's . . . redemptive possibilities."¹³⁵ Though not restricted to professional theologians or even the religious tradition of Christianity, this informed critical posture offers a way to see reality as it is, including an insightful account of the "dynamics of evil." It thereby gives wisdom to what can, does, and will happen when human beings misunderstand or misuse their passions toward self-securing—especially the desire to know.¹³⁶ The possibilities for redemption, accordingly, must recognize

---

133. Ibid., 11. Farley contends, that "the modern versions of the correctives of imagination, tradition, and praxis are not sciences or even university disciplines. They do not have their home in university departments."

134. *GE*, 197.

135. *GE*, 197. Consciousness of race in the pursuit and application of science is one instance Farley evidences. *FK*, 24.

136. For a discussion of how evil operates, see *GE*, 130–35.

not only what encourages the idolatrous passions of human beings to seek false satisfactions but also what supports the absolutization of the finite sphere of knowledge that perverts the very realm.

Besides the anthropological constant of idolatrous self-securing affirmed by the Christian mythos, another structural agent is problematic in university culture. This is apparent in his thesis: "the university is losing a tension that genuine knowledge requires—the tension between focused, cognitive abstraction and synthetic, relational correction—and that this loss is promoted by the hegemony of the specialty fields."[137] The problem with this new social entity bears upon the meaning of theology in the university insofar as it represents a paradigm regarding what education and knowing entail that Farley's constructive proposal seeks to overcome. To understand, then, the broad criticism of specialty fields and their role within the university, we must first grasp what Farley means by the aim or goal of university instruction—an educated person. For clarity, let me start with the end and work backward.

EDUCATIONAL *PAIDEIA* AND OVERCOMING THE UNIVERSITY SPECIALTY FIELD

The notion of an educated person is a goal, an aim, an ideal. Students should be shaped a certain way by their university experience. This formation is the process and product of education, what Farley suggests "a modern version of Greek *paideia* might be."[138] Unlike the aims of vocational training, this development does not concern "the production of capacities of technical functioning but the evoking of ways of existing in and interpreting reality."[139] Education, in other words, is not something directly quantifiable, measurable or technical; it denotes more reflective features.

> The aim of education is sometimes thought to be the transmission of knowledge concerning a content or subject matter. But when we ask about the purpose of the transmitted knowledge, we are referred to another order of aims, an order having to do with the use, function, and relevance of knowledge. Knowledge, in other words, lends itself to various agendas that attend human life, and it can improve the ways human beings exist in the situa-

---

137. *FK*, 30.
138. Ibid., 60.
139. Ibid.

> tion of life. Human life is constituted by a succession of *situations* that call for understanding and interpretation. "Understanding" is the more static, "interpretation" the more active, expression. The educational process, when successful, refines and disciplines the ways of understanding and interpretation.[140]

The specific, discrete content of academic education subordinates to the inculcated, interpretative habits and skills a properly formed mind applies to any subject matter.[141] An educated person must be self-conscious in her exposure to "the various types of knowledge and modes of thinking which occur in university education," namely, the "experiential, pluralistic, hermeneutic, critical, rational, political, and aesthetic dimensions."[142] But the types of interpretation these signify are not pursued arbitrarily but insofar as these modes and particular studies proper to them disclose something true about reality.[143] The key dynamic brought before students in terms of "the historical ideals of the university" is the "tension" accompanying any university subject or unit and the "synthetic relationality" required to properly grasp a specific reality's contextual complexity.[144] These perspectival dimensions represent coordinates for forming a "hermeneutic self-consciousness" of the student.[145] They also help map the diverse situational character of human existence and experience, serving as synthetic correctives to the multiplicity of scattered details and information considered in universities.

"What allows there to be education—what enables the disciplining of interpretation and the refinement of understanding—is that it is possible to abstract the different kinds of interpretation. That is, the various dimensions of human life can by conceptual art be so separated that they can be focused on, analyzed, and subjected to inquiry."[146] Sciences, disciplines and pedagogical areas are all precisely abstracted views in human experience that, when education actually takes place,

---

140. Ibid., 135.

141. Such skills are also called "hermeneutic orientations" and can include "historical, aesthetic, ontological, social, and linguistic, to mention a few." Ibid., 186.

142. Ibid., 60. Farley admits that this list is "tentative," so other aspects or dimensions can be added.

143. Ibid., 180.

144. Ibid., 29.

145. Ibid., 61.

146. Ibid., 136.

acknowledge their own limitations as a total explanation of something. Unfortunately, university education is not geared to forming the different dimensions of hermeneutic self-consciousness.[147] One main reason, correlative to the lack of any articulated educative ideal, is the current way knowledge inhabits university structures: the dominant position of the specialty field.

According to Farley, the "social carriers" of knowledge in universities tend not to be generalists or people of capacious learning but specialists whose loyalty and orientation—due to many factors—proceed toward "highly specialized cognitive endeavors" most evident in "research-oriented universities."[148] Specialty fields are reinforced and concretized by a certain quality of professionalism, the university reward system, the influence of "narrowed empiricism" upon scholarship at large and the consequences of scholarly isolation. Why this is important in university education and teaching, and why it inhibits a recovery of *theologia* results from the problem that these "specialty fields," are, by and large, neither sciences nor disciplines.[149]

"Science" can express something ideal or an actual reality for Farley. The former can "mean a discrete area of knowledge, methods, and procedures which can be situated on a comprehensive map of cognitive undertakings" (psychology, chemistry, physics, etc.). These range from the general to the more specific and are intelligible "on the basis of types or regions of subject matter and their correlative methods." The latter, namely, "an actual science," signifies a "corporate project, a cognitive exploration occurring in a historical situation, drawing on the past in a particular way, and dominated by paradigms of knowledge and reality."[150] Actual sciences occur in various settings and receive forms of social support from things like "the learned society" or "the department." As Farley describes its primary sense, when carried out by a group or individuals, "science" lacks a pedagogical or teaching component. When such a component is present, it is now a "discipline."[151] A feature of both ideal (or map) sciences and actual ones is that while each employs concentrated abstraction to resolve problems and effect discovery proper to its subject

147. Cf. ibid., 70.
148. Ibid., 35–36.
149. Ibid., 35.
150. Ibid., 33.
151. Cf. ibid., 109.

matter, each is aware of an "essentially unresolvable tension between the abstracted or focused aspect and the synthetic (concrete) character of what is under consideration." When science operates well, it evinces a "self-correcting movement between the abstract and synthetic poles." The science, in other words, is aware its investigation occurs within specified, narrow limits and so acknowledges "other aspects and dimensions" to the subject matter than its own applied principles and methodology.[152]

Other academic realities related to but not identifiable with sciences are disciplines and pedagogical areas. As Farley defines it, "'discipline' connotes instruction, teaching, learning."[153] Unlike science, its settings are confined to educational centers precisely because the teaching-learning dynamic occurs in concert with scientific research. There is an even greater distinction. He also states that "a discipline is necessarily a pedagogical area but a pedagogical area is not necessarily a discipline."[154] What defines disciplines is a pedagogical area combined with and "facilitated by the pursuit of scientific, scholarly inquiry."[155] Teaching or pedagogical areas, however, taken as something distinct from disciplines and science mean simply "focused areas of teaching" and therefore "are not sciences or even groups of sciences but perspectival emphases." Farley notes that, generally speaking, philosophy, religious studies, fine arts are precisely examples of pedagogical areas since no one specific "region of reality" comprises their "subject-matter." In contrast, commercial market research or genetic experimentation are sciences while high school biology or English are strictly "pedagogical areas." The former involves discovery while the latter is expository. The areas can consider or deal with all sorts of things due to their wide viewpoint.[156] The key difference, then, between disciplines and pedagogical areas turns on their relationship to advancing knowledge through appropriation of scientific methods and not simply the presentation of subject matters or kinds of knowledge.

The reality and influence of the specialty field as a social structure, however, does not deliver correctives to the acute subjects it examines or engender habits adequate to the tension between specificity and the syn-

152. Ibid., 31–32.
153. Ibid., 34.
154. Ibid., 109.
155. Ibid., 34. For example, "Although cooking, auto mechanics and reading are all teaching areas in schools, they are not disciplines."
156. Ibid., 34.

thetic relationality of educational *paideia*. Now the research, methods and dynamics of specialization and its fields are not the issue. It is rather that the elements which spawn them and maintain their dominance actually effects a twofold suppression of knowledge: dimensionality and the concern for truth.[157] Farley's contention applies most aptly to large research universities but his major points logically extend beyond them into institutions of higher education as whole. This is so because the credentialing and training process of past, present and future university professors devolves from the professional character of academic departments and graduate programs that form and distribute them. What occurs in the professional formation during graduate studies are skills and habits geared towards specialization—narrow pursuits. Taken individually, the social carriers of university teaching and research are attuned from the start not to complexity and multidimensionality but to an acute focus upon a highly specific subject matter (e.g., the dissertation). Hence, the specialty field's utility toward grasping "what is real" remains limited. Reflecting on specific objects as an illustration of this point, Farley asserts that

> all the concrete things we know—cats, rocks, human beings—include in themselves multiple contents, aspects, events, most of which remain unknown and unexperienced. Accordingly, nuclear physicists and microbiologists never study, perceive, or know all aspects of any actual thing. No one has exhaustively mapped even a single cell of a living thing. Because of the complexity of what is real, to confront the real is to acknowledge something we never master or manage. To study the real is inevitably an act of selection and focus, never the exhaustive comprehension of a totality.[158]

Reality emerges, then, from various perspectival emphases or self-conscious hermeneutic modes of interpretation.[159] But these modes, so crucial to university education, are significantly lacking because the very teachers who might impart and form such habits and skills in students are largely not taught to pursue them.[160] Such broader perspectives are

---

157. Ibid., 45.

158. *DS*, 58.

159. For a more detailed explanation of the term and meaning of "reality" in Farley's thought, see *GE,* 27–113 and *DS*, 55–73.

160. "If the reform of education in church, leadership, and college education is

not only minimized by the professional associations and publications proper to the specialty field but also by the "university reward system" upon which academic existence depends. The academic system demands original and frequent research for a scholar's survival. But survival largely means producing specialized scholarship quickly. The prescribed, rigorous abstracting necessary to produce what passes for legitimate scholarship (obtained in a short period) and thus ensuring future employment at colleges or universities opposes "synthetic relationality." The structures of professionalization, scholarship, and promotion to tenure cannot afford it.[161] It is not a theoretical objection but a practical necessity.

Specific subject matters and pedagogical areas assist, shape, and provide content for larger skills, interpretive abilities, ways of seeing. However, scholarly expertise in particular areas (dogmatics, bioethics, homiletics) precisely due to its narrowed abstraction and detail does not inculcate *theologia* or theological understanding. "Ordered learning," (which such specialized knowledge and progressive structure comprises) Farley argues, "does not create human reflective life. It instead disciplines and rigorizes reflective activity. The relation is the same between theological reflective interpretation and ordered learning. Ordered learning does not create either faith or the reflective responses to faith, that is, theology. It can, however, give faith's reflective interpretation tools and knowledge that will assist it in its constant negotiations with the complexities of reality. That is why theology, the reflective interpretation of faith, should occur in a pedagogical mode."[162] The unity and coherence of

---

to occur, teachers in these programs must be able to transcend their guild loyalties and specialist worlds . . . teachers in these schools must themselves be educated in the *paideia* of theological understanding. It is just at this point that graduate schools are deficient. While the quality of scholarly accomplishment varies from school to school, there is little doubt as to the commitment of these schools to the ideals of scholarship. This commitment is acted out specifically in the linguistic and methodological world of the specialty. Graduate teachers and their students, accordingly, are not only specialists in designated literatures and areas, but their overall thinking occurs in and through the conceptual world of the specialty. The primary unit of the specialty shapes and restricts the specialists' way of thinking. Thus, thinking is dominated by literary tests, cases, ontological structures, arguments, historical details, and so forth. This primacy of unit and method in a scholar's work appears to be inevitable, even desirable, as a concomitant of serious scholarship. It becomes problematic when it cannot be transcended, when it pervades all the postures, perspectives, and thinking of the specialist." *TH*, 199–200.

161. *FK*, 35–42.
162. Ibid., 134–35.

theological reflection in the university, then, does not just depend upon the content of theology's subject matter, what Farley holds in the broadest possible way to be the Christian faith.[163] What helps engender and form theological understanding is not mainly discrete and largely independent scholarly pursuits or units but "basic modes of interpretation."[164] Let me consider what these basic modes do not entail before proceeding to their positive attributes.

THEOLOGICAL UNDERSTANDING, HERMENEUTICS, AND THE UNIVERSITY SETTING

It follows, then, that theology in the university will not be a pedagogical area, a specialty field or a "science." If specialty fields mean narrow, "intensive," research into increasingly detailed problems, it necessarily suppresses the broader hermeneutic modes. Theological reflection, therefore, cannot be defined by specialty fields. This is especially the case for the latter since if by "science" one means a rigorous, ordered inquiry into a particular "territory" or "region" of reality such as biology or psychology and "the knowledge of which is publicly available and capable of withstanding continued public and critical scrutiny." Indeed, what orders and shapes these sciences is a clear "subject-matter, a piece of reality" and rational criteria—neither of which theology enjoys since it is not restricted to one paradigm or dimension of knowledge or subject matter.[165] The two models for theology as science, namely, the medieval notion of "an architectonic of sciences" or Schleiermacher's model for "positive sciences" connected to the legacy of the clerical paradigm are not good options.[166]

> The medieval framework, grounded as it was in a comprehensive world metaphysics, is neither available to nor viable for most modern churches and schools. Even if it were available, it would be incompatible with the modern view that theology is constituted by a number of discrete specialty fields. The clerical and professionalized framework is inadequate precisely because it is clerical and professionalized. For insofar as the specialty fields

---

163. Farley's position, he admits, fundamentally concurs with Schleiermacher's. Ibid., 144.

164. Ibid., 107.

165. Ibid., 116–17.

166. Ibid., 114–15.

occur on a map of clergy education, they cannot coincide with the structure of theological study as such. This is the case at least if theology and theological study occur in broader settings than schools of clergy education. On the medieval view we have a comprehensive science but not sciences. On the modern view we have specialty fields whose unity and justification are found in professional education, not in a comprehensive science.[167]

Moreover, let me also recall that Farley's understanding of theology attempts to recover an older meaning of *theologia* as "primarily an understanding and only secondarily a science or discipline" adapted to overcome the narrowness of specialized inquiry and co-optation of professional tasks.[168] In other words, theology is not a discrete activity of ministry or scholarship per se. Yet while overcoming professionalism and narrowness, Farley's idea seeks to work within the current academic structure of specialty fields, recognizing that fundamental change in how academic knowledge organizes and orients research is unlikely to happen. Its visionary thrust is sober.

On the other hand, though Farley finds it difficult to regard theology as a science, it can possess features that are "*wissenschaftlich.*"[169] It can be a rigorous, critical and scholarly undertaking. Further, if theology comprises basic modes of interpretation rather than specialty fields, it far more resembles the character of philosophy in a university setting. This is precisely because philosophy is neither scientific in the strict sense or limited in its range of possible subject matters and auxiliary resources.

> Like philosophy, theology in the academy annexes and pursues humanistic and social-scientific projects. But even when these pursuits become specialty fields (the archaeology of Palestine, structuralist exegesis), they are not parts of a science comprising subsciences. Nor is it helpful to think of ethics, theological anthropology, ecclesiology, theodicy, and the study of religious language as discrete sciences. They are, rather, ways of exercising a distinctive kind of thinking or reflection. For theology is like philosophy in having a preoccupation with mystery which resists partitioning. Theology's specific subject matters are not abstracted regions of reality but ways of penetrating the overall mystery of the world. The mystery with which theology is preoccupied

---

167. Ibid., 115.
168. Ibid., 64.
169. Ibid., 116.

> does not fall into one of the compartments of knowledge or reality, since it is the mystery of these things themselves. Theology, too, is a kind of meta-thinking, and it occurs at a distance from all the world territories and their sciences. So the reason that theology cannot easily occupy a place among the sciences is not that a heteronomous revelation calls it into being. Rather, it is that the mystery with which it is concerned is not confined to one of the world's territories.[170]

There is an acknowledgment here of theology's comprehensive reach into reality and an implicit affirmation of the doctrine of creation as a hermeneutic principle. The trajectory of theological reflection is towards a transcendent goodness in creation expressed as mystery.

More specifically, what are the specific hermeneutic modes that comprise theological understanding and why are they necessary? The modes of interpretation coordinate not only with elements specific to understanding a religion but also comprise an individual's situational (existential) orientation to reality. This connection opens up possibilities to overcome the narrow, idolatrous tendencies of academic or professional reductionism. At this point, it must be recalled that theology essentially means a *habitus*, a disposition of soul, a reflective activity of the person (the believer) and a religious community. Consequently, the aims and the subject matters of theological *paideia*, though related, are yet distinct. As the subject matters burgeon in diversity, Farley is precisely attempting to unify them through the aims. Aims and subject matter, therefore, if identical, fail to recover any unity to theologia as a reflective wisdom of believers. Subject matters properly embrace the means to theologia, that is, the knowledge of Christianity, the world, possible actions; aims, on the other hand, denote ways of seeing, holding, grasping—theological understanding (*theologia*). For Farley, the contents (subject matters) serve and assist the end—not vice versa. If the ends, then, are basic hermeneutic modes leading to theological judgments, what expressly are the working dynamics? In response, Farley lays out a broad schematic of interpretation.

There are "elemental types of interpretations" proper to human beings as such. These interpretations

> reflect perennial or recurring situational dimensions that are typically human and historical. It is characteristic of human be-

---

170. Ibid., 118.

ings to retain and interpret their past, especially their corporate and narrative past. And the human striving to survive, to secure oneself, to obtain a certain well-being, prompts interpretations oriented to the truth of things—for instance, to the behavior of the hunted animal, to the regularities (and irregularities) of nature, to the resources for healing. There are, it seems, elemental interpretations in a very formal and general sense which reflect very elemental types of situations which are characteristically human. In addition we can speak of interpretations which are basic to particular types of situations. This is because very specific situations have their "elemental" dimensions and these dimensions evoke the interpretations appropriate to them.[171]

Types of situations evoke different modes of interpretations and their specific dimensions. Naturally, these modes can be immensely varied as the complexity of situations themselves. Reflective interpretations when deliberate and involved in the educational sphere possess identifiable characteristics: "critical," "normative," "reality-oriented," "interrogative," "curious," "assessive." The situation for believers existing in the world is no different; they will also share the same characteristics accompanying their educational experience. But Farley seeks to uncover those "elemental dimensions" appropriate to one shaped by redemptive, ecclesial existence.[172] As we shall see, this dimensional and interpretive matrix is immensely significant for anyone engaged in theological understanding.

The conditions for redemptive existence actually help shape those modes of interpretation that structure theological understanding. Abstracting and isolating the critical elements to express the meaning of concrete redemptive existence, Farley offers a succinct distillation and a justification of their necessity.

> Faith comprises redemption as a mode of existence, with all that this entails—and thus the way tradition and gospel have to do with norms, warrants, idealities, and aims for action. Without ecclesia nothing would have occurred to make redemption possible or give it any content whatever. And without a content as a bearer of truth, the only reality reference that redemption involved would

---

171. Ibid., 136–37. Other "perennial features" that any human situation includes are "personal self-insight, the grasp of the corrupted elements in the social situation, and the possibilities of redemption." Ibid., 157.

172. Ibid., 138.

be to the life situations in which it occurred. Without gospel, tradition and faith would occur simply in the mode of indifference, since they would have nothing to do with the actual life and practice of human individuals and communities.[173]

Though each element can be considered as a theological category, they are also embedded within a believer's faith-life. They "are primordially present in faith and are not just created by education or scholarship." Farley concludes there are three elemental types of interpretation that structure the way people of faith make sense out of their lived situations: interpreting tradition, its truth, and finally how it figures in real life, that is, its effect on human "praxis."[174] Just like the aforementioned perennial types of interpretation proper to human existence as such (search for healing, well-being, etc.) so are these types of interpretation characteristic of the believer. And yet in terms of what theology means or how theological understanding is shaped, these three alone remain insufficient.[175] Their insufficiency stems from the situation that persons of faith exist in and toward a horizon of different realities much broader. Put more concretely, the human condition when seen on an individual level is formed by a multiplicity of responses to varied situations and the ways of being, seeing, and acting in each. Faith experience cannot be abstracted, therefore, from world experience.[176] This world experience concretely entails a succession of different situations. Hence, to adequately appraise and understand the primordial interpretations that attend faith, one must also consider "the comprehensive interpretive act of the believer, the interpretation of situations."[177] There must be a broader framework of understanding in which the more restricted types actually coinhere.

> This is the kind of interpretation that occurs constantly in the concrete life of the believer and in the corporate life of the church. It is the interpretation in which the other elemental types of interpretation distinctive to faith come together in concrete acts. If this type of interpretation became the subject matter for

---

173. Ibid.

174. Ibid., 138–39.

175. Ibid., 139.

176. An implication of the idea that faith and world are deeply connected means that a strict "fideist" position concerning theological argument and audience cannot be sustained. See ibid., 120–21.

177. Ibid., 140. For a more detailed analysis, see Farley, "Interpreting Situations," 1–26.

inquiry and pedagogy, there would have to be a concern with the formal or general structure of any situation and with hermeneutics as such, that is, with the distinctive way all the basic types of interpretation come together and function in the interpretation of situations involving faith.[178]

What Farley maintains here simply refers to a general hermeneutic consciousness, a sensitivity to, for example, the social, aesthetic, political, economic, personal, ethical, technical dimensions—among others—available in many human life situations and, therefore, candidates for abstraction, study, and disciplined as ways of seeing.[179] It is "the interpretation of an inclusive situation," in other words.[180] This hermeneutic encompasses the skills and perceptivities necessary to grasp a variety of situations. Indeed, this view of interpreting situations is precisely what Farley calls "theology's primary mode."[181] It presupposes a broad, liberal foundation and exposure to different strata of concrete, contextual meaning. "For situational interpretation is broader than the appropriation of the conceptual framework of a specific science, for instance, psychology. Constituting the believer's responses to things is interpretation in the sense of a self-conscious and disciplined reading of the complexity and dimensionality of what is interpreted."[182] Consequently, this comprehensively concrete type of interpretation is synthetic, it draws many different features into a certain coherency or intelligibility.[183]

Alongside this elemental type of interpretation, another merits inclusion, namely, what Farley calls the interpretation of "vocation." Whereas the comprehensive interpretation of situations marks a condition necessary for anyone to engage properly the more specific modes of tradition, truth, and praxis, so there is the more individual idea of "*primary occupations*" for the development of theological understanding. In part, vocation must be recognized in the lives of believers because

---

178. *FK*, 140.

179. Farley gives specifics. "For example, the marriage one takes for granted becomes an intensely focused subject matter when it is threatened by disintegration. Situations as problematic can range from very global situations (the crisis in planetary ecology) to "metaphysical" situations (the course and destiny of human history) to very specific situations of the individual (the onset of an illness)." "Interpreting Situations," 10.

180. *FK*, 156.

181. Farley, "Four Pedagogical Mistakes," 201.

182. *FK*, 157.

183. Farley gives the example of attending a theatre, see ibid., 156.

it is the "primary situation" in which they find themselves and which involves "specific situations, activities, and responsibilities that evoke interpretation."[184] Vocation balances the more general interpretation of situations, conceptually attending to the realities of believers within their dominant "life-world."[185] Taken together, then, there are five "primary hermeneutic modes" of interpretation "at work in the believer's situation."[186] Referring to their Latin roots, they comprise: "*mundus, vocatio, traditio, veritas, and actio.*"[187] The latter three are specific forms of theological interpretation while the first two, world and vocation, are modes of human interpretation that make sense of part and whole, that is, they are "synthetic."[188]

Theological understanding, its achievement as an end, cannot be equated with the myriad subject matters proper to each mode of interpretation. Farley insists that especially in ordered learning or a course of pedagogy judged "theological" that the aims precede whatever understanding considers and forms it.[189] When this fails, the core of theological understanding suffers.

> The education whose center is *theologia* is an ecclesial counterpart to *paideia*, focusing as it does, not on *areté*, but on a sapiential knowledge engendered by grace and divine self-disclosure. The view that education (the course of studies) means the exposure to sciences or realms of scholarship tends to promote a technological view of education. Education as mere scholarly learning

---

184. Ibid., 141. Italics his.

185. Farley's meaning here presupposes a more technical term borrowed and modeled on Husserl's philosophy. See *EM*, 85f.

186. *FK*, 148; 143.

187. Ibid., 142. Italics his. Each term subsumes an immense field of questions, problems, texts, knowledge and so forth. Let me offer a brief overview of what "tradition, truth, and action" mean. Tradition is shorthand for the effort to understand the complex dimensionality of Christian faith, namely, its "temporal, institutional, moral, intersubjective, linguistic" aspects. The "truth question" concerns the evidential claims that reality makes upon human beings, not simply abstract or philosophical controversy over certain philosophical conceptions or theories. As Farley puts it, this "is chiefly a question about whether the claims of faith are true and about whether our world is illumined by those claims." Interpretation of action concerns reading situations in order to effect concrete change or certain outcomes ordered toward the future and possessing the characteristic of responsibility. It is "an assessive and altering way of existing in a situation." Broader than all three, stand the synthetic modes. Ibid., 148–55.

188. Ibid., 148.

189. Cf. ibid., 142–43.

is not a process affecting and shaping the human being under an ideal, but a grasping of the methods and contents of a plurality of regions of scholarship. The loss, then, of *theologia* to theological study resembles the older loss of education as *paideia*.[190]

The basic modes of interpretation—theological *paideia*—must structure and enjoy a certain priority in programs ordered by specific pedagogical areas. It is precisely these five hermeneutic modes—the Christian tradition, the orientation toward reality and truth, the concrete practice in the world, the interpretation of situations and the more specifically individual framework of vocation—that become the personal habitus, the wisdom that is *theologia*. To repeat yet again, it is not restricted to scholars or professional classes of ministers. These immensely general coordinates constitute what theology involves structurally. Furthermore, it should be clear that "theological understanding is not one thing but many things."[191] The relevance of university education for theologia, why it belongs there, is partly because its sciences and subject matters help discipline these basic modes of interpretation and understanding.[192] The modes of interpretation are not created by the university: they are made conscious and sharpened in it and by it.

Understanding the meaning of Christianity, considering it insofar as it makes claims about reality, and then seeing how it concretely effects the human condition—these three comprise the "immanent elements" in a static view of *theologia*. Farley also offers a probative description of what the concrete activity of theologizing involves, calling it a dialectical activity. Though a qualified version since it "omits most of the issues which should be treated in such an account," his description crosses the different "social matrices" of theological study, namely, the life of the believer, clergy education and scholarly inquiry.[193] Five moments characterize this dialectic. Before the specific moments of the theological dialectic engage, what always precedes is the situation of the believer's living, the problems, issues, and social reality that "evoke response and interpretation." Then, from the concrete situation, theological reflection moves to grasp the rich content of Christian faith, seeking to thematize its "primary symbols, the themes of proclamation, the dogmas of tradi-

190. *TH*, 153.
191. Ibid., 157.
192. *FK*, 171.
193. *TH*, 164.

tion." In other words, the believer looks to the historical reality, evidence and claims of the ecclesial community to make sense out of the concrete situation. Second, theological understanding then refuses to give the situation of the believer (whatever it might be) absolute or normative status, making the issue a "candidate for theological criticism." The present, then, can be measured according to the past. Third, a critical principle emerges that not only prevents one from absolutizing elements within the situation but also recognizes this caution applies as well to the ecclesial tradition. It is, in brief, acknowledging the historicity and relativity proper to human existence. Given the complexity of the first three moments, Farley maintains that, nevertheless, theological understanding must struggle to discern "that about the persisting imagery, symbols, and doctrines of that mythos which expresses truth" namely, "some grasp of the way in which the Christian mythos is a mirror of truth and reality." How, in other words, is faith normative here? Finally, the fifth moment attempts to locate within the situation the "'kingdom of God,' *the situation* as God undergirds it, pervades it, disposes it, lures it to its best possibilities." Having proceeded from tradition, to criticisms of situation and ecclesiality and then seeking still normative truth and meaning in a relativized tradition, the fifth moment strives to locate the "theonomy" of what is occurring, namely, redemptive action.[194]

The meaning of theology as Farley understands it, accordingly, moves away from a narrow judgment of its genre as practical task or specialty field to the personal, reflective wisdom of the believer and the community of faith. The fivefold modes of interpretation that constitute theology's heuristic structure, therefore, extend beyond the social matrices of church and specialized scholarship to the university in the following ways: (1) as an intrinsic component in university study and teaching of religion and (2) as a critical corrective necessary to the health of university knowledge and science.

Farley maintains that theology cannot be separated from the serious study of religion. Because the context of Farley's treatment is the secular university, his reasoning presumes the acceptance of scholarly inquiry into the human phenomena of religion. And it is precisely within the teaching of religion that theology subsists necessarily, not as endowed chairs or designated theologians, but as intrinsic to its nature. Indeed, religion and theology cannot, it seems, exist independently. One defini-

---

194. Ibid., 166–69. Italics his.

tion of theology given indicates this clearly: "*Theology is the reflectively procured insight and understanding which encounter with a specific religious faith evokes.*"[195] Insofar as the scholarly investigation and teaching of a religion concerns its specific historical determinacy, attempts to understand its truth claims and "religion as an aspect of human existence," the investigation will effect and manifest a theological character. When the study of religion concentrates upon a concrete, historically conditioned religious faith, and faith entails modes of interpretation and self-understanding, "any thoroughgoing study of religion will face the tasks set by theological study: the understanding and interpretation of a subject matter (Jewish, Christian, Buddhist faith), and the grasp of basic modes of interpretation."[196] Put differently, when the study of religion is taught seriously, it cannot help but engage "those faiths at the point of their reality claims and their experiential dimensions (of theological hermeneutics)."[197] These issues will emerge even among the various principles and methodologies employed towards understanding it simply because, Farley insists, "religion" cannot be legitimately understood without them, without theological interpretation.[198]

To this end, it is possible and necessary for the study of religion to include, engage, and teach theology. But what is the difference between theology in a confessional setting and within a secular university? Farley does not emphasize the difference in content taught and studied so much as the aims.

> Within a faith, the aim of study is the disciplining of faith's actual reflective life; this occurs in the institutions and among the constituents of the religious faith. In the more distanced study of a faith, the aim of theological study is to understand the religious faith; this requires entering into specific hermeneutic modes to the degree that that advances the understanding . . . Although the educational aims of religious and nonreligious institutions are different, both kinds of institution must include studies that seek to understand and to be shaped by whatever wisdom and truth can establish itself, however historically specific its origin and context.[199]

195. *FK*, 64–65. Italics his.
196. Ibid., 179.
197. Ibid., 78–79.
198. Ibid., 180–81.
199. Ibid., 179–80.

Farley acknowledges, however, that the pedagogical order and priority will also differ between confessional and secular institutions. Specifically, the secular university will view the study of the Christian religion primarily from a historical perspective. Even so, within such a consideration, he affirms it would be studied according to "pedagogical areas" essential for proper scholarly inquiry: the historical, the social and the symbolic-linguistic.[200] Collectively, these areas cover fairly comprehensive topics like general and specific historical events, human individual and collective dynamics and everything related to the Christian mythos (doctrine, creed, imagery, etc).[201] The difference between the confessional and secular approach hinges on this: that the academic approaches the study of Christianity as a serious historical phenomenon while the confessional approach first privileges its truth claims.[202] In either setting, however, when the historical reality, sociality, and mythos of Christianity reduces to scholarly description or data management, ignoring its central claims to truth and reality, that reflection forfeits its theological character.[203] Such inquiries are easily assumed by specialty fields that disperse and fragment the basic modes of theological interpretation.

In terms of who can legitimately undertake "theological understanding," Farley does not impose confessional stipulations. This idea tends to derive from a fideist position that Farley defines as the view that "the cognitive and reality status of the witness—the images and narratives of a religious faith—is evident only to the participant, the believer, in the specific religious community." For such a position, those outside the confessional, ecclesial community cannot truly access the depth and meaning of Christian claims.[204] However, while acknowledging that the content of ecclesial life and witness is historical and communal, the claim that Christianity is not intelligible to non-believers or non-Christians cannot be sustained. "On what grounds," he writes, "does one human be-

---

200. Ibid., 183.
201. Ibid., 182.
202. Ibid., 181.
203. Cf. ibid., 70.

204. Ibid., 121. In terms of theology as a discipline, Farley concurs with James Gustafson and maintains that a program of fideist theological study results in the "ghettoization of theology." Ibid., 120.

ing tell another that he or she is incapable of understanding or insight?"[205] Another reason opposing a fideist position is that "every religious faith has already violated and transcended the principle of fideism." According to Farley, this is because "specificity is not simply territorial and cultural but temporal as well . . . If fideism were absolutely correct, there would be no way a religious community could appropriate its own past."[206] This remark already supposes the legitimacy of the Enlightenment critical principle concerning the historicity of human knowing, events and texts. Human beings can claim that religious traditions possess wisdom, insight, truth and meaning not necessarily bound by the historical-linguistic forms that express them. It is not necessary, for instance, to be a speaker of Koine Greek living in first century Palestine to understand New Testament claims. It is possible, therefore, that students in secular universities exposed to serious study of Christianity can also develop a theological habitus that not only concerns the reality of Christianity but can open to the evidencing realities of redemption in its claims.

Individually and collectively, as previously mentioned, the accent of the basic modes of interpretation for believers rests upon the appropriated truth and living out the commitments of the Christian mythos. Contact with other university disciplines and sciences should ideally help refine and hone the primary modes of world, vocation, tradition, truth and practice for the person who lives under the posture of commitment. For the student of religion, a theological hermeneutic not only enables accurate historical understanding, but opens up the possibilities of alternative forms of social and cultural criticism equally available to believers. The determination whether such theological hermeneutics effects spiritual or moral transformation, however, is not a topic Farley considers. But in keeping with his caution concerning who can legitimately understand, it seems reasonable to posit that answering such questions will remain elusive.

The other primary reason for theology's place in a university is what it brings to the pursuit and teaching of human knowledge and science. For Farley, the "essential instability of knowledge" concerns the loss of reality when a particular paradigm of knowing excludes others, such as the empirical without "praxis." But it also indicates something about human subjectivity. The critical posture of the Christian mythos holds that

205. Ibid., 65.
206. Ibid., 121.

there is a dangerous desire and attitude behind the pursuit of knowledge when it is thought to deliver human beings absolutely from their desire for survival and security. This second aspect can lead to idolatry or exaggerated hope and unrealistic expectations of success. When such efforts fail, there is an immense temptation to turn away from the pursuit of truth and reality towards a "cynicism about the cognitive endeavor itself."[207] What, then, can the presence of the Christian mythos do for the academic milieu and pedagogic undertakings in a university? It provides a penetrating account and vision of the horizon in which such pursuits, desires, correctives and successes exist.

> The Christian mythos engenders a criticism directed at both sides of this instability. It offers a posture that combines an interest in what is real and an interpretation of the corruption and redemption of all that is real. Compared with the formal critical principle (human knowledge requires constant correction) and various hermeneutical corrections, this is a third posture of criticism. Is this third criticism itself a hermeneutic, to be added to those of intuitive imagination, tradition, and praxis? I do not think so. The reason is that the hermeneutic correctives are created by the dimensions of real things. But what are set forth in the Christian mythos are less dimensions of reality than simply reality's corruptive and redemptive possibilities. The third principle is not so much a hermeneutic as a critical posture in which certain convictions, suspicions, and even hopes operate.[208]

The human tendency toward idolatry, evil, and the spurning of reality in favor of other interests subordinate to pursuing reality as knowledge and science receives illumination and clarification from the account given in the Christian mythos. It does not replace other correctives or insights, but simply offers a broader framework for their claims and intelligibility. Hence, insofar as there is a presence of the critical posture supported by the Christian mythos, there will also be the study of religion requiring proper theological understanding. Yet such an understanding does not require "belief in a doctrine" or a confessional commitment. It is a vision regarding the corruption and redemption of knowledge available to those with a serious disposition to the real.

---

207. Ibid., 23–24.
208. Ibid., 24.

CONCLUSION

The problems of theology's meaning and place in the university have been surveyed along with their solutions. Farley sees rich possibilities in rethinking what theology means beyond a confessional or authority paradigm, where argumentation must constantly refer beyond principles made problematic by historical consciousness to a more accessible theological hermeneutics. In this trajectory, theology becomes unhinged from a fideist position, on the one hand, and removed as a practical end or professional specialty field, on the other. This twofold removal is necessary to restore unity to the activity and subject matters of theological reflection in terms of their aims and also for its salutary assistance in discerning correctly the contours, the authentic relationships between human knowledge and the human condition.

The shift towards the guiding structure of theological reflection encompassing tradition, truth, and action attempts to broaden the range of theological reflection. It moves beyond a technological approach restricted to either the subject matter or professional institutionalizations to seriously reflective human beings—believers or not. Indeed, the threefold coordinates and the ability to think theologically are human givens, not accidents of nature or learning. We have seen how, in fact, the meaning of "ecclesial reflection" and conditions for knowing its divine references cannot be a priori dismissed of people not denominationally committed. If true, Farley views the possibility of applying a theological *paideia* to the university setting in terms of knowing a religious tradition per se and also applying theological perspective to the variegated dimensions of science, disciplines, pedagogical areas and problems that generate academic questions. Theology offers a deep reservoir for constructive criticism and insight lacking in other academic areas precisely because of its universalizable theological anthropology and focus on God's redemptive activity. In many ways, the "experience of redemption" is theology's formal object that helps restore to the experience of learning not fragmentation but a synthetic apprehension of creation. In turn, human science and learning further hone and refine general and more particular theological interpretative modes. This is how educational *paideia* trains student minds. In the end, the recovery of theology as a personal, existential habitus, in some sense, accords with deep structures of human desiring and knowing, so that the presence of the Christian mythos as a critical posture is not an intellectual imposition, but an existential freedom towards a deeper understanding of reality as such. It is also something older, a pre-clerical paradigm of theological understanding.

7

University Theology as Saving and Sapiential

> Under the name of truth I also included beauty, virtue, and every kind of goodness, so that for me it was a question of a conception of the relationship between grace and desire. The conviction that had come to me was that when one hungers for bread one does not receive stones.
>
> —Simone Weil

A PRINCIPAL TASK OF this book is to investigate the ways in which the nature and academic setting of theology according to Schleiermacher, Newman, Dulles, and Farley might reveal fundamental patterns of contrast and overlap to illuminate the current situation of theology in Christian universities. The first conclusion I draw is a point of contrast. The most important contrast is the tacit or explicit soteriology that determines the nature of theology. Schleiermacher, Newman, Dulles, and Farley give evidence that theology in the university corresponds to either an exclusive or inclusive soteriology. The second conclusion is one of overlap: theology is more of a wisdom than a science. These two points are related. The soteriological character that theology exhibits determines the nature of the wisdom that theology becomes. This relationship between soteriological character and sapiential form, long a part of Christian theological and spiritual tradition, has been insufficiently recognized in the current debate about theology and its academic meaning in the contemporary Christian university.[1] To establish the validity of these claims, I will show in this chapter: (1) why these points can be found in the work of Schleiermacher, Newman, Dulles, and Farley; and (2) investigate briefly whether a soteriological character and sapiential

---

1. For an overview of the sapiential tradition, see Barnhart, *Future of Wisdom*.

form of theology function as latent presuppositions in current thinking about theology and the university.

EXCLUSIVE AND INCLUSIVE SOTERIOLOGY AND THE SAPIENTIAL CHARACTER OF THEOLOGY

The Christian tradition has long exhibited a connection between theology and salvation. One significant formulation of this relationship in the history of theology has been that of Aquinas. In the first article of the *Summa theologiae*, Aquinas poses the question, "Whether, besides philosophy, any further doctrine is required?" He argues that yes, another doctrine is required—*sacra doctrina*. Aquinas's determination of the question reads as follows:

> It was necessary for man's salvation that there should be a knowledge revealed by God, besides the philosophical sciences built up by human reason. First, indeed, because man is directed to God as to an end that surpasses the grasp of his reason: *The eye hath not seen, O God, besides Thee, what things Thou hast prepared for them that wait for Thee* (Isa 64:4). But the end must first be known by men who are to direct their thoughts and actions to the end. Hence it was necessary for the salvation of man that certain truths which exceed human reason should be made known to him by divine revelation. Even as regards those truths about God which human reason can discover, it was necessary that man should be taught by a divine revelation, because the truth about God such as reason could discover would only be known by a few, and that after a long time, and with the admixture of many errors. But man's whole salvation, which is in God, depends upon the knowledge of this truth. Therefore, in order that the salvation of men might be brought about more fitly and more surely, it was necessary that they should be taught divine truths by divine revelation. It was therefore necessary that, besides the philosophical sciences discovered by reason there should be a *sacra doctrina* obtained through revelation.[2]

For Aquinas, *sacra doctrina* and the theology associated with it is "necessary for the salvation" of human beings. The *raison d'être* of theology is salvation. It is important, however, to recognize that *sacra doctrina* is

---

2. Aquinas, *ST* I, Q. 1, art. 1. I have modified the translation at the end to read *sacra doctrina* rather than sacred science, the latter being an inaccurate translation of the Latin.

not the only knowledge of God that is salvific (i.e., God teaching human beings) but simply the most efficient and most direct path to the truth of divine revelation. Given the historical context of the high Middle Ages and the comprehensive influence of Catholicism upon its culture, it is extraordinary that Aquinas would even admit that other people do come to important knowledge of God through reason independently of *sacra doctrina*. Knowledge not specifically derivative of Christian revelation can be salvific. The meaning of saving knowledge, however, has not always been univocal.

What I wish to describe now are general traits of an exclusive and an inclusive soteriological theology derived from Schleiermacher, Newman, Dulles, and Farley.

For Schleiermacher and Dulles, the predominantly ecclesial and specialized character of theology means that its intellectual prerequisites are directed toward religious self-understanding and theological research. In addition, Dulles and especially Schleiermacher regard theology as a strictly scientific, academic, and learned activity. It requires training, doctrinally based theological coordinates, ecclesial participation, and strict church oversight. For Dulles, theologians who consider themselves Catholic but depart methodologically and philosophically from the sources of revelation and the authority of the magisterium do not deserve and virtually forfeit the title of Catholic theologian. Schleiermacher holds that theologians by definition are prominent in church leadership. A layperson might embody the theological ideal but that is unlikely. It is safe to say that for both Dulles and Schleiermacher theology is largely a professionalized undertaking for academics and church leaders. For Schleiermacher, systematic, historical, and practical theology and their subfields provide the historical material (God, Jesus, Spirit, church) for theological understanding and judgment. Schleiermacher's conception of theology terminates in preaching that is directly and specifically soteriological. Dulles's concern with orthodox transmission of Catholic teaching as implicitly catechetical similarly displays a soteriological character. The aims of ecclesial-transformative theology may differ in proximate scholarly ends but should ultimately terminate in ongoing and salvific transformation on the part of teacher and student. Soteriology is embedded in Dulles's very definition of the nature of theology as "ecclesial-*transformative*."[3] For Dulles and Schleiermacher, in other words,

3. Emphasis added.

one cannot do theology without confessing faith in the living God revealed through Jesus Christ. Indeed, theological study and formation for Schleiermacher must terminate in ecclesial leadership manifest in preaching and practical theology. Theological activity carried beyond ecclesial ends—speculatively engaged, for example, with other academic disciplines—forfeits its distinctive theological character and becomes simply another scholarly discipline.

Dulles's underlying soteriology, interestingly, is more sympathetic to Schleiermacher's position than to Newman's or Farley's. Just as Schleiermacher views theology as something within but not integral to university culture itself because he regards philosophy (with Newman) as the basic principle of undergraduate education, so also Dulles establishes such ecclesial prerequisites as belief and habits of thought explicitly and consciously formed by the central Christian symbols for theological understanding within the university context. Not only does ecclesiality in the strict sense control the integrity of theological activity but it also becomes—at least in the undergraduate classroom—the primary focus of its existence, namely a form of advanced catechesis. This function of ecclesiality means that for Dulles, theology assists the Catholic university to preserve and maintain its historic religious character in several ways: by its presence in the curriculum, by its fidelity to magisterial influence, and by its pedagogical transmission of official Catholic teaching to Catholic undergraduates. The necessity of theology depends on its ability to spread, develop, and protect orthodox doctrine to ecclesially affiliated students while criticizing and judging threats to ecclesial life and values. As Schleiermacher evidences the protective dimension of theology's soteriological character in the forms of polemics and apologetics, so Dulles regards the threats from relativism, indifference, and secularism along parallel lines.

What has become a problematic and confusing point in recent years in Catholic circles stems precisely from such an underlying exclusive soteriological character: the gradual conflation of Catholic theology with catechetics. One suspects that the controversy generated by *Ex corde ecclesiae*'s demand that theologians receive a *mandatum* from their bishop has only exacerbated the confusion. Cardinal Dulles maintains that catechesis is an organic and inextricable part of the teaching of Catholic theology. It might be wise, however, to review the official Catholic teaching on the relationship of theology to catechesis.

In one of John Paul II's early writings on catechesis, *Catechesi tradendae*, written in 1979, it is striking that the word *universities* appears only once. The context of the term concerns a priest's pastoral work as a chaplain not as a theology professor. From the start, the paucity of references to colleges or universities makes it questionable whether catechesis operates within them in a formal way. Moreover, the pope distinguishes the work of theologians from that of catechists.

> Aware of the influence that their research and their statements have on catechetical instruction, theologians and exegetes have a duty to take great care that people do not take for certainty what on the contrary belongs to the area of questions of opinion or of discussion among experts. Catechists for their part must have the wisdom to pick from the field of theological research those points that can provide light for their own reflection and their teaching, drawing, like the theologians, from the true sources, in the light of the Magisterium.[4]

This document does not, therefore, maintain that the college or university is a common setting for Catholic catechesis. Indeed, in *Ex corde ecclesiae*, John Paul II distinguishes theology as a discipline in a Catholic university that has its own methods and conducts research with academic freedom. Indeed, he emphasizes once more the *difference* between theological opinion and official Catholic doctrine.

> Bishops should encourage the creative work of theologians. They serve the Church through research done in a way that respects theological method. They seek to understand better, further develop, and more effectively communicate the meaning of Christian Revelation as transmitted in Scripture and Tradition and in the Church's Magisterium. They also investigate the ways in which theology can shed light on specific questions raised by contemporary culture. At the same time, since theology seeks an understanding of revealed truth whose authentic interpretation is entrusted to the Bishops of the Church, it is intrinsic to the principles and methods of their research and teaching in their academic discipline that theologians respect the authority of the Bishops, and assent to Catholic doctrine according to the degree of authority with which it is taught.[5]

---

4. *Catechesis in Our Time*, 800.
5. John Paul II, *Ex corde Ecclesiae*, 60–61; par. 29.

The conclusion seems clear: John Paul II does not identify catechesis with theology. First, theologians are not the official teachers of Catholic doctrine—bishops are. Second, there is a nuance in the level of assent to church teaching that theologians may give. This statement seems reserved for experts, not the typical parishioner or those being catechized in the basics of the faith. Such a statement permits creative reinterpretation, assessment, and possible dissent from particular teachings based on theological argument.

This position is repeated in the *Ecclesial Instruction on the Vocation of the Theologian* (1990) promulgated by the Congregation for the Doctrine of the Faith and produced under the guidance of its then prefect, Josef Cardinal Ratzinger.

> The living Magisterium of the Church and theology, while having different gifts and functions, ultimately have the same goal: preserving the People of God in the truth which sets free and thereby making them "a light to the nations." This service to the ecclesial community brings the theologian and the Magisterium into a reciprocal relationship. The latter authentically teaches the doctrine of the Apostles. And, benefiting from the work of theologians, it refutes objections to and distortions of the faith and promotes, with the authority received from Jesus Christ, new and deeper comprehension, clarification, and application of revealed doctrine. Theology, for its part, gains, by way of reflection, an ever deeper understanding of the Word of God found in the Scripture and handed on faithfully by the Church's living Tradition under the guidance of the Magisterium. Theology strives to clarify the teaching of Revelation with regard to reason and gives it finally an organic and systematic form.[6]

From this statement, it is clear that the offices of theological research and the Magisterium are distinct and pursue different proximate goals. Both, however, share the final goal of evangelization. One should also note that the words *catechesis* or *catechize* appear nowhere in the *Instruction on the Ecclesial Vocation of the Theologian* or in *Ex corde Ecclesiae*. From the documents that comprise official Catholic teaching, catechesis and theology are clearly distinct and not to be confused. Theologians like Cardinal Dulles, therefore, can certainly differ from church teaching about the relationship between theology and catechesis. Yet there are

---

6. Congregation for the Doctrine of the Faith, *Instruction on the Ecclesial Vocation of the Theologian*, as cited in *Catholic Identity in Our Colleges and Universities*, 102–3.

strong historical reasons to see the distinct tasks of theology and catechesis as helping the church to realize the gospel in different but related ways. Let me return to the central issue of soteriology.

In an exclusive soteriology, the narrative and conceptual framework of the biblical symbolic world cannot be separated from the meaning and reality of salvation. I will offer two different examples. David Ford criticizes the descriptions of sainthood given by Edith Wyschogrod of St. Teresa of Avila and the Hasidim precisely on this point. Ford explains:

> First, from the point of view of St Teresa and the Hasidim, she seems to be reversing the order of the commandments to love God and love the neighbour. Their "experience" in terms of their "actual or envisioned acts" is most profoundly shaped through worship and prayer. Their bodies, which for Wyschogrod are the basic units of significance, are disciplined, energized and formed through worship. Their perception of the Other is as someone created by God in God's image. So how can acts articulated in the context of human need be "more important" than the conceptual framework which is inextricable from loving God with all their heart, soul, mind and bodily strength?[7]

Ford argues that Wyschogrod seeks a kind of "fundamental option" to explain and justify the specific acts of goodness that comprise holiness.[8] These acts would then be independent of the language and experience of identifiable worship—a mistake. In an exclusive soteriology, the meaning of "love of God" and "love of neighbor" can neither exist nor have salvific import without the conceptual framework that brings this reality into being. Michael Budde's description of an ecclesially based university provides a good summary of what an exclusive soteriology looks like when applied to the ends of liberal education. "The purpose of ecclesially based higher education is to make participants more fully into disciples shaped by the priorities and practices of Jesus Christ; to help them discern their vocation as members of the transnational body of Christ; and to contribute to the mission of the church—to help the church serve more fully and faithfully as a foretaste of the promised kingdom of God, on earth as is in heaven."[9] When the kinds of theology

---

7. Ford, *Self and Salvation*, 221–22; See also Wyschogrod, *Saints and Postmodernism*.

8. Ford, *Self and Salvation*, 223.

9. Budde, "Assessing What Doesn't Exist," 256, as quoted in Hauerwas, *State of the University*, 105.

researched and taught conform to this model, namely one that focuses on explicit discipleship, vocation, praxis, mission, and a confessional identity formed by participation, then that theology would be typical of a religious knowledge that helps to move the community toward eternal life with God. It is saving faith in the strict sense. Schleiermacher and Dulles, I suggest, would agree.

If Schleiermacher and Dulles exhibit traits of an exclusive soteriology, Newman and Farley display those of an inclusive soteriology. Newman and Farley regard theology as something more integral to the ordinary life of faith and the liberal formation of a mind that seeks meaning in life than a specialized field or clerical preserve. In the best sense, theology is a form of contemplation and a hermeneutic for discerning the activity of God in relation to the world, the church, and one's personal experience. It is accessible to and possible for anyone to undertake, unhindered by barriers of professional class, formal ecclesial functions, or a credentialing process. Despite Farley's intellectual departure from the "house of authority," the content of theological reflection that seeks to avoid reducing Christian claims to human philosophical views or isolated preferences must be the regulative principles of the Christian faith. At the center of these basic principles for Farley is the experience of redemption in Christ. For Newman, the God of natural theology provides the subject matter of theological reflection, not traditionally orthodox doctrinal topics. If we take the subject matter especially in an academic setting, where it possesses scientific, disciplinary, and pedagogical characteristics, dogmatics becomes something imparted as a more specialized and less integrated field of teaching. In terms of dogmatic content, Newman's understanding of revealed theology develops either as catechetical information or something restricted to clerical study. Indeed, it is something Newman simply considers not essential to a liberal formation of mind but rather as part of a general religious knowledge. It is perhaps most in terms of subject matter that Newman's conception of theology, at least in a liberal arts curriculum, shows a marked difference from those of Schleiermacher, Dulles, and Farley. Natural theology is not directly concerned with Christian salvation. Moreover, intellectual formation for Newman leaves moral conversion—its more concrete soteriological element—to the custodial role of the colleges. Dogmatic theology, as I have argued, does not figure as much within the regular teaching and aims of liberal learning. Insofar as a soteriological component informs Newman's understanding, it is at best indirect. Other indirect purposes for theology that embrace Newman, Dulles, and Farley are Christian criticisms of values and notions incompatible with human flourishing, whether they are economic, political, or social. Let me turn more specifically to the issue of ecclesiality, for this topic bears directly on soteriology.

Newman's view of theology in the university subordinates strictly ecclesial elements to the more proximate end of philosophical cultivation of mind. Ecclesiality or Christian identity, then, is not in the foreground but rather in the general presuppositions of a liberally educated human being. Intellectual formation and its philosophical approach to a correct vision and appreciation of reality's metaphysical and aesthetic features are paramount. Ecclesial participation is generally presupposed for Newman given his own historical context. Moreover, it is likely that Newman's own experience of ecclesial authority would certainly have modified his stance with regard to the scope and intensity of magisterial control regarding course curricula and theological pedagogy, thereby reducing further the direct and explicit ecclesial influence over the content of university theology.[10]

Defining what ecclesiality means for Farley transcends confessional or denominational boundaries. So although the correction, discipline, and intellectual freedom given theological understanding within the university is vital, Farley's expansive view of ecclesial experience makes the identification of *theologia* as distinctively ecclesial with a set of fixed principles difficult. Indeed, this is the reason why Farley is wary of using the term *church* to describe his notion of *ecclesia*. This is true for Farley despite the necessity of the historical content of Christianity for the hermeneutical trajectory of the self-understanding and gospel proclamation of theology. In this respect, Farley's opposites here are Dulles and Schleiermacher. *Theologia* for Farley is not simply for clergy or the learned professions but for the larger community of those participating in the ecclesia. Now while Dulles would certainly permit people beyond

10. Would Newman be so reluctant to lay down criteria for Catholic theology more explicitly ecclesial today? The key would certainly lie in the way in which Newman would define and understand academic and theological freedom in relationship to the bishop. It is a question, however, that requires evaluating Newman's ecclesiology in light of communion ecclesiology proposed by the Second Vatican Council. For a concise overview of the ecclesiology of communion, see Wood, "Church as Communion," 159–76.

the academically credentialed or ordained clergy to be theologians and do theology, he would not hold that a nonbeliever or inactive Catholic could do so. Dulles holds that common human experience is an insufficient resource to understand or justify theological claims about the Christian faith.[11] Authentic human subjectivity becomes something seemingly external to the sacred realm of ecclesial experience.

For Farley, like Newman, the aims of theology concern the integration of knowledge and a renewal of its corrective possibilities. But his view of theological understanding also represents liberation from outmoded, fragmented, clericalized, and contradictory ways of understanding traditional forms of ecclesiality and authoritative doctrine. University disciplines and modes of interpreting situations inform *theologia*, providing new and relevant ways for it to recover the historical material, judge and affirm its validity, and then seek to change the world understood through its threefold hermeneutic. In turn, like Newman's account, Farley's *theologia* offers the university disciplines a penetrating account of human limitations and idolatry—conditions that operate implicitly within all academic inquiries and human pursuits. Both Newman's and Farley's accounts of theology in the university reveal an underlying inclusive soteriology.

What does an inclusive soteriology entail more specifically? For elaboration, I will draw on important passages from Catherine Mowry LaCugna and Karl Rahner. Each theologian develops central theological ideas that inform the various ways an inclusive soteriology might be expressed. In speaking of the praise and worship of God, LaCugna sees the context for these activities beyond formal liturgy. Prayer and worship are lived out in human relationships. She interprets 1 Cor 10:31 and 1 Peter 4:9–11 to mean that in whatever human beings do, they are to do for the glory of God. Authentic prayer and worship entail living holy lives of service, love, kindness, and gratitude. LaCugna writes, "Everything that promotes fullness of humanity, that builds up relationships based on charity and compassion, glorifies God. Actively resisting injustice, prejudice and hatred can glorify God. Right relationship in every sphere, according to that which God has ordained, everything that brings human persons closer to the communion for which we were made, glorifies God."[12] This

---

11. "Christian faith . . . cannot be justified by public criteria offered in common human experience." *Craft*, 54.

12. LaCugna, *God for Us*, 343.

passage emphasizes the universality and transformative power of grace operative in *human experience*—not only within Christian experience. Grace is not restricted to believers or conditioned by ritual, creed, or explicit confession of faith in Christ. Genuine and authentic human praise points implicitly to the glory of God. In this sense too, salvation is the restoration of right relationships, of healing in concrete situations, of overcoming blindness and ignorance, and the like. The more technical justification for this view of salvation comes from an expansive understanding of grace as extending beyond explicitly Christian patterns of thought and practice. Karl Rahner explains:

> [A]ccording to Catholic teaching there is grace, and justifying grace, outside of the Church too, true though it is that this grace does, in an effective sense, originate within the Church and "orders" a man to the true Church whether he realizes it or not. There are without doubt people who are justified in the grace of God but not in the strict and complete sense members of the Church, as this word must be understood and employed today according to official usage. The Church is not, then, coterminous with humanity as embraced by God's grace; the area of the Church and the area of effective salvation do not, at this moment in the history of salvation, simply coincide.[13]

One feature of an inclusive soteriology, however, is the sense that it is effective in moving the human person toward real union with God. Put concretely, Rahner writes:

> In every conceivable historical and social situation of life a man can have direct and saving access to God without necessarily being required to leave his objective situation "de necessitate medii absoluta," in order to be able to discover the direct reality of God somewhere else. Naturally the actual discovery of this immediate presence demands "metanoia," faith, hope and love, but the universal possibility of salvation, as it is understood here, means precisely that the necessary turning to God can be achieved, either reflectively or unreflectively, from any conceivable existential standpoint, in so far as it is the given historical, cultural or religious situation which is in question.[14]

---

13. Rahner, *Christian Commitment*, 42.
14. Rahner, "One Christ and the Universality of Salvation," 203.

The implications of this teaching are still being worked out today in the theology of inter-religious dialogue and religious pluralism. Still, one of the significant features here is the notion that authentic human growth and development of whatever kind, intellectual, moral, or social, are related to Christian salvation because the providential grace of God is operative though hidden in these developments.

THEOLOGY AS WISDOM

The second claim that can be drawn is the consequent view of theology as a sapiential habit of mind. Newman, Farley, and more recently Dulles share this view. The most oppositional position is Schleiermacher's. For Schleiermacher, the predominantly ecclesial and specialized character of theology means that its intellectual prerequisites are oriented toward clerical and academic research. Schleiermacher sees theology as largely a *wissenschaftliche* undertaking. It is something studied and taught by experts who possess the necessary scholarly expertise and ecclesial authority. The endeavor of serious academic theology thus becomes confined to either the clergy or to those scientifically trained in specialized fields. This ecclesial and intellectual genealogy of theology affirms its position as a scientific discipline. For Schleiermacher, the engagement between Christian faith and culture is not clearly mutually informing but divergent. Christian faith, its beliefs, and its theological orientation serve the Christian community through preaching. Specifically, university culture is secular, distinct, and does not have an equal or decisive influence on the soteriological character of Christian reflection. Whereas both Dulles and Farley extend the subject matter of theological inquiry beyond confessional topics, Schleiermacher's definition of theology as a positive science means that it is ecclesial knowledge in the strict sense.

Farley agrees with Schleiermacher up to a certain point. Theology, as he argues, is a legitimate, professionalized, and scholarly undertaking. But this type of understanding generated, in his view, a clerical paradigm and the fragmentation of theological understanding from one integrated habit into a plurality of disparate fields, thereby marginalizing the relevance, efficacy, subject matter, and hermeneutical possibilities of theology. Farley views theology differently. The genre of theology is not a specialty field but rather a type of personal hermeneutic. The intellectual skills and understanding necessary to carry out the tasks of theology derive from a rigorous liberal education. Farley concedes the legitimacy of theology as an academic discipline but privileges theology as a sapiential wisdom by virtue of the practitioner's ecclesial experience and participation.

Newman's view is closer to Farley's than to Schleiermacher's on this point. Although Newman could presuppose a largely Christian audience at the time that he wrote, it is fair to say that even Newman's view of the content of natural theology resonates closely with the monotheism presupposed by Christian faith and takes its origin from it. Still, theology for Newman is not simply a field of knowledge but a corpus of habits and skills that refine and elevate the mind's synthetic appreciation of reality—a contemplation that aids a certain transcendence. Theology helps to achieve the philosophical and transcendental cultivation of the intellect. This transcendence is effected primarily through a sapiential elevation whose orientation is indirectly religious. That is, contemplative transcendence moves the student or the inquirer to the threshold of questions that are profound, serious, and indicative of religious depth.

Unlike Newman and Farley, Dulles views theology as wisdom but in a more restricted sense of the term. In a 2006 editorial symposium, Dulles replied to a group of scholars who made critical remarks on a brief article he had written. One of the invited scholars was Professor Christopher Ruddy. In Dulles's reply to Ruddy, he wrote:

> In the years following Vatican II, alert theologians were striving to avoid excessively rigid and naïve presentations of doctrine. But now that everything has been exhaustively questioned, the first priority is to rediscover and perfect the edifice of wisdom that stands firmly on the rock of faith. Like William Po[r]tier, Ruddy calls for a more evangelical style of Catholicism that does not eschew proclamation. But he does not settle for a new fundamentalism. He calls for a wisdom based on spiritual conversion and a deepening "encounter with the person of Christ." That is exactly what is needed, and what the Catholic tradition is best equipped to supply. The great doctors of the church offer as sapiential theology that speaks to the heart as well as the head.[15]

The need to recover a sapiential theology, as Dulles indicates, moves beyond the strict scientific understanding of theology construed by Schleiermacher. There is a more integrated and holistic understanding. For Dulles, this recovery of a sapiential theology is connected to

---

15. Dulles, "Catholicism 101," 328.

Christian evangelization.[16] Toward the end of evangelization, tied explicitly to the church's message of redemption, Dulles distinguishes between philosophical and theological wisdom.[17] He holds that philosophical wisdom "in the full and unrestricted sense of the word belongs to those who can discourse about reality in general, seeing all things in their mutual interrelationships, and assigning to each its proper place within an intelligible whole."[18] In contrast to this general philosophical wisdom, Dulles views theological wisdom, especially the highest form—namely infused wisdom—as restricted to a few. "The wisdom of theology, like that of philosophy, is rarified and abstract. It is the special vocation of a dedicated minority. As the Christian people, individually and in groups, strive to find God's will and work out their salvation, they should be able to receive some helpful guidance from the theological community. Theologians, as a responsible order within the Church, have an obligation not to mislead the People of God. They must be modest in their claims and faithful in their performance."[19] The view of sapiential theology in the fullest sense concerns the special grace theologians enjoy as believers. This special grace helps guide their reasoning and evaluate their theological conclusions. Lives of prayer, ascesis, participation in the Eucharist, and embodied holiness are correlative with infused wisdom. There is a clear link between this gift and explicit Christian identity and self-understanding.

It seems clear that these descriptions of theology as sapiential have a corresponding exclusive or inclusive soteriology. Dulles's understanding of theology as wisdom, especially as an infused grace, exhibits the features of an exclusive soteriology. In contrast, the theological accounts of Newman and Farley display correspondingly inclusive soteriological characters. Schleiermacher, as I have argued, understands theology as a positive science, far more cognate to a form of knowledge necessary for a technology of ministry, and so differs from an understanding of theology as a wisdom or particular habit of mind.

---

16. Dulles, "Evangelization of Culture and the Catholic University," 5ff.
17. Dulles, "Wisdom as the Source of Unity for Theology," 61–66.
18. Ibid., 61.
19. Ibid., 70–71.

Testing the Thesis

An immediate objection to my conclusion is that the connection between an exclusive and inclusive soteriological character and the nature of theological wisdom is simply coincidental and limited to the authors selected. This is a fair objection. So I must ask: Is there any further evidence one could provide to substantiate these claims more generally? Can my claims be established within the current debates concerning the nature and place of theology in the university? In response, I will test my thesis by briefly examining the recent approaches of Stanley Hauerwas, Gavin D'Costa, George Dennis O'Brien, and Michael J. Buckley, S.J., on the issue of the place of theology in the university.[20] My aim is to trace the relationship of a hidden or overt soteriology and evaluate whether it influences their view of theology in the university. This brief analysis should provide adequate evidence to support or refute the basic thrust of my argument.

Stanley Hauerwas

Hauerwas's book, *The State of the University: Academic Knowledges and the Knowledge of God*, offers a series of reflections that touch on the place of theology in the modern university. To understand Hauerwas's approach to this issue, one must first grasp his analysis of the relationship between church and world. Ecclesiology, it seems, determines the nature and priorities of how theology is cast as well as the nature of Christian ethics.[21] For example, Hauerwas subscribes to the view that "Constantinianism," a theologically charged term coined by the late Mennonite theologian John Howard Yoder, accurately portrays the current church-world problematic.

> Constantinianism is the name Yoder gives to the time when Christians confused the time inaugurated by the resurrection of Jesus with the time of the old age. The identification of the church with the world means that the eschatological character of the Gospel is now domesticated in the interest of promoting an

---

20. Hauerwas, *State of the University*; D'Costa, *Theology in the Public Square*; O'Brien, *Idea of a Catholic University*; Buckley, *Catholic University as Promise and Project*.

21. Cf. Hauerwas, *State of the University*, "Yoder's narrative, a narrative that obviously begs for detailed development and qualification, has the great virtue of helping us see that how Christians understand and evaluate the development of the secular, and in particular the secular state, depends on their ecclesiology" (173).

> ethic that is workable for anyone. Of course the Christian ethic is one Christians rightly think anyone can live by being redeemed, but Christians confused that understanding of the universal ethic with the presumption that the Christian way of life is open to anyone even if they are not a member of the church.[22]

It is vital to notice the implicit and explicit pairs of oppositions: church and world, Christian ethic and universal ethic, church member and non-member. Hauerwas emphasizes the difference between the elements of each pair. This emphasis indicates a tension between universality and redemption. A development of the present situation is what Yoder describes as "neo-neo-neo-neo-Constantinianism."[23] Summarizing Yoder, Hauerwas offers a description that reveals the kind of soteriology behind his theology.

> This last development makes explicit what all these efforts to defend the cause of the church before the bar of secular reason have in common: that the true meaning of history, the locus of salvation, is in the cosmos and only in the church to the extent the church's identity is absorbed by the wider world. Constantinianism is, therefore, to be identified by the convictions that the meaning of history lies outside the church whose agent is now the state. The eschatological tension between the two aeons is subordinated to a progressive view of history for which the only time available is that produced by state agency.[24]

There is a disjunction between "church" and "world" here such that the shift threatened by Constantinianism is precisely the possibility of Christian salvation that Hauerwas seeks to defend. What lies beneath this tension, I would argue, is the rejection of any assumption about human capacities that might be connected to a natural theology. Hauerwas states:

> The attempt to develop a natural theology prior to or as grounds for subsequent claims about God cannot help but be mistaken to the extent that such a project fails to help us see that there can be no deeper reality-making claims than the one Yoder makes: those who bear crosses work with the grain of the universe. Christians betray themselves as well as their non-Christian brothers and

---

22. Ibid., 172.
23. Ibid., 173.
24. Ibid.

sisters when in the interest of apologetics we say and act as if the cross of Christ is incidental to God's being. In fact the God we worship and the world God created cannot be truthfully known without the cross, which is why the knowledge of God and ecclesiology—or the politics called church—are interdependent.[25]

One can infer that salvation, then, becomes more restricted to conscious participation in the language, symbols, and formative practices of the Christian church. Indeed, the earlier quotation I offered from Michael Budde, indicative of an exclusive soteriology, is used approvingly by Hauerwas to describe the purpose of Christian higher education.[26]

If my characterization of Hauerwas as having an exclusive soteriology is correct, does this position influence his view of theology? I believe that it does. First, it follows from Hauerwas's acceptance of the real danger posed by Constantinianism and rejection of natural theology that the role of theology and theologians will be shaped by Hauerwas's interpretation of ecclesiology. "Theologians," for Hauerwas, "are servants to the Bishop charged with the task of maintaining the memory of the church so that the church may be one."[27] This view of the practitioner of theology is situated within a political context unfavorable to the Christian church. As the theologian works within a range of universal discourse unconverted by the particular language and effects of the gospel, the primarily responsibility of those in the church, especially the theologian, is faithful witness.[28]

Second, does this ecclesial responsibility give theology a certain form within the university context? Hauerwas affirms theology as a "subject" and does indeed say that "theology as a discipline is a constructive and normative mode of reflection on how and what Christians believe about the way things are in the light of our conviction that the way things are has been created by God."[29] He rejects the idea, however, that theology is a "specialized form of knowledge" and moreover, though theology is a subject, it is unlike other academic subjects.[30] "Theology properly understood as knowledge of God," writes Hauerwas, "means theology

---

25. Hauerwas, *With the Grain of the Universe*, 17.
26. Hauerwas, *State of the University*, 105.
27. Ibid., 103.
28. Ibid., 3.
29. Ibid., 12.
30. Ibid., 7.

cannot be restricted to one 'field.'"[31] Theology is not, then, a positive science in the tradition of Schleiermacher. Due to Hauerwas's Protestant commitments and intellectual debts to Yoder, what is striking about his approach in the first chapter of his book, "Theological Knowledge and the Knowledge of the University: Beginning Explorations" is that for guidance as to the purpose of theology in the university, he turns to Newman!

Hauerwas makes two revealing comments in his analysis of Newman's *Idea of a University*. First, he correctly perceives the relationship between Newman's view of liberal knowledge and contemplation.

> It is certainly true that Newman argued that "liberal knowledge" is that which "stands on its own pretensions, which is independent of sequel, expects no complement, refuses to be informed (as it is called) by any end, or absorbed into any art, in order duly to present itself to our contemplation." I do not think, however, that Newman is commending art for art's sake or knowledge as an end in itself; for the crucial word is "contemplation," and Newman being the good Augustinian that he was, knows that only God can be so contemplated.[32]

Hauerwas holds indeed that theology is not simply about what matters to the church; he maintains that "our theological task" should also "help the various disciplines of the university explore their limits, possibilities, and connections to other subjects."[33] Though Hauerwas's theology reveals an exclusive soteriology, he does not preclude dialogue with other university sciences or interdisciplinary engagement. Indeed, Hauerwas observes toward the end of his essay that "theology cannot be relegated to the theology or religious studies department."[34] Here, there is already evidence of something more like a wisdom or a broader intellectual hermeneutic. A final passage synthesizes both ideas:

> It is a good thing that theology bears the burden of proof before the epistemological conceits of the knowledges represented by the contemporary university. That challenge should not only make us more truthful and faithful theologians, but we might also discover different ways to think theologically because we cannot assume

31. Ibid., 6–7.
32. Ibid., 24.
33. Ibid., 29.
34. Ibid., 31.

the way theology was once done is the way we must do theology. Of course theology should never be done to pass muster in the university. Theology must be done in a manner that glorifies God and serves God's people. It has always been my conviction that when theology is so done, those in the university will take notice because what we have to say is so interesting.[35]

Hauerwas's understanding of theology, I suggest, is an anti-Constantinian ecclesial wisdom that follows from his exclusive soteriology.[36]

Gavin D'Costa

Professor of Theology at the University of Bristol, Gavin D'Costa's recent book, *Theology in the Public Square: Church, Academy and Nation* is an ambitious and theoretical attempt to "envisage what a Catholic university might look like," with theology playing a central role in unifying the academic disciplines.[37] His argument proceeds from a description of the problematic place of theology within the modern university to a proposal of a "desirable sectarianism" or a specifically Catholic "postliberal university system."[38] For D'Costa, this refashioned Roman Catholic university would follow the theoretical design advanced by Alasdair MacIntyre.[39] What then energizes and helps define this new type of Catholic institution is the function of theology to "theologize" not only religious studies but also "*all* disciplines."[40] My aim here is not to provide an overview of the entire argument—a rich and suggestive one—but simply to identify the kind of soteriology implied by D'Costa's position and the nature of theology that issues from it.

---

35. Ibid., 31.

36. My analysis of Hauerwas' theology might suggest to some that narrative theology is incompatible with an inclusive soteriological character. This is not the case. Paul Fiddes, a contemporary Baptist theologian at Oxford, uses the language of story to frame his reflections about Christian identity and theology but allows more interaction between the order of creation and the order of redemption. It is also telling that, like Hauerwas, Fiddes also appeals to Newman in making sense of theology in the university. See "Place of Theology in the Modern University," 82–86.

37. D'Costa, *Theology in the Public Square*.

38. Ibid., 144.

39. Ibid., 36. The formative influence upon D'Costa is Alasdair MacIntyre's views about a postliberal university, advanced in *Three Rival Versions of Moral Enquiry*. See also MacIntyre, "Catholic Universities," 1–21.

40. D'Costa, *Theology in the Public Square*, ix.

The situation of theology in the university today is untenable for D'Costa. The main heading of the first chapter reads: "Theology's Babylonian Captivity in the Modern University." Indeed, writes D'Costa, "Theology, properly understood, cannot be taught and practiced within the modern university."[41] The situation of Christian and Catholic universities in general, he argues, is no better: they are dying.[42] D'Costa finds a clear rupture between the sacred and secular reminiscent of Hauerwas's church-world dichotomy, which is detectable even in his stated aims. For example, he "will trace how university theology became prised from ecclesial life so that it now often succumbed to alien philosophies, methodologies, and models for its very life-blood, a blood that would subsequently infect Church life."[43] Again, D'Costa assumes the primacy of ecclesiology in determining an implicit soteriology. From the start, the world is characterized negatively as a dilution and potential poison in terms of intellectual influences. There are theological antecedents for this view that originated in the early church but developed more acutely during the medieval transition from monastic to university theology.

D'Costa's reading of the history of institutional theology gives some clues as to the kind of soteriology his argument assumes. He distinguishes three strands in the relationship between theology and other disciplines. The first is the tradition of Tertullian, which "stresses that all truth and salvation is to be found in the Bible, therefore pagan knowledge is fundamentally useless." The second strand sees pagan knowledge as preparing (*preparatio*) and educating (*paidagogos*) human beings toward Christ. Justin Martyr is a prime example of this tradition, though D'Costa places Augustine and Aquinas within it also. The third strand is that of Origen, who uncritically allowed pagan categories of thought to transform Christian teaching into heresy. Curiously, D'Costa puts Origen in this third strand as well as the second and does the same with Aquinas.[44] Generally speaking, one could describe these three theological approaches to secular knowledge broadly as isolation, critical appropriation, and accommodation.

D'Costa praises the monastic period and the cloistered setting of theology far more than he acknowledges the advantages gained through

41. Ibid., 1.
42. Ibid., 5.
43. Ibid.
44. Ibid., 7–8.

the shift from the monastery to the university.⁴⁵ As this story is well known, it need not be retold. Yet it is telling that D'Costa wholeheartedly accepts Jean Leclercq's reading of the shift from monastic to university theology as one of complex decline. He writes:

> Leclercq goes so far as to say that scholastic university theology, being wedded to the form of disputation and dialectics, eventually "lost contact with the life of prayer." This loss would eventually lead to the slow divorce between "knowledge and love, science and contemplation, intellectual life and spiritual life" and it would then become necessary to construct categories of mystical and spiritual theology, the worse for their separation from dogmatic theology. While there was admittedly what Grabmann has called "hyperdialectic" in university scholasticism, it would be wrong to characterize scholasticism . . . However, Leclerq's point is still pertinent to my argument, rather because of the *telos* of the institutional setting. . . .⁴⁶

This shift from the monastery to the university in terms of the setting of theology not only initiated the rupture between holiness of life and rational inquiry but also laid "the seeds of the fragmentation of knowledge."⁴⁷ D'Costa relies on Prudence Allen's analysis of this incipient decline as eventually giving birth to the secularizing and fragmenting university of the Enlightenment period.⁴⁸ The strength of the medieval university, namely that it would become "a place of considered disputation," allowing for the possibility of "lay theological education" and the place of theology in "harmonizing and integrating the other three faculties of arts, medicine, and law" seems less consequential for D'Costa than the legacy of scholasticism's defects.⁴⁹

Another major clue to the type of latent soteriology within D'Costa's argument appears in his chapter concerning the rationale for a kind of Catholic "sectarianism" that would lead to theological enhancement and the strengthening of Catholic identity within universities and colleges. In trying to explain and defend the type of sectarianism D'Costa wants, he writes at length about the ways in which those who are op-

---

45. Ibid., 6.
46. Ibid., 9–10. See also Leclercq, *Love of Learning and the Desire for God.*
47. D'Costa, *Theology in the Public Square*, 10.
48. Ibid., 11.
49. Ibid., 13.

posed to all forms of "sectarian" discourse or communities or identifies have been co-opted by a "rationalist modernity" that is equally sectarian in its secularizing tendencies.[50] In particular, D'Costa discusses the charges of sectarianism leveled by James Gustafson at the thought of Stanley Hauerwas. "Sectarian" in this debate reduces to the idea that Hauerwas's theological position does not allow legitimacy or value to nontheological discourse in terms of allowing Christian theology to be formed by and shaped by explicitly non-Christian value systems or ideologies.[51] In a sense, all contemporary uses of pre-Christian or non-Christian thinking must first be cleansed of whatever poison they might carry as a result of contamination by Enlightenment conceptions of reason, freedom, rights, and the like. This sectarian theology shuts out and insulates itself from human rationality as such. D'Costa notes that "one very important theological issue related to the use of this term [sectarian] revolves around the centrality of Christology for epistemology and ontology, and that this is perhaps the heart of the intra-Christian debate on sectarianism."[52] Thinkers allied with Gustafson's view of reason (David Tracy, Richard McCormick, Martha Nussbaum, and Edith Wyschogrod) allow that "by virtue of being human, all people encounter a common 'world,' which offers the basis for common discourse, the common good, and a 'public theology' on social, ethical, and other issues."[53] Hauerwas and his sympathizers (George Lindbeck, Michael Banner, Oliver O'Donovan, and John Milbank) reject this understanding of reason. On the contrary, they hold that

> ... the "worlds" encountered by different groups are culturally and religiously shaped, hence no such presumption of public discourse is *a priori* possible ... there is no shared moral language, although this need not mean that public discourse is not possible. In theological terms, the first group [Gustafson and his allies] believes that by the use of reason all people can discern and use common "natural" ethical laws, Christian or otherwise; the second group [Hauerwas and his allies] believes that such laws may exist, but are related to and properly disclosed in the self-revelation of God in Christ.[54]

50. Ibid., 81–82.
51. Ibid., 84.
52. Ibid., 83.
53. Ibid.
54. Ibid.

What underwrites the position of Gustafson is what D'Costa describes as a "doctrine of creation in natural-law terms." Hauerwas rejects this doctrine of creation. In articulating why Hauerwas rejects such a view of creation on natural-law terms as permitting shared discourse based on a common human rationality, D'Costa helpfully explains Hauerwas's position and then *agrees* with it. For instance, he writes that "For Hauerwas the order of creation is only understood in terms of its *telos*, understood eschatologically, and therefore Christologically. Ethics cannot be separated from its Christological and ecclesiological base and *telos*, and, therefore, neither can Christian discourse . . . the warrants for Christian discourse are necessarily Christian, based on revelation, and thereby *sui-generis* [sic]."[55] To say that the Christian claims are *sui generis* supposes a sharp break between the order of creation and the order of redemption. Indeed, it also presupposes a rupture between the church and the world that we have already treated in discussing Hauerwas. Moreover, D'Costa maintains that the notion of creation as somehow neutral, indeed as somehow "universally shared"—a position he attributes to Gustafson and McCormick—is not Christian at all but a product of "rationalist modernity."[56] So reading against the traditional theology of Genesis 1 regarding the intrinsic goodness of creation and human beings, D'Costa asserts: "My main argument in this chapter and book calls into question the assumption that any neutral reading of creation such as this is epistemologically possible, and in this respect Gustafson and McCormick rely on presuppositions that can be criticized theologically."[57] For D'Costa, the orders of creation and redemption, as evidenced in his support for Hauerwas and others who reject the possibility of a common rationality and shared experience of creation, are utterly divergent. There is no natural desire for God, no natural theology, no built-in desire for happiness that would count toward genuinely human acts of freedom, goodness, honesty, or virtue as having salvific content without explicit confessional faith. It is precisely the confessional faith and acceptance of revelation *a priori* that heals the damage to human rationality, enabling it to understand everything ecclesiologically and christologically. In D'Costa's description and analysis, an exclusive soteriology subtly emerges in which he sides with Hauerwas against other scholars.

55. Ibid., 86.
56. Ibid., 87.
57. Ibid.

If an exclusive soteriology functions as a latent presupposition, what are the consequences for D'Costa's understanding of theology? First, he is interested in "returning theology to a profounder integration with itself and with other disciplines in a manner not unknown prior to modern university 'specialization.'"[58] Second, D'Costa seeks a "tradition-specific theology" that "requires prayer as its epistemological presupposition, precisely because theology is primarily concerned with a communal love affair with the living God."[59] For the theologian, prayer is a *sine qua non* because it demands a personal knowledge of God mediated by liturgical participation in a community.[60] In turn, this formative prayer helps to guide theological reasoning and assist in judging the validity of the conclusions drawn.[61] Presently, the education and activity of theologians is reduced to concern with comparing and interpreting various texts but does little to actually form the necessarily faith-defined habits and skills required to do theology well. Theology must be broader than a narrowly specialized discipline. Indeed, D'Costa argues that theological formation should incorporate into its content, in addition to languages and the intellectual methodologies gained through the humanities, the knowledge of "saints, sinners, fasts and feast days, dogmas and doctrines, the repressed and explicit emblems of what communing with God might mean."[62] In other words, the intellectual and moral virtues that lead to holiness come to be defined and experienced through the gift of faith in "cohabitation with God."[63]

D'Costa claims that "by virtue of cohabitation with the living and triune God through prayer and all that it involves and the life of virtue, the theologian increases in love, and love is the lamp of knowledge."[64] As the theologian's love of God increases, so should the sensitivity and quality of her theology. The disciplined habits of loving God through prayer and communal participation lead unsurprisingly to D'Costa's appropriation of Aquinas' view of theology as wisdom. Indeed, he cites the same passages as Dulles to support the view that it is precisely the infused gift

58. Ibid., xii.
59. Ibid., 112.
60. Ibid., 132.
61. Ibid., 114.
62. Ibid., 119.
63. Ibid., 117.
64. Ibid., 126.

of the Spirit that configures the theologian to "connaturality with divine things." Though Aquinas distinguishes theological wisdom as the consequence of a cognitive process that one might acquire through study and training, D'Costa focuses on the infused gift of the Spirit. And it is clear that such an infused gift seems possible only within the explicit pattern of Christian prayer, practice, and communal participation that clearly shapes and integrates the intellectual and moral habits of faith. D'Costa's vision of theology as wisdom flowing out of a passionate love affair with God mediated by the liturgical, ascetic, practical, and aesthetic dimensions of the Catholic tradition is rich, compelling, and certainly evidence of an exclusive soteriology.

George Dennis O'Brien

Past president of the University of Rochester and Bucknell University, O'Brien has advanced, as he describes, a "provocative" argument about the nature of the Catholic university as an institution in contrarian opposition to the modern research university.[65] His interests extend beyond the issue of theology within the university to the broader problem of what a Catholic university might mean and provide within the context of higher education in which the usual view of truth is restricted to the scientific model. O'Brien attempts to move beyond a view of truth as scientific by distinguishing other modes, namely, the artistic and the "realm of existential presence" or the religious.[66] By contrasting these models of what counts as true in the academy, O'Brien seeks to deepen the legitimacy of science and art by exposing them to a realm defined by "a sacramental view of 'the real.'"[67]

Unlike Hauerwas and D'Costa, O'Brien returns repeatedly and explicitly to the topic of salvation. The following statement is typical: "Catholicism may support the ethical concern essential to the university, but in the long run religious claims extend beyond the merely ethical. To illuminate what *more* is involved, one must raise not just moral issues, but issues of 'salvation.' Even for the university."[68] It is not that one directly encounters the biblical doctrine of salvation through

---

65. O'Brien, *Idea of a Catholic University*, 9.

66. Ibid., 112; 8.

67. Ibid., 183.

68. Ibid., 96. O'Brien frequently capitalizes the term *Salvation* for emphasis: 16, 21–2, 29, 60, 77, 79.

reason or scholarship in the academy.[69] Yet O'Brien sees the biblical foundations of Christian faith as not opposed to but legitimating the knowledge pursued through the arts and sciences as something genuinely good. Because the biblical doctrine of salvation and university knowledge are justified theologically by the doctrine of creation, they are somehow connected.[70] O'Brien offers evidence of this connection when he states that the university cannot finally avoid questions about the meaning of life.[71]

Precisely because O'Brien seeks to show the harmonious character of faith and reason in the university context at large, he treats the statement of Jesus Christ, "I am the Truth" to highlight the central contents of Christian faith. In taking a chapter to analyze this christological statement, O'Brien explains how the presence of God and Christ differs from the transcendent observer's view of scientific data and the spectator's encounter with Duchampian anti-art. "In Jesus there is life to life, a presence as 'companion.' Jesus as life to my life is the heart of the Resurrection, the continuing *real* presence of Jesus to each and every person who calls him Lord."[72] What does this statement mean? To illustrate, O'Brien cites the writer John L'Heureux and his short story, "An Expert on God." What is fascinating about this example is O'Brien's stress on the theme of salvation. In the story, an unbelieving priest encounters an automobile accident and finds a young boy dying. Taking the boy into his arms, the priest at first falls into the official routine of prayer but finds it ineffective and unable to express the meaning and truth that the dying youth should hear. "[A]t once the priest, faithless, unrepentant, gave up his prayers and bent to him and whispered, fierce and burning, 'I love you,' and continued until there was no breath, 'I love you, I love you, I love you.'"[73] O'Brien's commentary on this passage reveals his soteriology.

> Life's final truth is chanciness, the blundering accident, the awesome density of existence, and suffering. If there is any Salvation, any "Word," it is to be held, to have the presence of the Other who says, "I love you." Note the irony of the title L'Heureux chooses for his story: An Expert on God. This expert, it seems is "faithless,

---

69. O'Brien, *Idea of a Catholic University*, 21.
70. Ibid., 20–22.
71. Ibid., 22.
72. O'Brien, *Idea of a Catholic University*, 78.
73. L'Heureux, "Expert on God," as quoted by O'Brien, *Idea of a Catholic University*, 78.

unrepentant." He cannot state a doctrine because he does not believe. Nevertheless, he asks whether it matters to hold a "crushed, dying thing" and say "I love you" until no breath remains? Being present to another, present to one unconscious and dying, saying "I love you"—all this may be nonsense, none of it may matter. Yet somehow the priest knows that it does matter. Jesus is *the* "expert on God"—not because he announces some hidden fact or message like a privileged witness, but because he is present to humans in all the blunder and chanciness of life. If we are held once and for all by the "expert" who says "I love you," there is Salvation.[74]

Salvation here is not delivered through the gospel story or the forming narrative that shapes a distinctive character, but through the love one person communicates to another as wholly and totally present. The encounter of the priest with the dying youth is an experience of the density of reality as overwhelmingly present. For O'Brien, such a situation is indicative of religious experience. He explains: "In the event of presence one has the experience that is characteristic of the religious, the revelation of the whole (me) to and in the whole (the external situation). It is an experience of *presence*: I am wholly present (in the sense that I am neither the scientific nor artistic spectator), and because I am wholly present external reality is now present in a manner that escapes factual assessment or artistic form."[75] What becomes central is the caring commitment, the movement of compassion of one person to another in pain and suffering. Put differently, it is an example of one's experience of the mystery of existence.[76] Such an experience of the mystery of existence is not unrelated to the university context insofar as the university is a locus for studies related to the dimensions of human life and thought. "The real" is precisely about those kinds of life choices that define identity and determine the meaning of existence.[77] The illustration and O'Brien's interpretation reveal, I suggest, an inclusive soteriology by intentionally stripping the characters from an explicit religious tradition and focusing upon profound human experiences that disclose central realities of Christian faith as a religious experience accessible to anyone, even the unbeliever, though it may not be self-described as such. Finally, O'Brien's

74. O'Brien, *Idea of a Catholic University*, 78–9.
75. Ibid., 82.
76. Ibid., 86.
77. Cf. Ibid., 119.

approval of Karl Rahner's notion of "anonymous Christians" in the context of the possibility of Christian salvation beyond Christian boundaries only confirms a broad view of human experience as potentially salvific.[78]

If this explicit and operative inclusive soteriology frames O'Brien's argument about the Catholic university, how does it influence the nature of theology? O'Brien argues that universities, especially Catholic universities, should embrace disciplines that connect different forms of truth (scientific and artistic) with experiences of totalizing presence that lie beyond "form and concept."[79] He discusses the role of theology more formally vis-à-vis other academic disciplines in a rich passage. O'Brien also reveals how his understanding of theology emerges from his inclusive soteriology.

> The first consideration for a *Catholic* university does not, then, bear upon the competencies of varied disciplines within the academy. Physics is physics is physics and so on. Existential dogma, Catholic or atheistic, only (!) positions the range of learned competencies and artistic achievements relative to "the real" and the issue of "salvation." It is not stretching a point or terminology to place any such consideration in the realm of "theology." Theology is that study which assesses "the real" and sketches out strategies for Salvation (if any) in the light of "the real." The question about the salvational range and capacity of normal academic studies does not in any direct way encroach on the academic freedom of the various disciplines.[80]

It seems a bit obscure to state that theology assesses "the real," but if we recall that by "the real" O'Brien intends more than scientific facts and artistic presentation to incorporate totalizing experiences of overwhelming presence, then theology is not simply another academic discipline.

O'Brien addresses the nature of theology in the Catholic university in the final chapter entitled "Practical/Praxis Postscript." Though theology pervades the book insofar as theological reasoning and language are used to differentiate the truth of science and art from the truth of presence, it is telling that the kind of "thing" theology comprises for O'Brien does not emerge until the end. He does hold, however, that theology is a

---

78. Ibid., 154.
79. Ibid., 113.
80. Ibid., 106.

meta-discipline and properly belongs in the undergraduate curriculum.[81] Furthermore, the substance of theology emerges from a kind of universal life experience of those who study it and those who (one hopes!) teach it. Indeed, O'Brien holds that "theology rests on some 'intuition' about the chaos, density, 'splendid waste,' utter givenness of life and 'the real'—and about how all this relates to our ordinary sense of reality—one cannot expect or require the sort of neat abstracted demonstrations that characterize less messy academic fields."[82] Theology seems accessible to its students by virtue of their own prior experience. It is not a practice restricted simply to believers who explicitly confess a creed. Moreover, theology is unlike other academic fields in terms of argument. One important feature of theology for O'Brien, at least at the undergraduate level, is the way in which it concerns the issue of what Charles Taylor calls "hypergoods," namely, "those actions in life that are superior to the 'domestic' goods of everyday life: the monk abjures sex and the soldier risks his very life, both in search of a hypergood."[83] O'Brien frames this issue of higher, more serious life values in terms of what a course in "fundamental theology" ought to consider: "the status of love, commitment, and decision."[84] In terms of pedagogical and theological method, O'Brien is making the case for introducing the grammar of higher values and realities that students already experience in order to build a more explicit treatment of dogmatic theology on this foundation. However, dogmatic theology—while important for a Catholic university in terms of course content—is not O'Brien's emphasis.

The kind of theology that O'Brien desires and emphasizes most strongly is what he calls "fundamental theology." Such a course would examine the way in which one lives, a way of life that encompasses the meaning and possibility of genuine love, meaning, fidelity, and then concrete action. While O'Brien leaves open the specific content of such a course to creative professors, he does suggest that several different conceptions of love, e.g., Stoic, Cynic, Christian, be included as well as patterns of life. Moreover, the course ideally would also incorporate a service-learning dimension to involve the students in concrete situa-

---

81. Ibid., 196–97.
82. Ibid., 198.
83. Ibid., 200.
84. Ibid., 201.

tions requiring commitment and decision making.[85] The course would be properly termed fundamental because it would provide the grammar of understanding and engaging in experiences that explore the meaning of life. The aim of this course is to open up deeper dimensions of the student's attitudes toward life for reflection and action. Indeed, in the final pages of the book, O'Brien links theology to the notion of a life vocation as distinct from a focus on job and career as an integration and culmination of the argument. So the characteristics of the course, one expects, help students to craft habits of thinking and life skills that lead them more deeply into raising questions of ultimacy leading to God, to the density of existence, to "the real." The purpose and aim of theology extend far beyond a course on "Love, Commitment, and Decision" to deeper reflective experiences that combine theory and practice overflowing into an examined way of life. It seems clear to me that O'Brien's view of theology more closely resembles a wisdom than a discipline, especially at the undergraduate level. Because of O'Brien's inclusive soteriology, it also follows that the course he describes is open to all students and presumes that salvific moments occur in the intersections of reading, reflection, and service.

Michael J. Buckley, S.J.

In *The Catholic University as Promise and Project: Reflections in a Jesuit Idiom*, Augustin Bea Professor of Theology at Santa Clara University, Michael J. Buckley addresses different but related topics: the relationship of the academic and the religious, social justice, humanism, academic freedom, the role of the liberal arts, philosophy, and theology. All of these topics have a central focus, namely, "the character and issues of the Catholic, Jesuit university."[86] Buckley's explorations combine a robust vision of the way in which liberal education possesses a religious orientation and the orientation of a religious faith that seeks academic expression. Buckley explains: "Any academic movement towards meaning or coherence or truth, whether in the humanities, the sciences, or the professions, is inchoatively religious. This provocative statement obviously does not mean that quantum mechanics or geography is religion or theology. It does mean that the intellectual dynamism inherent in all

---

85. Ibid., 201–2.
86. Buckley, *Catholic University as Promise and Project*, xxi.

inquiry initiates processes or habits of questioning that—if not inhibited—inevitably bear upon the ultimate questions that engage religion."[87] The human knowledge that academic inquiry values and pursues on the one hand and the religious faith that desires union with God on the other hand complete each other. For Buckley, one cannot separate the realm of human culture from what is Catholic, religious, or theological. Buckley criticizes the attempt to exclude what is not self-evidently religious or what appears to be purely secular from the nature of a Catholic university education as "extrinsicism."[88] An extrinsicist position inserts a false division between nature and grace. For Buckley, religious faith must be related to all of human culture in order to fully understand itself in relation to God. Likewise, academic inquiry pursues questions within a specific field or discipline that extend beyond themselves, seeking meaning in ever broader, more ultimate questions. "One keeps asking questions—unless this natural drive is repressed—until they lead to questions about ultimate explanation or intelligibility, about the truth of the finite itself, 'which all human beings call God.'"[89]

There is already present in these remarks a profound appreciation of the intimate relationship between the order of creation and the order of redemption. Buckley links this mutual relationship between the academic and the religious to its ecclesial origins; and it is here that he explicitly sounds the theme of salvation.

> Thus, it is no accident that historically the university issued out of the church —not out of the hierarchy alone, but out of the people of God, the community that is the sacrament of human salvation . . . The Catholic university is that academic community of higher education which issues out of the church and in which the church, in the words of the Second Vatican Council, "strives to relate all human culture to the announcement of salvation." This is "all human culture," comprising whatever passes for significant discourse, for philosophic, scientific, and humanistic inquiry, etc. What the Catholic university proposes is a union between the human and the divine, a union between culture and faith.[90]

---

87. Ibid., 15.
88. Ibid., 11.
89. Ibid., 15.
90. Ibid., 16.

The theological form of this relationship is analogous to the hypostatic union of the divine and human natures in Christ. Buckley states that "faith and human culture" find their "paradigmatic realization in Christ."[91] The type of soteriology that Buckley assumes and that will influence his understanding of theology is intensely inclusive. In large part, this inclusive soteriology is explained by Buckley's Ignatian commitments. For a Jesuit Catholic university—as Buckley argues—does not emerge from a prior philosophy of education but from a form of spirituality that sees God intimately involved in all dimensions of human culture.[92]

The establishment of a Jesuit view of higher education, according to Buckley, emerges from the experiences of God given in the life of Ignatius Loyola and articulated in his writings. Buckley points to the capstone of the *Spiritual Exercises*, namely, the "Contemplation for Attaining Love" as revealing "some apprehension of God's relations to human beings and all creation."[93] There are four ascending points given in the contemplation that indicate the graced experience of the human person and the divine activity of God. First, "all things are seen as gift." The totality of the created universe and the parts comprising it in one's daily life become not something alien but profound realities for human beings. For Buckley, being as such is metaphysically convertible to "gift." Being, life, and creation emerge as experiences of God's love for human beings.[94] So there is an inevitable personal relationship, a personal sensitivity to creation in this first point. Second, everything that is—creation—also possesses a sacred quality precisely because "God is immanent within creation, an indwelling presence in all things which God has given and transforming by this indwelling human life into that which is sacred, a dwelling-place of God."[95] In addition to gift, the unmerited experience of life and encounter with reality, there is also the immanent presence of God sensitizing the human person to His presence. Third, God is at work in creation for human beings "to achieve human salvation." Buckley calls this third aspect "providential" because it points to the historical dimension of God's activity in all things, not simply one location, to bring human beings to union with Godself. This image of God

91. Ibid., 17.
92. Ibid., 81.
93. Ibid., 81–82.
94. Ibid., 82.
95. Ibid.

here is that of a "workman" struggling on behalf of human beings. It is this aspect, Buckley notes, that is the uncommon element in Ignatian spirituality compared with other spiritualities in the Christian tradition.[96] The soteriological implications of this dimension are profound. "God as workman will found two critical characteristics of Ignatian educational theology: that God works in all things, in all events, and that one must assign a religious importance—a secondary importance, but real importance—to all natural gifts, talents, and endowments as those gift[s] through and in which God labors. God is present, immanently working within them all, and any theological appreciation of the value of created things and talents must register their place within this divine providence and the resultant sacred history."[97] Reality understood as gift, sacred, and providential helps move human beings toward God. Finally, Buckley describes the final point of the contemplation as how "things are seen not so much as moments in a human ascent to God as they are seen as participative realities descending from God."[98] This noteworthy aspect of Ignatian spirituality is called "descent spirituality."[99] Precisely in and from the perspective of a "descent spirituality," the human being "can find God in all things because all things descend from God and speak of God." In other words, one does not remove oneself from reality, cut oneself off or purify oneself from the matter and substance of family, work, or studies to find God—one can discern the activity of God precisely in and through created realities, life's pains, joys, achievements, and so forth. "In Ignatian spirituality, there is already an absolute priority given to the divine in "the first initiative in the order of good and salvation"—out of which comes everything and by which everything is given its religious density ... Nothing is finally profane. Precisely because of the divine origin of all things and the quality of the divine presence in all things, every aspect of nature is to be revered and treasured, every science and human development is in its integrity gift, sacred, providential, and of God."[100] In all human undertakings, the initiative is God's salvific will for human beings in all their dimensions of life.

96. Ibid., 82–83.
97. Ibid., 83.
98. Ibid.
99. For a fuller treatment of the difference between "ascent" and "descent" spiritualities, see Michael J. Buckley, S.J., "Spirituality and the Incarnate God," 23–38.
100. Buckley, *Catholic University*, 84.

So how does this spiritual vision and inclusive soteriology determine the nature of theology in the university? Again, Buckley mines the works of Ignatius Loyola to construct his view. First, theology is a "university discipline."[101] But for Ignatius and for Buckley, theology is also much more. Interpreting Ignatius Loyola's *Constitutions of the Society of Jesus*, Buckley states that as "wisdom constitutes the ultimate justification for the arts and sciences ... For Ignatius, what should emerge from a Catholic university was the integration of knowledge into a theological wisdom—the highest achievement of critical reasoning."[102] What kind of wisdom is this? Buckley explains.

> The history of philosophy supplies a term that may be applied to the Ignatian understanding of the function of theology within a Catholic university, i.e., as its specifying and integrating wisdom. It is a term whose origins lie with the division of the sciences in Aristotle, but which achieved its modern prominence in Kant. The term is *architectonic*, and it designates a kind of knowledge that brings order into the vast assemblage of human sciences and disciplines, subject matters and activities ... The architectonic nature of theology does not lie—as does that of the philosophy of science and of education—in the analysis of the foundations, axioms, and methods of the various sciences or in the location and distinction among the subject matters of these various disciplines ... Theology does not so much analyze the presuppositions as it synthetically reflects upon the conclusions of the sciences. Theology, then, must not be seen as one science among others, self-contained in its own integrity and adjacent to the other forms of disciplined human knowledge. It is much more like a place, a place within which the critical thought and developed habits of reasoning in the arts and sciences are encouraged and their ineluctable movement toward questions of ultimacy taken seriously.[103]

Buckley will go on to distinguish theology as wisdom from "a particular *Wissenschaft*," giving to its meaning a breadth and suppleness that extends to non-professional theologians[104] Indeed, one instance of the function of theology as an architectonic wisdom is to foster interdisci-

---

101. Ibid., 69.
102. Ibid.
103. Ibid., 71–72. Italics in original.
104. Ibid., 72.

plinary exchange regarding a common theme or issue that raises questions beyond the confines of any discipline such as physics or history or marketing to touch upon the deeper issues of human purpose, meaning, and religious transcendence.[105] In this way, the integrating wisdom of theology brings together different sciences or knowledges that engage the deeper realities of human life. Theology realizes its synthetic and indirectly salvific purpose for the university in such serious, collaborative inquiry concerning issues that may involve ethical, religious, scientific, and economic perspectives.

What I have been describing seems to fashion theology into what O'Brien might call a meta-discipline. Yet for Buckley the understanding of theology as wisdom does influence theology as a subject that people teach and study within a Catholic university. Besides the architectonic nature of theology as fostering interdisciplinary questioning, Buckley finds two more ways that theology can emerge as wisdom. First, one might return to requiring more "universal theological arts" within theological education. Arts here refers to "the medieval sense of disciplines and methods, skills which permeate and are employed in all theological reflection: systematic, constructive, moral, ascetical, liturgical, comparative, and legal. Among these arts, already present and busy, are four: hermeneutics or semantics, methodology, philosophy, and history. Each of them particularizes for theology those liberal arts or *studia humanitatis* which have entered into liberal or humanistic education in general. Each of them is present and active whenever theology is well done."[106] There is then a certain analytic and synthetic set of reasonings that pervades and is sharpened by the liberal arts so necessary for serious theology to become an architectonic wisdom. Here Buckley is not talking about the product of wisdom so much as he is describing a process to achieve it. The final suggestion is that theology take its questions and subject matter from beyond more traditional topics native to the Catholic tradition to more general issues that originate from "human questioning and longing." Buckley states: "Academic theology must attend more seriously and more carefully to the occasions of its existence and vitality in the religious implications of any human inquiry or engagement and to the experience and desires of men and women."[107] Human aspirations,

105. Ibid., 73.
106. Ibid., 174.
107. Ibid.

challenges, problems, and sufferings are to be the sources in which one discerns and articulates the revelation of God's mysterious self-communication. Theology, then, must be present—for its own life—within the range of university knowledge. In the final analysis, one would be pressed to find a vision of theology as wisdom more richly directed by an inclusive soteriology than Michael Buckley's.

If I have read these contemporary theologians correctly, there is a consensus that theology is a kind of wisdom and that an exclusive or inclusive soteriological character accompanies it in the Christian university. Still, the scope of this inquiry has not considered feminist, womanist, liberation, or postmodern arguments that might yield important corrections. I leave this task for others.

QUESTIONS AND IMPLICATIONS

In the current situation of higher learning, a liberal arts education is increasingly becoming a difficult proposition to defend against specialized vocational training. The social and economic pressures toward utilitarianism that threaten to diminish the liberal arts ideal stand before theology as well.[108] Consequently, the future position of theology in North American Catholic and Christian colleges and universities remains unclear. One can imagine a few directions that theology might take at different institutions. Theology may become increasingly confessional, a niche discipline, and thus more isolated from other academic disciplines. In this trajectory theology would become more self-consciously catechetical as it seeks a more defined ecclesial identity. On the other hand, theology may become more specialized and intellectually diffuse, leaving open the question of its purpose and the identity of its practitioners to internal contradictions and ever-changing intellectual trends.

The notion that theology is a kind of wisdom that possesses an inclusive or exclusive soteriological character and functions as a wisdom more than a university specialty field does not answer these pressing questions, yet it does bear upon them. Understanding theology as a kind of saving wisdom does clarify latent presuppositions that operate within diverse theological styles and underlie various appeals to the audiences of church, academy, and society. Though the project of Christian the-

---

108. The academic study of religion is not immune from social and ideological forces or the questioning of its legitimacy by other disciplines. See Hart, *University Gets Religion*, 6ff.

ology today embraces the gains and insights of pluralism, contextual theologies, and the growing consciousness of a world-church, I am convinced that in diverse ways an inclusive or exclusive soteriology exists within each theology's fundamental questions, concerns, and general conclusions. Insofar as there is reflective discourse about the human and the divine, the symbol or the idea or the experience of salvation will be somehow present. If this is true, then practical and pedagogical questions arise for the teaching of theology.

Can theology courses be offered to undergraduates with the honest expectation of competent engagement and understanding? Can a non-Christian or an unaffiliated religious seeker actually do Christian theology? Is the teaching of wisdom even possible? Should faith be counted among the departmental prerequisites for advanced courses in theology? Is explicit confession enough to guarantee theological understanding for interdisciplinary and interfaith reading and dialogue? Such questions may seem odd and recall concerns from an earlier time, but what are theology courses and their instructors promising and delivering to students who take their courses? If a professor's theological commitments express an exclusive soteriological character, does the academic standard of critical rationality become questionable? On the other hand, if one maintains a theology with an inclusive soteriological character, what more does a distinctive religious identity offer than another symbol system to select from and openness to authentic human experience? How does an inclusive soteriology approach the question of religious truth—for example, the unique importance of Jesus Christ in the redemption of the human race? A critical start to answering these difficult questions must in the end come from acknowledging the latent dimensions of what theology actually is in the university context and who can engage in its practice. That might be a wisdom that is saving.

Bibliography

Alexander, Thomas. *The Prussian Elementary Schools*. New York: Macmillan, 1919.
Anselm. *Proslogion; Monologion; And Appendix On Behalf Of the Fool by Gaunilon: And Cur Deus Homo*. Translated by Sidney Norton Deane. La Salle: Open Court, 1993.
Aquinas, Thomas. *Summa Theologiae*. 3 vols. Turin: Marietti, 1950.
Aristotle. *The Complete Works of Aristotle*. Edited by Jonathan Barnes, vol. 2. Princeton: Princeton University Press, 1991.
Aubert, Roger. "Catholic Thought Searching for New Ways." In *History of the Church*, vol. 8: *The Church in the Age of Liberalism*, edited by Hubert Jedin and John Dolan, 31–56. New York: Crossroad, 1980.
Augustine. *Confessions*. Translated by Henry Chadwick. Oxford: Oxford University Press, 1992.
———. *Teaching Christianity*. Translated by Edmund Hill, OP. Hyde Park: New City, 1996.
Aumann, J. "Contemplation." *New Catholic Encyclopedia* 4:258–63. New York: McGraw-Hill, 1967.
Barnhart, Bruno. *The Future of Wisdom: Toward a Rebirth of Sapiential Christianity*. New York: Continuum, 2007.
Barr, Colin. *Paul Cullen, John Henry Newman, and the Catholic University of Ireland, 1845–1865*. Notre Dame: University of Notre Dame Press, 2003.
Barth, Karl. *Anselm: Fides Quaerens Intellectum*. London: SCM, 1960.
———. *Protestant Theology in the Nineteenth Century: Its Background & History*. Reprint, Valley Forge, PA: Judson, 1973.
———. *The Theology of Schleiermacher*. Translated by Geoffrey W. Bromiley. Edited by Dietrich Ritschl. Grand Rapids: Eerdmans, 1982.
———. *The Word of God and the Word of Man*. Translated by Douglas Horton. Gloucester, MA: Peter Smith, 1978.
Barth, Ulrich. *Christentum und Selbstbewubtsein*. Göttinghem: Vandenhoeck & Ruprecht, 1983.
Bebbington, David. "The Secularization of British Universities since the Mid-Nineteenth Century." In *The Secularization of the Academy*, edited by George M. Marsden and Bradley J. Longfield, 259–77. New York: Oxford University Press, 1992.
Benne, Robert. *Quality with Soul: How Six Premier Colleges and Universities Keep Faith with Their Religious Traditions*. Grand Rapids: Eerdmans, 2001.
Bickman, Martin. *Uncommon Learning: Thoreau On Education*. Boston: Houghton Mifflin, 1999.
Blehl, Vincent. F. "The Spiritual Roots of Newman's Theology." In *John Henry Newman: Theologian and Cardinal*, 17–32. Brescia: Paidea Editrice, 1981.
Bonaventure. *Itinerarium Mentis in Deum*. Translation and commentary by Philotheus Boehner, OFM. Reprint, Saint Bonaventure, NY: Franciscan Institute, 1990.

Brown, William A., and Mark A. May. *The Education of American Ministers*. Vol 1. New York: Institute of Social and Religious Research, 1934.

Buckley, Michael J. *At the Origins of Modern Atheism*. New Haven: Yale University Press, 1987.

———. *The Catholic University as Promise and Project*. Washington, DC: Georgetown University Press, 1998.

———. "Spirituality and the Incarnate God." In *Spirituality for the 21st Century: Experiencing God in the Catholic Tradition*, edited by Richard W. Miller, III, 23–38. Ligouri, MO: Ligouri, 2006.

Budde, Michael. "Assessing What Doesn't Exist: Reflections on the Impact of an Ecclesially Based University." In *Conflicting Allegiances: The Church-Based University in a Liberal Democratic Society*, edited by Michael Budde and John Wright, 255–71. Grand Rapids: Brazos, 2004.

Burghardt, Walter. "Intellectual and Catholic? Or Catholic Intellectual?" *America* (May 6, 1989) 420–25.

Burtchaell, James T. *The Dying of the Light: The Disengagement of Colleges and Universities from Their Christian Churches*. Grand Rapids: Eerdmans, 1998.

Butler, Joseph. *The Analogy of Religion Natural and Revealed*. London: Dent, 1906.

Calvin, John. *Institutes of the Christian Religion* (1536). Rev. ed. Translated by Ford Lewis Battles. Edited by John T. McNeill. Grand Rapids: Eerdmans, 1986.

———. *Institutes of the Christian Religion* (1559). 2 vols. Translated by Ford Lewis Battles. Edited by John T. McNeill. Philadelphia: Westminster, 1960.

———. *Institutio Christianae Religionis*. Genevae: Apud Iacobum Stoer, 1637.

Carey, Patrick W., and Earl C. Muller, SJ. *Theological Education In The Catholic Tradition: Contemporary Challenges*. New York: Crossroad, 1997.

Carlen, Claudia, IHM. *The Papal Encyclicals 1939–1958*. Raleigh, NC: Pierian, 1990.

Carlyle, Thomas. *On Heroes, Hero-Worship, and the Heroic in History*. Introduction and notes by Michael K. Goldberg. Berkeley: University of California Press, 1993.

Collingwood, R. G. *An Autobiography*. Oxford: Clarendon, 1978.

Congar, Yves. "Théologie." *Dictionnaire de Théologie Catholique* 15:341–502. Paris: Librairie Letouzey et Ane, 1946.

Coogan, Michael. *The New Oxford Annotated Bible*. 3rd ed. Oxford: Oxford University Press, 2001.

Coulson, John. *Apologia Pro Vita Sua and the Grammar: Newman and the Common Tradition*. Oxford: Clarendon, 1970.

Cross, F. L. *The Oxford English Dictionary of the Christian Church*. Oxford: Oxford University Press, 1997.

Crouter, Richard. "Rhetoric and Substance in Schleiermacher's Revision of the Christian Faith (1821–1822)." *Journal of Religion* 60 (1980) 285–306.

Culler, Dwight. *The Imperial Intellect: A Study of Newman's Educational Ideal*. New Haven: Yale University Press, 1955.

Curran, Charles. *The Origins of Moral Theology in the United States*. Washington, DC: Georgetown University Press, 1997.

D'Costa, Gavin. *Theology in the Public Square: Church, Academy, and Nation*. Oxford: Blackwell, 2006.

Darricau, R. *La Formation des professeurs de séminaire au début du XVIII siècle d'après un directoire de M. Jean Bonnet (1664–1735) Supérior général del la congrégation de la mission*. Piacenza: Collegio Alberoni, 1966.

Dauphinais, Michael, and Matthew Levering. *Wisdom and Holiness, Science and Scholarship.* Naples, FL: Sapiential, 2007.
De Caussade, Jean-Pierre. *The Sacrament of the Present Moment.* Translated by Kitty Muggeridge. San Francisco: Harper & Row, 1989.
Degert, A. *Histoire des Séminaires Français jusque' à la Révolution.* 2 vols. Paris: Gabriel Beauchesne, 1912.
Dens, Petro. *Theologia ad Usum Seminariorum Et Sacrae Theologiae Alumnorum.* Mechliniae: H. Dessain, 1880–1882.
De Ridder-Symoens, Hilde. *A History of the University in Europe.* 2 vols. Cambridge: Cambridge University Press, 1992.
Deutscher, Thomas. "Seminaries and the Education of Novarese Parish Priests, 1593–1627." *Journal of Ecclesiastical History* 32 (1981) 303–19.
Dorner, J. A. *History of Protestant Theology.* Vol. 2. Translated by George Robson and Sophia Taylor. New York: AMS, 1871.
Drey, Johann Sebastian. *Brief Introduction to the Study of Theology.* Translated by Michael J. Himes. Notre Dame: University of Notre Dame Press, 1994.
Dulles, Avery Cardinal, SJ. *The Assurance of Things Hoped For: A Theology of Christian Faith.* New York: Oxford University Press, 1994.
———. "Can Philosophy Be Christian?" *First Things* 102 (2000) 24–29.
———. "Catholicism 101: Challenges to a Theological Education." *Horizons* 33.2 (2006) 303–29.
———. *The Catholicity of the Church.* Oxford: Clarendon, 1985.
———. "The Church and the Universal Catechism." *America* 3 (1990) 201–19.
———. *A Church to Believe In.* New York: Crossroad, 1982.
———. *The Craft of Theology: From Symbol to System.* New York: Crossroad, 1995.
———. "Criteria of Catholic Theology." *Communio* 22 (1995) 303–15.
———. "Disputed Questions: How Catholic is the CTSA? Three Views." Avery Dulles, S.J., Mary Ann Donovan and Peter Steinfels. *Commonweal* (March 27, 1998) 13–14.
———. "The Evangelization of Culture and The Catholic University." *Journal of Law, Philosophy, and Culture* 1 (2007) 1–11.
———. "Evangelizing Theology." *First Things* 61 (1996) 27–32.
———. "Hermeneutical Theology." *Communio* 6 (1979) 16–37.
———. "Knowledge, Wisdom, and Theology." *The Papin Festchrift: Essays in Honour of Joseph Papin*, vol. 2, edited by Joseph Armenti, 269–72. Philadelphia: Villanova University Press, 1976.
———. "Method in Fundamental Theology: Reflections on David Tracy's *Blessed Rage for Order.*" *Theological Studies* 37 (1976) 304–16.
———. *Models of the Church.* Expanded edition. New York: Doubleday, 1987.
———. *Models of Revelation.* Maryknoll, NY: Orbis, 1992.
———. "The Place of Theology in a Catholic University." In *Catholic Theology In The University: Source of Wholeness*, edited by Virginia Shaddy, 59–71. Milwaukee, WI: Marquette University Press, 1998.
———. "Principles of Catholic Theology." *Pro Ecclesia* 8 (1999) 73–84.
———. "Reason, Philosophy, and the Grounding of Faith: A Reflection on *Fides et Ratio.*" *International Philosophical Quarterly* 40 (2000) 479–90.
———. *The Reshaping of Catholicism: Current Challenges in the Theology of Church.* San Francisco: Harper & Row, 1988.

———. Review of *The Possibility of Religious Knowledge* by Jerry G. Gill. *Theological Studies* 33 (1972) 146–48.

———. Review of *Revelation and Theology: The Gospel as Narrated Promise* by Ronald Thieman. *The Thomist* 51 (1987) 169–72.

———. *The Splendor of Faith: The Theological Vision of Pope John Paul II.* New York: Herder & Herder, 1999.

———. *A Testimonial to Grace and Reflections on a Theological Journey.* Kansas City: Sheed & Ward, 1996.

———. "The Theologian And The Magisterium." *CTSA Proceedings* 31 (1976) 235–46.

———. "Theological Education in the Catholic Tradition." *Theological Education in the Catholic Tradition: Contemporary Challenges,* edited by Patrick W. Carey and Earl C. Muller, S.J., 10–22. New York: Crossroad, 1997.

———. "Tradition: Authenticity and Unauthentic." *Communio* 28 (2001) 377–85.

———. "Tradition and Creativity: A Theological Approach." In *The Quadrilog: Tradition and the Future of Ecumenism,* edited by Kenneth Hagen, 312–27. Collegeville, MN: Liturgical, 1994.

———. "The Two Magisteria: An Interim Reflection." *CTSA Proceedings* 35 (1980) 155–69.

———. "Wisdom as the Source of Unity for Theology." In *Wisdom and Holiness, Science, and Scholarship,* edited by Michael Dauphinais and Matthew Levering, 59–71. Naples, FL: Sapientia, 2007.

Eckhart, Meister. *Meister Eckhart.* Translated by Raymond B. Blakney. New York: Harper Torchbooks, 1941.

Edwards, Johnathan. *Religious Affections.* Edited by John E. Smith. New Haven: Yale University Press, 1959.

Elwell, Clarence Edward. *The Influence of the Enlightenment on the Catholic Theory of Religious Education in France 1750–1850.* Cambridge: Harvard University Press, 1944.

Emerson, Ralph Waldo. *The Collected Works of Ralph Waldo Emerson,* vol. 1, Introduction and notes by Robert E. Spiller. Cambridge: Belknap, 1971.

Evans, Gillian, et al. *The History of Christian Theology: The Science of Theology,* vol. 1. Grand Rapids: Eerdmans, 1986.

Farley, Edward. *Deep Symbols: Their Postmodern Effacement and Reclamation.* Valley Forge, PA: Trinity, 1996.

———. *Divine Empathy: A Theology of God.* Minneapolis: Fortress, 1996.

———. *Ecclesial Man: A Social Phenomenology of Faith and Reality.* Philadelphia: Fortress, 1975.

———. *Ecclesial Reflection: An Anatomy of Theological Method.* Philadelphia: Fortress, 1982.

———. *Faith and Beauty: A Theological Aesthetic.* Burlington: Ashgate, 2001.

———. "Four Pedagogical Mistakes: A Mea Culpa." *Teaching Theology and Religion* 8.4 (2005) 200–203.

———. *The Fragility of Knowledge: Theological Education in the Church and the University.* Philadelphia: Fortress, 1988.

———. *Good and Evil: Interpreting a Human Condition.* Minneapolis: Fortress, 1990.

———. "Interpreting Situations: An Inquiry into the Nature of Practical Theology." In *Formation and Reflection: The Promise of Practical Theology,* edited by Lewis S. Mudge and James N. Poling, 1–26. Philadelphia: Fortress, 1987.

———. *Practicing Gospel: Unconventional Thoughts on the Church's Ministry.* Louisville, KY: Westminster John Knox, 2003.

———. *Theologia: The Fragmentation and Unity of Theological Education.* Philadelphia: Fortress, 1983.

———. "Thinking toward the World: A Case for Philosophical Pluralism in Theology." *American Journal of Theology & Philosophy* 14 (1993) 51–63.

Ferruolo, Stephen. *The Origins of the University. The Schools of Paris and Their Critics: 1100–1215.* Stanford: Stanford University Press, 1985.

Ferry, Luc et Alain Renaut. "Université et Système: Réflexions sur les théories de l'Université dan l'idéalisme allemand." *Archives de Philosophie* 42 (1979) 59–90.

Feuerbach, Ludwig. *The Essence of Christianity.* Translated by George Eliot. New York: Harper Torchbooks, 1957.

Fichte, J. G. *Early Philosophical Writings.* Translated by Daniel Breazeale. Ithaca: Cornell University Press, 1988.

Fiddes, Paul. "The Place of Theology in the Modern University." *The Baptist Quarterly* 42.2 (2007) 71–88.

Flannery, Austin, OP. *Vatican Council II*, Vol 2. Rev. ed. Northport, New York: Costello, 1988.

Ford, David. *Self and Salvation: Being Transformed.* Cambridge: Cambridge University Press, 1999.

Fraser, James W. *Schooling the Preachers: The Development of Protestant Theological Education in the United States 1740–1875.* Lanham, MD: University Press of America, 1988.

Frijhoff, Willem. "Patterns." In *A History of the University in Europe*, vol. 2. Edited by Hilde De Ridder-Symoens, 43–110. Cambridge University Press, 1996.

Frost, Robert. *Selected Prose of Robert Frost.* Edited by Hyde Cox and Edward Connery Lathem. New York: Holt, Reinhart and Winston, 1966.

Gay, Peter. *The Enlightenment: The Science of Freedom*, vol. 2. New York: Norton, 1977.

Gerhardt, V. "Interesse." In *Historisches Wörterbuch der Philosophie*, vol. 4, edited by. J. Ritter. Basel: Schawbe, 1976.

Gerrish, Brian. *Continuing the Reformation: Essays on Modern Religious Thought.* Chicago: University of Chicago Press, 1993.

———. *Grace and Reason: A Study in the Theology of Luther.* Oxford: Clarendon, 1962.

———. *Tradition and the Modern World: Reformed Theology in the Nineteenth Century* Chicago: University of Chicago Press, 1978.

Gilley, Sheridan. *Newman and His Age.* London: Darton, Longman & Todd, 1990.

Gilpin, Clark W. *A Preface to Theology.* Chicago: University of Chicago Press, 1996.

Gleason, Philip. "Catholic Higher Education as Historical Context for Theological Education." In *Theological Education in the Catholic Tradition*, edited by Patrick W. Carey and Earl C. Muller, S.J., 23–33. New York: Crossroad, 1997.

———. *Contending With Modernity: Catholic Higher Education in the Twentieth Century.* New York: Oxford University Press, 1995.

González, Justo L. *A History of Christian Thought*, vol. 3. Nashville: Abingdon, 1987.

Grave, S. A. *Conscience in Newman's Thought.* Oxford: Clarendon, 1989.

Griffin, David Ray, and Joseph C. Hough. *Theology and the University.* Albany: SUNY Press, 1991.

Habermas, Jürgen. *Knowledge and Human Interests.* Translated by Jeremy J. Shapiro. Boston: Beacon, 1972.

Harrison, Peter. *"Religion" and the Religions in the English Enlightenment*. Cambridge: Cambridge University Press, 1990.

Hart, D. G. *The University Gets Religion*. Baltimore, MD: Johns Hopkins University Press, 1999.

Harvey, Van A. "On the Intellectual Marginality of American Theology." In *Religion and Twentieth-Century American Intellectual Life*, edited by Michael J. Lacey, 172–92. Cambridge: Cambridge University Press, 1989.

Hauerwas, Stanley. *The State of the University: Academic Knowledges and the Knowledge of God*. Oxford: Blackwell, 2007.

———. *With the Grain of the Universe: The Church's Witness and Natural Theology*. Brazos, 2001.

Hefling, Charles C. "Newman on Apprehension, Notional and Real." *Method: Journal of Lonergan Studies* 14 (1996) 55–84.

———. *Why Doctrines?* 2nd ed. Chestnut Hill, MA: Lonergan, 2000.

Hennesey, James, SJ. *American Catholics: A History of the Roman Catholic Community in the United States*. New York: Oxford University Press, 1981.

Hermes, Georg. *Einleitung in die christkatholische Theologie*. 2 vols. Frankfurt: Minerva, 1967, 1819.

Hernández, Francisco Martín, and José Martín Hernández. *Los Seminarios Españoles en la Epoca de la Ilustración: Ensayo de una Pedagogía Eclesiástica en el Siglo XVIII*. Madrid: CSIC, 1973.

Hinze, Bradford E. *Narrating History, Developing Doctrine: Friedrich Schleiermacher and Johann Sebastian Drey*. Atlanta: Scholars, 1993.

Hoitenga, Dewey. "Faith and Reason in Calvin's Doctrine of the Knowledge of God." In *Rationality in the Calvinian Tradition*, edited by Hendrik Hart et al., 17–39. Lanham, MD: University Press of America, 1983.

Hough, Joseph. "The Marginalization of Theology in the University." In Joseph Kitagawa and Robert Lynn, *Religious Studies, Theological Studies, and the University-Divinity School*, 42–43. Atlanta: Scholars, 1992.

Howard, Thomas. *Protestant Theology and the Making of the Modern German University*. Oxford: Oxford University Press, 2006.

Huber, Ernst Rudolf, and Wolfgang Huber. *Staat und Kirche im 19. und 20. Jahrhunderts: Dokumente zur Geschichte des deutschen Staatskirchenrechte*, I: 576–78. Berlin: Duncker und Humblot, 1973.

Hume, David. *Dialogues and Natural History of Religion*. Oxford: Oxford University Press, 1998.

Hutchins, Robert. *The Higher Learning in America*. New Haven: Yale University Press, 1978.

Jaeger, Werner. *Paideia: The Ideals of Greek Culture*. Translated by Gilbert Highet. Vol. 1. 2nd ed. New York: Oxford University Press, 1945.

Jedin, Hubert, and John Dolan. *History of the Church*, vol. 7: *The Church Between Revolution and Restoration*. Translated by Peter Becker. New York: Crossroad, 1989.

Jonas, Ludwig, and Wilhelm Dilthey. *Aus Schleiermacher's Leben. In Briefen*. 4. Berlin, 1860–3.

Jones, C., et al. *The Study of Spirituality*. New York: Oxford University Press, 1986.

Julia, Dominique. "Le Prêtre Au XVIII Siècle La Théologie Et Les Institutions." *Recherches de Science Religieuse* 58 (1970) 521–34.

Kaiser, James F. *The Concept of Conscience According to John Henry Newman*. Washington, DC: Catholic University of America Press, 1958.

———. *The Conflict of the Faculties*. Translated by Mary J. Gregor. New York: Abaris, 1992.

Kelsey, David. *Between Athens and Berlin*. Grand Rapids: Eerdmans, 1993.

Kennedy, Arthur. "Introduction of Theology in the Catholic Tradition." In Patrick W. Carey and Earl C. Muller, S.J. *Theological Education in the Catholic Tradition*. 81–97. New York: Crossroad, 1997.

Ker, Ian. *The Achievement of John Henry Newman*. Notre Dame: University of Notre Dame Press, 1990.

———. *John Henry Newman: A Biography*. New York: Oxford University Press, 1988.

Klauber, Martin I. *Between Reformed Scholasticism and Pan-Protestantism: Jean-Alphonse Turretin (1671–1737) and Enlightened Orthodoxy at the Academy of Geneva*. Selinsgrove: Susquehanna University Press, 1994.

La Vopa, Anthony J. *Prussian Schoolteachers: Profession and Office, 1763–1848*. Chapel Hill: University of North Carolina Press, 1980.

LaCugna, Cartherine Mowry. *God For Us: The Trinity & Christian Life*. New York: HarperCollins, 1993.

Lamm, Julia A. "The Early Philosophical Roots of Schleiermacher's Notion of *Gefül*, 1788–1794." *Harvard Theological Review* 87 (1994) 67–105.

Lauchert, Friedrich. "Liebermann, Bruno Franz Leopold." *The Catholic Encyclopedia* 9.235–36. New York: Appleton, 1910.

Leclercq, Jean. *The Love of Learning and the Desire for God*. 3rd ed. Translated by Catharine Misrahi. New York: Fordham University Press, 1982.

Lemaitre, J. "Contemplation." *Dictionnaire de Spiritualité Ascétique et Mystique* 2:1643–2193. Paris: Beauchesne, 1953.

Levinger, Matthew. "The Prussian Reform Movement and the Rise of Enlightened Nationalism." In Philip G. Dwyer, *The Rise of Prussia 1700–1830*, 266–75. Essex: Pearson, 2000.

Lexicon der Pädagogik, vol. 4. Freiburg: Herder, 1971.

L'Heureux, John. "The Expert on God." In *Celestial Omnibus: Short Fiction on Faith*, edited by J. P. Many and Tom Hazuka. Boston: Beacon, 1997.

Lichtenberger, F. *History of German Theology in the Nineteenth Century*. Translated and edited by W. Hastie. Edinburgh: Clark, 1889.

Liebermann, Bruno Franz Leopold. *Institutiones theologicae*. Moguntiae: Sumptibus Francisci Kirchemii, 1857.

Lill, Rudolf. "The Beginnings of the Catholic Movement in Germany and Switzerland." In *History of the Church*, vol. 7: *The Church between Revolution and Restoration*, edited by Hubert Jedin and John Dolan and translated by Peter Becker, 216–27. New York: Crossroad, 1989.

Lindbeck, George. *The Nature of Doctrine: Religion and Theology in a Postliberal Age*. Philadelphia: Westminster, 1984.

Lonergan, Bernard, SJ. *Method in Theology*. Minneapolis: Seabury, 1979.

Loyola, Ignatius. *Ignatius of Loyola: Spiritual Exercises and Selected Works*. Edited by George E. Ganss, S.J. New York: Paulist, 1991.

Luther, Martin. *Disputation Against Scholastic Theology*. In *Martin Luther's Basic Theological Writings*, edited by Timothy F. Lull. Minneapolis: Fortress, 1989.

———. "Lectures on Jonah, 1:5." In *Luther's Works,* edited by Hilton C. Ostwald, 19:3–31. St. Louis: Concordia, 1974.
Macauley Jackson, Samuel, editor. "Reinhard, Franz Volkmar," In *The New Schaff-Herzog Encyclopedia of Religious Knowledge*, vol. 9. New York: Funk & Wagnalls, 1911.
MacIntyre, Alasdair. "Catholic Universities: Dangers, Hopes, Choices," In *Higher Learning & Catholic Traditions,* edited by Robert E. Sullivan, 1–21. Notre Dane: University of Notre Dame Press, 2001.
———. *Three Rival Versions of Moral Enquiry.* Notre Dame: University of Notre Dame Press, 1990.
Madges, William. "Does Theology Belong in the University? The Nineteenth-Century Case in Ireland and Germany." In *Theology in the University,* edited by John Apczynski, 151–77. Lanham: University Press of America, 1990.
Magee, Bryan. *Confessions of a Philosopher.* New York: Modern Library, 1997.
Magill, Gerard. "Interpreting Moral Doctrine: Newman on Conscience and Law." *Horizons* 20 (1993) 7–22.
Mariña, Jacqueline. *Transformation of the Self in the Thought of Friedrich Schleiermacher.* Oxford: Oxford University Press, 2008.
Maritain, Jacques. *Distinguish to Unite, or, The Degrees of Knowledge.* Translated by Gerald B. Phelan. Notre Dame: University of Notre Dame, 1995.
Marsden, George M., and Bradley J. Longfield. *The Secularization of the Academy.* New York: Oxford University Press, 1992.
Martin, James, SJ. "Reason, Faith, and Theology: An Interview with Cardinal Avery Dulles, S.J." *America* (March 5, 2001) 6–8; 10–14.
Maynes, Mary Jo. *Schooling for the People: Comparative Local Studies of Schooling History in Germany, 1750–1850.* New York: Holmes & Meier, 1985.
McClelland, Charles E. *The German Experience of Professionalization.* Cambridge: Cambridge University Press, 1991.
———. *State, Society, and University in Germany 1700–1914.* Cambridge: Cambridge University Press, 1980.
McCool, Gerald. *Nineteenth-Century Scholasticism: The Search for a Unitary Method.* New York: Fordham University Press, 1989.
McGinn, Bernard. *The Foundations of Mysticism.* New York: Crossroad, 1991.
McManners, John. *Church and Society in Eighteenth Century France.* Vol. 1. Oxford: Clarendon, 1998.
Melanchthon, Philipp. *Melanchton on Christian Doctrine: Loci Communes 1555.* Translated by Clyde L. Manschreck. New York: Oxford University Press, 1965.
Merrigan, Terrence. *Clear Heads and Holy Hearts: The Religious and Theological Ideal of John Henry Newman.* Louvain: Peeters, 1991.
Misner, Paul. *Papacy and Development: Newman and the Primacy of the Pope.* Leiden: Bril, 1976.
Müller, Wolfgang. "Ecclesiastical Learning in the Eighteenth Century—Theology of Enlightenment and Pietism." In *History of the Church,* vol. 6: *The Church in the Age of Absolutism and Enlightenment,* edited by Hubert Jedin and John Dolan, 524–46. New York: Crossroad, 1981.
New Catholic Encyclopedia 4. New York: McGraw-Hill, 1967.
Newman, John Henry. *Apologia Pro Vita Sua.* Edited by I. T. Ker, London: Penguin, 1994.
———. *Apologia Pro Vita Sua.* Edited by Martin Svaglic. Oxford: Clarendon, 1967.

Bibliography

———. *Autobiographical Writings.* Edited by Henry Tristam. New York: Sheed & Ward, 1957.

———. *Certain Difficulties Felt by Anglicans in Catholic Teaching.* Vol. 2. Westminster, MD: Christian Classics, 1969.

———. *Certain Difficulties Felt by Anglicans in Catholic Teaching.* Vol. 2. London: Longmans & Green, 1900.

———. *Discourses Addressed to Mixed Congregations.* Westminster, MD: Christian Classics, 1966.

———. *An Essay on the Development of Christian Doctrine.* Notre Dame: University of Notre Dame Press, 1989.

———. *An Essay in Aid of a Grammar of Assent.* Edited by I. T. Ker, Oxford: Clarendon, 1985.

———. *An Essay in Aid of a Grammar of Assent.* Introduction by Nicholas Lash. Notre Dame: University of Notre Dame Press, 1979.

———. *Essays Critical and Historical.* Vol. 1. London: Basil Montagu Pickering, 1871.

———. *Essays Critical and Historical.* Vol. 2. London: Longmans & Green. 1897.

———. *Essays Critical and Historical.* Vol. 2. New York: Longmans & Green, 1907.

———. *Fifteen Sermons Preached before the University of Oxford.* Edited by James David Earnest and Gerard Tracey. Oxford: Oxford University Press, 2006.

———. *Historical Sketches.* Vols. 2 and 3. Westminster, MD: Christian Classics, 1970.

———. *Idea of a University.* Edited by I. T. Ker. Oxford: Clarendon, 1976.

———. *Letter Addressed to His Grace the Duke of Norfolk.* As quoted in *Certain Difficulties Felt by Anglicans in Catholic Teaching.* Vol. 2. London: Longmans & Green, 1900.

———. *Letters and Diaries of John Henry Newman,* Vol. 15. Edited by Charles Stephen Dessain and Vincent Ferrer Blehl, S.J. London: Nelson, 1964.

———. *Letters and Diaries of John Henry Newman.* Vol. 16. Edited by Charles Stephen Dessain. London: Nelson, 1965.

———. *Letters and Diaries of John Henry Newman.* Vol. 20. Edited by Charles Stephen Dessain. London: Nelson, 1970.

———. *Letters and Diaries of John Henry Newman.* Vol. 21. Edited by Charles Stephen Dessain and Edward E. Kelly, S.J. London: Nelson, 1971.

———. *Letters and Diaries of John Henry Newman.* Vol. 26. Edited by Charles Stephen Dessain and Thomas Gornall, S.J. Oxford: Clarendon, 1974.

———. *Letters and Diaries of John Henry Newman.* Vol. 27. Edited by Charles Stephen Dessain and Thomas Gornall, S.J. Oxford: Clarendon, 1975.

———. *Loss and Gain: The Story of a Convert.* Oxford: Oxford University Press, 1986.

———. "Memorandum About My Connection with the Catholic University." In *Autobiographical Writings,* edited by Henry Tristam. New York: Sheed & Ward, 1957.

———. *On Consulting the Faithful in Matters of Doctrine.* Edited by John Coulson. Kansas City, MO: Sheed & Ward, 1961.

———. *The Philosophical Notebook.* Edited by Edward J. Sillem, Vol. 1. Louvain: Nauwelaerts, 1969.

———. *Sermons Preached on Various Occasions.* London: Burns & Oates, 1870.

———. "The Tamworth Reading Room." In *Discussions and Arguments on Various Subjects.* Gracewing and University of Notre Dame Press, 2004.

———. *The Via Media of the Anglican Church.* Edited by H. D. Weidner, 3rd ed. Oxford: Clarendon, 1990.

Nietzsche, Friedrich. *On the Advantage and Disadvantage of History for Life.* Translated by Peter Preuss. Indianapolis: Hackett, 1980.
Norris, Thomas J. *Newman and His Theological Method.* Leiden: Brill, 1977.
O'Brien, David J. *From The Heart of the American Church: Catholic Higher Education and American Culture.* Maryknoll, NY: Orbis, 1994.
O'Brien, George Dennis. *The Idea of a Catholic University.* Chicago: University of Chicago Press, 2002.
O'Donohoe, James. *Tridentine Seminary Legislation: Its Sources and Its Formation.* Louvain/Boston: Publications Universitaires De Louvain, 1957.
O'Keefe, Joseph M., SJ. *Catholic Education at the Turn of the New Century.* New York: Garland, 1997.
Ogden, Schubert. *On Theology.* San Francisco: Harper & Row, 1986.
Ostwald, Hilton. *Luther's Works*, Vol. 19. Saint Louis: Concordia, 1974.
Paley, William. *Natural Theology; or, Evidences of the Existence and Attributes of the Deity.* 12th ed. Charlottesville, VA: Ibis, nd.
Paul, John II. *Catechesis in Our Time.* In Austin Flannery, OP, *Vatican Council II.* Northport, NY: Costello, 1988.
———. *Ex Corde Ecclesiae.* In *Catholic Identity in Our Colleges and Universities: A Collection of Defining Documents.* Washington, DC: USCCB, 2006.
Paulsen, Friedrich. *The German Universities and University Study.* Translated by Frank Thilly and William W. Elwang. New York: Scribner's, 1906.
Paulson, Michael. "Cardinal's Path to Faith Began Simply." *The Boston Globe* (November 3, 2001) B2.
Pieper, Joseph. *Leisure: The Basis of Culture.* South Bend, IN: St. Augustine's, 1998.
Plato. *Republic.* Translated by G. M. A. Grube and revised by C. D. C. Reeve. Indianapolis: Hackett, 1992.
Polanyi, Michael. *Personal Knowledge: Towards a Post-Critical Philosophy.* London: Routledge & Kegan Paul, 1958.
Ponticus, Evagrius. *The Praktikos & Chapters on Prayer.* Translated and introduced by John Eudes Bamberger, OCSO. Kalamazoo, MI: Cistercian, 1981.
Powell, Jouett L. "Cardinal Newman On Faith And Doubt: The Role Of Conscience." *Downside Review* 99.335 (1981) 137–48.
Press, Eyal, and Jennifer Washburn. "The Kept University." *Atlantic Monthly* (March 2000) 39–54.
Quenstedt, Johann. *The Nature and Character of Theology: An Introduction to the Thought of J. A. Quenstedt.* Edited and translated by Luther Poellot. St. Louis: Concordia, 1986.
Rahner, Karl. *The Christian Commitment: Essays in Pastoral Theology.* New York: Sheed & Ward, 1963.
———. *Encyclopedia of Theology: The Concise Sacramentum Mundi.* New York: Seabury, 1975.
———. *Foundations of Christian Faith: An Introduction to the Idea of Christianity.* Translated by William V. Dych. New York: Crossroad, 1982.
———. "The One Christ and the Universality of Salvation," *Theological Investigations XVI.* New York: Crossroad, 1979.
Rausch, Thomas P. "Divisions, Dialogue and the Catholicity of the Church." *America* (January 31, 1998) 21–29.

Redeker, Martin. *Schleirmacher: Life and Thought.* Translated by John Walhausser. Philadelphia: Fortress, 1973.

Reinhard, Franz Volkmar. *Vorlesungen über die Dogmatik,* edited by Johann Gottfried Immanuel Berger. Sulzbach: Seidel, 1812.

Reuben, Julia A. *The Making of the Modern University: Intellectual Transformation and the Marginalization of Morality.* Chicago: University of Chicago, 1996.

Ribadeneira, Diego. "A Spirited Study of Science, Religion." *The Boston Globe* (11/07/97) B1, B8.

Ringer, Fritz. *The Decline of the German Mandarins: The German Academic Community 1890-1933.* Cambridge: Harvard University Press, 1969.

Rouse, Ruth, and Stephen Charles Neill. *A History of the Ecumenical Movement 1517- 1948.* London: SPCK, 1954.

Roy, Louis. "Consciousness According to Schleiermacher." *Journal of Religion* 77 (1997) 217-32.

Sailer, Johann Michael. *Vorlesungun aus der Pastoraltheologie.* Munich, 1820.

Saine, Thomas P. *The Problem of Being Modern.* Detroit: Wayne State University Press, 1997.

Scharlemann, Robert P. *Thomas Aquinas and John Gerhard.* New Haven: Yale University Press, 1964.

Schelling, F. W. J. *On Universities Studies.* Translated by E. S. Morgan and edited by Norbert Guterman. Athens: Ohio University Press, 1966.

Schleiermacher, F. D. E. *Brief Outline on the Study of Theology.* Translated by Terrence N. Tice. Richmond, VA: John Knox, 1970.

———. *Christian Caring: Selection from Practical Theology.* Translated and edited by James O. Duke and Howard Stone. Philadelphia: Fortress, 1988.

———. *The Christian Faith.* Translated and edited by H. R. Mackintosh and J. S. Stewart. Edinburgh: T. & T. Clark, 1994.

———. *Der Christliche Glaube: nach den Grundsätzen der Evangelischen Kirche Im Zusammemhange Dargestellt.* Edited by Martin Redeker. Berlin: Walter de Gruyter, 1960.

———. *Dialectic or, The Art of Doing Philosophy: A Study Edition of the 1811 Notes.* Translated by Terrence N. Tice. Atlanta: Scholars, 1996.

———. *Hermeneutics and Criticism.* Translated and edited by Andrew Bowie. Cambridge: Cambridge University Press, 1998.

———. *Introduction to Christian Ethics.* Translated by John C. Shelley. Nashville: Abingdon, 1989.

———. *Jugendschriften 1787-1796.* Herausgegeben von Günter Meckenstock. *Kritische Gesamtausgabe,* erste Abteilung. Bd. 1. Berlin: Walter de Gruyter, 1984.

———. *Occasional Thoughts On Universities in the German Sense.* Translated by Terrence N. Tice and Edwina Lawler. San Francisco: EM Text, 1991.

———. *On Freedom.* Edited by Albert Blackwell. Lewiston: Mellen, 1992.

———. *On Religion: Addresses in Response to Its Cultured Critics.* Translated by Terrence N. Tice. Richmond, VA: John Knox, 1969.

———. *On Religion: Speeches to Its Cultured Despisers.* Translated by Richard Crouter. Cambridge University Press, 1988.

———. *On Religion: Speeches to Its Cultured Despisers.* Translated by John Oman. 1958. Reprint, Louisville, KY: Westminster/John Knox, 1994.

---. *On the* Glaubenslehre: *Two Letters to Dr. Lücke.* Translated by James Duke and Francis Fiorenza. Chico, CA: Scholars, 1981.

---. *Die Praktische Theologie nach den Grundasätzen der evangelischen Kirche im Zusammenhange dargestellt.* In *Sämmtliche Werke,* edited by Jacob Frerichs. Vol. 1.13. Berlin: Walter De Gruyter, 1983.

---. *Psychologie, Sämmtliche Werke.* Vol. 3/6. Berlin: G. Reimer, 1834–1864.

---. *Schriften aus der Berliner Zeit* 1796–1799. herausgegeben von Günter Meckenstock. Kritische Gesamtausgabe, erste Abteilung, Bd. 2. Berlin: Walter de Gruyter, 1984.

---. *Theologisch-dogmatische Abhandlungen und Gelegenheitsschriften,* herausgegeben von Hans-Friedrich Traulson, abt. 1, bd. 10. Berlin: Walter de Gruyter, 1990.

---. *Universitätsschriften. Herakleitos. Jurze Darstellung des theologischen Studiums,* herausgegeben von Dirk Schmid. *Kritische Gesamtausgabe,* erste Abteilung. Bd. 6. Berlin: Walter de Gruyter, 1998.

Schmidt-Biggeman, Wilhelm. "New Structures of Knowledge." In *A History of the University in Europe,* edited by Hilde De Ridder-Symoens, 2:489–530. Cambridge: Cambridge University Press, 1996.

Schubert, Frank D. *A Sociological Study of Secularization Trends in the American Catholic University: Decatholicizing the Catholic Religious Curriculum.* Lewiston, NY: Mellen, 1990.

Sheehan, James J. *German History 1770–1866.* Oxford: Clarendon, 1989.

Simpson, J. A., and E. S. Weiner. *Oxford English Dictionary.* 2nd ed. Oxford: Clarendon, 1989.

Sykes, Stephen. *The Identity of Christianity.* Philadelphia: Fortress, 1984.

Tackett, Timothy. *Priest & Parish in Eighteenth-Century France: A Social and Political Study of the Curés in a Diocese of Dauphiné, 1750–1791.* Princeton: Princeton University Press, 1977.

---. *Religion, Revolution, and Regional Culture in Eighteenth-Century France: The Ecclesiastical Oath of 1791.* Princeton: Princeton University Press, 1986.

Tanner, Norman P., SJ. *Decrees of the Ecumenical Councils.* Vol. 2. *Trent to Vatican II.* Washington, DC: Sheed & Ward, 1990.

Thandeka. *The Embodied Self: Friedrich Schleiermacher's Solution to Kant's Problem of the Empirical Self.* Albany: SUNY Press, 1995.

The Catholic Encyclopedia. New York: Appleton, 1910.

Thiel, John. *Imagination and Authority: Theological Authorship in the Modern Tradition.* Minneapolis: Fortress, 1991.

---. "Theological Responsibility: Beyond the Classical Paradigm." *Theological Studies* 47 (1986) 573–98.

Thoreau, Henry David. *The Journal of Henry David Thoreau.* Vol. 10. Edited by Bradford Torrey and Francis H. Allen. Boston: Houghton Mifflin, 1906.

Tice, Terrence. *Schleiermacher.* Nashville: Abingdon, 2006.

Tillich, Paul. *Systematic Theology,* vol 1. Chicago: University of Chicago Press, 1951.

Tracy, David. *Blessed Rage for Order: The New Pluralism in Theology.* Chicago: University of Chicago Press, 1996.

Twesten, August. *Vorlesungen über die Dogmatik der evangel.lutherischen Kirche.* 2 vols. Kiels, 1826.

Victor, Richard of Saint. *The Twelve Patriarchs.* Translated by Grover Zinn. New York: Paulist, 1979.

Vidler, Alec. *The Church in an Age of Revolution*. New York: Penguin, 1990.
Vizetelly, Henry. *Berlin under the New Empire: Its Institutions, Inhabitants, Industry, Monuments, Museums, Social Life, Manners*. Vol. 2. 1879. Reprint, New York: Greenwood, 1968.
Ward, Wilfrid. *The Life of John Henry Cardinal Newman*. 2 vols. New York: Longmans & Green, 1912.
Welch, Claude. *Protestant Thought In the Nineteenth Century*. Vol. 1. New Haven: Yale University Press, 1972.
Wheeler, Barbara G., and Edward Farley. *Shifting Boundaries: Contextual Approaches to the Structure of Theological Education*. Louisville: Westminster/John Knox, 1991.
Wildiers, Max. *The Theologian and His Universe*. New York: Seabury, 1982.
Williams, Robert. *Schleiermacher The Theologian: The Construction of the Doctrine of God*. Philadelphia: Fortress, 1978.
Wolff, Christian. Unpaginated dedication to the first edition of the "German Teleology," *Verünfftige Gedancken von den Absichten der natürlichen Dinge, den Liebhabern der Wahrheit mitgetheilet,* von Christian Freyherrn von Woff. Neue Auflage. Halle: Rengerische Buchhandlung, 1752.
Wood, Charles M. *Vision and Discernment: An Orientation in Theological Study*. Atlanta: Scholars, 1985.
Wood, Susan K., SCL. "The Church as Communion." In *The Gift of the Church*, edited by Peter C. Phan. 159–76. Collegeville, MN: Glazier, 2000.
Wyschogrod, Edith. *Saints and Postmodernism: Revisioning Moral Philosophy*. Chicago: University of Chicago Press, 1990.
Yearley, Lee H. *The Ideas of Newman: Christianity and Human Religiosity*. University Park: Pennsylvania State University Press, 1978.
Zwingli, Huldreich. *Commentary on True and False Religion*. Edited by Samuel Macauley Jackson and Clarece Nevin Heller. Durham, NC: Labyrinth, 1981.

Index

academic disciplines. *See* disciplines
academic theology. *See* theology
academy, the. *See* universities
academic freedom. *See* freedom
aesthetics, 17
agnosticism, 188, 205
Allen, Prudence, 309
Allies, T. W., 155
Anglican church, 104, 182
Anselm, St., 48, 159, 191
antecedent probability, 149
anthropology, 20, 45, 104, 106, 119
   theological, 20, 234, 267, 275, 287
apologetics, 21, 138, 184, 204, 212, 230, 247, 292, 305
apprehension, 104, 124, 126–28, 149, 183, 185, 196–97, 243, 287, 320
   notional, 107, 148, 150, 159, 179, 181, 185–86
   real, 148, 150, 152
Aquinas, Thomas, ix, 4, 10, 19, 38, 88, 134, 144, 178–80, 218–19, 259, 290–91, 308, 312–13
Arianism. *See* heresy
Aristotle, 4, 17–19, 34, 44, 82, 118, 124, 132, 174–76, 322
art, 17, 44, 164, 166, 171, 195, 306, 313–14, 316
   as craft, 46, 53, 66, 68, 82, 181, 194, 26
assent, 124, 148, 161, 197, 202, 227, 293–94
   notional, 127, 149, 195

   real, 124, 126–27, 149, 195
atheism, 118
atonement, 120, 123, 133
Aubert, Roger, 89, 93
Augustine, St., ix, 19, 37, 41, 141, 169, 174, 233, 308
authority ecclesial, 6, 8, 10–12, 100–101, 154–58, 194, 199, 202, 204, 208, 214–16, 222–25, 229–31, 238–45, 247–48, 250, 252, 287, 291, 293–94, 296–97, 300
   intellectual, 15, 218, 267
   government, 95, 154
   religious, 125, 132, 245–47, 287
   theological, 100, 164, 207, 224, 242–43, 250, 252
autonomy. *See* freedom
Avila, St. Teresa, 295

Banner, Michael, 310
baptism. *See* sacraments
Barr, Colin, 166
Barth, Karl, 15, 21, 37, 48, 59
Barth, Ulrich, 16–17
Baumgarten-Crusius, Ludwig F. O., 18
Baur, Ferdinand Christian, 26
belief. *See* assent
   personal, 47, 119, 137
   religious, x, 6, 46–47, 49–50, 95, 123–24, 141–42, 149, 161, 211, 226, 246, 286, 292
Bellarmine, Robert, 141

Bible. *See* Scripture
bishops, xii, 5, 10, 91–92, 118, 158, 292, 297, 305
   and ultramontanism, 92
Blachford, Lord, 156, 158
Blondel, Maurice, 209
Bonaparte, Napoleon, 75–76, 79, 92
Bonaventure, St., 37
Boniface VIII (pope), 157
Bonnet, Jean, 90–91
Bossuet, Jacques, 19
Bowles, Emily, 155, 158
Bretschneider, Karl Gottlieb, 18
Brown, William Adams, 7
Brownlow, William, 156
Brunner, Emil, 17, 235
Buber, Martin, 233
Buckley, Michael J., 105, 107, 118, 138, 213, 303, 318–24
Budde, Michael, 295, 305
Burghardt, Walter, 223
Burtchaell, James, xi, 213
Butler, Bishop, 118

Calvin, John, 19, 21, 38, 49, 81–84, 91, 104, 130
Cano, Melchior, 141
Carlyle, Thomas, 57–58
Carroll, John, 9
Catholic catechism, 9, 106, 180, 224
Catholic Church, ix, 10, 89, 104, 187, 189, 201
   Magisterium of, 159, 199–200, 203–4, 211, 216, 222–23, 225–26, 229, 238, 252, 291, 293–94
   triple office of, 155–59
Catholic priests, 5, 9, 89, 90, 92, 107, 186
Catholic seminaries, 9–11, 88–93, 159, 165, 185, 200, 258
Catholic studies, xii
Catholic University of America, 9
Catholic University of Ireland, 12, 166, 185

Chatterton, Lady, 186
Christian mythos, 262, 266–68, 282, 284–87
Christianity, 42, 44, 47–49, 51–54, 87, 105, 116, 129–31, 138–42, 144, 146, 155–56, 160, 182–83, 198, 201, 208, 238–39, 244–45, 247, 250, 256, 259, 267, 276, 281, 284–85, 297
   doctrines of, 7, 47
   essence of, 13–14, 21, 23–26, 48
Christology, 185, 225, 231, 310
Church Councils
   Chalcedon, 249
   Nicea, 160
   Trent, 89–91
   Vatican I, 158
   Vatican II, 8–10, 199, 206, 208, 220, 222, 297, 301, 319
Cicero, 18, 82, 168, 169
Collège de France, 63, 75
Collingwood, R. G., 113
Colmar, Johann Ludwig, 92
common good, 164, 216, 310
community(ies) religious, 25, 118, 230, 231, 242, 276, 284–85
communion of saints, 183
Congar, Yves, 88
Congregation for the Doctrine of the Faith, 294
conscience, 105
   and assent, 127
   and God, 118–24, 128–29, 131–32, 136, 140, 143, 149–50, 179, 185
   as affective and personal, 127–28, 134, 155
   as duty, 124, 129
   as moral sense, 124–26, 129, 133, 135
consciousness
   historical, 52, 245–46, 250, 260, 287
   historical-critical, 2, 53–54

consciousness (*continued*)
   religious 1, 15–16, 35, 40, 41–42, 45
Constantine, Emperor, 246
Constantinianism, 303–5
Constitutions of the Society of Jesus, 322
contemplation
   and liberal education, 107, 165, 170, 173–81, 186, 296, 301, 306, 309, 320–21
   as term, 173
conversion, 37, 83, 103–4, 120, 132, 195, 197, 217, 296, 301
cosmology, 245, 150
Coulson, John, 135
creeds, 19, 208–9, 241
   Nicene, 160
Crouter, Richard, 16–18, 57
crucifixion, 6
Cullen, Paul Archbishop, 151, 166
Culler, Dwight, 111, 173
Curran, Charles, 9

Dalgairns, John, 177
D'Costa, Gavin, 303, 307–13
De Caussade, Jean-Pierre, 38
de Wette, Wilhelm M. L., 18
Deism, 3, 103, 143
Delbrück, Johann Friedrich Ferdinand, 18
Demosthenes, 82
Dens, Petro, 88
dependence
   feeling of, 29, 31–34, 39
   feeling of absolute dependence, 15, 24, 26–29, 31–36, 38–44, 46
determinism, 245, 248, 251
dialectic, 61, 172
   and philosophy, 66–67, 70
   theological, 259, 281
Dilthey, Wilhelm, 17, 24
disciplines
   scientific, 59, 96–97

   secondary school, 61
   secular, 214, 222, 224, 227
   theological, 50–51, 86, 151, 192, 200, 211
   university, 2, 5–6, 8, 11, 23, 70–71, 77–78, 83, 85–86, 88, 93, 97–98, 102, 114, 115, 203, 219–23, 226, 256, 258, 260–61, 267, 269–71, 285, 287, 292, 298, 306–8, 312, 316, 322–24
dissent theological, 222, 227, 294
divinity schools, 6–8, 11, 200
doctors of the Church, 219, 301
doctrine
   "art doctrine," 53
   of atonement. *See* atonement
   Christian, xiii, 4–5, 8, 20–22, 33, 36, 45–47, 53, 55, 51, 77, 85–88, 104, 129, 130–31, 152, 157, 159, 184, 191–93, 196, 204, 207, 210, 220–22, 224, 226–27, 238, 241, 244–45, 259, 284, 286, 292–94, 298, 301
   of creation, 276, 311, 314–15
   development of, 70, 78, 154, 160, 222, 226
   of God. *See* God
   and holiness, 123
   and incarnation. *See* Jesus Christ
   Lutheran, 19
   and morality, 124
   of original sin, 119, 161
   philosophical, 17
   and revelation. *See* revelation
   as *sacra doctrina*, ix, 290
   of salvation. *See* salvation
   and threefold office, 155
   and tradition. *See* tradition
dogma, 131, 149, 182, 184, 202, 223, 238, 242–45, 296, 316
   as principle, 202
   and propositions, 25, 48
   and terminology, 55

dogmatic theology. *See* theology
Drey, Johann Sebastian, 89
Duchamp, Marcel, 314
Dulles, Avery Cardinal, S.J., xiii, 11, 187–229, 289–92, 294, 296–98, 300–302, 312

ecclesia, 155, 229, 231–32, 234–37, 246, 252, 277, 297
   and community, 236
ecclesiology, 87, 131, 135, 187, 198, 231, 275, 297, 303, 305, 308
Eccleston, Samuel, 9
Eckhart, Meister, 37, 41
Ècole Normale Supérieur, 75
ecumenism, 187, 222
education
   as *Bildung*, 85
   Catholic, 9–11, 93, 200, 319
   Christian, 200, 204, 305, 319
   clerical and seminary, 5, 8, 88, 90, 93, 165, 275, 281, 312
   elementary, 12
   higher (includes university), xi, 5, 12, 64–66, 68, 74–75, 79, 85, 95, 98, 100, 103, 107, 144, 151, 154, 163, 165, 169–70, 181, 216, 227, 259, 261–62, 267–70, 272, 275, 278, 280–81, 292, 295, 313, 319, 322
   liberal, 161, 163–67, 170–74, 176–78, 181, 183, 185–86, 212, 216, 295, 300, 318, 320, 323–24
   as *paideia*, 281
   philosophical, 15, 75
   philosophy of, 320
   religious, 96, 185, 204, 261, 272
   scientific, 3
   secondary, 61–62, 65, 171
   theological, 8, 15, 57, 85, 88–89, 200, 255, 258, 261–62, 309, 323
Edwards, Jonathan, 38
Emerson, Ralph Waldo, 57–58

encyclopedia, theological, 25
Enlightenment, x, 15, 20, 57, 75, 85, 86, 89, 92, 118, 138, 258, 260, 262–67, 285, 309–10
epistemology, 310
Ernesti, Johann August, 260
eschatology, 20
ethics, 23, 44, 83, 131, 249, 275, 303, 311
   philosophic, 17
   sexual, 10
   as social theory, 24–25, 27, 44, 67
Eucharist. *See* sacraments
Eusebius, 141
Evangelical
   and church, 52, 84, 87, 103–4, 106
   and faith, 19, 104
   students, 55
evangelization, 199, 205, 216–17, 227–28, 294, 302
evil, 81, 121–22, 131, 231, 233–34, 248–49, 253, 267, 286
evolution, 35, 69, 91
Ex corde ecclesiae, xi, 187, 219–20, 293–94

faculties, university, 59, 67–72, 74, 78, 85, 89, 92, 95, 192, 201, 213, 309
faith
   act of, 124, 161, 196, 217, 225, 230–32, 252–53, 299
   and adult formation, 200, 294
   articles of, 2, 197, 204, 223, 227, 259, 281
   Christian (religious), x–xiii, 10–11, 12, 19–20, 22–23, 47, 50, 52–54, 76, 78, 80, 82, 89, 93, 95–97, 101, 104, 134–35, 152–54, 158, 160–61, 187, 190, 193, 203, 207, 209–11, 213–15, 217–18, 224–25, 227, 230, 237, 242–43, 247, 251, 256, 258, 274, 277–78, 280,

faith (*continued*)
    283–85, 294, 296, 298–301,
    311–15, 318–20, 325
  community of, 25, 48, 142,
    197–200, 203–4, 207–8, 233,
    282
  and God consciousness, 14
  of Israel, 239, 247
  natural, 196
  non-Christian, 51–52, 283, 285
  philosophical, 1, 96
  and reason, 2, 19, 21, 60, 76, 81,
    83–84, 97, 130, 159, 195, 201,
    217–18, 220, 290, 294, 314
  sense of, 197, 202, 209
Farley, Edward, xiii, 7–8, 11, 181,
  187, 229–87, 289, 291–92,
  296–98, 300–302
Febronianism, 92
feeling of absolute dependence. *See* dependence
Feuerbach, Ludwig, 104
Ffoulkes, Edmund, 186
Fichte, Immanuel Hermann, 17
Fichte, Johann Gottlieb, 18, 20, 31,
  57–58
fideism, 285
fine arts, 172, 271
Foerst, Anne, 1
Ford, David, 295,
Foucault, Michel, 257, 267
fragmentation
  academic, 2, 256, 287, 309
  theological, 300
Francke, August Hermann, 260
Frankfurt school, 267
freedom, 144, 213, 248–49, 251, 288,
  310–11
  academic (intellectual), 55–57,
    72, 86–87, 203, 214–16, 222,
    226, 293, 297, 316, 318
  feeling of, 29–36, 39–40, 43
  and liberal knowledge, 172
  of opinion, 158
  religious, xii, 222, 232, 234
  of teaching (*Lehrfreiheit*), 56
French Revolution, 75, 92, 158
Freud, Sigmund, 113
Frey, Rebecca, 104
Frost, Robert, 195
Froude, Mrs. William, 157–58

Gallicanism, 92
Gerhard, Johann, 19
German Confederation, 79
Gerrish, Brian, 24, 42, 81
Gess, Friedrich, 17
Gilley, Sheridan, 104, 155
Gilpin, Clark, 6–8
Gleason, Philip, 9–10
God
  and causality, 248–51
  and deism, 103, 143
  doctrine of, 101, 128, 143, 183,
    185
  Holy Spirit, 80, 135, 183, 206,
    208–9, 211, 219
  and monotheism, 101, 103, 183,
    301
  natural knowledge of (also, *see* conscience), 118–21, 123,
    130, 136, 143, 150, 291, 311
  and philosophy, 82
  proof of, 105, 231
  and religious experience, 14–15,
    26, 36–40, 93
  and trinity, 207, 312
  Whence of absolute dependence,
    24, 33
Gnosticism, 16, 38
Görres, Johann Joseph, 89
Grabmann, Martin, 309
grace, 40–41, 80, 120, 130, 200, 202,
  210, 231, 289, 319
  justifying, 299–300
  and sacraments, 204, 225
  special, 219, 302
  and theology. *See* theology
Gustafson, James, 284, 310–11

Habermas, Jürgen, 47
habits
   philosophical, 116, 161, 167–69, 172–73, 181
   sapiential, 300
   theological. *See* theologian
Harrison, Peter, 117
Harvey, Van, 7
Hauerwas, Stanley, 295, 303–8, 310–11, 313
Hefling, Charles, 126–28, 244
Heidegger, Martin, 233
heresy, 159–60, 308
   Arianism, 160
hermeneutics, 16, 53–54, 86, 243–44, 247, 260, 267, 279, 283, 285, 287, 323
Hermes, Georg, 89, 93
Herms, Eilert, 17
higher education. *See* education
Hippocrates, 107
Hirsch, Emmanuel, 17
historical consciousness, 52, 245–46, 250, 260, 287
holiness, 123, 136, 295, 302, 309, 312
Holy Spirit. *See* God
Hope-Scott, James, 155
Hough, Joseph, 3, 8
house of authority, 238–41, 243–45, 248, 250, 252, 296
Howard, Thomas, 11, 69, 75, 89
Humani Generis, 221
humanism, and Christianity, 201, 222, 318
Humboldt, Wilhelm von, 56
Hume, David, 139
Husserl, Edmund, 17, 280
Hutchins, Robert, 2

Idea of a University, 69, 99–100, 102–3, 116, 130–31, 136–39, 144, 150–51, 155–56, 158, 174, 176–77, 180, 184, 306
Idealism, 20, 64–65
idolatry, 105, 132, 154, 233, 286, 298
Ignatius. *See* Loyola
Incarnation. *See* Jesus Christ
individualism, 15
inference, 124, 147
   formal, 145–46, 148–49
inspiration
   axiom of, 245
   biblical, 246
interpretation of scripture. *See* hermeneutics, 88
Islam, 38, 42, 44

Jacobi, Friedrich Heinrich, 16–18, 20, 22
James, William, 113, 232
Jesus Christ, 3, 13, 37, 134, 136, 199, 207, 212, 225–26, 235, 239, 242–43, 247–48, 251, 291–92, 294–95, 303, 314–15, 325
   and ecclesia, 235, 237
   and incarnation, 131, 183, 202, 206, 225, 240, 251
   and resurrection, 135
   titles of, 232
Josephinism, 92
Judaism, 38, 42, 44, 239, 246

Kant, Immanuel, 15–18, 60, 69, 322
Kelsey, David, 7
Ketteler, Wilhelm Emmanuel, 5, 10
knowledge
   correctives to, 160, 262, 264–67, 269, 271, 286
   as corrupt, 265
   empirical, 65–66, 71, 76, 263
   empirical paradigm of, 263–66, 285
   scientific, 106, 164, 319
   as tacit, 196–97, 209
   as *wissenschaftlich*, 24, 25, 59, 60–64, 68–69, 74, 76, 78, 86, 97
Komonchak, Joseph, 210

LaCugna, Catherine Mowry, 298
Lash, Nicholas, 123–24
law
    canon, 91, 249
    civil, 4, 57, 69, 216
    divine, 125, 239
    ecclesial, faculty of (schools), 3, 7, 69–70, 72, 78, 309
    moral, 57, 135
    natural, 311
    as subject matter, 26, 77, 182
Leclercq, Jean, 309
Leibniz, G. W., 3, 16–18
leisure, 169–70, 263
Lerins, Vincent of, 141
leveling, axiom of, 241, 245
L'Heureux, John, 314
liberal arts, 9, 164, 212, 296, 318, 323–24
    See also education
Liberius, Pope, 157
Liebermann, Bruno F. L., 88, 92
Lindbeck, George, 191–94, 196, 210, 310
liturgy, 44, 51, 53, 197, 202, 298
Lonergan, Bernard, 109
love
    and academic knowledge, 67, 309
    and contemplation, 180, 320
    as gift of the Spirit, 37
    of God and neighbor, 295, 314–15
    and salvation, 232, 249, 298–99, 315
    and theology, 114, 219, 312–13, 317–18
Loyola, St. Ignatius, 37, 142, 189, 320, 322
Lücke, Gottfried C. F., 16, 21, 32
Luther, Martin, 19, 80–84, 104

MacIntyre, Alasdair, 307
Magee, Bryan, 31
magisterium. *See* Catholic Church
Maritain, Jacques, 180, 209

marriage, 90, 195, 237–38, 279
Marsden, George, 2, 213
Martyr, Justin, 308
Marx, Karl, 265
May, Mark A., 7
Mayers, Walter, 104
McClelland, Charles, 69, 73, 75–76, 95
McCormick, S.J., Richard, 310–11
Melanchthon, Philipp, 19, 21
Meland, Bernard, 266
Mendelssohn, Moses, 18
Menken, Gottfried, 20
metaphysics, 4, 27, 83, 131, 175, 205, 274
Middle Ages, 37, 220, 256–57, 259, 261, 291
Milbank, John, 310
ministry, campus, 11
    of Jesus, 232
    professional (practical), 7–10, 36, 50, 91, 157, 202, 211, 226, 255, 258–60, 275, 302
Minsky, Marvin, 1–2
Misner, Paul, 158–59
Möhler, J. A., 89, 209
monasticism, 16, 37, 223, 257–58, 308–9
monophysitism, 225
monotheism. *See* God
Monsell, William, 184
morality, 11, 15–16, 53, 129, 131–32, 166
Moriarty, David, 151, 177
mysticism, esoteric 38, 173

nationalism, 60, 220
natural law. *See* law
natural theology. *See* theology
Nestorianism, 225
New Testament. *See* Scripture
Newman, John Henry, xii–xiii, 11–12, 99–187, 195, 200, 212, 218, 223, 262, 289, 291–92, 296–98, 300–302, 306–7
Nietzsche, Friedrich, 171

Norfolk, Duke of, 125, 159
Northcote, J. Spencer, 154
Nussbaum, Martha, 310

O'Brien, David, 10–11
O'Brien, George Dennis, 303, 313–18, 323
Odebrecht, Rudolf, 17
O'Donovan, Oliver, 310
Ogden, Schubert, 1–2
Origen, 141, 308

paideia, educational, 268, 272, 281, 287
   Greek, 256, 268
   theological, 6, 273, 276, 280–81, 287
Paley, William, 139–41
papacy (and popes), 92–93, 155–59, 199–200, 203, 248
Paul, John II (pope), xi, 187, 199, 219–220, 293–94
Paul, St., 37, 120
Paulsen, Friedrich, 3–5, 56
pedagogical areas, 269, 271, 273, 281, 284, 287
phenomenology, social, 233, 237, 246
philosophers, ix, 3, 10, 18, 20, 22, 56, 69, 82–83, 105, 118, 139, 143, 173, 184
   pre-Socratic, 173
philosophical spirit, 63, 68, 77, 98
philosophy
   as architectonic discipline, 59, 66, 76–77
   and dialectic, 66
   faculty of, 50, 56, 66–67, 69–72, 76, 184
   as field and general term, xiii, 3–5, 10, 18–26, 28, 45, 47, 61, 64–67, 69–72, 74, 80, 82, 86, 96, 107–9, 116, 122, 138, 150, 153, 155–56, 164, 173–76, 182–84, 191, 196, 204, 219, 221, 242, 259, 271, 275, 280, 290, 292, 302, 318, 320, 322–23
   of science, 267, 322
Pieper, Josef, 169
pietism, 15, 258, 260
piety
   as affective, 41
   and consciousness, 15, 24–32, 34, 36, 41–42, 44–46, 122, 143
   and religion, 38, 42–43, 92
   as social, 15, 44
   and theological *paideia*, 6
Pius IX (pope), 158, 221
Plato, 17–18, 28–29, 34, 82, 93, 107, 176, 267
Plotinus, 176
pluralism
   intellectual, 189–90
   philosophical, 233
   religious, 300
   secular, 212–14, 226–27
   theological, 198, 211, 325
Polanyi, Michael, 196
Ponticus, Evagrius, 37
Portier, William, 301
prayer, xi, 88, 122–23, 295, 314
   and soteriology, 298
   and theology, 197, 202, 209, 219, 258, 302, 309, 312–13
principle of identity, 239–43, 245, 249
professors of theology, 10, 93, 152;
   university, 67, 73, 76–78, 151, 185, 187, 272, 317
Protestantism
   and church, 5, 7, 20, 85, 87–89, 93, 95–96, 238–39, 255
   clergy, 76
   and ecclesiology, 87
   and scholasticism, 231
   and science, 85–86
   seminaries, 6–7, 11, 89, 91, 258, 261
   theology. *See* theology

Protestantism (*continued*)
   and tradition, xiii
   and universities, 5, 75, 260, 261
Providence, 38, 105, 121–22, 321
Prussia
   and church, 20
   and education, 95
   General Code of, 56
   and government, 79, 83
   universities, 18, 75
Pseudo-Dionysius, 257

Quenstedt, Johann, 88

Rahner, Karl, 129–30, 163, 194, 298, 299, 316
Rationalism, 5, 92
Ratzinger, Josef Cardinal, 294
Rausch, Thomas, 10–11
Realism, 194, 205
reason, 3, 19, 21, 24, 65, 68, 81–82, 100, 117, 124, 137, 141, 154, 172, 178–79, 264, 291
   Aristotelian, 80, 174–76
   and contemplation, 177
   Enlightenment (autonomous), 89, 178, 212–13, 227, 265–66, 304, 310, 314
   explicit and implicit, 140
   and faith. *See* Faith
   as fallen, 82–83, 267
   and idealism, 58
   as power, 167, 170
   and theology. *See* Theology
redemption, 13, 120, 131, 201, 233, 243, 253, 266–67, 277, 285–87, 296, 302, 304, 307, 311, 319, 325
   facticity of, 230–35, 237, 239
Reformation, 37, 91, 103, 117, 118, 245
Reinhard, Franz Volkmar, 19, 21
relativism, 188, 205, 213, 226, 292
religion, x–xi, 1–2, 6, 9, 12, 15, 16–17, 21, 24–26, 37–38, 83, 95, 99–102, 104–5, 112–13, 116–17, 123–24, 139, 147–50, 152, 155–57, 183, 185, 192–95, 213–14, 276, 282–83, 318–19
   and conscience, 116, 119, 128
   Evangelical, 104
   evidences of, 124, 131, 140–41
   as natural, 45, 117–23, 125, 130–36, 140, 150–52
   philosophy of, 183–84
   and piety, 38, 41–45
   as positive, 42
   as revealed, 99, 114, 117–18, 129–36
   study of, 214, 282–86, 324
   teaching of, 282
religious consciousness, 15, 35, 40, 41–42, 45
religious experience, 12, 26, 37, 39–40, 42, 44–45, 93–94, 104, 191, 195, 210, 232, 315
religious studies, x–xii 213, 271, 306–7
Renaissance, 117
resurrection. *See* Jesus Christ
Reuter, Hans-Richard, 17
revelation, ix, 2, 4, 15, 82, 100–101, 118–19, 123, 129, 132, 134–35, 138–39, 141, 146, 152, 154, 156, 161, 167, 184, 187, 191, 195, 197–200, 202–8, 210–12, 217–19, 221–22, 226, 241–43, 245, 259, 276, 290–91, 293–94, 310–11, 315, 324
   biblical, 20, 46, 82–84
   as *credenda*, 153, 160
   as *depositum*, 152
Ringer, Fritz, 56
ritual, 23, 197, 202, 299
Rohr, Johann, 17
Romanticism, 15, 57, 110, 264–66
Rousseau, Jean-Jacques, 44
Roy, Louis, 41
Ruddy, Christopher, 301

Sack, Carl Heinrich, 18
sacraments, 88, 204, 225, 236, 319
  activities, 237
  baptism, 161, 202, 237
  confirmation, 202, 237
  eucharist, 161, 202, 204, 302
  sacramental principle, 178, 202, 313
  as symbol, 238
  and theology, 90, 225
Sailer, Johann Michael, 89
salvation. *See* soteriology
salvation history, 239, 241–45, 248–50
Schelling, Friedrich, 16–20, 22, 57, 58
Schleiermacher, Friedrich, xiii, 11, 13–162, 187, 233, 274, 289, 291–92, 296–97, 300–302, 306
scholarship
  academic, 10, 57, 62, 86, 214–15, 260, 265, 270, 273, 278, 280–82, 314
  historical, 6, 8, 76
  humanist, 263
  scientific, 6, 56
  theological, 7, 49, 57, 275
schools
  divinity, 6–8, 11, 200
  elementary (and *Trivialschulen*), 56, 91, 95, 200, 203
  secondary, 56, 60–64, 200, 203, 260, 274
  secular, 182
  specialty, 75–76, 85
  vocational, 61
Schubert, Frank D., 214, 227
Schutz, Alfred, 237
science
  in academies, 62–63
  and architectonic, 65, 77
  and *episteme*, 257
  method of, 107
  natural (empirical), 15, 24, 139, 144–45, 166, 172, 223, 245

  and philosophy. *See* philosophy
  positive, 14, 59, 72
  related to the university or as university subjects, 56, 61, 64, 66–68, 70, 73, 76–77, 79, 103, 107–9, 111–16, 137, 142, 154, 164, 167, 169, 178, 181, 261, 270–71, 275, 279, 282, 285–87, 289, 313, 316, 321
  and theology. *See* theology
  and truth, 7
  as *Wissenschaft*. *See* knowledge 23, 24
scientific spirit. *See* theologian
Scripture
  and exegesis, 5
  and historical criticism, 10, 15, 222, 245, 260–61
  and inerrancy, 245
  and literalism, 88, 245
  and Mosaic authorship, 246
  New Testament, 54, 246, 285
  and revelation, ix, 83, 207, 233, 261, 308
  and symbols, 194
secularism, 190, 225, 292
seminaries. *See* Catholic and Protestant
Semler, Johann Salomo, 260
Shelley, John C., 24
Sigwart, Christoph von, 17
Sillem, Edward, 118
sin, 40–41, 104, 119–20, 131–33, 135, 161, 234, 240
Sixtus V (pope), 157
social justice, 200, 318
social theory, 24, 44
Society of Jesus, 9, 108, 318, 320, 322
soteriology, 11, 73, 81, 96–97, 104, 205, 222, 244, 247, 257–58, 290, 295–296, 299–300, 302, 304–5, 308, 313–16, 319–21, 325
  and history. *See* salvation history
specialty field, 181, 266, 270–71, 273–74, 282, 287, 300, 324

Spener, Phillip Jakob, 260
Spinoza, Benedictus, 17
Spiritual Exercises (Ignatius Loyola), 37, 142, 320
spirituality, 15, 37–38, 40–42, 45–46, 149, 173, 176, 320
  ascent and descent, 321
  Ignatian, 320–21
Steffens, Heinrich, 18
students
  and academies, 91
  Catholic, 11, 90, 204, 214, 216–17, 223–25, 227
  elementary, 92
  of theology, 10–11, 14, 18, 49, 52, 56, 93, 95, 161, 165, 183–85, 292
  university, xii, 3, 60–61, 65–68, 76–78, 161, 166–67, 170–71, 178–82, 268–69, 272–73, 285, 317–18, 325
Suarez, Francisco, 141
suffering, 41, 81, 121–23, 249, 314–15
symbols, 23, 44, 192–92, 194–98, 200–202, 206–7, 209–10, 230, 232, 234, 236, 238, 241, 254, 281–82, 292, 305

Tackett, Timothy, 90,
Taylor, Charles, 317
Tertullian, 141, 308
Thandeka, 16–17
theodicy, 248, 275
Theodoret, 141
theological anthropology, 234, 267, 275, 287
theologian(s) and academic freedom, 56, 86–87, 214–16, 222
  character of, 9, 15, 23, 49, 57, 94, 189–90
  disposition of, 160–61, 190, 196, 258, 261, 276, 286
  dogmatic, 152–53, 160, 159
  and ecclesial mandates, xii
  formation of, 14, 46–58, 70
  religious interest and scientific spirit of, 46–58, 65–67, 71, 75–77, 93–94
  rights of, 225
  schola theologorum, 156–57, 161
  as scholar, 48, 57, 68
  vocation of, 47, 49, 203, 206, 294, 302
  See also freedom
theology
  academic, 5, 8, 91, 212, 219, 221–23, 300, 323
  and anthropology. *See* anthropology
  as architectonic, 274, 322–23
  and catechetics, xiii, 11, 204–5, 211, 217, 292–95
  classical criteriology of, 242–43, 245, 250–51
  and clerical paradigm, 7, 230, 256, 261–62, 274, 288, 300
  courses, 10, 214, 224, 325
  and dialectic, 170, 172, 259, 281
  dogmatic, 9, 18, 20–22, 24–26, 45, 47–49, 80, 90–91, 137, 139, 150–51, 153–54, 159–62, 182–83, 185, 261, 273, 296, 309, 317
  ecological, 10
  and education. *See* education
  exclusion of, 2, 110
  faculties of, 69–72, 74, 77–78
  fragmentation of, 256, 300, 309
  fundamental, 317
  historical, 25
  liberation, 10, 237, 265, 324
  moral, 9, 88, 186, 261
  and mystery, 206, 253, 275–76, 315
  and narrative, 192, 295, 307, 315
  natural, 21, 99, 105, 137–53, 160, 181, 185, 296, 301, 304–5, 311
  and *paideia*, 6, 256, 268, 273, 276, 280–81, 287
  and pedagogy, 297
  philosophical, 25–26, 53–54

theology (*continued*)
  physical, 104–6, 110, 138–41
  and pluralism, 190, 198, 211, 213–14, 226–27, 233, 300, 325
  as positive, 14, 59, 72, 77, 84, 86, 88, 90, 93, 97, 212, 274, 300, 302, 306
  practical, 14, 25, 46, 48, 51, 60, 72, 84, 90, 95, 97, 192, 211–12, 254, 257–58, 260–61, 282, 291–92
  as *sacra doctrina*, ix, 4, 144, 290–91
  as science, ix, 14, 23, 72, 76–77, 84–86, 93, 102–3, 105, 112, 114, 116, 137, 139, 145–46, 150–52, 159, 163, 214, 218, 242, 260–61, 274–75, 289–90, 300, 302, 306, 322
  as scholastic, 88–89, 191, 260, 309
  and system 137, 153, 159, 218, 225
  theologia, 255–58, 261, 270, 273, 275–76, 280–81, 297–98
  theological dissent, 222, 227, 294
  theological method, 144, 152, 226, 229–30, 293, 317
  as wisdom, ix–x, 12, 81–82, 217–19, 230, 255, 258, 265, 276, 281–83, 289, 300–303, 306–7, 312–13, 318, 322–25
Thiel, John, 15
Thoreau, Henry David, 29
Tice, Terrence, 23–24, 47
Tillich, Paul, 129, 210, 233
Todt, Berhard, 17
Tracy, David, 193, 310
tradition
  Catholic, xi, 11–12, 206, 301, 313, 323
  ecclesial (religious), ix–xi, 7, 88, 104, 139, 189, 192, 194, 196, 199, 209–11, 215, 221, 223–24, 226, 229, 231, 236, 238, 241–42, 252, 265–67, 277–82, 285–87, 289, 290, 293–94, 315, 321
  Protestant, xiii, 13, 37–38, 80, 83, 96, (Calvinist) 104
  and spirituality, 38–41, 45
  theological, xii, 306, 308, 312
transcendence, 163, 165, 173, 176, 180–81, 186, 196, 234, 253, 301, 323
Trinity, 127, 148–49, 160, 206
truth
  moral, 121
  philosophical, 3–4
  revealed (divine), 2–3, 21, 50, 131, 152–54, 160–61, 201, 208, 210, 222, 241, 293
  theological, 3, 113, 157
Turner, James, 213
Twesten, August, 20

ultramontanism, 89, 92, 155
university(ies), xiv, 2
  Catholic, xi–xii, 8–10, 12, 75, 151, 153, 155, 166, 185, 213–14, 216, 219–20, 223–26, 292–93, 307–8, 313, 316–20, 322–23
  curriculum, 1–2, 8, 18, 67, 76, 165, 292, 296, 317
  disciplines. *See* disciplines
  faculty (schools) of law, 7, 69–70, 72, 78, 309
  faculty of medicine, 3, 7, 69–70, 72, 77–78, 85, 309
  German, 3–5, 60, 75
  and the humanities, 108, 312, 318
  Jesuit, 320
  and positive faculties. *See* faculties
  postliberal, 307
  Protestant, 5, 260–61
  research, 272, 313

university(ies) (*continued*)
  reward system of, 270, 273
  secular, xi, 11, 182, 216, 282
  and the state, xi, 56, 69–70,
    72–76, 78–79, 85
  students. *See* students
utilitarianism, 75–76, 181, 324

Verger, Jacques, 69
Victor, Richard of, 37
Vigilius (pope), 157
Virgil, 148

Wegscheider, Julius, 18, 21,
Welch, Claude, 15, 140
Wildiers, Max, 138
Wilhelm, Frederick III, 19
Williams, Robert, 27, 29

wisdom
  biblical, 82
  ecclesial, 307
  infused, 219, 258, 302, 312–13
  philosophical, 80–81, 83, 100,
    175, 217–218, 302
  and theology. *See* theology
Wissenschaft. *See* science
Wittgenstein, Ludwig, 192
Wolff, Christian, 3–5, 95
worship, 51, 96, 99, 134, 156, 176,
  209, 219, 236, 295, 298, 305
Wyschogrod, Edith, 295, 310

Yearley, Lee, 124
Yoder, John Howard, 303–4, 306
Yom Kippur, 120

Zwingli, Ulrich, 21

www.ingramcontent.com/pod-product-compliance
Lightning Source LLC
Chambersburg PA
CBHW071149300426
44113CB00009B/1137